STUDIES IN IMMIGRATION AND CULTURE
Royden Loewen, Series editor

Anna Enns Epp with ten of her forty-four grandchildren, 1958.

MENNONITE WOMEN IN CANADA
A History

MARLENE EPP

UNIVERSITY OF MANITOBA PRESS

University of Manitoba Press
Winnipeg Manitoba R3T 2M5 Canada
www.umanitoba.ca/uofmpress

Printed in Canada.

Text design: Relish Design
Cover design: Doowah Design

Library and Archives Canada Cataloguing in Publication

Epp, Marlene
Mennonite women in Canada : a history / Marlene Epp.

(Studies in immigration and culture 1914-1459 2)
Includes bibliographical references and index.
ISBN 978-0-88755-182-6 (bound).—ISBN 978-0-88755-706-4 (pbk.).

1. Mennonite women—Canada—History. 2. Mennonite women—Canada—
Social conditions. I. Title. II. Series.

BX8128.W64E76 2008   305.48'689771   C2008-902246-7

Studies in Immigration and Culture Series, ISSN 1914-1459, #2

The University of Manitoba Press gratefully acknowledges the financial support
for its publication program provided by the Government of Canada through the
Book Publishing Industry Development Program (BPIDP), the Canada Council
for the Arts, the Manitoba Arts Council, and the Manitoba Department of Culture,
Heritage, Tourism and Sport.

Financial support for the publication of this book has also been provided by
the Mennonite Historical Society of Canada, Divergent Voices of Canadian
Mennonites Program.

For my mother
Helena Louise Dick Epp

And my late father
Frank Henry Epp

CONTENTS

ILLUSTRATIONS

The author and publisher wish to thank the following institutions and individuals for permission to reprint the photographs in this book:

Centre for Mennonite Brethren Studies (CMBS); Essex-Kent Mennonite Historical Association (EKMHA); Mennonite Archives of Ontario (MAO); Mennonite Heritage Centre (MHC); Centre for Mennonite Brethren Studies (CMBS); the Waterloo Region Record, Ontario Canada; Anne Funk; David Hunsberger; and Chung Vang.

Frontispiece: Anna Enns Epp with ten of her forty-four grandchildren, 1958.
Illustrations following page 178:
Mennonite women, southern Manitoba, 1910s.
Postcard of Ontario Mennonite women at the beach, 1905.
Ontario wedding, 1902
Wedding photo, Manitoba, early 20th century.
Wedding photo of Ontario bishop Oscar Burkholder and Laura May Shantz, 1913.
Wedding photo, Manitoba, 1920.
Informal funeral photo, Manitoba, early 20th century.
Gender imbalance in class of 1946 at Ontario Mennonite Bible School, Kitchener.
Ontario women on their day off while working as domestics in California, 1911.
Helen Loewen Warkentin, missionary to India, c1920s.
Helen Willms, long time missionary nurse in northern Manitoba and Taiwan, c1950s.
Gathering at Mary Martha girls' home for Mennonite women workers in the city, Winnipeg, 1920s.
Helena Penner, first Mennonite woman graduate of University of Manitoba, with classmates, 1895.
City missionary Anna Thiessen and sewing class, Winnipeg, 1916.
Women's society, North End Mennonite Brethren Church, Winnipeg, c1930.
Women's sewing circle, Erb Street Mennonite Church, Waterloo, 1932.
Sorting material aid bundles at Mennonite Central Committee relief depot, Ontario, 1955.
Fraktur painting by Ontario artist Anna Weber, 1873.
Old Order Mennonite women quilting, 1978.
Susie Reddekopp, packing for return trip to Mexico from Ontario, 2000.
Hmong Mennonite women in traditional dress.
Ontario Mennonite woman who enlisted in the Canadian Women's Army Corps, 1942.
Midwife Frieda Isaak on her way to a delivery, northern Ontario, 1930s.
Mennonite women domestics in uniform, 1930s.
Making teaballs for Ontario Mennonite Relief Sale, 1970.
Selling eggs at the Kitchener Farmers' Market, 1948.
Mennonite woman picking raspberries in the Fraser Valley, British Columbia, 1948.

PREFACE

During one several-month period in the writing of this book, I frequently drove past an attractive sign near downtown Waterloo, Ontario, that pronounced 'Mennonite Women' in large bold lettering. The sign advertised an exhibit of original paintings by artist Peter Etril Snyder. Well-known especially for his watercolour and oil depictions of Old Order Mennonites in southwestern Ontario, Snyder had drawn together a collection of original artwork on Mennonite women. When a co-worker and I were in the gallery one day to purchase a gift for a colleague, we couldn't help but chuckle at ourselves, two 'Mennonite women,' in an exhibit devoted to, well, us! The sign proclaimed a certain monolithic theme—as if one could capture Mennonite women as a meaningful organizing focus—though the paintings themselves hinted at the diversity of experience and perspective that one might begin to discover if the women portrayed could give voice to their stories. At times I have felt it presumptuous for me to write a book on Mennonite women, as if I could even hope to paint a picture in words in which every Mennonite woman could see herself or her female ancestors, in the same way that I struggled with some amusement to find myself in that exhibit of paintings.

Had I found myself looking out from the canvas, I would have seen a second-generation Canadian whose Mennonite grandparents, both maternal and paternal, immigrated from the Soviet Union (present-day southern Ukraine) in 1924, settling as farmers in the southwest corner of Ontario and southern Manitoba, respectively. Because their ancestors established settlements in south Russia in the early nineteenth century, they, and so also I, are often referred to as 'Russian Mennonite,' a descriptor that collapses our religious and national identity into an historic label. However, my ethnic history is really not Russian or Ukrainian at all, since Mennonites in Russia and later the Soviet Union maintained and fostered a culture that was mainly north German in its origins. To the extent that I ever give myself a national label, I am Canadian.

Sharing that Germanic background, but with somewhat different origins, are the histories of many of my long-time friends from the Mennonite high school I attended when my family moved to Kitchener–Waterloo, Ontario in the early 1970s. Their Mennonite ancestors moved from Switzerland to Pennsylvania hundreds of years ago, and then to Upper Canada (present-day Waterloo region) beginning in the late eighteenth century. Their relatives are frequently called 'Swiss Mennonites' and include the Old Order—who appear most often in Snyder's paintings—a rural Mennonite subgroup that lives apart from society and opts not to follow many of its modern technologies, including motorized transportation. The woman who accompanied me to Snyder's gallery that day is also Mennonite, but finds her roots in the Swiss-origin Amish community that migrated directly from Europe to Canada beginning in the 1820s. And we are only two of many variations within the category of Mennonite women.

The differing roots of Mennonite women are echoed in the diversity of Mennonites themselves. Writer Katie Funk Wiebe offered this reflection after her immigrant family became Canadian citizens in the 1930s: "But what was Mennonite? Was that a religion, a nationality, or both—or neither? Maybe we were some strange new category."[1] At the beginning of the twenty-first century, Mennonites continue to wrestle with identity issues, what it means to be Mennonite, though questions of political and theological difference, and ethnic heterogeneity, have risen well above gender in priority and frequency of conversation. In one sentence, Mennonites are a Christian denomination with origins in the radical reformation of sixteenth-century Europe, called Anabaptists at that time, whose religious beliefs emphasize believers' baptism, nonresistance or pacifism, and a continuum of responses to separation from, or involvement in, the world. Motivated by religious persecution, a desire for community isolation, and in search of economic opportunities, Mennonites dispersed from their European origins to eastern Europe and later Russia, to North America, and to Central and South America.

A 500-year history of continuous migration, combined with an overseas mission program that began in the nineteenth century, has resulted in clusters of Mennonites across the globe. Indeed, in 2006 the number of Mennonites on the African continent outnumbered the population of Mennonites in North America. In Canada, there were approximately 131,000 Mennonite members in 2006, although government census figures that include non-baptized children within a household will be almost double that; for instance, the 2001 Canadian census reported 191,000 Mennonites.[2] Within Canada, there may be close to fifty different identifiable Mennonite subgroups that include, for example, modern yet politically conservative evangelicals; newcomer Canadians with Asian and Hispanic origins; Old Order and other conservative groups that use horse-and-buggy transportation or are visible by uniform dress; groups that connect strongly with historic ethnic Swiss or Russian origins; others who identify primarily with pacifist and social justice beliefs; and individuals who consider themselves 'culturally' Mennonite but do not relate to church institutions. Within these generalized categories exists a comparable diversity of Mennonite women. While I have attempted to present at least glimpses of this panorama of history and experience, I know some readers will find the book lacking in comprehensive representation of each 'group.'

As a Mennonite woman myself, I am only too aware of the challenges and opportunities of writing history from an insider perspective. While to a certain extent I share "fables of rapport" with some of the subjects about whom I write, I also know that many of those subjects are strangers to me in so many ways.[3] Though we may share a certain Mennonite 'world view'—albeit one that evolves continuously in response to changing global circumstances—as a woman who came to adulthood late in the twentieth century, I have had many different life choices to make from those made by my female Mennonite ancestors. Throughout the book, I occasionally draw on experiences and memories from my own family history—the lives of my grandmothers, my aunts, my mother—as I explore various topics applicable to the lives of Canadian Mennonite women. As Canadian historian Franca Iacovetta proposed in a

1999 article, centring oneself within the academic narrative acknowledges the close connections all historians have with their subjects and simultaneously decentres the "male authorial voice" that has tended to disavow those connections.[4] At the same time, I am well aware, as was American historian Hasia Diner when researching Jewish migration to America, that I might at times have "made greater claims for the shreds of evidence I found because doing so felt right." I admit to, but do not apologize for, bringing the personal agenda of myself as a Mennonite and as a woman to this project. I hope that in the end, again to quote Diner, "my mind-set as a scholar complements my sensibilities as an insider."[5]

I had already completed several topical studies on the history of Mennonite women when the Mennonite Historical Society of Canada approached me with the invitation to complete a book-length survey on the history of Mennonite women in Canada. This particular project would be one of several Society initiatives through which the Divergent Voices of Canadian Mennonites (as the subcommittee became known) would be explored. I am grateful to all the board members of the Society for their support, encouragement, and patience while they awaited the completion of the project, and also to Mennonite Central Committee Canada, whose generous financial support enabled publication of the book. Deep thanks goes to those individuals who read and offered constructive comments on the entire manuscript: Royden Loewen, Lucille Marr, Rachel Waltner Goossen, Leonard Doell, and Pamela Klassen. Warm thanks to Franca Iacovetta for offering an endorsement for the book. Director David Carr and his staff at the Press were enthusiastic about the project from the beginning, and also congenial and professional to work with as the book went through the publication process. I was fortunate to have helpful research assistance at several points during the writing of the book; in particular, I thank Linda Huebert Hecht, Agatha Klassen, and Bethany Seiling Leis. Archival staff at the Mennonite Heritage Centre, the Centre for Mennonite Brethren Studies (both in Winnipeg), and the Mennonite Archives of Ontario (Waterloo) were generous with their collections and with their knowledge. I have benefited from support and expertise elsewhere, including from my faculty and staff colleagues at Conrad Grebel University College at the University of Waterloo and other friends and academic colleagues too numerous to list here.

My mother, Helena Louise Dick Epp, and my sisters, Marianne Coleman and Esther Epp-Tiessen, each offered her own personal life example and insight into being a 'Mennonite woman.' Ironically, perhaps, it was my father, Frank H. Epp, who, as a well-known historian and churchman amongst Canadian Mennonites, first prompted me to research and write about Mennonite women when, in the year before he died, he handed over such an assignment to me because he didn't know where to find any information on such an unlikely topic.[6] Although I grew up in a family of women—my father was often absent—I now live in a household of men: Paul Born, and our sons, Lucas and Michael Epp Born, continue to nurture and challenge my thinking about egalitarian relations between men and women. Their love and support have helped to make this book possible.

MENNONITE WOMEN IN CANADA: A HISTORY

INTRODUCTION

The 'Curious Mennonite': Seeing Canadian Mennonite Women through Low-Lying Fog

Katie Funk Wiebe, a woman whose life and writing have inspired much of my thinking on Mennonite women, once described the important texts in Mennonite history as seeing women "mostly through a low-lying fog."[1] Indeed, women's invisibility in 'mainstream' historical texts was often cited as a crucial impetus to the agenda of women's history. As recently as 2004, two well-established women's historians commented that they sometimes "become depressed" at the difficulty of inserting women into the traditional historical narrative.[2] One doesn't need to look far to find numerous examples where the fog was and is particularly low and thick. In some accounts of Mennonite pioneers and immigrants in Canada, women are starkly invisible, although we know women were surely there.

For instance, in the book *Mennonite Memories*, published in 1974 on the centennial of Mennonite settlement on the prairies, an essay on "Home-steading at Rosthern [Saskatchewan]" does not list one woman's name, though names of male participants as 'heads of families' figure prominently.[3] An "historic picture" of pioneers who attended the first Mennonite church service at Yarrow, British Columbia, in April 1928 depicts twenty men, though one must assume that women were also in attendance and also contributed to "the start of a religious program which, through the years, has found expression in every phase of Yarrow's community life."[4] And when the Zoar Mennonite Church at Langham, Saskatchewan, was organized by settlers from Minnesota in 1910, the twenty-six founding members named were all men except for one woman, a widow; the wives of these men were not listed as founding members.[5]

One might be prompted to discount these depictions as products of an historical narrative that predated women's history as a critical discipline. Yet a congregational history published in 2003 also exhibits such an approach in portraying the church founders; two group photographs, one of men, the other of women, bear the captions "Some of the founding fathers" and "Wives of the founding fathers," respectively.[6] Rather than being viewed as equal participants in the project of church founding, women are defined by their marital relationship to the founders. Family histories, of which the Mennonite interest in genealogy has produced many, are markedly patriarchal in naming; my own family history, traced from my great-great-grandfather Heinrich H. Epp, and titled *House of Heinrich*, is only one typical example. His two wives, who collectively birthed eleven children, are immediately secondary players to the family 'progenitor.' Sometimes, an androcentric choice of words is quite amusing, as in a 2004 family history, in which the chapter about the first son in the family is titled "Fraunz: The First Male Fruit of His Father's Loins."[7] We know, of course, that the loins of Fraunz's mother went through considerable pain and effort in bringing him into the world!

A feminist historian's immediate questions include: What roles did women homesteaders play? How did the women of Yarrow and Zoar make possible the creation of a church? And what was Fraunz's mother's experience of child-birth? A main goal of this study is to explore women's roles, as prescribed and as lived, within contexts such as immigration and settlement, household and family, church and organizational life, work and education, and in response to societal trends and events. How did Mennonites prescribe the behaviour and 'place' of women within the church, family, and community, and how did women, collectively and individually, actually behave? Prescriptive sources about how women should act and also auto/biographical sources in which women's 'actual' experience is depicted are shaped by institutional and personal agenda. A church leader's admonitions that women keep their heads covered should thus be read with an understanding, first, that such admonitions were not just doctrinal in origin but were shaped by cultural events and social patterns, and, second, that the fervour of such pronouncements was usually met with equally intense reactions of both belief and practice. In his study of seventeenth-century German Mennonites, Michael D. Driedger concludes that official standards of Mennonite identity were by nature "contingent, dynamic, emergent, and situational." He further observes that, in the "daily lives of believers ... official, confessional standards of identity did not always have the permanent, enduring absolute significance that church leaders *sometimes* wanted them to have."[8] This contingency also held true throughout history for Mennonite women, whose responses to dictates about their proper place ranged from acceptance to rebellion. Sources reveal that women were constantly acting in ways that unsettled a clear delineation of their roles.

That roles shifted with some ease throughout history in response to unexpected or unusual exigencies reinforces the notion that gender roles are of human construction, are mutable, and are created to service particular interests during particular eras of history. Widowhood, war, migration, illness and death, economic crisis, for instance, all created sometimes profound disruptions to normative gender roles. In virtually all realms of women's public and private lives, I have found a juxtaposition between ideals of women's nature and behaviour with the exigency that allowed those ideals to be permanently or temporarily bypassed or subverted.

The historical lives of Mennonite women have been shaped by multiple identities and dichotomies. The tension between spiritual equality and social inequality present in Anabaptist beginnings continued to shape the lives of Mennonite women throughout the centuries. At times they acted as distinctly 'Mennonite' women, but at other, more recent, times they were clearly 'Canadian' women. Women experienced exclusion and victimization within their families and churches, but they also exercised influence and agency, and made vital contributions to the viability of both. The outward practices of their denomination may have alienated them, but their religious faith, as lived individually and expressed communally, also gave them at times hope, strength, and a sense of belonging. Women's relationships with their families, churches, and ethnic and local communities consisted of a dialectic dialogue, in which women were acted upon, but that women also helped to shape. They carved out spaces for themselves within the structures that constrained them, but also at times successfully subverted and resisted those structures.

OVERCOMING INVISIBILITY WITH CURIOSITY

Writing a Mennonite women's history is, first of all, an exercise in overcoming women's invisibility with feminist curiosity, about stretching our intellectual energy, and about taking women's lives seriously, to draw from one of the world's most inspiring feminist theorists, Cynthia Enloe.[9] Entering into such a demeanour of curiosity also prompts us to question the present, even when we are focused mainly on exploring the past. Such immediate questions, informed by historical patterns of gender inequality, will deconstruct the symbols, language, and behaviours of contemporary life and enable us to understand the existence of both progression and regression.

In 2004, a well-deserving Mennonite minister in Ontario was recognized with the title of pastor emeritus for his many years of service. As part of the celebration, he was given a stole or vestment on which were embroidered the names and logos of the institutions that were central to his work as a minister in the Mennonite church. As a testament to the support and partnership he had received from his wife, her name was embroidered on the 'underside' of one sleeve of the stole.[10] On the one hand, I understand this gesture to be an enlightened acknowledgement of the central role that the pastor's spouse played in his (usually 'his' if we are speaking historically) demanding vocation. Yet the symbolic implications of her name being on the 'underside'—thus hidden from public view—cannot help but cause some dismay. Despite the call, close to three decades old now, of women's history scholar Elise Boulding, to explore the underside of women's history, it would appear that many ongoing efforts in this direction remain at the level of compensatory history.[11] I don't want to focus too much on this particular example—I know the tribute being made is of the highest integrity, and one indeed that has been rarely made in the past—but it did confirm, in part, my sense that the state of the art of Mennonite historical writing on gender is still written mainly on the underside of the vestment. A sense of feminist curiosity compels me to turn over the many layers of history and critically analyze what can be found both on the surface and also underneath.

My interest in overcoming invisibility is tempered by a recognition of the significant developments in the field of Mennonite women's history over the past several decades. The increase in historical writing on Mennonite women responded to and followed the burgeoning field of women's history of the 1970s and onwards. Biographical collections of Mennonite 'women worthies' represented the first stage in discovering and recovering the particular experiences of women.[12] These were followed by topical analyses, in article or monograph form, that often emerged in the context of academic research papers or graduate theses.[13] A growing canon of literature, from a variety of academic disciplines, that emerged in the 1980s and 1990s demonstrated that there was much to say about the history of Mennonite women. More recently, we are seeing the emergence of institutional, congregational, and community histories that are informed by the theories and methods of women's and gender history, and thus give prominence to women's lives in hitherto unseen ways. Not only do these studies illuminate women as important actors in history, but the use of gender analysis, as it considers the presence of both femininity and masculinity as socially constructed factors, is compelling us to understand the creation and development of public institutions in new and fascinating ways.[14] Many of these secondary studies inform this book in important ways and I am exceedingly grateful for the work that has been done and that is underway.

PUTTING WOMEN IN CONTEXT

In 1995 a conference titled "Quiet in the Land?: Women of Anabaptist Traditions in Historical Perspective" was held on the campus of Millersville University in Pennsylvania. This event, described as path-breaking, as a watershed, with attendance that surpassed expectations, was exciting particularly for those of us embarking on academic careers in women's studies. I recall being startled and delighted with the profusion of topics and methodologies displayed at the conference. The collection of essays resulting from the conference and published in the 2002 book *Strangers at Home: Amish and Mennonite Women in History* was also described as a milestone and will likely be an important reference point for years to come. The book offers a rich range of chronology, geographic location, theoretical approach, and sampling from the evolving field of women's history, but there are no chapters on Canada. Hence, another motivation for this particular study is to explore and survey the distinctive historical lives of Canadian Mennonite women. While the experiences of Mennonite women in Canada closely parallel in many ways those of Mennonite women in other countries, the particular historical development of Canada, as well as unique dimensions to the Mennonite sojourn in this country, provides a divergent context within which to consider women's lives.

It is crucial to examine Mennonite women within their local and national communities so as to understand them as participating in forces other than just their religious or ethno-religious affiliation. M.J. Heisey has aptly argued that "nonconformist Anabaptists have largely borrowed their gender expectations from the larger society.... "[15] If this is true, it becomes necessary to understand how Mennonite women acted within the Canadian context, and to know how the lives of Canadian women were shaped by social, political, and economic forces during the past few centuries. Mennonite women experienced migration, settlement, marriage, childbirth, widowhood, education, career development, war, fashion, and so on, in ways sometimes unique to their ethno-religious ethos, but perhaps to a greater extent their lives resembled those of other Canadian women in these respects. I have attempted, at least in modest ways, to integrate the rich canon of macro-analysis that exists on the history of Canadian women into this micro-analysis of Mennonite women.

Conversely, to the extent that this is a study of 'religious' women, I hope that it will enrich the historiography on Canadian women, which has tended to shy away from the value of incorporating women's religious experience into interpretations of their overall lives.[16] Second-wave feminist scholars, many of them disillusioned with organized religion themselves because of centuries of female oppression within those structures, were reluctant to examine the participation of women within religious communities. In the late 1980s American historian Linda Kerber wrote that "no area is more inviting or more ignored than that of religion" in terms of understanding gender roles and boundaries.[17] Fifteen years later Ursula King wrote, in Blackwell Publishing's *Companion to Gender History*, that "Many disciplines are still extraordinarily 'religion-blind,' just as many studies in religion continue to be profoundly 'gender-blind.'"[18] Canadian historian Lynne Marks has similarly argued that binaries of interpretation, whereby religion represents either empowerment or repression in women's lives, have limited our ability to understand the real ways in which "ordinary people took what they wanted or needed from dominant religious beliefs, idioms and practices" in a kind of "lived religion."[19]

Mennonites are most fundamentally a religious body and so the history of Mennonite women must be explored, at least in part, with reference to Christian understandings of women and gender. The dual and contradictory understandings of women within Christianity have also influenced Anabaptist and Mennonite interpretations of women's roles. Christian and thus Mennonite women have lived for centuries with the confused and opposing emphases within biblical teaching that have alternately emphasized women's subordination as determined by Eve's sin in the garden and the subsequent human fall, versus later equality-suggestive teachings that pronounced 'in Christ there is neither male nor female.' While this study does not delve with any depth into feminist biblical interpretation or theological hermeneutics, it is my hope that case studies such as this one on Mennonites may enhance broader efforts to incorporate religious experience, both institutional and individual, into histories of women in Canada.

DIVERSITY WITHIN CATEGORIES

Mennonite women in Canada have lived lives shaped by other dichotomies than those explicit in Christian notions about women. One of these is their dual identities as women and as Mennonite, the interplay of which is central to this study. Over two centuries, their lives have paralleled those of other Canadian women, and often their gender identity as women has been more influential than their identity as Mennonites. But their experience as women is also mediated through their identification with an ethnic and religious minority. One shouldn't automatically conclude that women did not experience the events and issues chronicled in official histories, yet for many years it has been assumed that the sweeping surveys of Mennonite history have been genderless and spoke for all. As Frieda Esau Klippenstein commented, "Sometimes [the voices of women] speak in unison with the official histories, and sometimes they speak in significant and revealing counterpoint."[20] While Mennonite historical experience is of itself interesting, it certainly is not homogeneous and cannot be understood to represent the same things for men and for women, as Hasia Diner says about her history of Jewish women. In fact, because gender is *so* pervasive in human behaviour, it is too easily overlooked or undermined as worthy of thoughtful analysis. Gender is so "embedded," suggests Ursula King, that it can be "difficult to identify and separate out...."[21] The fact that gender is "omnipresent" in Anabaptist communities,[22] as Schmidt and Reschly have observed, should enhance, rather than minimize, the historian's curiosity about the constructed and relational lives of women and men.

In the same way that women's lives are different from men's because of gender, and as such, universal treatments of Mennonite history will always be elusive, trying to portray women as one category of analysis is fraught with the perils of generalization. Women who call themselves or are called 'Mennonite women' share some connection to a religious or ethnic framework, however that manifests itself in lived practice or memory, and also share a certain kind of embodiment, both in their sexed beings and in their gender-based conditioning. Yet the individual lives and experiences of Mennonite women are shaped by numerous factors: age, historic ethnic background, denominational subgroup, geographical locale, family history, sexual orientation, and individual personality. The disparate ways in which women experience and interpret the world around them is evident in two recent memoirs by women with nevertheless common Mennonite origins. Two remarkably parallel examples of women's biography, both published in 2003—one south, one north of the border—are the memoirs of Ruth Brunk Stoltzfus, *A Way Was Opened*, and Ruth Reesor's *Check Rein*.[23] The similarity in format, even appearance, of the books (both books have pale yellow covers with muted sepia-tone photos of each woman) but the opposite nature of their respective titles are perhaps representational of the nature of Mennonite women's lives generally: a common façade hides deep differences in character and experience. One woman may have seen doors open to her while another chafed against a check rein (a rein used on a horse to prevent it from lowering its head).

Mindful of the diversity that exists amongst Mennonite women, I recognize that in this study I've given least attention to Mennonite women who are new Canadians, to those whose ethnic/national background is non-Western, to lesbian Mennonites, to women living in poverty, and to those women within the most conservative, nonconformist groups. This neglect is partly due to the availability of sources but also reflects the smaller population numbers within these groups. As well, numbers and awareness of non-Western and gay Mennonites have arisen only in the last few decades of the twentieth century, a time period I have chosen not to explore except by occasional reference. Nor will I explicitly explore the histories of women whose ethno-religious identity is closely related to the Mennonites, such as Amish, Hutterite, or Brethren in Christ women. The brief stories at the outset of each chapter are intended to give the reader glimpses of this diversity.

GENDERING THE MENNONITE ETHOS

In keeping with the supposition that gender is omnipresent in Mennonite history, I also want to explore the notion that particular concepts, theological and ideological, that were, and still are, intrinsic to Mennonitism are also gendered. Various feminist scholars have begun to deconstruct these concepts, in order to think about how they might be understood from a woman's point of view. Such an endeavour follows European historian Joan Kelly's pointed and pivotal 1977 question, "Did Women Have a Renaissance?" She questioned the accepted schemes of historic periodization and, by extension, the normative impact of epochal transformations over time such as Renaissance, Enlightenment, Modernization, for example. In her critique of the third volume of the history of Mennonites in Canada, a volume that covered the years 1939 to 1979 and was subtitled *A People Transformed*, Frieda Esau Klippenstein questioned whether women's lives were 'transformed' during this period. Indeed, one text on Canadian women's history that covers almost the same historic period has the descriptive title *No Easy Road*.[24] Much as Kelly questioned the meaning of Renaissance for women, Klippenstein contested the way this period of Mennonite history had been interpreted, without reference to those spheres and activities that shaped women's lives most closely.[25] One could in fact argue that Mennonite women's lives were really not transformed in any significant ways until *after* 1970, when feminism as an ideological force prompted change in women's roles both inside and outside of church and community.

Many of the myths and images that characterize Mennonites should be read in newly gendered ways. Such an endeavour is potentially subversive because it attempts to deconstruct themes and ideals that are viewed as 'fundamental,' 'natural,' 'universal,' and 'core' to Mennonite thinking and praxis. Applying a critical gender perspective has the potential to destabilize, challenge, and pose uncomfortable questions of religious norms as traditionally lived and practised, as Ursula King has insightfully observed.[26] For Mennonites, such themes include favourite terms and phrases such as 'the Anabaptist vision,' 'the quiet in the land,' '*Gelassenheit*,' 'discipleship,' 'separation from the world,' and so on. Until recently (the last three decades or so), public articulation on these concepts has been almost exclusively male. But Mennonite feminist scholars, in particular, have begun to place these ideas and ideals under scrutiny with a theoretically gendered lens in the microscope.

The 1995 conference on Mennonite and Amish women's history, mentioned above, deliberately and provocatively placed a question mark after the main title *The Quiet in the Land* to become *The Quiet in the Land?*, and thus subtly encouraged participants and onlookers to wonder about this trope long applied to Mennonites. The phrase related to Mennonites' perceived historic withdrawal from interaction with culture and politics outside their communities, to their agriculture-based economy, and also to their overall obedience to the structures from which they nevertheless withdrew. It was originally applied to the Anabaptists (the Mennonites' religious ancestors) when their movement went underground to escape severe persecution in mid-sixteenth-century Europe. Yet the ideal has carried itself through time. For instance, Mennonite women who worked as domestic servants in Vancouver, British Columbia, in the mid-twentieth century were reminded to be "the quiet ones in the land," to be an example of modest decorum amidst the intemperance of city life, to submit to their employers, and also to remember their proper societal roles despite their self-sufficiency far away from families.[27]

Related to this concept are theological ideas of *Gelassenheit* and suffering, the former meaning "yieldedness to God's will, self-abandonment, the (passive) opening to God's willing, including the readiness to suffer for the sake of God."[28] Adopted by the early believers to enable them to bear suffering and martyrdom when faced with arrest, torture, and execution by religious and state authorities, such concepts become highly gendered when a model Christian-Mennonite demeanour is interpreted to be one of humility, submission, yieldedness, and readiness to suffer. Mennonite theologian Carol Penner has provocatively argued that the uplifting of suffering and submission and an ungendered emphasis on nonresistance has reinforced women's inability and their community's unwillingness to speak out against domestic violence.[29] One Mennonite woman commented that Mennonite ideals absorbed during her upbringing taught her "to not speak out, to always be nice, to turn the other cheek, to carry my cross. I was socialized into powerlessness."[30] As some Mennonite women have argued, the *Gelassenheit* and passivity that characterize the Mennonite world view and disposition have been reinforced by gendered characteristics of obedience and subordination. A Christian Mennonite faith orientation that included ideals of submission, self-denial, and humility coalesced and overlapped with comparable gender traits, thus for women adding an extra layer of expectation regarding belief, conduct, and, indeed, personality.

Along similar lines of inquiry, theologian Lydia Harder has proposed that Anabaptist/Mennonite ideals of discipleship—following the example of Jesus in serving and helping others—when interpreted as "obedience, service and self-denial" had the effect of supporting "the silent role of women." The expectations of a Christian disciple—"love, nonresistance, cross-bearing and separation from the world"—also coincided with the role of women in patriarchal society, she says. For men, on the other hand, applying models of discipleship allowed them to challenge the status quo of power relations in the world.[31] An emphasis on discipleship as a Mennonite ideal emerged especially during the Second World War when, in response to a high rate of military enlistment on the part of Mennonite men, Harold S. Bender, professor at a Mennonite college in the United States, presented and later published an address titled "The Anabaptist Vision." This Anabaptist vision was inspiring to many mid-twentieth-century North American Mennonites, prompting a renewal of the church's peace position and sparking a new interest in mutual aid and relief work. But the 'vision' had nothing to say specifically to women, who had no military service obligations to their country, about how they might live out nonresistant beliefs within their sphere of activity.

Also central to the Anabaptist and later Mennonite ethos was a call for the church and its members to separate from the forces of evil and secularism in the world, 'the world' being everything outside the community of true believers. The phrase 'in the world, but not of it,' derived from New Testament injunctions against participating in the evils of the world, is another long-standing historical descriptor for Mennonites. Often called 'nonconformity' or 'rejection of worldliness,' separation could have both spiritual and material manifestations. To the extent that principles of separation often were articulated with reference to that which was 'of the spirit' versus that which was 'of the flesh' (in keeping with Mennonites' propensity for the dualities of church and world), it became easy to associate the flesh with those things that were material, physical, and closely related to women's lives. Women were participants alongside men in a common project of establishing boundaries that would uphold those separation ideals. Yet, because religious authority was vested in male leaders, women had no official voice in establishing normative practice within their church communities. Mennonite women thus actively participated in ordering their lives within ethno-religious and sectarian communities, yet historically were simultaneously subject to the constraints and proscriptions, often gendered in nature, of those groups. Because men and women historically participated in 'the world' in different ways, the church's emphasis on separation could clearly have gendered consequences.

Mennonites were able to effectively separate from 'the world' because they lived out their religious beliefs not as isolated individuals, but within the context of community, or *Gemeinschaft*, as it was described in German. Ideals and images of community have been highly important for Mennonites; indeed, some subgroups refer to themselves as a community rather than a church. A theology of community helped Mennonites separate themselves from the world and create social boundaries and behavioural accountability deemed necessary in the quest for a pure church vis-à-vis the evil world. By emphasizing community, Mennonites accordingly de-emphasized the individual and in fact often demanded the subordination of the person to his or her community. Community ideals were maintained by means of external nonconformity and internal conformity and were enforced by varying degrees of church discipline. Disciplinary action towards those who broke community/church standards ranged from complete social and spiritual isolation, called 'shunning,' to excommunication from church membership, to short-term public embarrassment and humiliation. While the community often created positive contexts in which women were appreciated and valued for the important roles they played, community also, for some women, stifled creativity and allowed for patterns of behaviour that were destructive to women. As one woman stated it strongly, "The Mennonite community has molded many of us into doormats and made us so susceptible to abuse.... It is the community that has silenced women for too long."[32] Ideas and ideals about church as community—*Gemeinschaft*—thus also reveal themselves as dichotomous in the lives of women.

The symbolic order of Mennonitism has, on the other hand, also been used by feminist analysts to justify the so-called 'liberation' of women from subordinate positions within a patriarchal order. For instance, equalizing impulses found in the sixteenth-century Anabaptist movement were used to theorize about women's place in the late twentieth century. In the context of the 1970s women's movement that spawned historical studies of women, and inspired by the language of equality in some Anabaptist writings, some investigators of sixteenth-century gender relations suggested that the radical reformation offered an early modern model for gender equality. They pointed to a 'priesthood of all believers' theology that rejected the necessity of a mediating clergy between God and the individual and that made the reading and interpretation of scripture accessible to the entire laity. The recovery of the possible 'liberating' qualities of early Anabaptism gave Mennonite women of the 1970s and 1980s a foundation on which to put forward their case for the greater involvement and authority of women in public church life, including as ordained ministers. This idea of a 'priesthood of all believers' suggested that the Anabaptist movement offered women a more elevated position than was available to them in other Christian denominations. And indeed, there were women within the movement who hosted clandestine worship services, interpreted and taught scripture to those gathered, travelled and evangelized to bring their faith to others, baptized new believers, and were arrested and executed for heresy. For instance, Helene of Freyberg was an Austrian noblewoman who purportedly sheltered Anabaptist fugitives on her estate and eventually separated from her own family to join the radicals.[33] A collection of stories, called *The Martyrs Mirror*, of 930 Anabaptists who were killed for their religious beliefs, includes entries for about 300 women, leading some historians to suggest that women were active as leaders in the early stages of this radical religious movement.[34]

The initial celebration was followed by more nuanced studies, such as M. Lucille Marr's important 1987 article, which suggested that while Anabaptist women may have been "peers in the faith," they nevertheless remained "subordinates in marriage."[35] That is, while the Holy Spirit made no gender distinctions in bringing spiritual rebirth to individuals, the social order of the earthly church and family was stratified according to sex. More recently, Patricia Harms suggested that even if Mennonite women never experienced true social equality, the religious belief, rooted in Anabaptism, that "every person has something to contribute" perhaps had the effect of endowing women with an "atypical sense of self."[36] Recognizing the imperative of gendering religious experience, Marion Kobelt-Groch suggested that, amongst the sixteenth-century Anabaptists, it was easier and more likely for men to follow biblical injunctions to "renounce all earthly obligations" to follow the divine will than it was for women, whose ties to children made it difficult and sometimes impossible to leave behind 'hearth and home' to follow their religious convictions.[37] More research is needed to discern the role of women within early Anabaptism, asking, for instance, whether Anabaptist women were more constrained in joining the radical faith movement because of their maternal responsibilities. If taking along children was not an option when flight from authorities was necessary, did women opt to give priority to care for their children above their newfound religious beliefs? Do we know about women who recanted, not because they inwardly renounced their beliefs, but because they could not bear leaving their children behind, or felt a zealous compulsion to raise their children secretly to follow Anabaptism? At any rate, many of the initial studies on Mennonite women's roles, past and present, used the radical reformation as a springboard, hoping to find within the Anabaptist past an egalitarianism, both religious and social, that might undergird an assertion of women's rights in the late twentieth century. But, as the introduction to *Strangers at Home* concludes, "the record is ambiguous."[38]

The possible equalizing tendency in early Anabaptism was accompanied, and perhaps offset, by a strong emphasis on the Bible as the final authority for Christian thought and practice and, as well, literal readings of scripture passages. While looking for egalitarianism in sixteenth-century radical religious reform, biblical scholars and theologians also searched scripture for passages that could be interpreted as calls for equality, spiritual and social, between women and men. The Anabaptist emphasis on reading and interpreting scripture as the prerogative and responsibility for all believers meant that certain biblical texts could be used as clear prescriptions for women's elevated position within the church. On the other hand, an affinity for biblical literalism has also been used by Mennonites to support women's subordination and silence within churches and homes. This biblical literalism, variously interpreted in particular cultural contexts over time, took at face value such biblical admonitions that women submit to their husbands, remain silent, and keep their heads covered.

Furthermore, during certain eras of history, outside cultural and theological influences reinforced conservative readings of biblical statements on women. Especially in the first half of the twentieth century, the Protestant Fundamentalist movement was perhaps the strongest force in creating rigid definitions of gendered behaviour.[39] Fundamentalism, eagerly taken up by some Mennonite leaders in North America and filtering down to local churches, was characterized by a penchant for hierarchy in the creation order. God was on top, then men, then women, then children. An ironically militant language of domination and submission was used to reinforce this universal order, and was especially applied to prescriptive pronouncements regarding the relationship between man and woman. Equalizing tendencies in Anabaptist and Mennonite history have often thus been offset and counterbalanced by a persistent patriarchy, which has in turn been undergirded by societal norms and a range of theological and cultural influences.

One could explore many other symbols, including ones that go well beyond the limits of Mennonitism. Cynthia Cockburn, an analyst of war's impact on women, has observed that the 'ploughshare,' as opposed to the 'sword,' is a wonderful image of anti-war sentiments, yet both are nevertheless masculine tools not generally associated with women's tasks.[40] In applying a feminist curiosity to the lives of women in the past, it thus becomes important, indeed essential, to explore the possible double meanings inherent in community symbols. As I am neither a theologian nor philosopher, but a social historian, the discussion that follows focuses on the social manifestation of the impact— sometimes clash—of ideological myths and symbols, rather than deconstructs the concepts themselves, an endeavour that will require a new feminist and gendered reading of Mennonite theological history and historical theology.

BIAS, METHOD, AND SOURCE

While a gendered reading of core notions of Mennonitism underlies this book, it is equally important to understand the ways in which deliberately gendered movements of thought have conversely influenced Mennonite women and their communities. Here, of course, I am referring to the feminist movement of the late twentieth century, an ideological and activist movement of thought and action that caused distinct discomfort for Mennonites, but which nevertheless challenged and transformed the understanding and role of women within families and institutions. The growth of women's history in the 1970s and 1980s, an academic pastime inspired by the feminist movement, provided an impetus also for Mennonite historians to discover and recover the stories of Mennonite women. It is curious, perhaps remarkable, that little acknowledgement is given of the fact that the interest in Mennonite women was spurred on by the rise of feminism in academe and in the church—indeed, in society generally. The establishment of a Women's Concerns desk at Mennonite Central Committee and its highly successful but now defunct *Report*, as well as the first ordinations of female pastors, beginning in the late 1970s, were all denominational responses to wider social phenomena. Recent historical retrospectives on these eras seem surprisingly cautious in addressing such secular ideological influences.

In her review of the essay collection by Mennonite women leaders, *She Has Done a Good Thing*, Carol Penner questions why, in 2001, the words 'sexism' and 'feminism' are avoided as though they might embarrass or cause offence.[41] Similarly, a 2003 collection of reflections by women pastors in Ontario Mennonite churches, while extremely important as a narrative document, falls short of a gendered analysis of the challenging social and church context in which women felt called to be Mennonite ministers. Personal stories address 'pain,' 'obstacles,' or 'difficulties,' but few women leaders or pastors flesh out the gendered nature of the challenges they faced. The common 1970s qualification, 'I'm not a women's libber but … ,' seems to be resurfacing in this post-feminist age. In fact, the early literature was much more likely to acknowledge an ideological impetus to the emergence of historical writing on Mennonite women than are recent retrospectives on that era.

Any historical examination of women's lives must necessarily be back-grounded by an awareness that women's lives have never been homogeneous, but in particular changed dramatically in the second half of the twentieth century, and especially following the 1960s. The feminist movement of the 1960s and beyond was perhaps the strongest force in changing women's lives within their families, society, and the church. Particularly within institutional spheres, change occurred more by default and outside pressure than by inten-tional denominational decision. In this sense, the church and community were reactive, rather than direction-setting, within the wider society. The feminist movement challenged Mennonite families and churches, just as it challenged society in general. Debates over the changing roles of women did not exactly *rage* within the Mennonite media, but they certainly surfaced in pressing ways. As a woman who entered young adulthood during the heyday of second-wave feminism in the late 1970s, who made choices and developed opinions and perspectives that were fundamentally shaped by the movement for women's equality, I cannot write a book about women that isn't informed by a feminist perspective. As a graduate student in women's history, I embraced feminist ideals even more as I learned over and over again of the injustices and cruelty meted out to women in the past specifically because of their sex. Now, as a middle-aged professor of university students, I am well aware that 'feminism' is a loaded term and one that is soundly rejected by some of my female and male students. And yet I hope that a book like this one will help them develop their own vision for the twenty-first century, a vision that imagines and expresses transformational relationships and institutions that in no way perpetuate discriminatory power inequities based on sex.

The impact of second-wave feminism, and its societal repercussions, resulted in monumental changes in the family, work, and religious lives of Mennonite women. And so their histories as lived in the last two decades of the twentieth century and into the twenty-first differed significantly from the lives of their mothers and grandmothers. For the sake of identifying an historical moment at which to complete this particular narrative, I end the book at approximately 1980. Just one year prior marked the first ordination to ministry of a Mennonite woman in Canada. This pivotal event, and the numerous ordinations that followed, symbolize Mennonite women's entry into positions of seniority and authority within Mennonite churches and institutions, and into public and professional life generally. I briefly address the intense debate over 'women in ministry' in chapter 3, but I do not explore it in depth, nor do I probe the histories of late-twentieth-century Mennonite women—my own generation—to any great extent. The sources are too numerous, the time period too recent, and the themes and topics too multiple for me to attempt to bring this study up to the present, at least for now.

This book is structured on parallel and, I hope, poetic, triads of activity that I consider central to the historic lives of Canadian Mennonite women. In the first chapter, I examine women as 'pioneers, refugees, and transnationals,' recognizing that historically, Mennonite women began their Canadian lives as immigrants and refugees from elsewhere; their migratory experience shaped their lives and ethnic self-understanding in important ways. Both men and women create their most fundamental relationships as members of families. The second chapter on 'wives, mothers, and others' gives prominence to women's life cycle within their nuclear families, as they chose spouses or chose not to be married, as they gave birth and raised children, and as they lived within other family formations. The third chapter gives attention to women's historic activity within Mennonite churches and related institutional structures; as 'preachers, prophets, and missionaries,' they served as wives to ministers and later became ministers themselves, operated women's organizations, and found a myriad of other venues in which to live out their religious identities.

The fourth chapter discusses those women who lived their daily lives in the context of a Mennonite identity that posed ideological challenges and opportunities that were specifically gendered. As 'nonconformists, nonresistors, and citizens,' the women of this study were distinctly Mennonite as they responded to and incorporated the beliefs and prescriptions of their church community into their individual and collective lives. The fifth chapter, which looks at 'quilters, canners, and writers,' explores Mennonite women's material and creative activity with respect to their domestic productivity, their artistic expression, and their choices regarding education and work outside the home. Structuring a narrative that revolves around arenas of activity in which women lived out their daily lives will enable us to see Mennonite women as individual and collective actors—who believed fervently, questioned constantly, expressed themselves in a myriad of ways, and produced creatively and energetically.

A wide variety of sources has been used for this study. I have been over-whelmed by the numerous research paths I took, or could have taken, when gathering information for this study. The secondary studies discussed earlier have of course been a rich starting point and each journal article or published monograph has directed me to other literature as well as useful primary sources. Women's diaries, while not plentiful, are increasingly surfacing in private collections and within archives, as well as becoming available in published form. These personal documents provide, as Anne Yoder observes, "a myriad of images and facts about what women wore, how often they attended church, and what they believed about God, what they read, and how they amused themselves."[42] The rise of social history and women's history helped to validate the use of oral interviews as a means of learning about the lives of 'ordinary' people. The use of these, some of which I conducted myself, and others collected in various archives, offer factual, anecdotal, and reflective material that simply isn't to be found elsewhere. Denominational newsletters and newspapers provide insights on women's interface with public Menno-nitism, whether through the first-hand perspectives of women writers, or in articles about issues and events that illuminate women's experience. I have also found many "scraps of information in the margins of other studies"[43] such as church and community histories, family genealogies, and memoirs, published and unpublished, of both men and women. Sources that are not strictly histor-ical, such as fiction, poetry, cookbooks, and obituaries, have also been mined in limited ways, for factual detail in the case of the latter, or for creative musings on women's lives, in the former.

While the choice of sources for this study was relatively easy—everything and anything that would illuminate Mennonite women's lives—the choice of language presented a greater dilemma. When one is writing history, one must be mindful of how language is used, since words themselves have a powerful ability to uphold structures, or, at a minimum, leave us with an uncritical perspective. As Cynthia Enloe has noted, words like 'natural,' 'tradition,' 'always'—all terms that might easily and frequently pervade a discussion of Mennonite women—have served as "cultural pillars" that prop up "familial, community, national, and international power structures, imbuing them with legitimacy, with timelessness, with inevitability."[44] For instance, tradition is an oft-used term that must be nuanced carefully. In speaking about roles, I, and others before me, frequently use the descriptor 'traditional' to refer to models, norms, and patterns that have been 'stable over time' or that have reference to gender relations and roles that were/are based on historic and long-standing constructions of inequality between men and women. Words like 'conserva-tive,' 'progressive,' 'modern,' and 'radical,' all used regularly by Mennonite scholars, also present challenges in usage, since so-called 'conservative' groups like the Old Order may have envisioned women within a framework of 'being different but equal' and called for comparable yieldedness on the part of both men and women, while certain so-called 'modern' Mennonite groups uphold a rationale for subordination that is rooted in the fundamentalism of the Chris-tian religious right wing and thus are not 'progressive' at all in their attitudes to women. Other highly gendered terms and phrases are used with caution; these might include 'leadership,' 'household head,' 'pioneer,' for instance.

The naming of women, or the lack thereof, has always been a puzzle for historians. The following Mennonite example from a 1952 source is typical of how absurdly invisible women can be: "Among our women who are attending the [Mennonite] World Conference in Basel, Switzerland, are Sisters Allen Erb, Anson Horner, Paul Mininger, Amra Hostetler, Raymond Wenger, John Alger, Nelson Kauffman."[45] Within some extended Mennonite families, the perhaps subconscious desire to preserve a genealogical line meant that all the children in a family were given, as a middle initial, their mother's birth surname. Historian Lorraine Roth discovered that, among nineteenth-century Amish Mennonite women, it wasn't uncommon for widows to revert to the use of their 'maiden' names.[46] Writer Elaine Sommers Rich may have captured all dimensions of naming when she referred to her cousin as "Mary (Sommers Gingerich, Mrs. Irvin) Erb." This is not an approach I will attempt. As much as possible, I use a woman's full name, including her surname before marriage if I am able to ascertain that, even if she wasn't likely to use it herself. Only if her first name is absent from sources do I use 'Mrs' or refer to her by her husband's or father's name. I have also attempted to limit the amount of

'insider' terminology, whether that is German language expressions, or institutional titles and acronyms, or labels that define the numerous Mennonite
subgroups. The glossary at the end of this book may be a useful reference.

Writing a Canadian Mennonite women's history represents one approach
to incorporating gender history more broadly into the canon of Mennonite
history. Writing about gender has potential outcomes that go beyond the
immediate task of examining the ideological process through which individuals are positioned and position themselves as men and women. What gender
history has contributed to the broader craft of doing history is the sense of
temporariness and impermanence, the "implicit sense that things are not
over,"[47] and encouraged us to understand historical actors and the events they
created as socially constructed and variable over time. It is important for me
that Mennonite women read this book and see themselves and their foremothers reflected in it. I want them to read their own experience as an integral
part of the historical canon. My wish for this book is that men and woman will
read and discuss it and, in so doing, begin to see through and burn off the low-
lying, lingering fog of historical neglect and thus better understand—indeed,
become more curious about—themselves and Canadian Mennonite women of
the past.

CHAPTER ONE

Pioneers, Refugees, and Transnationals: Women Immigrate to Canada

In the early fall of 1824, Barbara Schultz Oesch (1803–1881) of Bavaria joined a small settlement of four Amish families that settled in Wilmot Township, just west of present-day Kitchener–Waterloo, Ontario.[1] Barbara Schultz was only sixteen years old when she married John Oesch in 1820; she gave birth to her fourth child one year after migrating to Canada and fourteen more children after that. Barbara's years in Upper Canada were characterized by the demanding and constant physical labour of subsistence production and the equally constant bodily changes she experienced from continuous reproduction. As well, she carried the responsibility of being married to a leader in the church, as her husband John was ordained minister in 1829 and later bishop. This meant running the household in his absences, setting an example of piety within her own large family, and acting as frequent host to the newcomers who arrived from Europe and the United States. After twenty years in Wilmot, Barbara may have been content to rejoice in the many obstacles they had overcome, but with so many sons and not much land, John decided they should push further into the frontier. And so, with Barbara heavily pregnant with her last child, the family moved to Hay Township near Lake Huron. Only four days before that child's first birthday, John died, possibly of appendicitis.

Fifty years after Barbara arrived in Canada, Katherina Hiebert (1855–1910) followed, but from a very different place of origin and to a different destination. Katherina was among a migrant group of approximately 8000 Mennonites who left their predominantly Mennonite settlements in south Russia and settled on reserve lands in the newly established province of Manitoba. She immigrated in 1875, just four months after marriage to a widower twenty-two years her senior, who had five children, the eldest daughter only two years younger than Katherina. While working with her husband to establish their own farm and giving birth herself within the first year of arrival in Canada, Katherina became one of the first midwives to serve the pioneer women, French, English, Métis, and Mennonite, of southern Manitoba. In a rural prairie settlement that was remote from centres of population and where travel was primitive, virtually all women gave birth at home with assistance from relatives or neighbours and, if they were fortunate, with a trained midwife present. Katherina was mainly self-taught; she ordered medical books from Germany and the United States and received advice from nearby Aboriginal women. Katherina was also well-known as a healer of many maladies and roamed the woods and meadows collecting "Swedish bitters, chamomile, and thyme" for her herbal remedies. Midwife-healers were crucial to the health and well-being of early immigrant communities, and it is said that "almost every day somebody called for Katherina." Her daughter recalled that "She was always away, day and night, summer and winter, tending the sick."[2]

Susie Reddekopp's (1979–) ancestral origins were very similar to those of Katherina Hiebert. However, the environment in which the two women grew up was very different. Susie's great-grandparents were among those Mennonites who migrated to Canada from south Russia in the 1870s, though her grandparents opted to join a subgroup that established homogeneous and somewhat isolated colonies in northern and central Mexico in the 1920s. Desiring greater control over their children's education and rejecting the militarism and modernization that were pervading Canadian society, these Mennonites sought an environment in which they could reinforce rigid cultural boundaries between themselves and the world. Born in Mexico, Susie and her husband Henry, with their two children, chosen to 'return' to Canada in the 1990s, hoping to escape bleak economic conditions and increasingly legalistic authoritarianism in the church. After Henry died tragically in a farm accident, Susie, a widow at the age of twenty-one, chose to return to her family in Mexico. With no husband, limited education and English-language skills, and little money, she considered her options in Canada to be narrow. Yet even while she prepared to move south to live with her parents, she mused about the possibility of coming back to Canada, perhaps to Alberta where her sister lived.[3] Susie became part of a migrant group that was transnational, with ties both physical and psychological in more than one country, and with a diasporic sense of impermanence and a constantly shifting sense of home.

Barbara Oesch, Katherina Hiebert, and Susie Reddekopp are all Canadian Mennonite women, though there is much about their life stories that is very different. Yet they share stories of diaspora, of uprooting, migration, and settlement, that are central to the histories of many Mennonites who made Canada their home. Early in their history, Mennonites developed a tendency towards mobility and migration in search of locales where they could establish relatively isolated communities. Driven by persecution and/or beckoned by religious freedoms and economic opportunities, they moved often to geographical frontiers to re-establish themselves. Indeed, since their sixteenth-century European beginnings, Mennonite communities have been created across the globe, sometimes following international migration trends, but also following their own agenda of seeking new environments in which their particular religious beliefs could be practised without impediment. From their earliest locations in Switzerland, Germany, and the Netherlands, some Mennonites moved east towards the Russian empire while others joined the mass movements west to settle North America. In the twentieth century, the Mennonite diaspora spread to the southern hemisphere, as war and repression in the Soviet Union, and assimilative pressures in Canada and the United States caused Mennonites to negotiate new settlement agreements in Central and South America. As well, a mandate to develop overseas missions that began in the late nineteenth century has seen a Mennonite presence grow in parts of Africa, India, and Asia.

The first permanent Mennonite settlers arrived in what would soon become Upper Canada (present-day Ontario) in 1786, creating a community at a location called The Twenty on the Niagara Peninsula. They were persuaded to leave their homes in Pennsylvania by government promises of military exemption and, especially, by the availability of large tracts of fertile land. Part of a larger movement of 'Pennsylvania Germans' to Canada during this era, Mennonites gradually settled also in York County north of the city of Toronto and along the Grand River in the present-day Waterloo region. In the Waterloo area, Mennonites were the first white settlers and lived in close proximity to Aboriginal peoples. Mennonites from Pennsylvania were followed closely by Amish families who immigrated directly from Europe, beginning in the 1820s. A small group of Swiss Mennonites, as the Ontario settlers were also known, owing to their European origins, went west in the early twentieth century and created communities in Alberta and Saskatchewan.

A second pioneer migration occurred beginning in 1873 when approximately 8000 Mennonites from south Russia—sometimes referred to as 'Kanadier'—were granted two blocks of reserve land in southern Manitoba. Like the Pennsylvania German Mennonites, the 1870s newcomers were pulled to Canada by a combination of religious, economic, and social factors. Their unique community and village settlement pattern, whereby Mennonites could live in relatively isolated concentrations, yet in close proximity to each other, was important to the development of the social and cultural life of these early prairie immigrants. Two further waves of Mennonite immigrants from Russia (later the Soviet Union) arrived in Canada in the 1920s (about 21,000) and after the Second World War (8000, including also a small number from Poland and Prussia). These twentieth-century arrivals found homes in Ontario and westward eventually all the way to British Columbia.

At about the same that these latter two waves of Mennonites were arriving in Canada from the Soviet Union, some Mennonites left Canada for Central and South America, mainly to preserve certain religious traditions. Other twentieth-century movements saw Mennonite refugees arrive in Canada after spending years in Paraguay and other nearby countries, where they sought refuge from Europe immediately after the Second World War. And beginning in the 1950s, a return migration of Mennonites, mainly from Mexico, continued well into the twenty-first century. While some Mennonites in Canada today can cite a family history characterized by permanent settlement over several hundred years, others can point to a story of ancestors who were on the move in almost every generation.

The motif of migration has been central to Mennonite self-description and self-understanding to the extent that paradigms of religious persecution, courageous uprooting, and successful settlement and adaptation have clearly become part of a collective consciousness. Mennonites have been described as a "mobilized diaspora" with "a strong corporate identity" and a leadership that represents their interests.[4] With respect to the Mennonites' many global migrations, the story has been one of adventurous and visionary community leaders, all male, guiding a particular group forward historically to a new land where the integrity of religious belief and ethnic custom could be preserved. Thus, migration became deeply rooted in myths of progress and purity; that is, from the perspective of those who led particular movements. The perspectives of followers, especially women, or those left behind, for that matter, are not included in the 'social memory' of migration and thus we know little about the extent to which they shared in the myths of forward movement.

To the extent that the concept of diaspora "disavows essentialist and unchanging notions of identity and emphasizes interconnectedness across borders," it is also useful for understanding the "tensions, negotiations, and contestations" over gender identities that women experience in the process of relocation.[5] Several recent studies of Mennonite migrations, informed by gender analysis, have demonstrated that immigration frequently destabilized normative gender roles and, in some cases, presented women with opportunities to exert high degrees of power and influence.[6] For Mennonite women, the outcomes varied greatly according to time and place. Furthermore, for women migrants in particular, whose social roles were closely tied to family and domestic space, an ongoing sense of "being simultaneously 'home away from home' or 'here and there,'"[7] may have been especially strong. This chapter will look at Mennonite women arriving and settling into new lives in Canada, whether as pioneers, refugees, or transnationals.

LEAVING HOMELANDS

A discourse of 'mobilized' diaspora that reflects the agenda of male leaders emphasizes push and pull factors in migration that leave little room for ambiguity or indecision, yet women may have experienced migration differently from men. For some women, migration was not an unequivocal decision. Anna Jansen, whose father was a leader of the 1870s migration from Russia, writes in her diary about a woman who blamed her husband for bringing them to North America and who threatened to return to Russia with the children.[8] Analyzing the diaries of several women migrants, Esther Epp-Tiessen suggests that "the reasons for the move were not of primary concern to them."[9] Characterizations of Mennonite movement, with emphasis on group identity and authoritative leadership, tend to make invisible those experiences and choices that depart from the collective discourse established by the writings of leaders. Women, whose mental place was culturally encoded in familial relationships and domestic spaces, were often individually 'looking backward' even while collectively 'moving forward.' Even while many Mennonites migrated in family and village groupings, both extended and nuclear family ties were disrupted in the process of migration and homes were left behind. For women, "loss and hope" existed together as "a defining tension"[10] in which they shared anticipation of the future with husbands and fathers, while also regretting separation from gardens, neighbours, and family members.

Margaretha and Anna Jansen, emigrants from Russia in 1874, both wrote in their diaries about their feelings of loneliness and homesickness for friends and family left behind. At Easter in Canada, Anna wrote that they had painted eggs, a custom that revived memories and caused her to remark: "I do not know very well why, but I am homesick very often."[11] Her sister Margaretha's pessimism over migration was even more profound. Four and a half months after arriving in Canada, she wrote the following on New Year's Day 1874: "We have started this new year in America and how dark the future lies before us."[12] Another family memoir states that when the David and Aganetha Klassen family arrived at the site of their new home on the banks of the Scratching River in Manitoba in 1874, the women of the family began to "weep uncontrollably. It was unbearably hot and the mosquitoes were attacking them ferociously."[13] Sarah Sawatzky Funk was "beside herself with grief" when in 1926, only a year after her mother died, her father and all her siblings chose to join an emigration from Canada to Paraguay. It is said that "Often she would walk to her parents' yard and weep for the family she missed so dearly."[14] Suse Martens Unruh, who arrived in Canada from Russia in 1928, recalled that "I ... cried so many times. A young woman, twenty-two years. And ... the baby ... was colicky, always sick and sick and sick. Not knowing the language. I cried so many, many, many times. But there was no way to go back."[15]

Analyzing women's perspectives on migration in a gendered manner may reveal that they thought about and experienced uprooting and settlement in disparate ways from their menfolk. Yet a woman's outlook may not only have been cautionary; she may indeed have been the one who pushed her family to go, perhaps because she feared for the future security of her children, or perhaps because she had an adventurous spirit. Barbara Reiff, a Pennsylvania woman whose husband Isaac died in 1802, opted to move to Canada in 1808 with the three youngest of her nine children. They settled on a farm of "bush and flies," according to her young son, who also said that his mother was "robust and of a quick turn," who, at the age of sixty, "would mount her pony like a young man."[16] While some women regretted the decisions of their menfolk to uproot and resettle in the New World, and others acquiesced while keeping their fears and doubts to themselves, other women expressed their views in favour of migration strongly and sometimes acted alone. For instance, Margaretha Harder, a fifty-four-year-old unmarried woman, wanted to migrate to Manitoba from Russia with her Kleine Gemeinde church group in the 1870s but was opposed by her brothers, who were guardians of their sister and her significant inheritance. She sought help from colony administrators and eventually her brothers allowed her to go—in exchange for her money.[17] Helena Jansen, another Kleine Gemeinde member, was reportedly "influential" in the decision of her village group to emmigrate to Manitoba rather than Nebraska in the 1870s.[18] As a life-changing family decision, migration could create significant tension in a marriage, when one spouse wanted to stay and one wished to move, as Katherine Schroeder observed in her account of the 1948 migration of Mennonites from Canada to Paraguay.[19]

Whether women were naysayers or promoters of migration, the experience of diaspora offered a point at which gender roles were destabilized and reconstructed according to the limitations and possibilities of a woman's social and religious environment.

PIONEERS IN EMERGING CANADA

Historian Lorraine Roth, in her book on early Amish settlement in Wilmot Township, Ontario, says the following about gender relations among pioneer immigrants: "The settler (usually male) was the head of the household, and his wife was an accessory, albeit an indispensable one."[20] This of course was the dominant portrayal of gender relations in immigration historiography[21] and in histories of Mennonite mobility as well. In pioneer agricultural communities, such as were established in Upper Canada by Mennonite and Amish immigrants from Switzerland and southern Germany from the late eighteenth through to the mid-nineteenth centuries and on the prairies by Mennonites from Russia beginning in the 1870s, there was a certain egalitarianism that sometimes occurred when institutional structures were less a priority than the physical subsistence labour demanded of women and men, young and old. To the extent that uprooting and new settlement demanded full participation of all family members and allowed women to create things new—sometimes including new roles—pioneering new lands, whether in

Upper Canada or Manitoba, may have had an equalizing tendency in terms of the value attributed to the respective contributions of men and women. It could also, at least for a time, destabilize entrenched gender roles that were limiting for women.

Women and men were collectively engaged in milking, making hay, setting up sheaves of grain, and filling the cellar with food for the winter. If men's work was located mainly in the fields, and women's mainly within the house, while the barn and garden were sites where their work paths crossed, the agrarian household economy would nevertheless not have functioned if the labour of either was missing. And during such work-intensive times of year as harvest, older girls and women might be found more often in the fields, while younger girls of the household ensured there were meals for a busy family. Maria Klassen reminisced that during harvest, "My husband and I did a great deal of work together...." and that "Meal-making took second place ... [lunch consisting of] raw cured ham, vinegar, raw onions, and thick sour milk."[22] On visiting new Mennonite settlers in southern Manitoba in 1877, a secretary in the Canadian Department of Agriculture, John Lowe, observed that "women were ploughing in the fields, thatching roofs and girls were plastering houses."[23] By the same token, the long winter months may have seen male family members participating in indoor tasks often deemed to be 'women's work.'

In pioneer economies that revolved mainly around subsistence production of both farm and household, women's productive and reproductive work was necessary and valued. It is argued that this has always been true of the rural farming enterprise, where production and household are closely tied—indeed, overlap—in contrast to urban economies where productivity is equated with waged labour in the marketplace. Some scholars have taken the question further, arguing that not only did women 'share' in a multitude of farming tasks, they actually "hauled a double load." Women who worked alongside their menfolk in the barn and on the fields may have had a sense that gender didn't matter on the frontier but, as Frances Swyripa has pointed out, for Ukrainian women in western Canada, the heavy labour and material hardships were considerably greater than in the Old Country and thus hardly welcome.[24]

The empowerment that sometimes occurred for pioneer women nevertheless took place within communities that remained largely male-dominated. Furthermore, as male-run institutions such as churches and schools developed and competed with the family farm in terms of their centrality to community life, and as mechanization changed the labour demands on the farm, and as the economies of Mennonite communities diversified, one could argue that women's roles were privatized within the domestic household and accordingly their labour was of lesser value. As historian Kathryn McPherson has pointed out, analyses of women and agricultural settlement—thus far ranging mainly between frameworks of 'frontier equality' and 'frontier inequity'—should recognize that the frontier experience was profoundly different among women, depending on their region, race, and class.[25] For example, Mennonite women may have lacked access to the rights and privileges allowed to Anglo-Canadian women homesteaders, but, as in Russia, where they positioned themselves socio-economically above their Russian and Ukrainian peasant neighbours, in Canada the frontier was certainly 'good' for Mennonites vis-à-vis their Aboriginal neighbours.

The first Mennonite pioneering families in Canada began arriving from Pennsylvania in the late eighteenth century. They would first settle at Twenty Mile Creek on the Niagara Peninsula and, in the early nineteenth century, move further inland to townships north of Toronto and to land along the Grand River in the present-day Waterloo region in southwestern Ontario. A second wave of pioneer immigrants were the Amish, most of whom arrived directly from Europe and settled, like Barbara Schultz Oesch, on the lands west of present-day Kitchener–Waterloo, Ontario. Then, in the 1870s, approximately 8000 Mennonites left their homes in south Russia to settle on reserve lands in southern Manitoba. Some twenty years later, another group arrived from Russia to homestead in Saskatchewan. All the women in these various stages of migration had little sense of the environs into which they were heading. They were all taking risks by leaving the security of established communities, even if circumstances such as land shortages and pressures of militarism were impinging on the quality of life for their families and future generations, thus prompting the move. In the earliest years, they were all venturing into lands that were sparsely populated by Aboriginal peoples and only a few other white settlers. All had dealt with the adversities of travel, over oceans and treacherous rivers, through swampland, and overland on rough trails. Whether they arrived at dense forest or open prairie, the building of shelter for people and livestock, digging of wells, and construction of rudimentary cooking ovens were the most pressing tasks.

The stereotype of the pioneer wife as a spiritless drudge is based on the reality that her life was one of almost incessant hard work. In this, the experiences of Mennonite women differed little from that of other newly arrived immigrant women in pre-Confederation and early Canada. Waterloo County historian Elizabeth Bloomfield noted that the highest compliment a woman could earn in the Mennonite community was "How she works!"[26] The first and, indeed, second generation of Mennonite women in nineteenth-century Ontario and on the prairies lived lives that were a morning-till-night succession of mostly arduous tasks to keep families warm, fed, and sheltered. From planting and harvesting huge gardens, butchering and preserving meat, to making soap and candles, weaving and sewing—all were undertaken from scratch. Fortunately, large nuclear families and nearby extended families meant that the larger tasks were often undertaken as communal efforts or 'bees.' Family and community memoirs are full of detailed descriptions of pig-butchering bees in particular, where several families would join together to prepare and preserve the many animal products that resulted, men and women assuming gender-specific and well-understood roles in the process. As well, a woman could more easily harvest from her garden and put away large quantities of dried and pickled foods with the help of several daughters or that of her neighbours or relatives.

Living on the frontier was not just about hard work, but also dealing with the kind of dangers that living close to nature meant. One young woman, preparing supper alone in her log cabin, poured boiling water on the noses of wolves that were attempting to dig their way through the floor.[27] Another recollection tells of Sarah Boese Loewen, newly married and homesteading in Alberta in 1904, chasing a coyote down a hill with a butcher knife to protect her sheep.[28] And oral tradition is full of stories of women, and men, killing rattlesnakes in their way as they journeyed to their assigned plots of land. Some historical accounts present encounters with Aboriginal peoples as one of the many dangers faced by white settlers, yet it is more likely that Mennonite women benefited from what they could learn from Aboriginal women and men, in adapting to a new environment. Knowledge gleaned from indigenous peoples in terms of native plants and herbs that were edible or could be used as dyes or for medicinal purposes was crucial for survival, as midwife-healer Katherina Hiebert (profiled above) was quick to learn when she began providing healthcare to her immigrant community in Manitoba in the late nineteenth century.

Pioneering women lived with close awareness of the physical elements of climate, crops, and daily sustenance, and with an almost unimaginable litany of daily tasks in running a household. The diaries of nineteenth-century Mennonite women are organized around such seemingly mundane yet labour-intensive routines and events as butchering, livestock births, selling of produce, harvesting and preserving foodstuffs, and the regular tasks involved in preparing meals, and keeping a house clean and family clothed. Maria Reimer Unger, a southern Manitoba midwife who bore thirteen children by age forty-three, offered a day-by-day account of her many tasks in 1919, which included weaving, sewing, making soap, butchering, writing letters, hosting and visiting an extensive network of kin and neighbours, and numerous other farming routines.[29] Laundry could consume the better part of a week and was among the most laborious tasks in nineteenth-century households: potatoes had to be ground for starch, gallons of water hauled and then boiled over wood fires, clothing scrubbed by hand, and then heavy water-soaked fabrics had to be wrung out and hung outdoors, no matter what the season. Then irons were heated and reheated in a day-long regime of ironing. Other regular tasks included whitewashing walls and polishing earthen floors with a mixture of cow dung, sand, and water.

The 'pioneering' experience continued well into the twentieth century for some Mennonites, as new migrant groups arrived and as already resident groups sought new farming opportunities and/or social isolation in frontier settings. Indeed, Sara Brooks Sundberg points out, a "female farming frontier" persisted at least until 1922 in Manitoba, since the mechanization of male farm labour progressed at a much faster pace than for women. For example, very few farm women benefited from running water in either kitchen or bathroom; and even by 1931, less than 2 percent of Manitoba farms reported these amenities.[30] In 1925, a recently arrived group of migrants from Russia attempted to establish a community called Reesor along the CPR rail line in northern Ontario, not far from Kapuskasing. With no roads yet built, and land uncleared, settlement conditions were harsh and arduous. Women inevitably experienced greater isolation, since men would occasionally make trips into town or be together in the bush cutting trees much of the time. Anna Berg Klassen recalled the severe challenges faced by women in this isolated setting: "The winters were long and very cold.... For [the women with small children] it was impossible to get out. In winter the men, when cutting pulpwood, were gone from dawn to dusk, this left the women with the chores of not only looking after the family but also to tend the stove, bring in the firewood, baking, cooking, melting snow for water, and milking the cows. These responsibilities left the women in complete exhaustion, both mentally and physically." Another Reesor recollection concurs that the "mothers of large families with young children [had] hardship beyond all imagination."[31] The difficulties of daily and routine tasks were compounded when disruptions such as death and illness visited a household. For instance, new immigrants on the prairies, already impoverished during the Depression, suffered even more when waves of illness hit their families. The household of Gertrude Epp was quarantined during the winter of 1933–34 when she was pregnant and all five of her children contracted scarlet fever. When a physician refused to visit, the local Mennonite bishop brought medication and information regarding proper care for the sick.[32]

The significant amount of work required in the pioneer and rural household meant that most families sought servant girls to help out. Sometimes they were teenaged girls from another Mennonite family that needed the income or didn't require their daughter at home. Non-Mennonite girls from nearby towns were also hired for this purpose. Laura Shantz's 1918 diary makes frequent mention of Minnie Humphrey, a sixteen-year-old English girl who worked off and on as required in the Shantz household, such as on heavy wash days or when Laura was bedridden for a week.[33] Families with many daughters were advantaged because of the many household tasks that were gendered as female. Maria Reimer Unger's 1919 diary offers a glimpse, on a daily basis, of the numerous and varied jobs that her daughters performed, both indoors and out. For instance, on July 4, "the girls cleaned, baked and weeded"; on August 13, "The girls canned plums in the forenoon and then stooked sheaves"; on August 23, "The girls made ketchup and pickles and canned cherries and blueberries"; on October 1, "The girls cleaned the henhouse and whitewashed it"; on October 14, "The girls did various things, like ironing the wash, canning tomatoes, cleaning and sealing the windows, etc."[34]

While tasks on the farm household were fairly gender-specific, the degree to which rigid divisions were maintained sometimes depended on the number of boys and girls in any given family. For instance, Maria K. Plett had twelve children, only two of whom were boys, and so "the girls had to do the work of boys" such as "choring, making hay, plowing, and whatever else needed to be done."[35] And while girls were expected to do 'boys' chores, it was less likely that boys were called upon to help with female tasks like baking and ironing, for instance. As Sheila McManus observes of Alberta farm women, which probably also applied to Mennonites, "The allocation of various tasks was flexible, but the division of responsibility remained clear: women were responsible for the inside work, and men were responsible for the outside work."[36] If a woman did not have her own daughters to assist her in the house, she was more prone to seek a hired girl than expect her sons to do the work of women. Indeed, one Amish woman in Ontario recalled that she helped with outdoor farm work when they had a maid, because "Girls were easier to get than men to work for you."[37] Other accounts demonstrate, however, that crucial female domestic help on the farm could be a scarce commodity. This may have been especially true in communities with a high birth rate, where 'maids' were in high demand, and where men may have travelled up to fifty kilometres to find a girl to help out.[38]

Women frequently added to tasks of sustenance by generating income through the sale of garden produce or handmade goods. And sometimes the women's small-scale food production was crucial to the economic viability of the rural family enterprise. For instance, diaries from early immigrants in southern Manitoba refer to the sale of "chickens, butter, eggs, sauerkraut, onions, and potatoes" in Winnipeg, and that income generated from these sales accounted for more than half the annual income of some rural households.[39] As household producers and reproducers, women's work was essential to the success of the rural household and may have "provided them with a significant degree of meaning, status, and power"[40] to offset the patriarchism of Mennonite church communities.

Women without husbands who were 'heads of families' took on additional responsibilities and crossed the boundaries of gender in order to accomplish necessary tasks. They also had to use their ingenuity to generate income needed to support their families. Elizabeth Witmer Groh migrated to Upper Canada (Ontario) as a forty-seven-year-old widow with seven children from Montgomery County, Pennsylvania, in 1804. Her husband had cleared and planted six acres in Waterloo Township the previous year but then fell ill and died when returning with his family. Interestingly, of thirty-one family heads who arrived in the first phase of settlement in Waterloo Township, Elizabeth was the fourth in terms of amount of land purchased, with 450 acres assessed.[41] Esther Bleam Steckle also had to take leadership in maintaining her family when her husband John was disabled in a logging accident in the 1840s. She did much of the "lathing and plastering" of their log house and was known as a "remarkable horsewoman" for her ability to carry a spinning wheel on horseback as well as fill her saddlebags with eggs to sell.[42]

For communities that were oriented to agriculture almost exclusively, land ownership and inheritance practices could have a significant impact on women's status and on their economic security. This was often particularly so for widows and single women. The early settlers in Upper Canada were identified according to the location and amount of land they owned. Susannah Erb Brubacher was the only woman named as a shareholder in the German Company, the group of Mennonites from Pennsylvania who purchased 60,000 acres of land in Waterloo Township in 1805. Mennonites who migrated to Manitoba from south Russia in the 1870s brought with them a distinct tradition of 'bilateral partible' inheritance that, according to historian Royden Loewen, "presented women with tools to exercise important degrees of influence at crucial points in the household's life cycle."[43] Under this custom, estates were divided equally among a deceased owner's heirs and, more importantly, land was inherited equally by males and females.[44] This differed from the more common European practice whereby land was indivisible and would be passed on to one heir, usually the eldest son. How this worked, in the case of a married man's death, for instance, was that his widow would receive half the estate and the remaining half would be divided equally—whether in land or equivalent cash—amongst the children, both sons and daughters.

The implications of the practice was that it ensured some economic security for widows, and for daughters who did not marry. It was thus not uncommon for unmarried women to be landowners, nor for women to bring inherited land to their marriage. Matrilocal households then became more common when a woman with land and more local familial ties than those of her new husband was able to attract him to live in her village community. Even if daughters did not receive land outright, the division of a deceased parent's estate could bestow on her substantial sums of money and, accordingly, a measure of economic autonomy. The practice also offered the potential for 'upward mobility' for poor boys who married wealthy girls. Significantly, Mennonite churchmen who outlined these inheritance procedures used biblical texts to undergird the practice. In particular, I Peter 3:7 was cited, which exhorted that if men and women were "joint heirs in the grace of life," then "how much more of temporal goods?" What it meant in terms of women's economic autonomy and status is hard to estimate. It did ensure that a widow did not become completely dependent on her church or family for support, although she was reliant on the integrity of a male guardian chosen to oversee the devolution of her husband's estate.

Amongst Swiss Mennonite pioneers in Upper Canada, similar inheritance practices meant that females inherited land as well. John and Catherine Brubacher, who owned a sizeable 1100 acres in 1831, were able to set up most of their children on substantial farms. According to their youngest daughter, each of the boys received 200 acres of land and each of the girls 150 acres.[45] Jacob Schneider, another land-wealthy Mennonite, bequeathed equal shares of his estate to his sons and daughters. That the practice of equitable inheritance was also distinctive among the Swiss is suggested by the analysis of Joseph S. Stauffer, who remarked, "In contrast to their English and Scottish neighbours, some of whom by tradition believed that boys were entitled to more than their sisters, in any division of property, the Mennonites, in all financial affairs, treated their sons and daughters equally." Stauffer goes on to suggest that, since primogeniture (inheritance by the eldest son) was not the prevailing norm, women became good administrators of property. To ensure equitable division of parental assets, families would maintain a record of the debits accrued by both daughters and sons who left the household. For instance, when a daughter married, the assets and gifts she took to her new household were debited in her parents' family book. One family book recorded the following debits placed against a daughter upon her marriage to a nearby farmer's son: "to [sic] span of horses; two cows; one heifer; twenty sheep; one colt; three pigs; sleigh and cutter; one second hand harrow; furniture outfit."[46] When the last child was left with the farm, he (usually a son retained the farm) was obliged to pay out to his brothers and sisters an amount to equal the value of the farm, minus debits they had accumulated. This also ensured that sons and daughters ended up with comparable assets from their parental home.

Land inheritance practices could be especially crucial among agrarian groups with large family sizes, such as the Mennonites. Perhaps even more central than her role as producer was a woman's role as reproducer. Certainly Mennonite women, like other pre-industrial women, spent a large portion of their adult years childbearing. Pioneer settlers like Barbara Schultz Oesch had a particular settlement agenda that was oriented towards reproduction as much as to agricultural production. Her willingness to risk death by bearing eighteen children grew out of her desire to 'people' a new land; she knew the importance of generational succession in ensuring that a community flourished. As Nanci Langford says of the Canadian West, "Women literally risked their lives to establish their families and a future for their children. . . ."[47] The male-centred analysis of early immigration and settlement that focuses on land cultivation rather than people production prevents us from seeing Barbara as an equal participant. But particularly in a pioneering setting with a sparse European population, Barbara's reproductive capacity was crucial to the success of her community's settlement. Family formation was central in the pioneer agenda, and one aspect of this was raising large families that provided labouring hands for their parents' farm. When those children then established themselves on nearby farms of their own, not only the family but the entire community extended its presence, in terms of both land owned and population growth. Some evidence suggests that family size did indeed increase in frontier settings.

The transplantation of social customs from the Old World, like that of the inheritance patterns described above, could have a variety of outcomes for women. On the one hand, cultural traditions brought to Canada from south Russia, Pennsylvania, and Switzerland provided women and their families with a sense of continuity in the midst of otherwise drastic changes to their environment that required adaptation on many levels. As scholars of diaspora have proposed, the memory of places left behind, whether stored inwardly or enacted in transplanted tradition, have "often served as symbolic anchors of community for dispersed peoples."[48] One historian has suggested that Mennonite women were central to the transmission across the globe and preservation of cultural artefacts, such as storage trunks and dowry chests.[49] Another example of transplanting symbolic anchors occurred on the prairies, where the establishment of reserves with rural villages and agricultural land laid out according to a street-village model used in Russia may have been a significant factor in alleviating the isolation that was so common for other homesteading immigrant women on the prairies who may have sometimes pondered whether "to drown myself now or later."[50]

The street village (*Strassendorf*), as it was known, was created when ten to thirty families combined their homestead allotments, then built their homes and barns (the two buildings often connected) closely together along a central road, sometimes on both sides, sometimes on only one side. The surrounding pastureland and fields were then divided or worked commonly. With their homes only a short distance apart, women could connect easily with their neighbours, who were, at least in the early years of settlement, often members of their extended family. In this, the Mennonite women who arrived on the prairies in the 1870s had a distinct advantage over other British and European immigrant settlers. Being able to walk a short distance to one's neighbour and kin undoubtedly allowed for the sharing of advice, household supplies, childcare, and community news in ways that were simply not possible for households separated by several kilometres. Female networks were able to flourish when women lived close to one another and allowed for regular activities such as quilting, canning, and cleaning bees, as well as sewing parties and sister circles. Knowing that a neighbour or relative was only a short distance away helped to diminish fears of childbirth and other illnesses on the frontier. And simple customs such as passing the wedding invitation door-to-door was made easy when doors were only a short walk away. At the same time, the physically close village layout may have reinforced watchfulness over behaviour that then placed pressures on women to conform to community norms that could limit creative expression and individuality.

Especially in the early years of pioneer settlement, the household was the social unit that shaped the identities of Mennonite women more so than the church. Because women's roles were so closely tied to family and domestic space, the centrality of the household over and above the church, its related associations and those community institutions that were slower to be established, may have afforded women a certain status in those early years that diminished as house and home were privatized. Many of the patterns that shaped women's lives in early immigrant communities continue to exist in the more rural, isolated, and sectarian communities, such as the Amish and other Old Order Mennonite subgroups. Among conservative groups, where there is little distinction between the 'church' and the 'community,' families play a major, indeed primary, role in passing on and expressing religious beliefs. For the Old Order Amish, who have no church buildings but hold worship services in homes and sheds, church and household come together most directly. It could be argued that because the community, church, and household are so closely related amongst conservative Mennonites, there is more gender equality and greater value attributed to women and their work.

Women also played a primary role in nurturing kinship and other social relationships across huge geographic spaces, since migration inevitably divided Mennonite communities and, quite often, extended families as well. Because they possessed a high rate of literacy, Mennonites were prolific letter and diary writers and women in particular nurtured kinship relationships across many kilometres through regular letter writing. This remained true even for later 'pioneers' such as Helen Esau Froese, who migrated from Canada to Paraguay in 1948 but was able to reduce the psychological and emotional separation from her three sisters in Canada through three decades of conversation via letters and cassette tape recordings.[51]

Yet, even while certain customs enhanced communication in rural areas, other social patterns impeded women's ability to orient themselves to life in Canada. In the rural Manitoba community where my grandparents settled, evening English classes were held for men in order to equip them to talk with their English neighbours and do business transactions in town. Such classes were apparently not considered necessary for women, who only went to town accompanied by their husbands. Because of her social isolation, my grandmother, Maria Driedger Dick, was one of many Mennonite women immigrants who never became fluent in English.[52] Among 1870s immigrants from Russia, only 17 percent of married women on the East Reserve (Manitoba) could speak English in 1900, compared to 73 percent of men.[53] Their lesser capacity to converse and write in English than could their husbands and children, and thus their great isolation as newcomer Canadians, is mentioned in numerous female immigrant narratives. Helene Funk, who immigrated to Saskatchewan in the 1920s, would often say to her chattering children, "If only I could buy an English tongue!"[54]

Pioneer and rural settlements, because of their physical isolation from more urban areas and social boundaries that limited interaction with non-Mennonite neighbours, afforded a certain legitimacy to women in vocational roles as midwives, chiropractors, and undertakers, for instance. Indeed, in pre-industrial Canada generally, women's domestic vocations as healers and midwives were among their most important roles. As there were no resident doctors in Waterloo Township until the 1830s, early Mennonite settlers relied on such individuals as Esther Bleam Steckle, who was "well versed in the medicinal values of wild plants, being the local home doctor of the community."[55] Agnes Meyer Hunsberger, mother of fourteen and an immigrant from Pennsylvania to southwest Ontario in 1800, was "remarkably gifted in the healing art" and "answered all calls as physician or nurse." According to a family genealogy of 1896, she visited the sick on her "favorite chestnut mare, a most intelligent beast [that] carried her safely through the wilderness at all hours of day or night on the errands of mercy."[56]

Maria Eitzen Penner was known as a "Mother of Israel" among southern Manitoba settlers who would come to see her in times of "trouble, sickness, or otherwise."[57] Anganetha Dyck Bergen Baerg was a Saskatchewan woman who had no formal training but wore the hat of nurse, midwife, and undertaker as needed in her rural community; the last task involved confirming a death, and cleaning, dressing, and preparing bodies for burial.[58] Katherine Born Thiessen, a popular 'doctor' in southern Manitoba in the late nineteenth century, was served with a $50 fine by the Manitoba College of Physicians in 1895 for practising medicine without a licence. A male writer to a Mennonite newspaper called on the community to help her pay the fine, since "it is very strange that a woman who has tirelessly worked to dispense her own wisdom should be persecuted."[59] Thiessen was highly valued for her skills as a midwife, bone-setter, and naturopath, training she had begun in Prussia as an eighteen-year-old.[60]

Healing skills were frequently passed on through generations and even after the initial decades of settlement, women with particular abilities to cure all manner of ailments remained much sought-after in rural areas. Maria Dueck Ginter, considered a "special woman with a special gift," learned her bone-setting skills from her father, but her practice included varied treatments such as 'turning' women's wombs to enable them to become pregnant. When she was sent a letter from the government, prohibiting her from charging fees as she was unlicensed, she simply allowed patients to give whatever they could, in money or in gift.[61] Especially in the early years of settlement in Upper Canada and Manitoba, Mennonite women healers learned many of their skills from Aboriginal women. For instance, Katherina Hiebert, profiled at the outset of this chapter, gained "considerable herb healing information" from an Aboriginal woman. When Katherina developed breast cancer, she stayed for several weeks with the woman for treatment that included poultices made from herbs and bark. Apparently she was completely cured.[62] These kinds of interactions, so rarely documented in written sources, point to a need for further research and analysis into the relationship between white Mennonite newcomers and Aboriginal people in nineteenth-century Canada.

In the early decades of settlement, be it in southwestern Ontario in the early nineteenth century or on the prairies seventy-five years later, or in many other parts of Canada in the twentieth century as new waves of agricultural settlers arrived, Mennonite pioneer women performed a multitude of roles— thatching roofs, harvesting crops, bearing children, and curing maladies—that were central to the survival of their immigrant communities. In later decades, Mennonite women who migrated to the city were also a vital link to the economic success of their families and ethno-religious communities.

MIGRANTS TO THE CITY

By the mid-twentieth century, Mennonites were gradually becoming decidedly more urban than rural, as census figures and other documents note. But single Mennonite women began to urbanize already in the 1920s and, indeed, a large migration of Mennonites from the Soviet Union was followed by a migration of women to Canadian cities. The First World War, the Bolshevik revolution of 1917, and the years of civil war, anarchist violence, famine, and disease that followed caused significant trauma to the 150-year-old Mennonite settlements in south Russia. Death touched most families through starvation, an epidemic of typhus, and, in some villages, horrific massacres by vengeful bandits.[63] By the early 1920s, the future for Mennonite religious and economic institutions looked uncertain, prompting many families to consider searching for a home elsewhere in the world. In Canada, the immigration gates were opening up again after a several-year ban on the admission of Mennonites and other pacifist sects following the war.

Beginning in 1923 and until 1930, approximately 25,000 Mennonites left the Soviet Union for North and South America. Most of the 21,000 immigrants who arrived in Canada between 1923 and 1929 attempted to establish themselves on farms, though some were drawn to the increasing demand for waged labour in urban factories, especially in southern Ontario, where established Mennonites were already living in semi-urban environments. Many of the newcomers from the Soviet Union, in fact, were given accommodation and employment for as long as a year in the Waterloo region by long-resident Swiss Mennonite families. On top of the challenges in generating income for daily sustenance, all the families arrived in Canada with travel debts owing to the Canadian Pacific Railway. In this context, women's labour became a significant source of family income.

As families struggled to establish themselves in rural areas, many sent their daughters, some as young as thirteen years old, to nearby cities to fill the high demand for domestic workers. Some entered domestic labour immediately on disembarking at train stations, responding to the agents and employers who were ready to hire women on the spot. And the demand was great. Domestic service was the dominant waged labour option for women in Canada from the nineteenth century up to the Second World War. Immigrant women—British, Irish, Finnish, German—were a popular source of labour that was constantly in short supply. Unlike women from some other immigrant groups, Mennonite women were not known for their 'defiance' or class-conscious resistance to exploitative treatment on the part of employers. Indeed, Mennonite women were in high demand because of their reputations for "cleanliness, submissiveness and honesty." As Ruth Derksen Siemens remarks, Mennonites were desirable as domestics because "they were white, submissive, quiet, hardworking and their lifestyles appeared as clean as their floors."[64] In Kapuskasing, Ontario, "well-to-do families ... valued the Mennonite girls as maids [because they] had been well-trained at home."[65]

The hundreds of young women working in cities then sent almost all their wages home, a contribution that meant the difference between survival or not for some struggling immigrant households, especially during the years of the Depression. As well, the wages of the domestics were crucial to the success of Mennonite immigrant families in repaying enormous travel debts owing to the CPR. Three of four daughters in a 1924 immigrant family worked as domestics in Winnipeg, sending their wages home to rural Manitoba to pay for their parents' house and the family's travel debt, which was finally paid in full in 1941.[66] As Frieda Esau Klippenstein has noted, this scenario created "an uncomfortable, if not bewildering, role reversal" whereby young women were supporting their fathers economically—and, in the case of the travel debts, their entire community—and thus upsetting the patriarchal order of financial dependency.[67] Katherine Friesen and her sister also went to work as domestics in Saskatoon during the Depression years to help ease the financial burden of their farming family. Katherine described the working conditions that were common to all her different positions. The work day was fifteen hours long and wages averaged $20 per month. A deferential demeanour towards employers was definitely required, as she explains:

> We were called maids and were treated as servants. The door between the kitchen and dining room was to be closed at all times. When summoned by a bell, I entered only to change the courses. I always ate my meals alone in the kitchen after they were finished. My sleeping quarters was usually a make-shift room in the basement. I entered the house by the back door.... The rule was that the servant should get Thursday afternoons and two Sunday afternoons a month free. There was more trouble with this than anything else. Usually an extra amount of work was found that had to be done on Thursday, so my half-day started at 3 or 4 p.m.[68]

Thursdays became significant days for women workers and their families alike. The sheer number of young Mennonite women who entered domestic service in cities in the 1920s and 1930s meant that the routines of rural

Mennonite communities and churches were shaped around the women's days off. Mariechen Langemann Klassen, who in 1928 moved with her family to North Kildonan, on the north edges of Winnipeg at the time, said, "We girls all worked in Winnipeg. A whole row of girls." Their church held choir practice on Thursday evenings and service on Sunday evenings, the only two days the women were able to return home.[69]

In addition to upsetting the normal roles of economic 'provider' in their families, young female workers were also upsetting a mental framework in which an agricultural lifestyle brought Mennonites closer to God. Mennonite leaders viewed cities as dangerous places where numerous vices lay in wait to bring about the downfall of innocent men and women and also lead to a breakdown of Mennonite community and insularity. There was a certain irony in encouraging young women to leave their families, to work for wages, and to do so in the city, all of which ran counter to the normative ethos of Mennonite community life. Yet the financial exigencies faced by immigrant households and the obvious opportunities that the domestic service labour market presented quickly sidelined traditional ways of life. Fearful for the morality of young women amidst the perceived evils of the city, Mennonite churches created boarding houses or "girls' homes" (*Mädchenheime*) in Vancouver, Calgary, Saskatoon, and Winnipeg. The homes functioned as employment bureaux, connecting young Mennonite women with potential employers, the supervisors also doing their best to monitor employment situations. Since most domestic situations were live-in, the girls' home offered lodging for newcomers to the city in search of employment and also held weekly gatherings—usually Thursdays, which were known as 'maids' day off'—that included singing, sewing, socializing, and devotionals. At the Saskatoon home, the evening typically ended with the singing of the hymn "Blessed Be the Tie that Binds," followed by "a lengthy prayer" in which the home's director and city minister J.J. Thiessen "lifted up the particular concerns expressed by the women present."[70] Several of the homes also formed the nuclei of urban congregations.

Once established, the girls' homes became immensely busy, as the Mennonite reputation for reliable domestic service grew, and as rural parents, comforted by the knowledge that such supports existed, sent their daughters to the cities in greater numbers. At the Bethel Home in Vancouver, the number of women registered grew from 53 in 1934, to 81 in 1936, and 350 at its peak in 1956.[71] The first venue for the girls' home in Saskatoon was a two-bedroom apartment, which quickly became too small for the seventy-five women who attended the weekly gatherings, never mind those who needed overnight lodging.[72] Each girls' home functioned as a 'home away from home,' providing sanctuary and protection for women in the unfamiliar and sometimes threatening urban environment. It was at the girls' home where women spoke a shared language, where they could meet friends and relatives, and where they could perform familiar cultural and religious rituals, such as doing needlework together and meeting with a city minister for devotions.

But the homes also were mechanisms of social control, watching over and curbing the behaviour of any young woman who exhibited decorum contrary to Christian Mennonite standards. Life in the city was considered to be replete with worldly entertainments and vices that could potentially tempt vulnerable and naïve young women. During the 1940s, one British Columbia minister expressed the concern that the possibilities for "frivolous living" were enhanced by the presence of military personnel in Vancouver, the higher wages, and the independent attitude of employees.[73] Canadian Mennonite conference leader Jacob J. Thiessen, together with his wife Tina, opened a girls' home in Saskatoon in 1931 and became a 'father' figure for many Mennonite domestics in that city. "J.J.," as he was known, felt a paternalistic responsibility towards unmarried women working in the city and demonstrated a "zealous interest" in their lives that extended to reprimands if he disapproved of the company they kept or entertainment they attended. While some women appreciated his concern, the comment by one woman that "We couldn't do anything that he didn't know" suggests that others may have resented his attentiveness.[74] Though the homes did not explicitly include matchmaking in their mandate, directors such as J.J. and Tina Thiessen played an important part in steering women away from potential suitors of whom they disapproved—non-Mennonite men in particular—but also in arranging church-related functions that introduced the numerous single Mennonite women in the city to young rural men brought to town specifically to meet and interact with the women in a supervised context.[75]

Since the homes were under the supervision of male-run Mennonite conferences and mission boards, the authority of patriarchy remained in place, even though many of the homes were effectively run by women. Unmarried women like Anna Thiessen and Helen Epp, each of whom worked for several decades as matrons and administrators of girls' homes in Winnipeg, Manitoba, found opportunities for a church-related vocation that was unavailable in their own formal congregations.[76] These matrons saw it as their responsibility to ensure the women were placed into suitable situations, and that they weren't mistreated or expected to perform tasks that were against Mennonite principles, such as serving alcohol. Anna Thiessen also lobbied city officials to obtain adequate time off for live-in domestics. At the same time, Thiessen and other home administrators were watchful over the behaviour of the young women, seemingly well aware that city life offered mysteries and excitement that might be attractive to girls freed from the constraints of family and rural church community. Thus, Thiessen also found a challenge in winning potentially 'lost souls' to the Lord. Families more easily released their daughters to the city knowing that they were safely in the care and control of the girls' homes, as the following comment affirms: "Imagine, some 250 noble souls, virgins, our daughters, 'dumped' into a large city by conditions beyond their control, without the home!"[77] The motto of the Bethel Home in Vancouver—"Thou God Seest Me"—was both a promise of God's protection and a reminder to the women that their behaviour, at the home and outside it, did not go unnoticed by the home's matron.[78]

The existence of the girls' homes helped parents and rural church leaders justify the incongruity between their agrarian theology and the practical reality that saw young woman go alone to the city. Many families also felt the divergence between their own experience of employing hired help in Russia and their situation in Canada that saw their daughters hired out in the same manner. As a way of reconciling these class differences and discomforts, parents, church leaders, and women themselves constructed a service-oriented theological framework around domestic work in the city that allowed them to view and thus justify such labour activity and its location in spiritual, as well as material, terms. The role of women in the city took on the elements of a missionary enterprise, whereby the female domestics were sent into private homes to bring employers and their children to Christianity, by either example or direct teaching. Furthermore, to the extent that women's labour was viewed as Christian 'service' to their own families and to the ungodly city dwellers they worked for, women were less likely to resist poor working conditions or view their situations as demeaning. If women individually or even collectively felt overworked and underpaid, they were not, like some immigrant domestic workers, explicitly class-conscious. The discourse was evident in such material items as quilt blocks, embroidered by young women domestics, with proverbs that situated what might have otherwise been viewed as an exploitative and underpaid work environment within a context of service to God and humanity, and as "shedding light in a dark city."[79]

The homes did their best to provide an environment in which women would remain firmly connected to their Mennonite/Christian beliefs and traditions, but, especially for those who spent significant amounts of time living in non-Mennonite households, the influence of their employers was also strong. The Mennonite domestics learned language, styles of cooking, home decor, cultural customs, and ways of thinking from their employers and their children. One woman described these cultural influences as follows:

> Suddenly I was wearing a black and white uniform and emptying ashtrays and serving cocktails at a dinner party. I'd never even heard of hors d'oeuvres before, let alone made them. And a cucumber sandwich! What kind of thing was that to eat? At home we had always spoken German and now I had to answer the phone, place orders at the butcher shop, and deal with the milkman, the baker and the Eaton's delivery boy. I learned English pretty quickly.[80]

Women then incorporated these influences into their own households later in life, or carried them back to rural Mennonite communities where the 'new ways of doing things' were sometimes met with dismay. For instance, in one recollection, a woman's potential as a good marriage partner was questioned because she was pejoratively considered a "city girl."[81] Another unintended consequence of the urban work experience of Mennonite women was to enhance their sense of independence and provide them with viable alternatives to a life as wife and mother on the farm. Significant numbers of women chose to remain in the city as wage earners, even after their financial obligations towards families ended. A few saw domestic service as a means to earn enough money to support further education and vocational training for themselves. While, at one level, domestic service might be considered menial drudgery made necessary only by the temporary circumstances of new immigrant families, at another level it opened the door for women to step out of conventional roles and confining rural environments, whether for the short term or for the rest of their lives.

Women within this Mennonite immigrant community were at the forefront of an urbanizing trend that continued through the twentieth century. As such, they played a significant role in altering a Mennonite ideal that considered a rural lifestyle and agricultural vocation practically akin to religious belief. The vast majority of women who migrated to urban areas to work and who remained 'upright' Mennonites were evidence that city life did not have to bring about the ruin of a Christian woman. And, as some of the girls' homes evolved into urban Mennonite congregations, the city was soon viewed as a mission ground for growth of the Mennonite–Christian church. As Frieda Esau Klippenstein also demonstrates, the female domestics paved the way for Russian Mennonite immigrants to enter into Canadian life and contributed to wider social acceptance of the group as a whole. At the same time, the gradual closure of the various girls' homes in the late 1950s and early 1960s signalled the end of an immigrant era, in terms of the mass migration of destitute families across the ocean from the Soviet Union, but also in the sense that living in the city was less and less demonized. As Klippenstein states,

> The closure of the girls' homes was an assertion of the male leadership, reclaiming men's functions as providers and communicating a clear call to the young women to return to hearth and home. They were also a statement about Mennonite aspirations. Community reputation, which had previously been enhanced by the girls' homes, was now perceived to be negatively affected by them, for the homes had become a symbol connecting the community with a place in society it wished to rise above, and a chapter in its story that it wished to leave behind.[82]

In western Canada, the creation and operation of the girls' homes were formalized under the auspices of Mennonite church conferences. The homes received their initial impetus from the mass migration of Mennonites to Canada in the 1920s and saw renewed activity in the late 1940s and through the 1950s as another wave of newcomers from the Soviet Union arrived, the latter migrant group being mostly female and more prone to take up residence in cities. But given this domestic labour sector's predominance among Canadian women workers generally through much of the twentieth century, domestic service also drew rural Ontario Swiss Mennonite girls into local towns and cities, and prompted individuals in that province to create church-related venues with which women workers could connect. In 1936, Elizabeth Brown Kanagy, who had experience in urban mission work in both Toronto and Chicago, began a biweekly meeting called the Fidelia Club for Mennonite girls working as domestic servants in the towns of Preston, Hespeler, and Galt, Ontario.[83] The Mennonite mission in downtown Toronto, serving mainly evangelistic purposes, also functioned as a "drop-in centre" for domestics in that city.[84] Urban boarding and gathering homes for working women were also established by single women, outside any particular denominational mandate. For instance, in Kitchener, Ontario, Susannah and Alberta Shantz lived with and cared for their father until he died in the late 1920s, at which point Susannah turned their large house into a "home away from home" that boarded as many as sixteen young working women at a time; according to one account, "Many parents were grateful for Susie's care for their daughters in the big city."[85]

An important purpose of girls' homes and also less formalized drop-in centres was to offset one of the biggest drawbacks to domestic service, which was loneliness. Anna Hildebrand was only fifteen years old when she left home to work for a family thirty miles away. Having always worked alongside her mother and sisters at household labour, she found it challenging to work at such tasks alone, since "she had never heard of one person doing all the laundry and ironing by herself." She was desperately lonely away from her large family of "lively brothers and sisters."[86] Those young women who had access to a Mennonite-run girls' home eagerly anticipated their days off when they might leave the isolation of their employer's home—however benevolent the family might be—and spend a few hours with friends and other women who shared their culture and situation.

An even greater drawback, indeed a danger, of performing domestic service in private households was the potential for sexual harassment and abuse. As researchers of domestic service have concluded, sexual molestation was the most feared hazard of working as household help. Among the large numbers of young Mennonite immigrant women who went to cities to earn wages as domestics, undoubtedly many were subject to lewd looks, suggestive comments, and physical molestation by their male employers. Sometimes the abuse would extend to rape. For instance, at the age of fifteen, Suzy was repeatedly raped by her employer. She commented that many girls like herself feared they would not be believed if they reported the violence. In her words: "He used me—a couple of times a week.... He took me—threw me on the bed.... I was so ashamed. Who would believe me? So many girls didn't report it because they don't believe them.... His wife knew. She never helped me. Only came to see if I was pregnant six months later."[87] Another immigrant woman who arrived in Canada in 1948 worked as household help in a variety of temporary situations. At one placement, where she helped out before and after the arrival of a new baby, she was repeatedly molested by her male employer, who also happened to be a distant relative; she recalled, "with my milk pails full of milk he pressed me to the wall and squeezed me and even gave me a kiss. I was so very ashamed.... I was very uncomfortable. But I had to stay there. They gave me forty-five dollars a month."[88] Like many immigrant domestics, this woman was caught between a repugnant situation and her need to earn money to repay her debts and help her family out financially.

If Mennonite church leaders and workers in the girls' homes expressed concern about what would happen to young Mennonite women on the streets of Canadian cities, they offered less comment on the potential dangers these women might face in the private homes of their employers. Occasionally, if a woman was confident enough to approach the girls' home supervisor about harassment she was experiencing, the supervisor might quickly intervene to facilitate a change of placement. It is likely, however, that many incidents went unreported, as Mennonite domestics were too embarrassed and ashamed to admit that they had been subject to sexual advances or abuse in their place of employment.

Single women, whether immigrants from another country or 'migrants' from the farm, were at the forefront of the earliest movement of Mennonites to the city. Adult women who were not caring for husbands or children and were no longer needed on the family farm, or moved along with aging parents who retired in town, found an increasing number of work opportunities—in offices, in factories, in their own cottage industries—during the years of the First World War and beyond. Historian Laureen Harder observes that it was the many "women-led" households in Berlin (now Kitchener), Ontario, that provided a threshold for Mennonites to move from farm to town early in the twentieth century. Further, she suggests that the employment opportunities in town allowed "female-headed families" to stay together.[89]

Urban migration had other facets for women. Even when families moved to the city, creating small Mennonite urban enclaves, household work might be just as labour-intensive for women as in rural areas. And they may well have had to do much of that labour on their own when husbands had jobs in the city. Liese Peters, commenting on the early years of settling the community of North Kildonan on the edges of Winnipeg, noted some of the hardships for women: "There was the getting of water in two pails, the fetching of fire wood and coal, the melting of snow and the heating of water on a wood and coal stove for the wash and the bath. In spring there was the large garden which had to be looked after and in the summer the canning of the garden produce, and ever deep down the gnawing fear: 'If my husband should lose his job, what then?' ... And forever there was the dirt and mud on the streets and yard, for the children a source of joy, for the mothers grief and extra work."[90] North Kildonan, today fully enveloped by the city of Winnipeg, was a final destination for many Mennonites arriving directly from the Soviet Union in 1929 and 1930. The struggles they experienced as new immigrants were exacerbated by the onset of the Depression. Mary Enns Ediger, who grew up in North Kildonan recalled,

> The people that I felt most sorry for really were the mothers. You know, when I think of my own mother. How she struggled in those first years! Of course, it was unfortunate that ... those dirty thirties happened at the same time as our moving out there, the beginning of the whole Mennonite settlement. That made it, of course much harder for the mothers. I mean none of them could speak English. They had no means of going out and learning it because they were housebound, you know. They had children and that was about it.[91]

The gradual merging of the city of Winnipeg with the frontier of North Kildonan may have brought welcome amenities such as paved roads, plumbing, and electricity that eased the labour burden for Mennonite women, but the absorption of their communities by urban society also introduced cultural influences that inevitably altered their traditional ways of life. For some Mennonite subgroups the encroachment of non-Mennonite society caused sufficient concern to generate new migrations.

WANDERERS TO NEW FRONTIERS

While many Mennonites gradually moved into towns and cities over the course of the twentieth century, some farming families opted not to move to the city, but instead followed relatives and other Mennonites to regions in Canada where they anticipated better economic opportunities for themselves and their children. Often these moves further into the frontier, especially when undertaken in denominational or village groups, were also motivated by a desire on the part of church leaders to separate from the influences of modernity that were believed to tempt young people away from their religious community as well as compromise the beliefs and practices of that community. These patterns of internal migration were not unlike moving across oceans in terms of the psychological impact that resulted and socio-economic adjustments that had to be made. In selecting locales for settlement, it was common for all-male delegations, or the male family head, to go first to investigate prospective locales and, in many cases, also to purchase property before returning home to fetch entire families. It was not unusual, then, for women and children to arrive at their new homes with little sense of what awaited them.

Beginning in 1902, small groups of Swiss Mennonites left southwestern Ontario to take advantage of homesteading opportunities in rural Alberta and Saskatchewan. Then, beginning in the dry 1930s, many Mennonite families left the poverty-stricken and drought-ridden prairies for the fruit-growing regions of Ontario and British Columbia. For instance, Johan and Maria Klassen, who had lived through meagre times in southern Saskatchewan for well over a decade, began sending their teenage daughters to Yarrow, British Columbia, in the late 1940s in response to a shortage of berry pickers there. The parents soon followed, after selling their land, household goods, and machinery, and purchasing a two-tone turquoise car for the price of eighty acres. Unfortunately, the family had barely established themselves when they, and others like them, were devastated by the 1948 flood in the Fraser Valley.[92] Also in the mid-1930s, groups of conservative-minded Mennonites established remote communities in the Peace River region of northern Alberta.

Following a similar yearning for greater control of their social environment, as many as 6000 Mennonites actually left Canada in the early 1920s and latter 1940s for Mexico and other countries in Central and South America; such was the migratory background for Susie Reddekopp, profiled at the outset of this chapter. For women participating in such movements, whether within Canada or across national borders, the pioneering experience with all its hardships might begin all over again. Living in such settlements, often idealized as 'utopias' and in which the parameters were created by men, women were obliged to serve both family and community. As one scholar of utopian communities has observed, "dreamers of utopia have been flesh and blood men, who have woven their fantasies into social fabrics that have perpetuated the power of people like themselves."[93] Thus, the gender hierarchies within utopian sectarian communities were frequently reinforced and advanced. Living in utopia also usually meant the enforcement of social controls and regulatory measures that served to define and enforce the boundaries between the community and the outside world. And often the Mennonite desire for isolation and separation had the effect of further isolating women. Utopias do not always succeed, however, and for many Mennonite families that joined colonization efforts in Mexico, economic and social conditions, combined with intolerable levels of rigidity and legalism in their particular church subgroups, prompted a return migration to Canada beginning already in the late 1950s. Initially, many families spent the summer months in Canada, employed as migrant agricultural labour, and returned to winter in Mexico. Eventually, a 'transnational' process occurred (and continues in the early twenty-first century) that saw some families eventually settle permanently in Canada while others continued to move between north and south on a regular basis.

Amongst Mennonites who made repeated pilgrimages back and forth between Canada and Mexico, women were often the ones who kept families together. In the context of a family ideology that set men at the top of a hierarchy ordered by power and authority, coupled with socio-economic circumstances that undermined the self-sufficiency of those men, women frequently became the unofficial 'family heads.' Susanna Enns had worked with her family as migrant labour in southern Ontario, returning to Mexico in the winter but at least in one season leaving her husband Frank behind: "As he drinks a lot, it's usually better if he's not around," she said. With her six children, she had earned $1300 over six months and in Mexico was also able to generate some profit by selling goods purchased at yard sales in Ontario.[94] For her part, Susie Reddekopp did not feel she could successfully 'make it' in a new land without her husband after his death in a farm accident in Ontario. Not unlike nineteenth-century immigrants such as Barbara Schultz Oesch, Susie complied with her husband's initiative to move to Canada in search of a better life, but in his absence considered her options limited and so chose to return to her family in Mexico. For her, a member of a traditional and highly patriarchal church community, the success of migration depended on the presence of a healthy patriarch who could provide for the family. Even so, she found entrepreneurial strategies to support herself and her daughters that included filling her Mexico-bound van with buckets of peanut butter to sell on arrival. Mennonites of Canadian heritage living in Mexico developed a pattern of migration to Canada to escape a harsh and legalistic church and a life of poverty but in Canada were faced with other obstacles, including discriminatory attitudes, unemployment, and a jarring disjuncture between their 'old world' ways and a modern society. Among the numerous other socio-economic obstacles faced by this migrant group, women were especially isolated by rigid dictates regarding appropriate social spaces for their sex, and also by practices that position women as the primary purveyors of their religious culture.

Though immigration as a process is oftentimes accompanied by a deconstruction of gender roles in families and social groupings, for those subgroups
that sought to reinforce particular ways of living perceived as 'tradition' by
relocating to out-of-the-way places, an entrenchment of normative gender
roles frequently occurred as well, including a renewed emphasis on female
subservience and subordination. Mennonite women who were part of invol-
untary or forced migrations as refugees, however, were able to shake off,
even if only temporarily, the rigidity of gender definitions that limited their
choices and autonomy.

REFUGEE NEWCOMERS

The Mennonite population in Canada's growing urban centres as well as
smaller towns received a boost with the arrival of refugees from eastern
Europe and present-day Ukraine in the aftermath of the Second World War.
This third significant wave of Mennonite immigrants from the Soviet Union
(the first two being in the 1870s and 1920s) had a uniquely gendered impact
on existing Mennonite communities in Canada. Among the approximately
8000 Mennonite refugees who came to Canada over a decade beginning in
1947 was a high percentage of widows with children and an overall ratio of
women to men of about two to one. This gender imbalance was due primarily
to the arrest and exile or execution of large numbers of adult men during
several waves of Stalinist repression towards Soviet Mennonites and other
minorities—indeed, towards all Soviet citizens—in the late 1920s and through
the 1930s. Further losses occurred as men were evacuated from their homes
eastward to labour camps as the German army advanced into Ukraine in
1941, while others went missing on the war front after being conscripted into
either Soviet or German armies.

For those families that remained in the Soviet Union after the large emigration in the 1920s, the next decade represented a new cycle of famine, repression, and terror.[95] Many individuals recall in particular the height of the so-
called Stalin purges in 1936 to 1938 when a black car—called the 'black
raven'—of the Soviet secret police would arrive at their door at night to take
away fathers, brothers, and husbands. Indeed, entire truckloads were taken
from a village in any one night. Some sources state that by the outbreak of the
Second World War, an average of 50 percent of Mennonite families were
without a father. At any rate, a family that was intact was a rarity. Mennonite

settlements in Ukraine experienced the war close at hand as first the German forces moved in from the west in 1941 to occupy portions of Ukraine until a rapid Soviet advance from the east in 1943 prompted a German retreat. Those Mennonites who hadn't been exiled or arrested prior to the war, or deported eastward during the war, followed the German forces west, in a journey known as the 'great trek.' As the war ended in Europe, thousands of Mennonites were overtaken by Red Army forces and sent to labour camps in the eastern Soviet Union. The minority that safely made it to Allied zones of occupation eventually migrated, 8000 to Canada, and 4000 to Paraguay. Several thousand Mennonites displaced from homes in Prussia and Poland also migrated off the continent after the war, mainly to South America.

The resultant diaspora consisted of hundreds of fragmented families, many of which were headed by widows or unmarried young women. In post-war Canada, the impact of this diaspora of 'women without men' was significant to churches and communities, while the predominance of women and children meant that gender roles of necessity were challenged and transformed.[96] Having lost husbands, fathers, and brothers, these households of women, children, and the elderly learned how to adapt socially conditioned gender roles to accommodate the demands of child rearing and income generating in the context of non-traditional family structures. And they did so, having survived horrendous wartime conditions as refugees, in a post-war environment that idealized domesticity and the patriarchal nuclear family in which a male as proper head was the norm. Women whose husbands were dead or missing found themselves performing traditionally masculine roles—breadwinner, protector, moral and spiritual guide, rescuer, and strategist—during their refugee sojourn in Europe and then as new immigrants to Canada. This in addition to being mothers and often caretakers of elderly parents, younger siblings, and sometimes other dependents who had lost family.

Once in Canada, such refugee women negotiated through a societal terrain in which certain stigmas were attached to their sex and marital status, as well as a personal terrain of independence and self-sufficiency that derived from their life experiences. Within the Canadian context, whether in the Fraser Valley or Niagara Peninsula, women operated farms, purchased houses (often without the assistance of banks that would not issue loans to women), learned to drive cars, and, by their sheer presence, began to question the restricted role for women within Mennonite churches. However, as often happens in the process of uprooting and resettlement, the limited emancipation that accompanied immigration was also met with resistance and discomfort at the presence and actions of self-supporting women who had stepped out of dependent gender roles.

Unbeknownst to them, the women who fled their homes in the Soviet Union and eastern Europe, and were among the 200,000 displaced persons who arrived in Canada in the half decade after the war, had much in common with later groups of Mennonite refugees. The face of Mennonite churches and the characteristics of Mennonite women became more multi-faceted in the late twentieth century with the arrival of refugees and political exiles from countries in Central and South America, Southeast Asia, and from the African continent. Although somewhat beyond the stated time frame of this study, the expansion of the category 'Mennonite women' to include women whose ethnic and national background is neither Swiss-German nor Russian-German is a significant development of the later twentieth century and should be recognized. For instance, uprooted from their homes in Laos and El Salvador, Laotian and Hispanic women and their families sought refuge in Canada in the late 1970s and through the 1980s, often sponsored by Mennonite churches across Canada. Those who then became church members may have had little in common with other Mennonite women in terms of language and ethnic or religious ancestry, yet they nevertheless had experienced many of the same forces of migration that shaped the lives of women in earlier Mennonite diasporas. However, their ethnic and national identity created a different self-identification as Mennonite women. Miriam Ambrosy de Ruiz reflected on this as follows:

> When I hold up my role as a Mennonite woman in my new society, I don't think I measure up to the traditional role. Although I have a strong desire to work for peace, justice and equality in this needy world, I do not relate to traditions of baking, quilting, and playing the "Mennonite name game." I respect the beautiful traditions that have shaped Mennonite women and their families to become what they are, but I belong to a new breed of Mennonite women, anxious to practice our faith in the social field through service to a hurting world.[97]

Perhaps wishing to convey something else, Miriam nevertheless in fact raised up for herself a calling that characterized the activity of Mennonite women for at least most of the twentieth century; that is, alleviating suffering in a hurting world.

The story of Gloria Gonzalez is illustrative of both disparate histories of ethno-religious identity and shared family and gender experiences amongst immigrant Mennonite women. Gloria was raised in a family of eleven children in a poor neighbourhood in San Salvador, El Salvador.[98] Her mother was the primary provider and caretaker of the family, since her father's alcoholism disabled him from those roles and, despite the family's poverty, made it a priority to send her children to an upper-class school in the hopes that a better education would give them a better future. Motivated by her Catholic religious faith and desire to help the poor, a teenaged Gloria and committee of friends became active in the underground distribution of food and other goods to needy families. Under an oppressive right-wing dictatorship, this work branded her as subversive and a threat to the state. She continued in this work, despite escalating tensions in El Salvador in the late 1970s and early 1980s. During this time, her two older brothers and father disappeared and were presumed to have been executed by the national guard. Gloria herself was arrested and held for questioning for several days, after which she took the advice of her priest and family members and decided to immigrate to Canada. She did so in 1989, with her husband and their four-year-old daughter. Despite several attempts, Gloria and José had not yet been legally married, since each time they had planned an appointment with the justice of peace, they were warned of a possible arrest. In fact, Gloria had not seen José for at least two years prior to their reunion at the airport, since living together was too dangerous for both of them.

When they arrived in Kitchener, Ontario, they faced the usual challenges of new immigrants: learning English, finding jobs and housing, acquainting themselves with new systems and rules. A priority for Gloria was finding a church that met her spiritual needs and possibly a faith community like the one she had known in El Salvador. Eventually, Gloria connected with a Spanish-speaking Mennonite congregation with many members who were also immigrants from Central America. She became a member and, after a six-year separation, legally married her husband José there. Gloria's life story, including family dynamics that saw women—herself and her mother —assume the 'head of household' role (in deed if not in word) parallels that of numerous other Mennonite women of the past. If her language, her cultural traditions, and 'homeland' were different from theirs, her sense of being a woman wanderer, trying to find security for her children and a community for her family, was much the same.

Mennonite women newcomers, whether they arrived in Canada in the early nineteenth century or late twentieth century, experienced the process of immigration in ways much like other Canadians. They dealt with the environmental and physical adversities faced by all pioneer settlers, confronted the loneliness of separation from family and friends—those left behind in the 'homeland' or those living in the country while daughters 'worked out' in the city—and adapted as best they could and as necessary to a new language, cultural customs, and pressures to accommodate their traditions to a different societal context. They gradually became Canadian, even while they maintained ties, emotional or material, to places and events of the past. Those pre-migration experiences might be idealized as 'golden' eras of security and prosperity or recalled with horror as times of violence, death, and loss. Either way, their past lives shaped women and their communities in numerous ways ranging from formal persistence of cultural traditions to the pain of unspoken memories.

Whether pioneers, urban migrants, refugees, or transnationals, Mennonite women experienced immigration to Canada in ways that were oftentimes quite similar despite vast differences in chronology and ethnic origin. For all women, the diasporic experience—that of uprooting, wandering, and settlement—provided a site at which gender meanings were destabilized and challenged. Occasionally, circumstances demanded that gender roles were irreversibly deconstructed. Perhaps more often, however, women's roles as 'cultural carriers' and their gendered roles within families were reinforced to ensure community survival in a new society. In the end, the common aspects of women's experiences as Canadian immigrants were nuanced in important and evolving ways by their gender, locale, and by the multiple identities held by different Mennonite groups.

CHAPTER TWO

Wives, Mothers, and 'Others':
Women within Families

Susan Heinrichs Klassen (1902–1989) spent the better part of her adult life bearing and raising children. Married in 1920 at the age of seventeen, she bore her first child when she was eighteen, and fourteen more over the next twenty-four years. Descended from immigrants from Russia in 1875, she married a man who became a well-known Mennonite church leader in southern Manitoba. A candid woman, she at times expressed resentment at the overwhelming demands of the household and child-rearing labour that she carried almost alone, as her husband was often taken away, physically and mentally, by his church work.[1] Today, the baseball-team-size family is a rarity and an oddity, but in early twentieth-century rural Mennonite communities, families like the Klassens were only slightly larger than most; my own grandmother raised thirteen children while her neighbour bore twelve.

Mary Snider (1863–1930), who lived in the Waterloo, Ontario, area, never married. In 1896 she became matron of the newly established Berlin (now Kitchener) orphanage, an institution that undoubtedly created for Mary the sense of herself as mother to a "busy household of children." She eventually adopted a baby boy who was left in a basket on the doorstep of the orphanage, and thus stood outside the norms of her era by choosing single parenthood. Her son Edward died suddenly in his mid-twenties, and Mary, reportedly "broken-hearted," died herself on the day of his funeral.[2] Mary had created a family for herself by unconventional means, within her own home and workplace as well.

Maria Redekop Wall (1901–1974) arrived in Canada in 1948, a widow with six children, the youngest ten years old at the time.[3] She was born in south Russia (present-day Ukraine) and came to adulthood and marriage during tumultuous years of revolution, war, famine, and political repression. Her husband Jacob disappeared at the hands of Soviet secret police in 1937 and was never heard from again. Maria led her children out of the Soviet Union through the violent, chaotic Second World War-front of eastern Europe and eventually the family was sponsored by distant relatives to immigrate to Canada as displaced persons. Like many women of her migrant group cohort, her marital status was nebulously described as 'widow,' although her husband's death was never confirmed. Despite offers of marriage from potential suitors in her chosen province of British Columbia, Maria remained a widow until she died. This meant she also lived with the contradictions of being a household head in a Mennonite church community that gave no voice to women except through their husbands, and that responded to widows mainly with sentiments of pity. For their part, Maria's children grew up with only memories of a father, but were quite familiar with the fragmented and blended family structures, predominantly female-headed, that characterized their immigrant community in Canada.

Whether married, single, a mother, or childless, Mennonite women have been part of families throughout history. While different historic time periods have generated varied family forms and the relative value given to those different structures, women more than men have consistently been identified by their position within a family. For nineteenth-century pioneer women, marriage, childbirth many times over, and widowhood shaped adulthood in predictable and all-consuming ways. Until well after the mid-twentieth century, Mennonite women were expected to marry for life, bear and raise children, and deal with the likelihood that they would end their lives as widows. Women who chose not to marry, for whatever reason, or who did not bear children, were departing from normative gendered behaviour. They fell into the awkward and marginalized category of 'others.' Increasingly common towards the late twentieth century were Mennonite women who, like other Canadians, opted not to bear children, or women who entered same-sex unions. Over the course of the twentieth century, a Western transition occurred "from a world in which it was common for some people to have large families while others never married or reproduced, to a world in which almost everyone married and had a small family."[4] Mennonites fit this model in part, though probably large families were more common and more prolonged amongst Mennonites and perhaps the rates of marriage higher than in the general population.

The Mennonite family, either nuclear or extended, was a central institution for organizing community life and transmitting beliefs. A family functioned as an economic unit, a migration unit, and was the building block for village and settlement formation. There has been little historical analysis of family ideology specifically within Mennonite communities, but sociologists have generally agreed that the family has been a "near-sacred institution" for Mennonites.[5] As other studies of Christian families have found, the relationships within Mennonite families were the basis for church and community patterns. As such, the family could not really be considered a privatized realm totally separate from other spheres of governance. Local church congregations developed an ethos largely reflective of the collection of its member families; a Mennonite family in turn was shaped by and responded to the dictates and practices of its local church and broader denominational body.

Family life represented, historically, the context within which Mennonite women were defined by their communities and churches but also strongly influenced their own perceptions of themselves as individuals with particular roles and status. Her position as mother, wife, and community matriarch could, on the one hand, provide a woman with a sense of her essential value and purpose. Indeed, some interpretations of Mennonite women's roles have pointed to examples of strong and influential women as evidence of a matriarchal social order that offset a woman's subordinate position in church structure and religious doctrine. The centrality of family to Mennonite community life offered women a venue in which they had substantial influence. This may have been especially true in some pioneer settings, where "kinship lines" were more important than "church lines."[6] One could, of course, question whether hidden power and influence, unrecognized in formal community structures, were really power in any meaningful sense. Yet it was often within the circles of family, nuclear and extended, that women could shape customs and decisions. A woman's family was thus a source of comfort, enjoyment, and sometimes empowerment. But family life, as defined and prescribed by societal and community norms of a particular time and place, could also be limiting and constraining, and indeed a site of fear and danger. For each woman profiled above, her experience of family represents one snapshot during a century that saw dramatic changes to humankind's most significant social structure. This chapter will look at Mennonite women's historical experience with regard to their places within families.

For women, as for men, their first life stage within families was as children. Their primary family relationships were with parents, siblings, grandparents, and with an extended group of kin that were near or far. Girls were expected to help their mothers with the household until they were ready themselves to marry, bear children, and 'begin their own families.' The Mennonite doctrine of believers' or adult baptism meant that until individuals formally joined the church as teenagers or young adults, there may have been a certain degree of latitude in the extent to which children and adolescents departed from the rules of the church. For boys, especially those within conservative communities that had a clear *Ordnung* (rule of order), this pre-baptismal period may have meant owning a radio, making occasional trips into town, or playing billiards or cards. Girls, perhaps because of an assumed lower level of rebellious instinct, were given less room to stretch the boundaries of church-sanctioned behaviour. Also, because of their close ties and responsibility to the inner, domestic household, girls had fewer opportunities to test the world. While this disparity in expected standards of behaviour were and are more pronounced in conservative groups, girls in all groups generally had less latitude in stepping outside the boundaries of church rules. While boys, generally considered more prone to rebellious behaviour, were known to 'sow their wild oats' and indulge in 'worldly' behaviour contrary to church standards, girls were less likely, or at least less expected, to test the world in so-called masculine ways. When they did cross boundaries, they were more likely to be reprimanded. For example, Aganetha Plett Warkentin recalls only one time that her mother punished her: when she and her sister were caught smoking cigarettes rolled from old catalogues and dried leaves.[7]

Despite the fascinating religious differentiation between children (pre-believers) and adults (believers), there has been minimal investigation into the history or sociology of childhood in Mennonite communities, and even less into the gendered nature of that life stage.[8] Until the post-Second World War era, Mennonites lived primarily in rural settings where children's lives were shaped by their participation in a household agricultural economy. Girls, like boys, spent many hours in labour that supported the subsistence of a farming family. Like farm-based conservative groups today, girls were apprenticed by their mothers in the tasks of gardening, food preservation, clothing making and maintenance, and other household arts. They attended school, but education beyond grade eight or perhaps high school was a rarity for girls, who were expected to have 'careers' as wives and homemakers well beyond a turning point when employment and career opportunities for boys had broadened beyond the farm.

COURTSHIP AND MARRIAGE

Having received her vocational training in domestic arts under the tutelage of her mother and possibly grandmothers and older sisters, a young Mennonite woman was ready to turn her thoughts to marriage and the creation of her own family unit. Until the latter part of the twentieth century, women were generally expected to assume a passive formal role in finding a life partner, waiting until she was 'chosen' by a young man, even though informally she was behaving in ways that would ensure she would be chosen by the right one. Little has been written about courtship practices and norms in Mennonite settings, but historically it occurred mainly in private or in sanctioned church settings, and with certain expectations of proper process and decorum attached to the rituals of matchmaking. Mennonite approaches to courtship combined religious and pious restraint with European custom that could border on the raucous and bawdy. For instance, the practice of 'bundling' was one brought to Ontario by Swiss Mennonites and Amish, though its practice is rarely acknowledged in public or private writings. Bundling was a common southern European and Pennsylvania German custom whereby a young couple would 'visit' in the girl's bed—albeit fully clothed and sometimes with a board or blanket barrier between them—as a way of keeping warm late at night when the fire was low and the rest of the family asleep. In an 1874 diary entry, Russian immigrant Margaretha Jansen commented on the unusual courtship customs among her Canadian Swiss Mennonite hosts: "When we drove home from choir practice that evening, somebody drove behind us very silently without bells. I was wondering about that, but the others were quiet. Now I know what it was. Susanne had a visitor. It seems so strange to me. A person, whom she did not know, comes that late in the evening when all the others had already gone to bed! But that is a custom over here!"[9]

Young women and men in rural settings became acquainted through relatives and friends but most often in the context of church activities, such as at weddings, picnics, young people's meetings, choirs, and other religiously sanctioned social settings, of which there were plenty. As one woman recalled, "Many a romance began after a Sunday night service."[10] At some of these events, women were clearly disadvantaged by the ratio, such as at a 1951 "M[ennonite] B[rethren] Beach Party" on the west coast, attended by 200 women and 50 men. One female party-goer wrote to her sister, describing the situation as "desperate" and noting that "R.P. managed to snare the only ... eligible man there."[11] Relationships also developed from the flirtation that occurred for hours on end as young people worked together picking hops or berries in British Columbia or hoeing beets on the prairies, for example. Thelma Reimer Kauffman describes the advantage a young woman had if her boyfriend worked at the same hop yard:

> If you were lucky, as I was one summer, your boyfriend might be hauling sacks of hops by truck to the kilns, and he would use his break time to come and help you pick. And if your boyfriend was a very fast picker, as mine was, your basket would fill up like a yeasty loaf rising. You would also get to face one another and look at each other to your heart's content, and perhaps, say a few useless words. What a heady, marvelous feeling, to have a tall, handsome young man spend time generously with you in public. When weighing time came around, there would be smiles and raised eyebrows as my bursting sack was lugged to the weigh-up circle and the pounds were announced.[12]

Prolonged courtships that consisted of frequent and private dates were rare. Recalling his proposal and brief engagement to Sarah Martens in 1942, Abram J. Esau of Yarrow, BC, recalled, "In those days we were taught by word and example of our pastors and others, that a long courtship is a poor testimony for Christians. In our more closed communities ... everybody knew everybody, so there was no need [to] tak[e] time for extended courtships or [to get] acquainted. I knew I would get a good rating by our pastor if I did my proposing & marriage in a quick, more conservative and 'appropriate' manner."[13] For new immigrants, both men and women, marriage sometimes had to wait until economic stability was attained. For instance, Helena Neufeld, newly arrived in Saskatchewan in 1923, refused Diedrich Epp's several requests of marriage because she first wanted to repay her CPR (Canadian Pacific Railway) travel debt and purchase a sewing machine, as did immigrant Elizabeth Fast, who delayed her marriage until her debt was completely paid.[14]

Young adults made decisions about a marriage partner within the context of family influence, and mainly under the approving or disapproving eyes of parents. Some sources refer to the common practice of a young man nervously seeking permission from his hoped-for bride's father; in other memoirs, a young couple would together approach both sets of parents to announce, or ask for their blessing on, a marriage union. For Mennonites, what may have been the most important factor in sanctioning a couple's decision to unite was their religious and denominational compatibility. Until the latter decades of the twentieth century, women were most likely to marry within the Mennonite fold. Endogamy—marrying within one's group—was prevalent amongst Mennonites partly because their patterns of social separation meant that a young woman was more likely to meet Mennonite men than otherwise. One woman commented that marrying another Mennonite would help her to live out her cultural and faith heritage.[15] But it also represented continuity with the Anabaptist belief that forbade marriage between believers and unbelievers. In the sixteenth century, those categories represented fairly rigid distinctions between Anabaptists and others and were aimed at keeping the church community pure and 'without spot or wrinkle.' The consequences of marrying outside the fold could mean discipline or excommunication, or, if an individual was baptized into the church when already married, one's loyalty to church and God could take precedence over an unbelieving spouse.[16]

Mennonite regulations against 'mixed' marriage, as it was perhaps absurdly viewed, given the small Mennonite population, became very strict within certain Mennonite groups. For instance, the Mennonite Brethren refused to marry a couple if either one had not been baptized by full water immersion according to that group's practice, even though their respective Mennonite churches and possibly families shared historic roots in south Russia; this prohibition was not officially lifted until the 1980s. Other Mennonite subgroups also forbade marriage outside their membership at various points in time. Not only was it deemed mandatory for most of history to marry another believer— that is, within the Mennonite church and indeed within one's particular subgroup—but in some locales it was preferable if an engaged couple came from the same district so that "both partners could be close to their families and get the support they needed," and even more desirable if they attended the same church.[17] Mennonite endogamy declined throughout the twentieth century, from 93 percent in 1921 to 61 percent in 1981, though the latter figure is still remarkably high; among religious groups in Canada, only Jews had a higher rate of endogamy than Mennonites, according to the 1981 census.[18] In many districts and among certain groups, and still today among the Old Order Mennonites, for instance, mixed marriages are practically non-existent.

Even though Mennonites had a higher than average rate of endogamy well into the last century, 'mixed' marriages were part of almost every family's experience at some point. In early nineteenth-century Upper Canada (Ontario), when religious services were held cooperatively amongst settlers from different Protestant denominations, it is said that "many of the [Mennonite] young people married persons from different religious backgrounds."[19] The way in which marrying outside the faith and fold was treated varied across eras, locales, and between church groups. Generally, if a woman married a non-Mennonite who then submitted to baptism into the Mennonite church, there was little problem. Statistics that compare the numbers of mixed marriages between Mennonite women and men have not been generated; one might speculate, however, that men were more likely to marry non-Mennonite partners than were women because they moved more often in the non-church realms of town, business, and education, and, also, because fewer nonconformist standards of conduct were enforced on males. For instance, in one oral history, a woman recalled that Ontario men increasingly married outside the Mennonite church during the era of strict plain-dress regulations for women. Despite rigid positions adopted by some Mennonite groups against mixed marriages, the actual practice of church members usually tempered the degree to which those positions were enforced. In his study of Mennonites in seventeenth-century northern Germany, Michael D. Driedger found that the ongoing practice of mixed marriages resulted in an increasingly diverse community and served to modify the stances taken by leaders.[20] Private sources, like the diary of Laura Shantz, reveal a fair number of marriages between Mennonites and non-Mennonites in early twentieth-century Ontario.[21]

If courtships and marriage proposals required male initiative, weddings were within the future bride's domain. From the nineteenth through the twentieth centuries, weddings underwent a cultural transformation from a home-based community event that was nevertheless primarily a religious union, to a church-based but commercialized reflection of popular culture. In the nineteenth century, home-based weddings were the norm and, indeed, the Mennonite church as it existed in pioneer settings had minimal involvement in the marriage ceremony. Until 1831 Mennonite clergy in Upper Canada did not have the legal right to perform marriages. Prior to this, Mennonite marriages were performed by Anglican clergymen or justices of the peace.[22] The migratory history of Mennonites meant that in the early phase of settlement, there might be an absence of either ministers to perform marriages or local recognition of Mennonite credentials to do so. This had been the case in seventeenth-century Europe, in eighteenth-century Russia, and in nineteenth-century Canada. In such circumstances, it is possible that the Mennonite particularity of the marriage ceremony was of less concern, or that the official sanctioning was sufficient for a union to be recognized by the faith community. Furthermore, for much of the nineteenth century, performing the wedding within an explicitly Mennonite context may have been less important, since it was not uncommon for both bride and groom not to be baptized, and therefore not church members, prior to marriage.

Like courtships customs, many of the wedding traditions practised in ethnic Mennonite communities had their origins in European custom. For the Swiss, such customs might have their origins in Swiss regions, whereas for Russian Mennonites these practices can be traced to Ukraine, Prussia, and the Netherlands. In both cases, these folk traditions were predominantly rural and began to disappear when Mennonites moved to towns and cities and as wedding practices themselves were aligned to a newly developing North American popular and commercialized culture. Customs such as the 'Polterabend' or the 'Charivari,' both of which involved groups of young people making a great deal of noise by breaking old dishes or banging pots and pans, evolved from common European folk traditions. The Polterabend was generally held the evening before the wedding, and might include a program of humorous poems and stories, as well as gift giving. The Charivari was held after the wedding, and had the purpose of interrupting and making public the newly established privacy and intimacy of the married couple, and also highlighting in circus-like fashion the sexual act that was about to take place. Variations on these rituals were common in both Russian and Swiss groups. Such traditions allowed for community intervention and made public a rite of passage that by the late twentieth century was considered very private. The condemnation of these practices by Mennonite church leaders and their gradual demise indicated a growing involvement of church authority in wedding planning, and also reflected an increased modesty and puritanism that ran counter to the thinly veiled sexual innuendos of such folk rituals.

When weddings were held in homes, they were huge events and could mean a significant amount of work in preparation and on the actual day. Helena Penner recalled that when her older sister was married in the 1880s, the guests began to arrive before noon for a two o'clock wedding. After the ceremony they served afternoon coffee, a full supper meal, refreshments at midnight, and breakfast for whoever was still there in the morning. Her mother hadn't been to bed at all and didn't suggest sleep until the last guests had left and the wedding couple departed on their honeymoon. The wedding itself was quite an event. A new carriage house was cleaned out and decorated with evergreens and wildflowers, and a platform built for the musicians that included fiddle, harmonica, and drum. In Helena's words: "they danced and they danced all night through. Some wedding!"[23] The significant work involved in preparing for a wedding was lessened by the communal aspect of the event, whereby relatives and neighbours of the bride would assist in food preparation, such as the custom in which the mother of the bride prepared large batches of bun dough, which were then retrieved by community women who would shape and bake the wedding buns in their own homes. The passing of the handwritten wedding invitation from house to house (that included a list of invitees) also generated a sense of community responsibility for the successful outcome of the wedding.

Many traditional wedding customs began to disappear in the 1920s and onwards as professionalism crept into the wedding industry. With the introduction of printed, embossed invitations in the 1920s, the custom of passing one handwritten invitation from house to house began to disappear. Baking the wedding meal ceased to be a shared endeavour among neighbouring women, though they became important fundraising opportunities for church women's groups. Wedding gowns and bouquets were purchased from department stores or specialty wedding shops, and, at one reception, bologna and store-bought cookies were considered a treat.[24] Mary Konrad "spent nights looking at wedding dresses to order from the Eaton's catalogue" and had her bouquet made of organdy (fabric) flowers rather than common July garden flowers, since, in the words of her sister, "artificial was better." She was also encouraged by a British war bride friend to include a "Canadian" wedding cake; that is, a dark fruitcake with "tiers and little pink icing roses" at her 1943 wedding.[25] Nettie Sawatzky's 1936 wedding may have represented a

transitional moment in wedding culture: while her dress for the marriage ceremony was store-bought at Eaton's bargain basement in Winnipeg and black in
accordance with the practice of her Sommerfelder church group, her wedding
dress for later festivities was homemade and white and was matched with white
shoes. The food served during the day was a combination of traditional, epitomized by the buns baked collectively by community women, and the modern,
which included store-bought bologna and marshmallow cookies.[26]

Historian Laureen Harder also noted the transition in at least one Ontario
congregation whereby the "traditionally low-key" home-based nature of
weddings in Swiss Mennonite culture gave way in the 1950s to events in which
"Couples were married in the church amid flowers and candles ... the brides
wore special dresses and had attendants, solos were sung, the organ was played,
rings were exchanged, and a reception held at a home or a hotel."[27] At Shantz
Mennonite Church in Ontario, the first church wedding was held in 1931.
However, the minister's daughter, who married the same year, had her wedding
at home because her father "didn't want his daughter to set a precedent for the
rest of the young people."[28] As weddings modernized, their communal character began to fade. Greater work fell to the mother of the bride, who became
responsible for organizing all the food preparation, or, in some cases, preparing
everything herself or giving direction to the church's catering group. Even
though the planning and execution of the wedding came more under the
purview of the woman to be married, and perhaps more so under her mother's,
her control over the products associated with the wedding—invitations,
garments, food, and flowers—diminished as the dictates of popular wedding
culture created new ideals of the perfect wedding. While modernization in
household technology lightened the workload for women in caring for their
homes, other aspects of an increasingly consumer-oriented society may have
diminished the contribution women had traditionally made in various aspects
of community life, such as at weddings.

For Mennonites, the nature of popular wedding practices was tempered by
a religious belief system that warned against following societal trends, that
demanded modesty and simplicity, and that called church members to separate
themselves from worldly things. Since the wedding dress was (and is) the
primary external symbol of the ceremony's intended character, the style and
colour of dress was an important marker of the particular Mennonite subgroup
of which the couple were members and the degree of religious nonconformity
maintained by that group. In the Chortitzer church, a small conservative group

with roots in the 1870s migration to southern Manitoba, wedding dresses had to be in dark colours and not fancy or ornate in any way. Similarly, the Sommerfelder Mennonites, of the same roots, were differentiated from the Bergthaler Mennonites, from whom they had split, by their choice of black wedding dresses. For most groups, simplicity and conservatism were greater in Canada in the twentieth century than had been the case in nineteenth-century Russia, as Mennonites sought to differentiate themselves from the modernization taking place in virtually all aspects of daily life. Some women, who had known more elaborate wedding traditions in Russia, were surprised by the simpler customs in some Canadian communities. For instance, Anna Bartsch was forewarned by her intended husband about the customs in Dalmeny, Saskatchewan, and so she wore a half-length green silk gown with a flower attached, rather than the long white dress with train, a bouquet of flowers and a ring, as was the custom she had recalled from Russia. This caused her some small discomfort because, since childhood, she had associated the train with a woman's virtue and wedding rings with a couple's faithfulness.[29] The Dalmeny community may well have followed the Swiss Mennonite practice, whereby wedding rings were considered worldly.

Another wedding custom common in Russia (mainly amongst the larger, culturally modern groups) but gradually disallowed in Canada was the wedding dance. Like Helena Penner's late nineteenth-century wedding, Nettie Sawatzky's mid-1930s wedding day also included a dance at which a band of local musicians played "polkas, scottisches and square dances" until four o'clock in the morning. When Nettie's brother Jakob married a decade later, however, a wedding dance was considered inappropriate, given that many of the family's neighbours had sons who were in the military overseas and might "never dance with their sweethearts."[30] One Mennonite subgroup attempted to clamp down on wedding dances by denying church membership to a couple who held a dance at their engagement party; the leadership then locked the doors of the church on the intended day of the wedding.[31]

The shift away from wedding dances as an acceptable and assumed part of the overall marriage event reflected a new sense of sobriety and decorum that was increasingly applied to Mennonite weddings over the course of the twentieth century. The emphasis on nonconformity extended from a call for simplicity and, in some cases, peculiarity, in dress and appearance to warnings against worldliness in all aspects of living. One area that seemed to become an acute concern for all Mennonite groups was weddings. The wedding industry became a booming one in the post-war era as the institution of marriage itself received new attention and as material prosperity allowed fancier dresses along with cakes, flowers, attendants, and elaborate receptions. Many ministers reacted to what they considered a departure from the wedding ceremony as a Christian ordinance and the adoption of secular forms. Wedding rituals, which more and more mirrored outside society, became a contested site where the church met the world. As Pamela E. Klassen observes, "A cyclical relationship developed between religious leaders condemning increases in 'materialism' and women embracing ready-made and labor-saving clothing."[32]

While the content of the wedding ceremony remained fundamentally a religious event, the form of a wedding was modelled on cultural tradition and evolved according to societal trends. Because wedding practices often reflected the latter, they frequently came under attack by church leaders as manifestations of worldliness. And because the planning and executing of weddings was largely a female function, church admonitions were often directed at women. Lavish wedding dresses and veils, bridal attendants, parade-like processions, jewellery, make-up, receptions with entertainment—such accoutrements all seemed to undermine the solemnity and spiritual nature of marriage, according to some pronouncements. Wedding trends such as short stand-up ceremonies and the practice of the father 'giving away the bride' also caused tension and conflict in church and home. As Klassen also notes, Mennonite church leaders objected to the shift from "Christ-centered weddings" to "Bride-centered weddings."[33] Much of their objection was rooted in recognition that Mennonites generally were acculturating, especially during the post-Second World War era, and losing many outward symbols of separation from the world.

Written and spoken advice about wedding practices were especially prominent during the 1940s and 1950s when modern wedding practices were increasingly evident in Mennonite weddings. In 1941 already, the Mennonite Conference of Ontario warned its female members against "worldliness" in wedding gowns.[34] A set of "Wedding Regulations" accepted by the Bergthaler churches in Manitoba demanded a sermon of at least twenty minutes not flavoured with jokes, no attendants except children, no giving away of the bride, no short sleeves or low-cut dresses, no lipstick or nail polish, no toasting at the reception, and no noise-making in the streets after the wedding. Such warnings were especially exacting because they were intended to resist a trend that saw young women drawn into imagining the fantasy wedding that was a necessary beginning to the 1950s domestic ideal.

The strict pronouncements from the Bergthaler church are of special interest to me since, as a child in southern Manitoba in the early 1960s, I well remember spending hours with my best friend, the daughter of a prominent Bergthaler minister, describing our future weddings, which, in all our imaginings, included numerous bridesmaids in lavish dresses of velvet and satin (the identity of the groom was of little concern at that point). Pamela Klassen suggests that prohibitions about sexual activity and codes on modest dress were intrinsically linked in prescriptive statements on wedding dresses. She concludes, "Given the ambivalence and sinfulness surrounding sexuality among Mennonites, and the preoccupation with modest, Christian attire, it is not surprising that weddings provoked such conflict over the clothing of the bride—a woman in transition from tempting virgin to sexually active wife."[35] Of course, if sex was a subtext, it was not explicit in church statements that focused on the drift away from Christian simplicity and towards the frivolity and excess of modern culture. Symbols of religious separation and worldly sexuality could, of course, overlap and present unique conundrums to Mennonite women. For instance, as the snowy-white wedding dress became a key signifier of a woman's virginity, what mixed messages may have been received by young women whose particular Mennonite group insisted upon dark-coloured dresses?

The planning of weddings became a site of conflict between women and church leaders, and often their own family members as well. It became such perhaps because the wedding, while a central rite in Mennonite religious life, was one of the few, if not the only, public church function in which women were the centre of attention. This was the case especially from the mid-twentieth century on, when the planning of a wedding became an all-consuming agenda for women. When church leaders decried the pageantry of weddings, they also undermined the centrality of women's roles. In response, women pushed at the boundaries of what was acceptable, caught, one might argue, between their church's call for 'simplicity'—interpreted by one woman as a "lack of appreciation for aesthetic things"—and the commercial marketplace of wedding culture. As the same woman said about her own 1960s wedding, "I went for whatever I could manage to have," which in her case meant a beaded, white satin wedding dress, three bridesmaids in gold velvet, and a veil over her face.[36] The wedding dress became symbolic of this woman-centred event, since more thought and consideration went into the purchase or design and sewing of the wedding dress than in any other activity. And on the day itself, all eyes were on the bride as she made her entrance. One woman commented: "Getting into that white dress does signify something very important, 'I'm queen for the day. This is my big day.' It really symbolized a break with my home and my family, my parents."[37] While the material functions of wedding planning accorded very much with appropriate gender roles—food preparation, clothing creation, decor—they were performed in a very public manner and thus drew attention to a woman, as well as the other women involved. Not only were their decisions public, but, to the extent that women chose to defy the admonitions of church leaders and or their own parents, their choices were also political.

CHILDBIRTH AND MOTHERHOOD

Once the intensity of wedding preparations and the gaiety of the actual event were over, the long-term reality of married life set in. Perhaps the most immediate benefit of marriage for never-married young couples was a full sexual relationship, normally begun on their wedding night. Within the context of a church community that condemned premarital sex, most couples were celibate prior to marriage, or at least maintained the appearance of such. The wedding night was thus something to be at once dreaded and anticipated. Accounts of a woman's first sexual experience are rare, but, if discussed, were referred to obliquely or with euphemisms. For instance, Maria Dueck wrote in her memoir that when she married she had been naïve, but "it went."[38] Honeymoons were rare, especially during years of early settlement, or poverty and hardship. If a wedding trip was possible, it often meant visiting extended relatives or perhaps a short road trip to a nearby park or lake. After Mattie Leis Bast's 1923 wedding, she went to live with her new husband's parents and helped with chores the next morning.[39] Olga Hepting Rempel spent the day after her 1932 wedding helping her new mother-in-law pluck geese while her new husband hauled sugar beets.[40] Margaret Heinrichs Groening also went to live with her husband in his mother's home for ten days following the wedding.[41] Abram J. Esau, who married Sarah Martens in Yarrow, BC, in 1942, seemingly couldn't even anticipate the wedding night: "In those days 'Honeymoon' was still somewhat of a No-No.... I brought Sarah back to her mother, kissed her good night and went back to my home to sleep by myself once more." The next day, with her brother and his truck, Abram picked up Sarah and their collective belongings to move to their new home.[42] Engaging in sanctioned sexual intercourse was at one level pleasurable, but, given the privacy and indeed taboo around the topic of sex, there are almost no sources that illuminate women's experience—positive or negative—about their sexual lives within marriage. Alongside the pleasure, or pain, was the potential for pregnancy that women now dealt with for the duration of their adult, fertile lives.

The association of marriage with parenthood was much stronger for women than for men. Well into the late twentieth century, Mennonite women who married were expected to turn their thoughts and intentions towards bearing and raising children. Being a mother was so intrinsic to a woman's identity and others' perception of her that the role itself has hardly been analyzed. Author Katie Funk Wiebe offered a simple, but poignantly telling, description of who her mother was: "Mother was always at home waiting for her family to come to her from the outside.... Mother worked at home cooking, cleaning, sewing, and mending. Mother worked and waited. I thought all mothers did only that."[43]

Regardless of how they viewed motherhood in their specific circumstances, most Canadian Mennonite women in history gave birth and raised children. Giving birth was a central experience in the lives of Mennonite women, especially for rural women on the frontier. Pregnancy (or the avoiding of it) and childbirth was perhaps the most significant life cycle event for adult women of child-bearing years up to the 1960s and after. The impulse to have children was considered 'natural' but also followed Christian–Mennonite understandings of biblical statements regarding the purpose of conjugal relations and woman's highest purpose: to 'be fruitful and multiply' was a command taken very seriously by men and women in Mennonite church communities. Despite the centrality of child bearing for Mennonite communities and women's lives, the physical aspects of those events were spoken of very little and indeed were almost hidden. Pregnancy was just one of many subjects too delicate to talk about. Even women used euphemisms to talk about pregnancy amongst themselves, saying "she is like that again," or she is "showing" or "she is in flower."[44] The modesty and embarrassment associated with pregnancy meant that many women avoided being seen in public—even at church—and wore clothing that concealed their growing wombs as long as possible. As one woman born before 1927 said: "You wore a garment or corset and hid that you were pregnant as long as you could and never ever told your other children that you were going to have a baby."[45] Despite the frequency of childbirth in Mennonite house-holds, and the fact that most births occurred at home, children often didn't know what was going on when it came time for their mother to deliver the next offspring. Usually, children were sent to a neighbour's or nearby relative's home when Mother went into labour, then returned to find, to their surprise, a new brother or sister at home.

In my father's family of thirteen children, because their mother was a stout woman and wore loose dresses almost always covered with an apron, they didn't always know when a new sibling was expected. Even fourteen-year-old Olga Hildebrand, the third of ten children, didn't know what was up when she and her siblings were hastily sent to the neighbours; the "lump" under her mother's apron was, she thought, just an indication that the woman had been eating too many "homemade noodles with cream gravy." When Olga returned home to find a new baby sister, she was told that the red mark on the infant's forehead resulted from a too-small suitcase with which the stork had delivered the baby.[46] Gordon Bauman recalled that four siblings were born after he was into his Old Order family but each was a total surprise. They always seemed to arrive during the night because in the morning, his mother would be in bed, "a baby could be heard, and Grandmother Bauman was present, having served as a midwife along with the doctor who by this time had left."[47] Another man recalled that when his brother was born, there wasn't time to send him to the neighbours, and so his father hastily hid six oranges in the wheat in the granary and challenged the boy to find them all, a task that took some time; when he returned to the house with the oranges, he discovered a new baby brother.[48]

Children were sent to the neighbours because, until the 1930s and 1940s, almost all Mennonite—like most Canadian—births took place at home, hospitals being too distant, too expensive, or only for the indigent. For many early immigrant women, childbirth could be an extremely isolating and, indeed, dangerous experience. Conditions for giving birth were extremely primitive in some locales. For instance, Russian immigrant Margaret Loewen Isaac gave birth to her first child in November 1874 in a hut built of reed grass where the temperature was minus seven degrees Celsius.[49] Given such circumstances, a woman and her midwife had to be prepared for a death as fully as they had to be prepared for birth. Prior to the Second World War, maternal mortality rates in Canada were high[50]—indeed, higher than in most other Western countries except the United States—and childbirth-related death was second only to tuberculosis in cause of female deaths. Referring to the late nineteenth- and early twentieth-century period, Nanci Langford says, "Perhaps no other aspect of life on the Prairies endangered women as much as did the birthing of their children." This reality was so great that in one case, Langford says, a woman readying herself for giving birth also laid out her wedding gown in readiness for her burial.[51] One Mennonite recalled the cemetery that was next to her childhood home in Manitoba, in which "many young mothers and infants lay buried, mute testimony to the harshness of the pioneer years."[52]

The fear of death in childbirth was heightened in rural, isolated areas, where assistance by either midwife or physician or both was far away. Katherine Martens, in her oral history of childbirth in Mennonite communities, notes that if sex and death are difficult to talk about, childbirth, carrying associations of both, may be even more secretive. Martens notes that for the twentieth-century women in her collection of stories, "Even in normal birth and delivery, there is a sense of moving into the unknown that some of the women ... associate with death."[53] As this statement might suggest, the nexus between life and death in the context of childbirth held certain religious connotations as well. Annie Reesor in fact chose to be baptized into the church during her second pregnancy. Her first experience of childbirth had been "so difficult that [she] felt she needed to make a decision about making her peace with God."[54] The death of a young mother in childbirth, or later of related complications, was devastating for families. The 1932 death in childbirth of Justina Goertzen Plett, aged thirty, was described by her father-in-law in this way:

> That was a very difficult Sunday for us. At 5 o'clock in the morning Jakob [her husband] came to get us, and, likewise, the doctor was immediately brought; and thus she had to suffer severely and ... soon said that her breath was hard ... and that she wanted to be laid somewhat differently, but it was already not for long, and then, one and a half hour after the birth, she at the end fell asleep calmly, namely, at 2 o'clock after dinner ... she left behind in life her spouse who had come to love her deeply and three children; the fourth, which was stillborn, we could lay in the coffin together with her.[55]

In 1934, thirty-year-old Maria Poetker died of haemorrhage following the delivery of a stillborn child, her seventh birth in ten years; her eldest child was only eight at the time. In a letter to his siblings describing his wife's death, Maria's husband told how she had begun bleeding in the night two months before her due date. Two doctors had worked to deliver the dead child but then could do little for Maria but give her sedatives. She died within only twelve hours, during which she had repeatedly said good-bye to her husband Jacob and asked forgiveness "for everything." In his letter, which was unusually emotive, he said, "I can hardly grasp it, how everything happened so quickly. Oh how lonesome it is for me! Every time I come inside I have the feeling that she will come to the door to meet me, but she does not come.... I cannot describe my feelings; my heart was almost breaking."[56] Jacob Poetker was not alone in experiencing such tragedy. Until medical knowledge and technique that reduced infection and haemorrhage were widely available from the 1940s and on, death of a mother and/or her infant were familiar events.

Given their settlement patterns that saw the first Mennonite immigrants from Russia establish homesteads within bloc reserves with farm buildings and houses situated close together along a village street, as on the prairies, or where families settled in close proximity to one another in other parts of the country, Mennonite women may have been at an advantage when facing the dangers of childbirth. A female culture already nourished by kinship networks was further reinforced by the frequent ritual of childbirth in Mennonite communities. Women in these settings relied on experienced and/or trained midwives, the assistance of family members and neighbours, and hoped for uncomplicated births. In rural pioneering communities up to the mid-twentieth century, Mennonite midwives played a central and essential role in healthcare, primarily assisting with childbirth but also performing a myriad of other functions.

In her survey of childbirth in Canada in the first half of the twentieth century, historian Wendy Mitchinson proposes that, "Midwifery lasted longest in cohesive communities that were isolated from the pressures of modern industrialized society as a result of geographic or cultural separation."[57] For instance, in Canadian communities such as Newfoundland, midwifery lasted much longer than elsewhere in the country; 50 percent of births were still under the purview of midwives in the second decade of the twentieth century. This appears to be true for Mennonites as well. Furthermore, immigrant women predominated amongst midwives in both the United States and Canada during the era of high migration from Europe at the turn of the past century.

One such Mennonite immigrant—possibly the quintessential Mennonite midwife—was Sarah Dekker Thielman. Sarah Dekker was born in 1878 in a German-speaking Mennonite village in south Russia (present-day Ukraine). Her family later moved to a Mennonite settlement called Samara, farther east, near the Volga River. She married David Thielman in 1911 and they moved to another settlement called Barnaul in Siberia (Asiatic Russia). She gave birth to three sons, one of whom died in childhood. They moved to Canada in 1929, in the final year of a significant Mennonite migration to North America during the 1920s, settling first in Glenbush, Saskatchewan, then moving to Beamsville, Ontario, in 1941. In the early years of the twentieth century, Sarah went to St. Petersburg, Russia, to be trained as a midwife and in 1909, still a single woman, she began recording the births at which she assisted in a midwife's journal, a carefully handwritten document in German Gothic script. When the journal entries end in 1941, Sarah had assisted at 1448 births, or at least these were the ones recorded. After moving to Ontario, she ceased her labour as a midwife, but continued offering her chiropractic and other healing skills to the local community.

Some Mennonite midwives fit Lesley Biggs's category of the 'neighbour-midwife,' a woman who operated within a relatively small geographic area and whose expertise as a 'baby-catcher' was gained primarily through self-teaching and personal experience.[58] Yet, Sarah Thielman's career, as that of other Mennonite midwives, reveals that professional training and skill in childbirth procedures were common amongst Mennonite women practitioners, even within nineteenth- and early twentieth-century immigrant communities, and were valued by women giving birth. Such training may, in fact, have been more common amongst immigrants, whose homelands may have offered closer access to institutions with obstetrical and related education programs than did early rural Canada. In Sarah's case, she left home as a single young woman in the first decade of the twentieth century to obtain midwifery training in St. Petersburg, several thousand kilometres from her family.

Katharina Born Thiessen studied midwifery, bone setting, and naturopathy in Prussia in about 1860, also studying to 'catch babies' well before she bore any of her own. After immigrating to Canada in the 1880s, she sought further medical training in Cincinnati, Ohio, in 1895. Eventually, an expanded 'practical' medical practice and newly built house included a reception area, pharmacy, operating room, and overnight rooms for her patients. Elizabeth Harder Harms, after training for two years in the city of Riga, Latvia, was certified as a midwife in 1912, and the next year was hired to be the official village midwife in the Mennonite village of Schoenfeld in Ukraine. When Elizabeth immigrated with her husband to Canada in 1925, she continued to practise community midwifery, although her husband did not consider it proper for her to work in a hospital when she was offered such a job.[59] One small indication of the perceived professionalism inherent in a midwife's labour is the fact that in the 1933 obituary of Manitoba midwife Anna Toews, she is referred to as an "obstetrician," though other biographical information notes that the source of her knowledge and training is unknown. The sheer number of births at which some Mennonite midwives assisted confirms that for these particular women, midwifery was a career and not just an occasional act of caring volunteerism for a neighbour and relative. For instance, Anna Toews delivered 942 babies, Sarah Thielman delivered more than 1400 infants in a thirty-two-year period, and Aganetha Reimer assisted at close to 700 births.

Midwives who did not have institutional training often took short courses or apprenticed with an older midwife or even a male physician. Barbara Zehr Schultz was trained in midwifery and herbal medicine by her grandfather, a licensed Ontario doctor, but also had the 'gift' of charming, a traditional folk healing practice.[60] In Steinbach, Manitoba, when the need for a local midwife was felt "very badly," Dr. Justina Neufeld was brought from Minnesota to offer courses in birthing as well as in the use of various home remedies.[61] Helena Klassen Eidse began to assist at deliveries at the age of thirteen when a local physician, Dr. Robert McTavish, enlisted her as an interpreter when he was called to German-speaking Mennonite homes in Manitoba. Gradually he trained her in the basics of medical care and she went on to a sixty-three-year career as a midwife, chiropractor, nurse, and undertaker. Initially she charged twenty-five cents per delivery, but in later years that sum rose to two dollars. Recalling that some people were indignant when she charged money for her services, apparently Helena had remarked that it seemed "babies aren't worth salt on an egg."[62] Helena's brown leather medical bag (still existing) contained such items as pills for fever, liquid medicine to stop haemorrhaging, scissors and ties for the umbilical cord, needle and thread, olive oil for greasing the birth passage, rubbing alcohol, and non-childbirth-related medical items.[63]

Midwives spent a considerable amount of time with their 'patients' both before and after the birth and saw their role as greater than only the delivery of babies. Katherina Hiebert regularly brought bedding, baby clothes, and food along to deliveries, and she didn't seem to have qualms about prescribing roles for husbands of women in childbirth. One story is told of how, just after a baby was born, the woman's husband brought the cow to the door, demanding that his wife milk it, as it was her duty. Katherina apparently gave him a good scolding and instructed the woman to stay in bed.[64] Aganetha Barkman Reimer's services included baking biscuits and making chicken noodle soup, in addition to the tasks surrounding the childbirth. Midwives also offered women knowledge about non-medicinal methods to deal with the harshness to their bodies of almost constant childbirth: this included such things as chamomile tea to ease cracked nipples during breastfeeding, and rubbing pig fat on bellies and legs to "loosen everything" in anticipation of labour.[65] Chamomile was also put in the bathwater of newborn babies to prevent heat rash and given to postpartum mothers to promote healing.

Midwives were 'working mothers' in an era when few married women with children worked for pay outside their homes. Because midwifery was considered an "extension of women's domestic duties, and in the traditional rhythms of rural life,"[66] however, it lay outside the category of female professional life, or at least has not been considered thus in histories of women's labour. In a setting in which women gave birth often, and other medical services were nonexistent or far away, midwives performed crucial functions, and, as such, women with these particular abilities and training were able to step out of gendered roles that might have tied them to their own households. Women who took on a life career of midwifery were usually women who were undaunted by challenges and had few fears, nor were they especially concerned about upsetting normative gender roles. Manitoba midwife Anna Toews regularly drove their Model T car because her husband Peter was "too nervous to drive" and so was always seen in the passenger seat. But she relied on him to crank-start the car and so he often accompanied her on her midwife visits just to start the car.[67] Not unlike what was experienced by the families of church ministers, the families of midwives coped with the ramifications of a parent's demanding career and with the frequent and sudden disruptions to family life that occurred when Mother was called away to 'catch' a baby. Margaretha Enns's daughters may have resented the extra household demands placed on them and the fact that they were unable to pursue higher education as a result of this: "The family often felt that everything revolved around their mother's career; family birthdays and Christmas gatherings were frequently interrupted when she was called away. Relatives who attended these gatherings recall her being summoned while she was in the midst of distributing Christmas gifts and homemade fudge to the grandchildren. She would drop everything, pick up her brown bag, and leave on her mission."[68]

If having a midwife in the family meant more housework for husband and children, it might also have meant greater household income. Evidence suggests that Mennonite midwives charged for their services; some were satisfied with payment in the form of chickens or garden produce, especially during hard times, while others had set fees. Many were likely willing to take whatever a woman could offer. In her memoir, Maria Klassen describes her good fortune at being a neighbour of Agatha Schellenberg, midwife in rural Saskatchewan in the 1930s: "For us it is handy that Agatha lives next door for she is a well-reputed mid-wife. We trust her because she has delivered hundreds of babies including our other three." She was also described as a "caring and efficient helper" who was willing to come at any time of day or night. Schellenberg didn't charge a specific amount but took what was offered. Maria's husband Johan paid her six, eight, and seven dollars, respectively, for three of their children.[69] Decades earlier, Helena Klassen Eidse charged only twenty-five cents for a delivery. For some new immigrants, the cost of midwife and doctor was prohibitive enough that women opted to manage their own births, with the assistance of neighbours or family members. Gertrude Epp was pregnant with her first child when she and her husband immigrated to Canada in 1924. That child was born in Ontario with a neighbour helping out, since the midwife arrived too late. When the child was only three weeks old, they ventured west to a farm in southern Manitoba. When Gertrude's next child was born a year and a half later, they had to pay the attending doctor thirty dollars, an enormous sum for the newcomers. Too poor to continue paying that amount, Gertrude's next four children were born with help only from her sisters-in-law. In each case, her preparations arose from what she had learned at previous births, including boiling a piece of binder twine with which to detach the cord. Her eighth child was born in the hospital, because by then they had "a bit more" money.[70]

By the late 1930s and onwards, hospital births became more and more common. The shift from home to hospital for childbirth during the first half of the twentieth century was dramatic; in 1926, 17.8 percent of Canadian births occurred in hospitals, while in 1950 that percentage increased to 76.[71] The increased medicalization of health care as well as the greater accessibility of hospital care and physicians meant the end of a career for many midwives. When Steinbach's hospital opened in 1938, Aganetha Reimer's local career as a midwife began to gradually see its end.[72] Although she gradually ceased attending the birth itself, Catherine Wagler Lichty, a midwife in southwest Ontario in the 1920s and 1930s, made a point of being at the home of a new mother when she and infant returned from the hospital.[73] Better roads and motorized transportation meant that women began choosing the hospital as a place to give birth. For instance, Tina Schulz's eighth and last child was the first to be born in a hospital in 1937 in Manitoba, as was Elizabeth Klippenstein's tenth child in Saskatchewan.[74] Anna Barkman's last of fourteen children was the first one who was born in a hospital, in 1931.[75] Margaret Sawatzky remarked that as her family grew, going to the hospital to give birth was preferable, since taking six or eight children away from home during the birth was increasingly problematic.[76]

Women's attitudes to the hospitalization of birth could be very different. Some women welcomed the mandatory rest imposed by the hospital stay, which, well into the post-Second World War period, was in the range of ten days. They were happy for the sense of security induced by the nearby presence of professionals and equipment required should intervention in the birth be required, especially as medical experts promoted 'painless' births through the use of anaesthesia and sedatives. Other women preferred the home birth setting, where they remained near their other children, could have their newborn child close, and where they were visited regularly by the midwife. They could also choose for themselves whether to stay in bed or resume their daily routines when they were ready.

Despite the overall trend towards hospital births through the twentieth century, some aberrations to this direction did occur. For instance, in the transition between home births assisted by midwives and the physician-attended hospital birth, some communities established birthing homes, sometimes referred to as 'cottage hospitals,' that had the function of creating a setting away from home in which women, for various reasons, could give birth. In Gretna, Manitoba, sisters Helen and Sarah Heinrichs ran such a home, while ten kilometres away in Altona the Nickel sisters offered such a service.[77] In 1928 a group of Mennonites in north Winnipeg decided to open a five-bed maternity hospital specifically to service a new neighbourhood of Mennonite settlers; it was initially directed by two sisters, Sara and Tina Koop. In later years, these same sisters operated a "midwifery" nursing home in Vineland, Ontario, from 1941 until 1954, where 732 babies were born. Interestingly, these birthing homes were often operated by single women, likely because it was viewed as an acceptable profession for women. Ironically, the shift to a hospital or centralized birthing home meant that for some rural women, the dangers of childbirth associated with travel presented new challenges that didn't exist for women in labour who waited at home for the arrival of a midwife only a few kilometres away. For instance, Mary Konrad planned the birth of her first child in 1945 at Johanna's Maternity Home in Sexsmith, Alberta, thirty-two kilometres from home. Four days prior to the birth, Mary and her husband made the wintry journey by horse and sleigh on unploughed roads through deep and drifting snow; she recalled how she shivered in the "strong icy wind" despite a heated stone at her feet.[78]

Sometimes urban women opted for childbirth at home, even though hospital proximity and physician availability wouldn't have been an issue as it was for rural women. Louise Martens Fehderau gave birth to all her children at home in 1930s Kitchener, Ontario, "because we had no means to pay for the hospital." She recalled that the doctor brought a Victorian Order nurse with him, who sterilized all the bedclothes and stitched together a thick layer of newspapers for underneath. After the birth of her first child, Louise recalled that "I was suddenly overwhelmed by the responsibility ... and worried about how things would work out," yet she went on to have three more children within five years.[79] For later immigrants, some of whom opted to settle in more isolated locales, midwives continued to be essential service providers, even when most Canadian women were giving birth in hospitals. For instance, Anna Wiebe was a midwife amongst Russian Mennonite immigrants on Pelee Island in Lake Erie during the years 1925 to 1950,[80] and was likely the one who helped bring my own mother into the world on the island in 1930. Similarly, when a small group of Mennonites attempted to establish a remote settlement called Reesor in northern Ontario in 1925, the nearest hospital was in the town of Hearst, over thirty kilometres away and accessible only by a daily train. And, since the "main support needed was at the time of birthing," the small immigrant group soon looked to women within their own community to serve as midwives. One of these was Frieda Isaak, who had prior midwifery experience in Ukraine, and whose first delivery in Reesor was a set of twins who were born after a very difficult labour. Isaak, who was called an "angel of mercy," travelled on skis or with dog and sled with supplies on her back when called to a childbirth during the long winters of northern Ontario.[81]

In the second half of the twentieth century, when home births were uncommon and midwifery almost obsolete (until legalization in the 1980s), a few Mennonite women who felt called to take up this profession took their skills with them into work overseas, often under the auspices of a missions initiative. Elsie Cressman, from the Waterloo region of southern Ontario, spent twenty-two years as a missionary nurse in Africa. Along the way she went to England to study midwifery and by the time she returned home to

Kitchener in 1976, she had assisted with at least 1000 births. In the 1980s, though in her sixties, Elsie persuaded another former missionary nurse, Alice Ropp, to join her in a midwifery practice. Elsie became an inspiration and mentor to numerous midwives who were trained and licensed in Ontario, beginning in the 1980s. The services of Elsie and Alice quickly appealed to Old Order Mennonite women who had no such trained individuals within their own community. The medicalization of childbirth had a particular impact on rural conservative women such as the Old Order, who were compelled to travel to urban hospitals to give birth when doctors ceased their practice of visiting homes to assist women in labour. One Old Order woman commented that "the delivery room, with the doctor up on his high chair ... looks like a slaughterhouse. Stirrups are for horses, not for women." The resurgence of services for home birthing generally also reinforced, for Old Order women, their desire to stay away from the impersonal and modern environment of hospitals and to maintain their values of "biblical simplicity."[82]

The fact that midwives were fairly plentiful and midwife-assisted child-birth common amongst Mennonites perhaps longer than in the general population relates to a number of factors, including their rural isolation and their desire for separation from non-Mennonite services and institutions in society. But it also may well have related to the sheer number of births that took place in Mennonite households. The size of Canadian families generally has, of course, declined significantly over the past century. Yet, throughout much of the twentieth century, Mennonite women continued to bear more children than did the national average. While rates of childbirth in Canada had dropped from 7.02 in 1851 to 3.54 in 1921, evidence from family genealogies as well as averages deduced from the census would indicate Mennonite women were on average bearing a few more in the 1920s. In the 1941 Canadian census, Mennonites had the highest percentage of adherents under the age of fifteen among other religious groups—38.7 percent—an indicator of large families. Larger families were more common among rural and newly immigrated Mennonite communities. In Ontario, where the more established Swiss Mennonites predominated, the percentage of adherents under age fifteen in 1941 was less, approximately 31 percent, while on the prairies, where newer immigrants from Russia were the majority, the number was about 40 percent.[83] Mennonite birth rates were 40 to 50 percent higher than national rates in North America until about the 1970s, at which point they began to decline to meet societal averages.[84] However, it is important to keep in mind, as Angus McLaren argues in his history of contraception, that in different historic eras, "what constituted a 'large' or 'small family' was a question of perception" that arose from a variety of cultural factors.[85]

Mennonite women, especially those who were rural immigrants, had remarkably high levels of fertility and sustained pregnancy and childbirth in numbers that are amazing for twenty-first-century women such as myself, a mother of two, to consider. Barbara Schultz Oesch's family was the second Amish-Mennonite family to migrate directly from Europe to Wilmot Township, Upper Canada, in 1824. She gave birth to eighteen children altogether, fifteen of them in Canada, and still outlived her husband John Oesch by thirty years.[86] Large families seemed especially common amongst rural Mennonites who migrated from Russia to Manitoba in the late nineteenth century. Judith Klassen Neufeld, the youngest in a family of fifteen children, was five years old when she immigrated and would herself bear ten children over nineteen years. One historian has noted that Mennonite families that arrived in Manitoba at the end of the 1800s actually increased in size when they were transplanted from the 'Old World' in Russia to the 'New World.' A decline in the age of marriage for Kleine Gemeinde women from an average of 22.0 in Russia in the 1850s to 19.3 in Manitoba in the 1890s was a significant factor contributing to a higher birth rate in the first generation of settlement.[87] For instance, Maria Stoesz Klassen, an 1874 Russian immigrant to southern Manitoba, bore sixteen children, twelve of whom were girls.

Rural families that were already large increased in size when remarriages after spousal deaths resulted in even larger 'blended' families. As an example, in 1921 widow Susannah Schroeder married widower Abraham Hildebrand; she had two daughters and he ten children from their previous marriages and during the first seven years of their marriage, Susannah gave birth to six more children; a total of eighteen children![88] When widow Anna Dueck Friesen married widower Peter P. Reimer in 1935, they each brought ten children to the marriage for a total of twenty offspring. A close-knit community of large extended families meant that one of Anna's daughters was also Peter's daughter-in-law.[89] The fact that all these individuals likely participated in the same church community reinforced the strong and overlapping linkages between religion and kinship that existed amongst Mennonites.

The 'many hands to run the family farm' adage was certainly operative amongst some Mennonite rural pioneer families. Large families were an economic asset, as both boys and girls were put to work at the many and assorted tasks involved in running a rural household and farm. This is evident in the rural household of Maria Reimer Unger, a midwife with thirteen children of her own. Her 1919 diary entries consist mainly of accounting for the daily tasks of herself and her children. For instance, on Tuesday, June 24, she wrote the following: "Papa, with the boys, worked in the barn; Johann ploughed; I baked; Elizabeth sewed; Anna, Tina hoed."[90] The unpredictable gender balance in households of course necessitated adjustments in normative gender roles and economic circumstances. When Peter P. Heinrichs shopped for a large amount of cloth at Eaton's in Winnipeg, the clerk offered him yard goods for free when it was discovered that the cloth would make dresses for Heinrichs's nine daughters. Because there were no sons in this farming family, two of the daughters were called "the boys, Pete and Bill" and helped their father in the barn and with the fieldwork.[91] In the Heinrichs family, not all the girls were needed at home all the time, so most of them 'worked out' at some point during their adolescent years. Farm and household economies that were mainly subsistence-oriented and had minimal mechanization needed a good supply of manual labourers that were best found among one's own children.

If a rural household had only a few children, it could become necessary to hire outside help. Of course, large numbers of small children in a household also necessitated additional help for women. Large families were made more manageable by the presence in most households of hired help and/or extended family members. For instance, in 1933, at the age of forty-one, Lovina Weber gave birth to twin boys, her eighth and ninth children. Daughter Selina, who was about fourteen at the time, recalled that "Angelina [their live-in domestic help] claimed baby Amos for her baby while she was with us, which came in very handy for mother. I remember very well how much I helped with the twins which I enjoyed. I love to read, often I had a baby on each arm and a book to read while they went to sleep...."[92]

Even today, the value of children to farm operations with little mechanization is evident amongst Old Order Mennonite families in Ontario, for whom there are special provisions that allow children to leave formal schooling after grade eight in order to enter 'vocational training' on the family farm. Amongst such rural, technology-resistant groups, family size is still higher than within the general population, although the average number of children per family might be five rather than ten, as in previous generations. The continued perception that large families go together with Mennonite culture is revealed in a study of Hmong refugee women who migrated to Canada in the early

1980s. Many of these newcomers felt an affinity with, and thereby joined, the Mennonite church less because of doctrine or religious belief than because of a sense of common family values: several Hmong women reportedly said, "Mennonites like lots of children, like us."[93]

The high mortality rate amongst pioneer families also meant that high fertility rates would ensure at least some generational succession. Childbirth was one site at which death was always a possibility. But in large families, the death of a child was also a common occurrence, especially up to the mid-twentieth century. When a diphtheria epidemic hit her family in the 1880s, Helena Penner lost three of her siblings in two weeks: "There was Margaret, a tall slight girl with long fair braids, about 2 ½ years older than Erdman, and an extremely intelligent child, the brightest of us all. And Abram, 2 years younger than myself, a sturdy, red-cheeked little fellow, the apple of my father's eye. And Sara, a perfect cherub of a little child, with lovely blue eyes ... and a mass of golden curls."[94] Anna Bartel Eidse lost three of her first four children: the first at birth, the second (a twin) in a kerosene fire, and the third during the flu epidemic of 1918. Her sixth child, a girl, was born prematurely and died shortly after. Anna then had five more children who survived.[95] Those women who lived through difficult years in the Soviet Union and Depression on the prairies could order their personal lives around the frequent occurrences of both births and deaths in their household. Susanna Kehler Wiebe, who immigrated from Russia in 1927, bore thirteen children, three of whom died in infancy or early childhood; one of her daughters later remarked: "Mother had many weary years just dealing with births and deaths."[96]

Indeed, it was rare if a nineteenth- or early twentieth-century family did not lose at least one of their children to illness or accident. Even on the eve of the First World War, 15 percent of Canadian babies died before the age of one.[97] Pennsylvania immigrant Esther Stauffer, wed at the age of fifteen, gave birth to four children before she was twenty-one, but then lost all of them within a few months in 1813. She would bear fourteen more in the years following, three of whom died in infancy. Esther herself died at the age of forty-five when her youngest child was just nineteen months old.[98] Helena Wiebe, an immigrant woman who died in 1896, gave birth to twelve children in just sixteen years, only six of whom lived to adulthood.[99] Because of the likelihood that at least some children would die young, the birth of additional babies was viewed as a way to replace those inevitable losses. In an 1874 letter written to Russia, Anna Klassen Goossen directed the following comment at her sister-in-law: "My beloved sister, I have heard that the Lord has given you twin sons. It was so hard for you with your son, Johann. Now He has given him back to you and another with him."[100] Even my own mother-in-law, a refugee who saw much death and suffering in her childhood and adolescence, advised that a couple should always have at least three children; in case one died, then at least there wouldn't be an 'only child' left. In one collection of reminiscences, it was remarked that before provincially financed medical care came to Saskatchewan, the father in a household was the first priority in receiving medical care, since the livelihood of the family depended on his labour. Mothers came next in priority, followed by children, who, because of their numbers, were rarely taken to a doctor.[101] A dramatic decrease in the rate of infant mortality that occurred in the years between 1921 and 1951 would also have contributed to the trend towards fewer pregnancies among Mennonite and other Canadian women.

Large families also resulted from the incorporation of orphans, labourers, and relatives into one household, a type of family culture that was common a century ago, but perhaps enhanced in Mennonite communities by strong kinship networks and sectarian tendencies. In time periods when birth and death were frequent events, a static notion of the nuclear family was not very strong. For instance, in early twentieth-century Russia, one young woman assured her older sister that she would share children from her own large family, given the elder's inability to bear children of her own. The younger, Elizabeth, promised Justina that "if you cannot have any children, then I will have a large family when I get married and will give some of my children to you." This promise was actually fulfilled when Elizabeth's infant daughter was adopted by Justina and her husband.[102] In 1891, Margaretha Plett Kroeker's southern Manitoba household contained, in addition to her husband (their own children were married and lived elsewhere), a thirteen-year-old foster child, an older disabled woman, a male German Lutheran servant from Winnipeg, and a female servant from a nearby village.[103]

Amongst pioneer families, in which death by accident, epidemic, or other causes was almost an everyday occurrence, taking in and raising orphans was common; adopting or fostering children from non-Mennonite families also occurred and may have reinforced the lesser degree of sectarian separation that existed in the very early years of settlement. For instance, a cholera epidemic in Waterloo Township in the 1830s killed both parents of an English family named Hembling, and so their six children, aged two to fourteen, were adopted into Mennonite families.[104] Because widows and widowers especially were expected to remarry, so-called blended families were commonplace, as noted earlier. Aside from the resultant extra-large households, this could also create some fairly challenging family dynamics. For instance, Agatha Wiebe, a forty-year-old professional nurse who had never married, gained an instant family in 1927 when she wed a widower with eleven children who had lost his wife in childbirth two years earlier. She became stepmother to children aged three to twenty-one. However, the older daughters, who had become accustomed to running their father's household, found it difficult to defer to Agatha, herself bewildered by her new status. In her mid-forties, Agatha gave birth to two children of her own.[105]

The large size of some Mennonite families had utilitarian purposes, mainly economic, as well as biblical, foundations, and also emerged from an urge, however subconscious, towards group survival. However, continuous child bearing also had negative consequences for women's physical and psychological health, and, in some families, the number of children exceeded their parents' ability to care for them properly. When Luise Konrad gave birth to twins—her ninth and tenth children—in rural Saskatchewan during the poverty years of the mid-1930s, she reluctantly agreed to send her thirteen-year-old daughter to live for a while with a neighbour's childless relatives. However, when the Konrads learned that the couple was intending to keep the young girl until she was sixteen, Luise's husband promptly brought her home.[106] Historian Royden Loewen suggests that high birth rates among Mennonite women in Manitoba in the late nineteenth century resulted in a significant demand for wet nurses, who might receive as much as fifty cents a day for their services.[107] Some women who had large families could hardly separate one pregnancy and birth from the next. I was amused when reading Anna Thiessen's birthing accounts of her ten children, her only certainty being that she had given birth to ten: "After the twins I had *about* three yet. I had ten children all together. I don't *think* I ever lost one"[108] (emphasis mine). My own immigrant grandmother, who birthed thirteen children during the years of Depression and following, was, by some accounts, self-conscious about the size of her family, commenting, "I enjoy much more going to families with many children; they understand us better."[109] One woman who married in the late 1950s or early 1960s recalled that her desire to use birth control arose in part from her embarrassment over growing up in a family of fifteen children.[110]

Despite the large amounts of time spent in child bearing and regular contact with animal births on the farm, in many groups sexual functions and activity were not discussed—except perhaps in the context of crude barnyard humour—and considered sin by some. This of course reflected a Protestant puritanism not unique to Mennonites, but perhaps reinforced by Mennonites' dual-world theology that placed sexual matters in the realm of a fallen world. Yet in those settings where high birth rates were common, women spent significant amounts of their adult life concerned with their physical bodies: with menstrual cycles, breastfeeding, fertility control, and with the problems that might result from repeated child bearing. Few sources provide evidence of how women experienced and dealt with constant physical changes to their bodies, but there are some glimpses in diaries and letters. For instance, in 1960 Luise Konrad wrote to her pregnant daughter, offering advice that included drinking plenty of water and eating sufficient fruit and vegetables, wearing warm and non-constrictive clothing, avoiding high heels, and reading "positive literature" including a passage from the Bible every day.[111]

Some sources suggest that women struggled with and even resisted the expectations and demands that child bearing represented, even though they may have welcomed each new arrival. Anna Jansen, writing in her diary in 1876, refers to her pregnant sister's frequent vomiting, and declares that if being married consists of so much vomiting, she will never get married.[112] Anne Konrad, whose mother had been pregnant eleven times, recalled asking why there were so many children in their family. Her mother's reply had been, "And which one would you want unborn?"[113] Women appeared to have been philosophical about their fertility, and considered their large families to be a blessing from God. Modern analysts generally associate such high rates of child bearing as an indicator of women's subordinate position, and indeed repression, within a given society. Efforts that reduce these rates are thus viewed as advancing women's status and sense of self-determination. But especially within religious communities in which women were denied access to formalized leadership and whose position in the universal order was beneath both God and man, the ability to successfully reproduce in abundance may have also garnered women community recognition and admiration and honed their own sense of accomplishment. This, of course, does not lessen the tiresome labour, in child bearing and in domestic chores, that were the lot of life for women with many children.

Understanding their frequent pregnancies and many children within a religious framework may have helped women make sense of the difficulties associated with high levels of child bearing and confirmed that they were behaving as good Christian women. Included in that religious framework, and reflective of the Mennonites' literalist reading of scripture and their rejection of societal trends, was an official condemnation of birth control well into the second half of the twentieth century. Large Mennonite families, then, also resulted from attitudes towards sexuality that encouraged ignorance about fertility management, but that also responded to prescriptive warnings against 'modern' forms of contraception. Mennonite women were not unlike other Canadian women in having limited knowledge about how to regulate their pregnancies; or at least, that knowledge was securely lodged in private and informal realms. Many early twentieth-century Mennonite women, such as those interviewed by Katherine Martens for her oral history collection on childbirth, asserted that they knew nothing about birth control. The woman who was determined to limit her own pregnancies after growing up in a family of fifteen recalled that inquiries from close relatives regarding contraception revealed four choices: abstinence, withdrawal, the rhythm method, and the vinegar douche. She recalled that she and most of her peers found themselves with unplanned pregnancies. She said the "constant fear of pregnancy was a major source of frustration."[114]

Sex education that did take place was usually framed in terms of warnings about the consequences of sexual activity. Anna Bartel Eidse apparently told her children "the facts of life" when they were young, with the primary purpose of protecting her daughters from hired hands.[115] As one woman said, "My mother always cautioned me to never let a boy tamper with me and the consequences that would follow."[116] When Helen Wedel's granddaughter asked her about birth control, Helen referred her to biblical knowledge: "You know, we didn't have any birth control except for the Biblical ones. God already told Israel, the women have their times, and for such and such a time men are not to come to the women."[117] Women did what they could to space childbirth by insisting on abstinence during their fertile times (if they knew when that was) and by hoping their husbands would practise withdrawal. While such things were officially not talked about, women secretively also learned from each other such methods as vinegar douches after intercourse, the use of herbs, or vaginal sponges. It is even more difficult to determine what kind of treatments or practices were observed that induced miscarriages. One family history is remarkably transparent in an anecdote about an immigrant mother wishing to end a pregnancy; in a letter to her sister in Russia, Agneta Klassen confesses that "on becoming pregnant and not wanting another child with all the other work involved during the first difficult years in the new country, she had prayed to God that He take the child away if He so willed." Agneta's wish was granted, even though she considered it "morally wrong."[118]

Combined with ignorance was discouragement, sometimes outright prohibition, against the use of birth control. Based on their literalist reading of the Bible, church leaders pointed to scriptural passages that commanded God's people to be fruitful and multiply. As an example, in his 1942 manual of sex education (the very writing of which was, despite its overall message, a rather enlightened initiative), Ontario minister Clayton F. Derstine stated, "To refuse to multiply is rebellion against the divine order in the moral universe" and referred to another writer who associated "intentional childless homes through the practice of birth control" with "concubinage."[119] Another male Mennonite writer said that it was "women's ordained responsibility to bear children willingly and rear them in the fear of the Lord."[120] And as late as 1964, one Mennonite periodical carried an article that reinforced the long-held adage that "motherhood is the highest calling to which a woman can attain."[121] To consciously and artificially limit family size not only went against what Mennonites understood to be God's command to fill the earth, but it also threatened a way of life that was structured around the family farm and sustained by extensive kinship relationships. Aside from biblical justifications, the rationale used by those who opposed the use of birth control was that it was 'worldly' and only one of many ways in which secular society was threatening the Mennonites. For instance, in 1953 the Ontario Mennonite Brethren ministers and deacons condemned birth control as "conforming to the world."[122]

Maintenance of the patriarchal order was also an underlying factor in vehement assertions against contraception. Without saying it, by condemning a woman's right to control her fertility, leaders were also asserting their rights as men to control women's bodies. A Birth Control Committee, appointed by the Mennonite Conference of Ontario in 1944, is a prime example of an all-male decision-making body exerting such control. That year the Conference passed a resolution voicing "opposition to the aims, philosophy, and particularly to all the artificial methods of the modern Birth Control Movement as contrary to the Biblical conception of family life."[123] The following year the three-man committee brought a five-page report to the Conference. While the Bible gave no specific directives about birth control, the committee found there were plenty of references in the spirit of Genesis 1:28 that called on the human race to "be fruitful and multiply and replenish the earth." The committee declared itself in opposition to modern birth control for a number of reasons. It resulted in a decline in population that was clearly at odds with God's injunction. Birth control was seen as evidence of materialism and the related factors of urbanization and employment of women. Not only was "race suicide" seen as the natural result of birth control, but the committee feared the impact of smaller families on the church: "If families continue to decrease in size as they have in the last generation, in twenty years our mission board meetings and conferences will not have the blessing of a large proportion of young people in attendance as they are now."[124] Birth control was thought to encourage immorality and was associated with a variety of "women's diseases." The committee also pointed out that "normal" marriages were blessed with children. Furthermore, the association of the birth control movement with certain atheist individuals and communist organizations only reinforced the committee's resolve that it should be avoided.

The Evangelical Mennonite Conference (EMC) also dealt with this question during the 1950s. Their report pointed out that the Bible offered no clear prescription on contraception. However, the fact that birth control and divorce were acceptable in the Soviet Union, a communist state, was proof that birth control rested on a system of unbelief. The report argued that children were a blessing from God, and that a woman with many children was not necessarily less healthy than a woman who had deliberately limited her child bearing. The report further suggested that if a woman accepted her role as mother content- edly, and nursed her child as a mother should, children would be spaced in a natural way. This argument, of course, rested on the false security that breast- feeding was a reliable form of fertility control. Above all, the EMC statement called for moderation in the sexual relationship, particularly on the part of the husband, whose sex drive was thought to be naturally stronger than that of his wife.[125] Given the limited female involvement in the public ordering of the EMC it is highly unlikely that women had any input into this report. One family memoir recounts how the question of birth control was met with "deafening silence" until a prominent minister rose and offered a quote from scripture: "Be fruitful and multiply and fill the earth," to which his wife—mother of fifteen children—publicly responded, "But where does it say that we have to do it all alone?"[126] Few sources offer such frank perspectives, but it is likely that women had opinions on birth control that were rarely heard in formal church discussions of the topic. These they discussed amongst themselves, perhaps sharing thoughts that countered the official position of their church, or privately feeling guilt when they took physical measures to controvert what they were told was God's natural law for married women.

Despite the fact that in the 1940s and after, birth control became an issue that seemed to warrant official investigations and statements on the part of church groups, this is not to say that it wasn't used prior to the obvious decline in family size amongst Mennonites. Nor should one discount the idea that women who did not give birth ten or more times or more were using some form of fertility control, while those who were repeatedly pregnant may have made conscious choices for many children. Certainly, not all women bore many children. Ironically, early in the century, one of Canada's foremost producers of contraceptive devices was also an important employer of Mennonites. A.R. Kaufman was a philanthropist and rubber factory owner in Kitchener, Ontario. One of the factory's nurses was Anna (Sophie) Weber, a sister to Irwin K. Weber, general manager at Kaufman's, and also Urias K. Weber, minister at First Mennonite and later Stirling Avenue Mennonite Church in Kitchener, Ontario. Anna was director of the Parents' Information Bureau established by Kaufman to find ways to alleviate the poverty experienced by many of the large families in his employ. The bureau employed nurses across the country who visited poor homes to discuss family planning and gave out free birth-control devices produced by Kaufman's. At a time when the dissemination of birth control information was illegal, Anna Weber was sued and briefly imprisoned for promoting such advice at the Kaufman rubber factory. At the highly publicized 1936 trial of one of her colleagues, Anna Weber said, "All mothers should have the privilege of voluntary motherhood."[127] Quite a few Mennonite women were employed at Kaufman's, and, according to one church historian, these women caused controversy in their urban churches because they refused to wear their prayer coverings to work. It is not surprising that Anna, like some other liberal-minded, single Mennonite women of her generation, had left the Mennonite church.[128]

The decline in the size of Mennonite families struck at what had hitherto been a fundamental part of Mennonitism, that is, large nuclear and extended families that were the basic unit of a community-oriented faith. However, the reality was that in an urban setting, and also on increasingly mechanized farms, large families were an economic liability. And so Mennonites, like the rest of society, increasingly chose to limit and space the number of children they had. As was often the case, official church concern and formal statements on the issue were responding to exactly this trend. Prescriptive warnings against birth control were not pre-emptive, but were in fact reactive to women's declining number of pregnancies and their apparent desire to control the number of children they would bear and raise. The quiet disappearance of this issue from the official denominational agenda—perhaps about the same time that birth control was legalized in Canada in 1969—was indicative of the modified views of leadership but even more so, the behaviour of women (and men) themselves. The removal of birth control from the category of sin was perhaps a revolutionary moment for Mennonite women, though it is difficult to determine to what extent women were using artificial methods of contraception all along, despite the warnings of church leaders. The ability and recognized right to regulate reproduction are crucial to women's autonomy within patriarchal families and communities. And it is likely that, like other Canadian women, Mennonite women who wished to avoid pregnancy or space their children sought information about fertility control from mothers, sisters, and other close relatives and friends.

The increased use of birth control in the 1950s and beyond led to smaller families, which in turn had other repercussions in church and community life. Families with few children were more likely to urbanize, and, as Katie Funk Wiebe perceptively suggests, declining family size meant smaller church membership rosters. In this, the fears expressed by the Mennonite Conference of Ontario committee were realized. Churches could no longer rely on biological reproduction to fuel church growth and so needed alternate strategies to prevent church membership from remaining static in numbers.[129] Referring to such strategies within Mennonite churches in the mid-twentieth century, historian Royden Loewen points to research that has linked fertility decline with the rise of pietistic evangelicalism, a change that encouraged women to think of having "few children of greater spiritual quality."[130]

While the majority of Canadian Mennonite women actively practised some form of reliable contraception and thereby reduced family sizes towards the latter half of the twentieth century, a minority of Mennonites continued to surpass global averages in birthrate. Large families remained common into the twenty-first century for some Mennonite groups characterized by family norms that included a patriarchal family order and prohibitions against the use of contraception. For instance, conservative Old Colony Mennonites in

Mexico, many of whom began a return migration to Canada in the latter decades of the twentieth century, are reported to have a birth rate among the world's highest.[131] In this church group, families with ten or more children are not uncommon, even though they represent an economic liability rather than a support, as most families do not operate the kind of labour-intensive, large-scale farming operations as were common a century earlier. This also holds true for a group of conservative Mennonites (Kleine Gemeinde) who moved to Nova Scotia from Belize in 1984. In this group, which also stresses the biblical subordination of women, "women are advised not to use birth control other than the natural rhythm method, unless both partners agree to abstain for a period of time."[132] One conservative Mennonite woman in Ontario, whose minister had made the comment that "contraceptives belong in the barn," was confronted by the local bishop when she announced her intention to teach in a Mennonite school after being married; he "hoped that [she] wasn't thinking of birth control."[133] For such groups, religious motivation to not limit the number of children given by God intersects with internal community gender norms and cultural resistance to external practices perceived as secular and modern.

SINGLENESS AND WIDOWHOOD

The discouragement of fertility control and the affirmation of large families reflected an overall Mennonite world view that considered marriage between a man and woman that resulted in procreation as the normative and preferred state of family relations. For women in particular, marriage and motherhood were (and still are, one might argue) considered to be the best and highest achievement. In this, they were little different from other Canadian women. And so for women who did not marry, or who did not bear children, or who spent a good part of their lives without husbands, as widows or as divorced women, there was a significant stigma attached to their family position. In the context of an idealization of the nuclear family structure, women in these categories were 'othered' and marginalized. Women who made alternate choices to marriage or motherhood, or whose lives simply took different turns, carried the psychological and emotional burden of being aberrations from the family norm. In a family memoir set in mid-twentieth-century Alberta and British Columbia, Anne Konrad describes her perception of both the norm and its aberrations:

A very few Mennonite teenagers who got pregnant were whisked out of school and invariably gave up their babies to adoption. In our community divorce was almost unheard of, except in novels, and single persons were not suspected of being gay.... Until the many women with children arrived as Displaced Persons after WW II ... the norm was two-parent families with children, each living on a small farm.... Single adults continued to live at home with their parents.[134]

While there are few sources prior to the 1960s that reveal the sentiments of earlier generations of women who made choices that departed from the expected, more recent reflections do exist. One woman, who, with her husband, decided to remain permanently childless after nine years of marriage, remarked that her situation seemed to put her in the "never-never land between the world of parents and the world of single persons." She said it was difficult to 'admit' that they had made a conscious choice to not become parents.[135] In 1976, a thirty-five-year-old woman reflected on the possibility of never having children and realized her inner struggle over what was "a response to society's message to me that the very essence of my female being could only be fully realized through marriage and child bearing."[136] Another woman who adopted two children reflected on the burden of infertility, which she felt was greater when one was Mennonite, "because in the Mennonite community there is more nostalgia, more sentimentalization, more romanticizing about the actual experience of childbirth. Why that is I don't exactly know, but I believe it to be a reality of being a woman in a Mennonite community. Perhaps because the less power you have in the structures that there are, the more you emphasize the power you do have, which is to bear a child and to produce that child."[137]

Perhaps most stigmatized were women who bore children outside marriage. It is impossible to determine the frequency of unmarried motherhood amongst Mennonites in comparison to the general population, but anecdotal evidence indicates that, of course, such cases existed in Mennonite communities throughout history. In many of these instances, the circumstances and outcomes surrounding a woman's pregnancy were tragic at worst or painful at best. For instance, Laura Shantz's 1918 diary refers to an unwed mother whose baby girl was "almost frozen [as it] was pitched out the window."[138] The baby later died, and the mother baptized into the Mennonite church after she had confessed and received forgiveness from the community. A Winnipeg woman said she became pregnant at the age of sixteen "when the war came and the soldiers and the sailors ... were very attracted to us girls. I don't have to explain it further." She noted that there were "two others before me" whose families "quickly up and left" the city. She chose to keep her baby but was "totally ostracized" and her mother was harassed on the telephone by people from their church. The child too was bullied as she grew up because she had no father. In later years, the woman reflected that she "weathered a very rough life" because of her premarital pregnancy and thought that perhaps it would have been better had she given the child up for adoption.[139] In most cases of pregnancy outside marriage, the couple involved—sometimes just the woman—were expected to make a public confession before their church community and possibly be subject to some form of discipline such as forfeiting their church membership or being excluded from communion and other church rites. One woman had to return to the rural church where she was a member, though no longer attending, to confess a premarital pregnancy, an event she recalled as a "ritual of humiliation."[140] If they remained within the church, most single mothers were nevertheless treated with contempt. In one reminiscence, two single mothers decided to sit together in their Mennonite church in Winnipeg, because then the congregation wouldn't "have to crane their necks in two directions to stare."[141] Helen Dueck Enns became pregnant in her mid-twenties after moving to Winnipeg to work. She chose to keep the baby, but according to her granddaughter, the experience "was a scarlet letter that would follow her for years within her small religious community."[142]

Of course, some cases of pregnancy outside marriage resulted from rape; the response of the church in such instances varied from sympathy to condemnation. "Marie," the eldest of eleven children, was born in 1900 into a Saskatchewan Mennonite Bergthaler home. When she was seventeen, she was raped by the hired man on their farm. She became pregnant and was excommunicated from her church, and the child was given up for adoption. Marie married a Mennonite man and was allowed to join his church. Apparently the rapist was taken to court in 1917 by Marie's father, though the outcome is unknown.[143] Most women who were raped while in domestic service (a not uncommon occurrence) but did not become pregnant kept the traumatic event a secret for the rest of their lives.

Other victims of sexual assault were counted among Mennonite women refugees who had fled violence and turmoil in the Soviet Union in the 1920s and 1940s. Many Mennonite families that arrived in Canada as displaced persons from the Soviet Union and eastern Europe after the Second World War were 'fragmented' or 'grab bag' families. That is, virtually every household had lost members due to arrest and exile in the Soviet Union, or because of illness and starvation during years of deprivation before and during the war, or were killed or went missing in the midst of wartime violence itself.[144] Most of the missing were adult men, and as a result, these families, about 8000 individuals, were composed mainly of women, children, and the elderly. The numerous single mothers in this group—most weren't quite considered widows because they had no definitive knowledge of a husband's death—struggled to integrate into Mennonite communities that, like other Canadians of the 1950s, were eager to settle into post-war domesticity that idealized a whole, nuclear family. Among the newcomers were women with children who had never been married, but had conceived prior to immigration as the result of wartime alliances, consensual relationships, or sometimes rape. These situations were gossiped about privately, but generally shrouded in silence in the postwar era. One woman living in the Russian zone of occupied Germany at the end of the war gave birth to a daughter after trading sex with a Soviet officer for food and protection for herself and her three other children. After immigrating to Canada in 1949, the woman knew that people talked about her past, although nothing was said directly to her. When the 'illegitimate' daughter grew up in Canada, negative rumours surrounded her own morality—she was thought to be "loose" and "easy"—simply because she was born out of wedlock.

In another case, a young immigrant woman, following the Mennonite practice of adult baptism, asked to be baptized but was refused by Mennonite churches in Alberta and Ontario. As an unmarried mother with a young son, it was expected that she repent of her 'sin' before being baptized. She had in fact married the child's German father during the war but had sought an annulment when she discovered that he already had a wife from whom he was separated but not divorced. The complicated circumstances of her marriage and her own stubborn personality prompted the woman to withhold this information from the church, allowing church members to instead think of her as an unwed mother.[145] For the most part, these female-headed family units, whether they had lost a husband/father or never had one, settled quietly into Mennonite communities (some left altogether), enduring the unspoken questions, rumours, or ostracism, and struggling with mixed inner emotions of defiance and guilt over their difficult past.

The most common way in which Mennonite women departed from a normative family trajectory was not to get married, whether by deliberate choice or due to the circumstances of her life. Certainly not all women entered into heterosexual marriage relationships and bore children. In fact, latter twentieth-century statistics showed that Mennonite women remained single at a significantly higher rate than men. Sociological studies done in 1972 and 1989 of modern Mennonite churches in North America revealed that women remained unmarried at higher rates than men; the study also showed, interestingly, that Mennonite women were also widowed and divorced at slightly higher rates than men, so that the overall population of single Mennonite women was higher, at least during the period of that study. But even prior to this later quantitative study, anecdotal evidence from earlier historical periods reveals a higher prevalence of never-married women than men. Historical literature on the family in Canada reveals that while marriage was an 'option' for women, for men, marriage was the only 'choice.'[146] Singleness for women has long received greater societal sanction, even while single women themselves were viewed pejoratively. A group of unmarried sisters living together, or female friends or relatives sharing a home, was considered acceptable, even if the women themselves were seen as oddities. For their part, a household of single men was pretty much unheard of.

There are many factors that may account for singleness among Mennonite women, some of which are of course common to other ethnic and religious groups. The reasons given for singleness were, however, seldom related to a woman's personal choices against marrying. In rare instances, a woman's own inadequacies were connected to her reduced marriage options; for instance, Anna C. Reimer, a woman in Russia, reportedly remained single "because as the result of a fall from a chair while picking cherries she was left with a stiff arm."[147] One certainly wonders why such a handicap would have eliminated her opportunities for marriage, except if potential husbands saw Anna as unable to perform the kind of physical labour expected of wives and mothers. Inability to conceive or bear children may have also been seen as a barrier to marriage, as is implied in Ontario minister Clayton F. Derstine's 1919 written statement that he had "respect for a woman that doesn't marry" since "There may be physical reasons."[148]

For some women, marital choices were precluded by caregiving demands presented by aging parents. Caretaking obligations meant that some women remained in their parental home beyond the typical age of marriageability. My own Aunt Agatha was the last to move out of my grandparents' home several decades after both of them had passed away. One family history includes an anecdote about a Mennonite woman whose father refused to allow her to marry her suitor because he wanted her to "nurse and serve" him in his old age.[149] Mary Ellen Reesor's father disallowed her from going to Colorado for nurses' training after her mother died in the early twentieth century, and so she stayed home and cared for him until he remarried, at which point "she was no longer needed."[150] Yet some single women who chose to remain in their parental home were thereby freed up to do other things. When her father died only two years after the family immigrated to Canada in 1923, Katie Hooge took on the responsibility of living with and caring for her mother and thus never married. Yet because her mother looked after the household, Katie was able to develop her own career in office administration, as assistant to the Canadian Mennonite Board of Colonization from 1923 to 1964. About Katie it has been said, "Without her efficiency and dependability these men would not have been able to function as they did."[151] At the same time, women who never married were never really deemed independent either, and for a long time were considered part of their parental home, no matter how old, financially secure, or professionally independent they were. One single woman, after returning to Canada from overseas mission work, remarked that "when single women come home they are expected to move in with relatives or a parent, whereas married couples are always provided for by the church and sometimes extensive preparations are made for their return."[152] Indeed, in her research on women missionaries in Puerto Rico, Beth E. Graybill describes the frequent trips home that single workers made in order to care for parents or deal with other family emergencies.[153] In addition to caring for aging parents or other dependent family members, single women took on the informal roles of "family kin-keeper, maintaining heirlooms and sharing the family history."[154]

Instead of, or in addition to, caring for parents, some women had vocational aspirations that could be followed only outside marriage, since for women, marriage, homemaking and child bearing were considered a life calling. Until the later twentieth century, women with vocational aspirations other than marriage and motherhood often had to choose between career and family. Esther Goossen, with an adventurous career that eventually resulted in a PhD in biochemistry, wrote the following in a 1951 letter to her parents, regarding her many suitors: "A couple of young punks have been giving me somewhat of a chase lately—O me, O my, children or sugardaddies all love me: They're either too young or too old; they're either too grey or too grassy green!!"[155] Susan Peters, a relief worker in Denmark during the Second World War, had similar thoughts about men and marriage: "I just can't see why people want to work so hard to get a ring ... I am a confirmed old maid."[156] Salome Bauman, one of the first teachers at Rockway Mennonite Collegiate when it opened in Kitchener, Ontario, in 1945 and later principal of the secondary school for two years, was another example of a woman who chose career over marriage. In one recollection, apparently when teaching a health class to high school girls, she addressed the topic of marriage but made it clear that single-ness was also "a viable option."[157] At about the same time, Agatha Klassen of British Columbia also chose a teaching career over marriage, and broke off an engagement to pursue her vocational dreams.[158] An even more acceptable career option for single women was to enter into overseas mission work under the auspices of a Mennonite church organization. Because they didn't have a husband and children to care for, single women also experienced greater latitude in working within the church. For instance, Erica Epp Koop recalled that it was more acceptable when her unmarried sister was voted onto a church committee than when she, a married woman, was put in that position because it "really ought not to be my place."[159]

Many single women found and created meaningful family relationships outside the traditional nuclear family. Gertrude Klassen, for instance, main-tained a popular practice as a chiropractor in southern Manitoba from the 1920s through the 1950s. About her professional identity, it was reported: "There is no card or name plate at her door, but her appointment book is filled months in advance; her large clientele runs into large figures, and her talented touch for resetting twisted joints has become legend." Throughout her adult life, Gertrude also fostered numerous children, particularly those who were orphaned or had health problems. Her first charge was her seven-year-old nephew, disabled with infantile paralysis, whose own family was unable to care for him. She took in fifty-three children over thirty years. She was single but certainly not alone.[160]

Even while some women chose not to marry, that didn't mean they didn't want to be mothers. While giving birth to a child out of wedlock was grounds for removal from the church, a few single women made even more unconven-tional choices by adopting a child, such as Mary Snider, profiled at the outset of this chapter. Among Mennonite refugees who came to Canada from the Soviet Union after the Second World War were many women who had never married, but nevertheless were guardians of children whose parents had died or disappeared during the years of Stalinist repression. For example, Kathe and Agathe Neumann arrived in Canada in 1948 with the five children of their brother and his wife, who were presumed to have died in the Soviet gulag sometime after 1938.[161] Single women also found community with each other, as women with similar interests, common goals, and shared identity markers as women without husbands. Throughout her life, Agatha Klassen maintained a close connection with ten to fifteen women with whom she had grown up, most of whom had chosen to remain single: "All cherished the freedom to pursue their careers and interests." For Agatha, such freedoms included a summer-long driving trip with three friends, criss-crossing the United States.[162] These women may well have thrived on close female friendships that were much more difficult for their married peers to maintain.

While single women themselves often flourished in their independence, career success, and non-marital relationships, lifelong singleness was historically viewed in mainly disparaging ways. Even while women who eschewed marriage were sometimes viewed in a sacrificial sense—especially those who cared for elderly parents—the common attitude towards single women was that of pity that they had not managed to achieve life's greatest goal for women. They were called spinsters, old maids, "unclaimed blessings," and "*die blieb sitzen*" (one who remained seated, or a wallflower).[163] Sometimes the labelling could be quite amusing, as in an 1875 diary, in which two sisters, aged eighty-six and seventy-eight, were referred to as "two maidens." Single women often found themselves on the fringe of church life, even when it came to exclusive women's organizations; in some churches, there were separate women's societies just for single women. During the era when women had no franchise within the church, single women, even if financially self-supporting and contributing to the congregation, were thus eliminated from decision-making processes. In an extreme expression of the marital hopes for single women, a practice existed within some communities whereby when an unmarried woman died, she would be dressed all in white "as if she was prepared to meet her groom in heaven" and would wear a myrtle vine wreath on her head as if at a wedding.[164] One Manitoba woman recalled the death of a twenty-one-year-old unmarried woman who, in the coffin, was dressed in "a long white dress like a bride" with a veil.[165]

Whether singleness was viewed as a blessing or a curse, it was clear that never marrying was a women's issue, and much less relevant to men. A two-part article in the *Canadian Mennonite* in 1957 spoke about the difficulties, but interestingly, also the advantages of being a 'single girl.' Advantages included freedom, job opportunities—which at that point were still largely filled by unmarried women—travel, and so on. No mention is made of the single male, since singleness for men was rarely considered an issue of concern, partly because of its rarity, but also given that marriage was not considered intrinsic to male self-identity as it was for women.[166] While men who remained unmarried for life rarely reflected in writing on their status—and indeed there were many fewer men who were bachelors for life—women often felt bound to apologize for or explain their singleness. Frequently, they sought to present the advantages so as to defend their choice. Sara Spenst, a woman living in Russia in 1929, wrote to Canadian relatives questioning the immigration restrictions being implemented by the Canadian government: "they now run the risk of barring their doors to some of the most desirable persons. Wouldn't it be better for them to welcome more people like me, though single, than inviting couples, and run the risk that some of the husbands would prove to be lazy?"[167] Another advocate for singleness was Saskatchewan author Margaret Epp, who wished young people the best in choosing a life partner, but also said that "if God called us to be single, we could be happy in that role as well."[168] Women were also more likely to articulate, in letters and diaries, their disdain for marriage, as did Susan Peters mentioned earlier. Another example is that of nineteen-year-old Marie Schroeder, who ended her diary entry of 4 November 1926 with the following comment: "No I'm not married yet and I don't expect to be either."[169]

Marie Schroeder did not in fact get married, but died at the age of twenty-eight after a short illness. Had she lived, the odds would have seen her married and, like most other Canadian women then and now, she would have outlived her husband. Katie Funk Wiebe, widowed in 1962 as a young mother of four children, once commented, "I am convinced that aging, poverty and widowhood will always be women's agenda."[170] Given the longer average lifespan of women compared to men, the majority of Mennonite women who married spent a portion of their latter years as widows. Today women in Canada live five to ten years longer than men, a longevity gap that developed only after the mid-nineteenth century, before which time men in Western nations actually lived longer than women.[171] During the writing of this section of the book, my own mother marked twenty years as a widow. For her—healthy, economically secure, children all grown up—widowhood has been a positive time during which to nurture a career and develop relationships and interests without the parameters of compromise that marriage necessarily entails. Widows of past eras, however, faced perhaps different challenges, specifically those related to financial stability and to raising children who were likely still dependent.

Economic security was undoubtedly the most important issue for widows, at least in the years before the Canada Pension Plan offered a regular and stable, albeit small, income for widows in their senior years. Amongst late nineteenth-century Russian Mennonite immigrants on the prairies, unique inheritance practices created the potential for substantial income for some widows. Upon the death of her husband, a widow inherited half the estate and the other half was divided amongst the children. Historian Royden Loewen has noted a number of wealthy widows in southern Manitoba who owned and managed farms comparable to the average farm acreage, or, if they had chosen to sell their land, were in a position to lend money to poorer community members.[172] An institution called the *Waisenamt* (orphans' office), transplanted with the Mennonites from Russia, oversaw the management of property and financial estates following the death of a parent. While the existence of such an institution had the potential to offer an objective 'third party' voice in the devolution of property within large families, the autonomy widows obtained by being self-supporting landowners could have been offset by the oversight of the 'goodman' appointed by the *Waisenamt* to provide counsel and oversee business transactions conducted by widows. The function of the 'goodman' included monitoring a widow's financial affairs and also serving as a guardian to her 'orphaned' children.

While the assistance this unique institution offered was undoubtedly welcomed by most widows at one level, it was based on limited notions of female financial prowess and also shaped by measures of social control that were likely also chafing to women and their children. In the case of Aganetha Barkman, whose father died when she was twelve, the guardian appointed to assist her mother was also charged with disciplining the daughter; apparently Aganetha had rebelled against the authority of a new stepfather and so the guardian's son warned her, "My Dad's going to whip you good."[173] When Elizabeth Reimer Toews became a widow at the age of thirty-nine in 1882, she had eight children between the ages of one and twenty years. Initially the church recommended that her youngest be fostered out to her extended family, and, within a year of her husband's death, her church's *Waisenamt* appointed a neighbour as a guardian for her younger children. The neighbour was given the duty to "see that the children were raised and nurtured in the Christian virtues and that they were properly treated in accordance with Isaiah 1:17 and Ecclesiasticus 4:10 which states: 'Be as a father unto the fatherless.'"[174] It is difficult to know what right of refusal or objection a widow may have had when the *Waisenamt* made its recommendations. On the one hand, a twenty-first-century mindset would react with consternation and judgment at a widow allowing her children to be fostered out. But in a separatist community with close kinship relationships, having a neighbour or extended family member care for one or two children within a large family may have been met with some relief and perhaps minimal worry.

In the last half of the twentieth century, government and commercial programs such as family allowances, pensions, and life insurance policies came to replace church-administered programs. Mennonites responded to the 'social safety net' with ambivalence and, in some groups, outright rejection. Gertrude Reimer, a 1926 immigrant from the Soviet Union, was the first person in Canada to receive 'mother's allowance' under a new law permitting the widow of someone who wasn't a Canadian citizen to receive benefits. Her husband died only five years after they immigrated, leaving her to support seven children with mother's allowance payments and what she earned cleaning houses.[175] This followed provisions for mother's allowances for widows with small children, newly implemented in five provinces. For Reimer's refugee migrant group from the Soviet Union, there may have been less resistance to financial aid from secular institutions, given the impoverished state of many of these newcomers.

Government programs could indeed make a huge difference in the lives of widows. But such programs were also premised on certain expectations of how a widowed family should live. A young widow with four children (her husband having been killed by a drunk driver), Elizabeth Wall supported her family with income from a large fruit and vegetable garden, and the produce of chickens and livestock. In the late 1930s she was receiving a widow's allowance of eighteen dollars per month; this was suddenly discontinued in 1943 when Elizabeth purchased her first car, a 1928 Model A.[176] Financial crisis was perhaps even a greater concern for widows within Mennonite subgroups that maintained gender understandings whereby the husband was considered, by nature and by God's command, to be the breadwinner and his wife the homemaker. Obtaining the kind of waged labour that would allow a widow to support a family would be viewed pejoratively in such cases. At the same time, conservative Mennonites in the past and today, because of their stance of suspicion towards state assistance, often maintained a greater sense of responsibility to look after extended family members in need. And as such, a widow may have felt a sense of security, knowing that there were community and familial obligations in place to look out for her and her children.

Widowhood frequently brought about economic hardship for women and loss of status in their community, and also meant great emotional grief as well. Susannah Betzner Cressman, widowed at the age of fifty-five with four daughters, expressed this poignantly in a 1912 diary entry: "A very sad day for me, 1 year ago today Papa left us, and oh what a sad lonely year it has been and the hardest year of my life."[177] Some women, anticipating economic security within a marriage relationship, married later in life only to find those expectations shattered by life as impoverished widows. Maria Braun, trained and working as a nurse-midwife in Russia, immigrated to Canada with her parents in 1924. She worked at factory and housekeeping jobs until, at the age of sixty, she married a British Columbia widower, apparently tired of being a housekeeper and longing for a home of her own. Maria cared for her new husband for two years before he died and left her without any financial support. She married another widower and moved to Winnipeg, but was again left a widow with minimal financial stability, living in one room and cooking her meals on a hotplate in a home she had shared with her husband but was now rented out by his children. Eventually she retired to a seniors' home in British Columbia, supported in small ways by her brother and his family, though apparently nothing was forthcoming from her last husband's children or grandchildren.[178]

Yet ironically, the loss of a husband also opened up new opportunities as the constraints that marriage placed on women were lifted. Lorna Shantz Bergey, married in 1940, experienced this gradually, when her husband became a semi-invalid following a farm accident and then died at an early age. While her husband became the primary caregiver to their two young sons and assumed many household tasks, Lorna took over the family cheese-selling business that took her frequently away from home. Many years later she reflected, "Making necessary accommodations in role sharing made our marriage extremely nontraditional for the 1950s."[179] Similarly, painter Mary Klassen, whose artistic aspirations were sidelined as she raised four children and supported her husband's academic career, found that her husband's early death opened opportunities that wouldn't have been possible otherwise. In 1961 she opened an art studio in her home, despite some criticism—one friend remarked, "Have you forgotten John so soon?"—something that gave her and her family financial stability. Later she remarked, "Those ... years spent thus gave me great pleasure and pain. Up to this point I had been a helper (except in our home)—now I was to be a leader."[180]

Historically, the need for economic stability and assistance in raising large families was frequently the overriding factor that compelled both widowed men and women to remarry shortly after the death of a spouse. The 'blended' family that is the bane of many contemporary advocates for the 'traditional' family was actually very common in Mennonite communities with large families, in eras where death came much earlier than it does today, and where potential marriage partners with common ethnic and religious identity were plentiful and close at hand. Family histories and genealogies offer evidence that in the nineteenth and early twentieth centuries, a man would often marry the sister of his deceased wife. In earlier years, it was not uncommon for both men and women to become widowed more than once and thus to remarry more than once. It was also quite ordinary for women to marry widowers who were significantly older. Susanna Loewen, who married twice, tried it both ways. When she was an eighteen-year-old in Russia in 1871, she married a widower ten years older with two young children. When he died in 1887, Susanna again was proposed to by a man fifteen years older than she. A mother of five girls at the time, she purportedly said to her daughters, "I believe that younger men are available. I'll wait." Her hopes were realized and two years later, at the age of thirty-seven, Susanna married a nineteen-year-old man.[181] Later her two oldest daughters married the brothers of their stepfather. Sometimes remarriage could result in significant age differences. For instance, Katherina Hiebert married a widower twenty-two years her senior and with five children, just a few months before immigrating to Canada in 1875. His eldest daughter was only two years younger than Katharina and so they became "the best of friends."[182] Such multiple relational connections within large Mennonite families were not uncommon in earlier years.

Though men were more likely to remarry soon after the loss of a spouse, widows also remarried, often to enhance their economic stability. When Susannah Schroeder, a widow with two daughters, married Abraham Hildebrand, a widower with ten children aged a few months to nineteen years, in 1921, her socio-economic status improved. She moved from the small town of Lowe Farm, Manitoba, to the large 320-acre Hildebrand farm, where finally she could "work for [her]self and not for other people."[183] Though her two daughters had resisted the marriage, Susannah believed it was God's will, after a dream in which a man resembling her future husband appeared at her bed. More widows, however, were likely to remain single than were widowers. Maria Martens Klassen, widowed at the age of sixty, declined an invitation from the friend of a distant relative to "come courting" nine months after the death of her husband. Twelve years later she did go ahead and marry her neighbour and a man she had known since their childhood in Ukraine, whose wife had died the year before; in deciding to accept his proposal, she reflected on the pros of remarriage: "He is a believer and belongs to our church. He is seventy-eight years old, but seems healthy, although his hands tremble. He has firm opinions on many issues, but he isn't radical."[184] Even when remarrying, widows were often identified with reference to their deceased spouse. For instance, in a 1919 diary entry, Maria Reimer Unger refers to the wedding of "P.R. Reimer and the widow Mrs. Gerhard H. Schellenberg."[185]

Mennonite churches generally approved of remarriage for a surviving spouse, provided that an appropriate period of mourning was observed (though this might be barely several months). But for post-Second World War immigrant 'widows' who were unsure about their husbands' fate, hopes to marry again posed significant difficulties. Between the peak years of post-war migration, 1947 to 1949, widows represented 15 percent of the total number of immigrants registered with the Canadian Mennonite Board of Colonization. This number is not insignificant, given that the number of married immigrants (20 percent) and number of single adults (23 percent) were only slightly higher and included both men and women; at the same time, the number of widowers was negligible. These refugee widows, many of whom were quite young, experienced the ambiguity of their own personal strength, independence, and resourcefulness, having led their families through tremendous hardship and tragedy, and the weakness and dependency attributed to them in community attitudes. Particularly for those who had lost their husbands in the Soviet purges of the 1930s or during the war, their marital status remained in a grey area, most women having received no confirmation of their husband's death. Many of these 'widows' chose never to remarry, either holding out hope that their spouse would be found alive, or eschewing the hierarchical gender relations that another marriage would impose on them.

Those who did seek to remarry, whether for companionship or economic stability, faced opposition within many Mennonite churches that emphasized a woman's obligation to be faithful to her first husband, even while treating her like a bona fide widow in every other respect. Within congregations that received a significant number of post-Second World War refugees, the question of remarriage became one of the most painful and divisive issues in the 1950s and 1960s. Initially, some Mennonite denominational bodies and individual churches took the position that a woman who chose to remarry without positive confirmation of her husband's death would be excommunicated—that is, lose her church membership—even though the Canadian government allowed that a seven-year absence was a sufficient time to declare someone deceased. Some women who went ahead and remarried simply left the Mennonite church as a result, while others continued to attend church as marginalized participants.[186] In choosing to remarry, with or without knowledge of a first spouse's death, some widows may have been trying to create a 'normal' family, either one that existed in memories of the past or one that emulated the families of their relatives and neighbours in Canada during an historical era that exalted the intact, nuclear family.

In attempting to construct 'whole' 'normal' families for themselves, postwar widows were also trying to escape the stigma attached to their marital status, one that plagued women without husbands in all eras. Within Mennonite churches, widows were perceived with some pity and also sidelined from full participation in congregational life. Katie Funk Wiebe found that when her husband died, "all contact with the church's decision-making processes had been cut off."[187] This was the case since, in the decades when women were disallowed from attending and/or voting at church business meetings, women had to convey their opinions and receive information via their husbands or fathers. Furthermore, families headed by widows were often viewed as incomplete. In his conclusion to a sociological study of Mennonite families based on data from 1972 and 1989, J. Howard Kauffman stated that in Mennonite beliefs about marriage and family, "fatherless homes are viewed as deficient."[188] The many female-headed families among the postwar migration were in fact referred to in German as *schwach*, which meant weak, precisely because the adult male in the family was missing and the household was considered to be without a 'family head.'

Because families without fathers were perceived as weak, there was often a community perception that the eldest son would fulfill some of the roles and duties of an absent father. Gertrude Rempel Epp, who lost her husband just before the birth of their last of eight children, was known in the Yarrow, British Columbia, community as "widow Epp." According to her son George, this gave her a "sense of identity," albeit a "simple one." He recalled that it was his eldest brother who was instructed by his mother to administer corporal punishment in the absence of their father. He also recalled that she compensated for the imposed silence on women in church meetings with extra zeal and volume during public prayer times.[189] Gertrude wasn't the only Mennonite woman whose self-identity and community label were tied to the fact that she was husbandless. The title of one woman's 1991 memoir, *Memories and Reflections of a Widow*, is indicative of the way in which a woman's familial status was directly tied to her relationship with a husband. Similarly, another widow titled her memoir *Under His Wings, Events in the Lives of Elder Alexander Ediger and his Family*, thereby giving the false impression that the book is a biography, and not in fact the story of her own life.[190]

FAMILY DANGERS

Until the last few decades of the twentieth century, Mennonite women who were single had this status because they were widowed or never married. By the early twenty-first century, divorce has become increasingly commonplace amongst Mennonites, though individuals (men and women alike) within conservative subgroups will still today lose their church membership should they divorce their marriage partner. There is very little written about divorce in Mennonite communities. The occurrence was minimal because until late in the last century, most Mennonite churches condemned it and divorce most often resulted in excommunication from the church within all Mennonite groups. Census figures from 1981 reveal that Mennonites had one of the lowest divorce rates among religious groups in Canada, at 3.3 percent compared with the Canadian average of 7.7 percent.[191] This doesn't mean that Mennonite marriages were any happier than in groups, ethnic or religious, in which divorce was more common. But a strong religious sense that marriage ended only in death and an explicit church condemnation of divorce meant that marriage difficulties were dealt with privately and quietly, or were suppressed. Divorced women who remained within the church carried the double stigma of being single and also morally fallen in the eyes of the church.

Along with adultery, one of the earliest and only grounds for divorce was physical abuse. While her family, nuclear and extended, offered a setting in which a woman might exercise some domestic leadership and autonomy, the private life of family and household was not without its dangers and hazards for women. The nonresistant stance of Mennonites has at times led to the assumption that Mennonites rejected violence in both public and private realms. Condemnation of violence in Mennonite prescriptive literature has sometimes led to the incorrect conclusion that as a result violence was not tolerated in communities and households. However, violence did occur within households where patriarchal family relations were combined with literal interpretations of biblical commands that women submit to their husbands and children to their parents.[192] Such violence took the form of severe corporal punishment towards children, wife-battering, incest, and sexual abuse. Few historic sources offer evidence or reflection on personal experiences of violence within households.

Recent studies of the issue, however, make observations that may be useful in considering the past. A 1990 pastoral counselling study proposed that Mennonite beliefs and behaviours "contribute to family violence," specifically "beliefs about separation from the world, denying the existence of certain emotions like anger and sexual feelings, adhering to a hierarchy moving from God to Christ to man to woman to child, and upholding a discipleship/perfectionism model."[193] A year later, a Mennonite pastor in Winnipeg, Manitoba, published a study on domestic abuse that concluded, perhaps not surprisingly, that "there is evidence of domestic abuse among Mennonites in Winnipeg."[194] One feminist Mennonite theologian suggests that Mennonite theological teachings in fact contributed to the oppression of women. In a 1999 thesis, Carol Penner concluded that "Traditional Mennonite theology has conveyed a gendered message which perpetuates the conditions leading to violence against women."[195] In particular, Penner argues, Mennonite perspectives on the concepts of forgiveness, obedience, and suffering have been interpreted with very gender-specific meanings for women dealing with violence in their lives. In this interpretation, biblically mandated submission became a Christian-Mennonite woman's highest virtue, even while her husband's exertion of power was an abuse of scripture.

Ideals of submission, especially of women to their husbands, were taught in explicit ways, most public perhaps in the sermons and writings of church leaders. Teachings on Mennonite marriages followed the order of benevolent patriarchy—considered God-ordained—in which husband and wife had specific and well-defined roles and in which the husband was clearly the head. In a two-part 1954 article in the *Canadian Mennonite*, B. Charles Hostetter outlined the responsibilities husband and wife had for one another. The

God-given duties of a wife were to regard her husband as the head of the home, to convert the house into a home, to assume the responsibilities of motherhood, and to provide a normal sex life for her husband. Hostetter's prescription for the husband, in turn, was to make the marriage a partnership, to assume the role as senior partner and high priest of the home, to love his wife as Christ loved the Church, and to provide a normal sex life for his wife. He followed this by saying that the main reason for unhappy homes lay in contemporary woman's unwillingness to submit to her husband as God had commanded. Of particular note is Hostetter's statement that "When a wife will not live in subjection to her head, she is disobeying God and will suffer consequences."[196] He didn't specify what those consequences would be.

Similarly, though several decades earlier, prominent Ontario Mennonite minister Clayton F. Derstine, in a 1919 sermon on "The Home," observed that the home should be like a "kingdom" in which the father ruled; "Show me a home where woman is the head," he stated, "and I will show you a defective home."[197] Many published sermons and articles by well-known church leaders echoed this perspective. Amongst conservative groups today, male and female roles are officially well-delineated and founded on literal interpretations of certain parts of scripture, such as Corinthians 1. This is true whether they are Old Order (Swiss) Mennonite or Old Colony (Russian/Low German) Mennonite. Within these groups, it is clearly understand that women exist in a God-ordained position of submission to men, whether reflected in their exclusion from official leadership or participation in the formal decision-making bodies of church, or whether in the hierarchies that exist within the home. These understandings exist apart from any female 'influence' or 'matriarchy' that arise from personality and particular family dynamic. A minister within a Kleine Gemeinde community, who moved to Nova Scotia from Belize in 1984, stated it quite plainly: "According to Scripture, [women] should be submissive to their husbands. Too many women now want to be equal with the men. Of course, they should not be our slaves, either."[198]

The message of submission was also incorporated into Mennonite women's culture in more subtle ways. For example, Ruth Derksen Siemens, who examined the biblical proverbs that women working as domestic servants stitched onto quilts, observes that texts that emphasize purity before and submission to God functioned to bring shame upon women who were subject to acts of impurity and also reinforced submission to authority, be it father, minister, or employer.[199] As well, submission was ingrained both socially and theologically in regulations on head coverings for women and in prohibitions on female participation in church decision-making structures. Even when submission was understood in non-repressive ways, women understood the hierarchical order clearly. As one writer recalled of marrying women of the mid-twentieth century, "our duty in life was to serve God, our husbands, and humanity."[200] Another woman, growing up in North Kildonan in the 1930s, recalled the nature of her parents' and other marriages: "My dad was strict, too. Most Mennonite men were that way.... And the wife was obedient to her husband. There was no thought of divorce if you had a misunderstanding."[201]

While wives were taught to submit to their husbands in the context of a 'partnership,' daughters also grew up fully aware of the bestowed and lived authority of fathers within the household. Fathers played a central role in patriarchal families, and were dominant if also benevolent. Immigration leader Cornelius Jansen figures prominently in the diaries of his two daughters, who seemingly organized their activities around the plans and desires of their father. Anna Jansen wrote the following in 1875: "Aunt and I had a big wash day, because we had not washed for a whole week.... We prefer to do the big work like washing when Father is not at home, because he does not like to be inside all by himself when everybody else is outside."[202] It was always daughters who had the job, undoubtedly sometimes unpleasant, of washing their fathers' feet, occasionally in preparation for the annual footwashing service at church. Elizabeth Dueck had this task at the young age of five, when her 350-pound father became too large to bend over to wash his own feet or tie his own shoes.[203] Footwashing wasn't part of my upbringing, but I do remember that one of my tasks as youngest daughter was to shine my preacher-father's shoes to a shiny black in preparation for church on Sunday; I don't recall performing any such service for my mother. The strong hold that fathers had on the lives of daughters, indeed the entire household, is suggested in the reflection by two contemporary Mennonite women poets, Sarah Klassen and Di Brandt, who said they were unable to write until their fathers died.

Many women resigned themselves to what was presented to them as a God-ordained relationship of authority and submission within marriage. But they secretly—and sometimes not so privately—recognized that such a partnership was ultimately unsatisfying. Maria Reimer, born in 1904, stated it as follows, when reflecting on her experience of childbirth:

> He had authority over me, but if only he could understand me better! But what can you expect from a man who has never been pregnant?

... I sometimes think a woman should not expect too much from a man. She can love him, be submissive to him, and make him happy, but she should not expect too much. If she feels she has to pour out her heart, she has to do that with another woman, and they can understand each other better.[204]

Maintaining obedience to a husband's authority could be difficult when a woman felt her husband's judgment to be faulty. Anna Bartsch and her children were instructed by her husband Heinrich to stop changing the temperature in the barn where they were raising baby chicks. One day when the temperature for the chicks became excessively hot, Anna struggled inwardly between her husband's warning and the well-being of the chicks: "I would have opened the windows but for the warning which we had received and which also applied to me. Opening the window was such a trivial thing—but why contradict? I could pray!" Fortunately for the chicks, Anna's husband arrived home shortly thereafter and she was relieved of her inner conflict.[205]

This sort of traditional and patriarchal ordering of roles within marriage may be one reason for the unusually high rate of never-married adult women within Mennonite churches. According to one source, a neighbour to a Mennonite family commented that they would love to have their sons marry Mennonite girls, but would never want their daughters to marry Mennonite boys.[206] This suggests that while marriage was good for men, it was not always good for women. Some women, on the other hand, willingly incorporated ideals of submission into their religious lives and thus also into their relationships with men. By acquiescing to a God-given gender hierarchy—as it was presented to them—women could claim an uplifted sense of themselves as Christian women and feel more sanctified as a result. They could also thereby 'give over to Jesus-God' any discontent or conflict they experienced in their domestic life, even if such a pious approach did not change their material circumstances in any immediate way. Such an orientation was reinforced in the late twentieth century, as conservative evangelical Christian women sought, through ideology and organizations, a means to balance old models of biblically based gender relations with new expectations about women's rights and need for self-actualization, a sort of "dialectic of female submission and empowerment."[207] Some Mennonite women, like many other Protestants, were drawn to evangelical Christian organizations such as Real Women or Women Aglow that emerged in the 1970s, groups that emphasized that "true liberation is found in voluntary submission to divine authority."[208] Contemporary evangelicalism, and the 'traditional' roles for women that it extols, may allow Mennonite women to recast biblically based ideals of submission within a modern context that makes the resulting gender relations more palatable.

As with many other social issues, Mennonites followed secular societal initiatives in responding to the issue of violence against women, as well as sexual abuse in homes. In the 1980s Mennonite institutions began to issue official statements of condemnation towards violence against women. In this, as with many other related issues, Mennonite churches and organizations were reacting to a wider social movement that was increasingly intolerant of violence against women. Prior to this public acknowledgement of domestic violence and sexual abuse, however, they were among those issues that were dealt with privately or, most often, were just kept secret by women and children. When incidents did come to the attention of church leaders, some form of church discipline might be enacted towards the perpetrator, or couples would be encouraged to 'work it out' with the help of prayer and religious renewal.

In keeping with the theoretical arguments linking violence in the home with Mennonite beliefs and behaviour, as discussed above, certain Mennonite subgroups have perhaps experienced more incidents of violence and abuse than others. Groups whose interpretation of the Bible and Mennonite beliefs have led them towards authoritarianism and legalism in both church and community, that have notable histories of seeking separation and isolation from wider society, and that have particularly patriarchal (one might argue misogynistic) understandings of social order, seem especially prone to violence and abuse within the household. One such group that came under close scrutiny towards the end of the twentieth century was the Old Colony Mennonite community, a group with a significant history of diaspora and isolation, and that began a return migration from Mexico, and Central and South America to various parts of Canada beginning in the late 1950s. One woman of Old Colony background talked about family incest for the first time after immigrating to Canada. "There are only two people who know about this. The first time I was raped was when I was nine. It was someone close to me, someone in my family. Someone I see often now. He knows and I know, but I never told anyone else before."[209] Another woman of the same background recalled, "When my father was drinking, he would get very angry. He would yell and chase my mother with a big butcher knife sometimes. He used up all our money for his drink. We usually went to bed hungry. He still drinks too much, and still gets very angry. It is not safe for my mother to live with him."[210]

Violence within the home could have its ongoing effects on children who witnessed cruelty towards mothers. The fact that the Old Colony Mennonites have received greater scrutiny on this issue has the effect, unfortunately, of lesser attention to violence that occurred (and occurs) in the homes of other conservative groups, and indeed amongst Mennonites generally.

One story written anonymously in the Mennonite Central Committee's *Women's Concerns Report* in 1987 described the cycle of violence in the home of a rural Mennonite family in Canada. After 'Mary' left her husband 'John,' a meeting at her Mennonite church trivialized the abuse she was experiencing. She felt that her decision to leave her husband was blamed on "women's liberation, feminist theology, on my practise of journaling and on my inability to forgive and forget."[211] The Mennonite health institution they went to for counselling blamed her for provoking her husband's anger. Similarly, Tien Wolfe (not her real name), an Old Colony woman in Ontario, contravened the norms of her conservative, patriarchal church by reporting her husband's sexual abuse of their daughters to the police. Not only was she undermining his authority in the family, but she was going against her minister's caution that "difficult domestic situations" should be dealt with by church leadership, not by the state.[212] It is risky, of course, to make generalizations about Mennonite family life based on the dysfunction of some individuals within some families within some subgroups. And, given the lack of a comparative study, there is no reason to believe that Mennonite families had or have higher rates of domestic violence than other Canadian families. Localized family relations, nevertheless, provide a useful site for considering how religious and cultural teachings and understandings shape the practice of family life.

Over the past two centuries, the lives of Mennonite women within families went through changes that paralleled the evolution that occurred within Canadian families generally, albeit perhaps at a slower pace. In pioneering and immigrant settlements, women spent most of their adult lives combining child bearing and child rearing with the dawn-to-dusk labour that was part of rural subsistence living. Like other Canadian women, over the course of the twentieth century, Mennonite women gradually increased control over their fertility so as to reduce the number of children they would have. Most women married, and a woman remained in that state until the likely death of her spouse before her, at which point she might remarry, but more probably she lived out her life as a widow. Within the religious framework of Mennonite belief and culture, women acquiesced to, rebelled against, or negotiated their way through dictates that they submit to husbands and fathers, who were thought to be closer to God in a divinely ordained gender hierarchy. Those women who chose to live outside the parameters of what was considered 'normal' family life—single women, widows, and lesbians, for instance—were continuously marginalized within Mennonite churches and communities, regardless of how deliberate their choices or how productive and fulfilling their lives were within a variety of non-traditional relationships.

Their lives within families could be, alternately and simultaneously, rewarding and repressive for Mennonite women. A community belief system and cultural ethos that placed much emphasis on family lineage, on genealogy, and on the kinship that existed within large extended families could offer a woman a sense of belonging and place, and the comfort of numerous close relationships that were supportive materially and emotionally. A woman who bore and reared numerous children carried the knowledge that she was a significant contributor to community identity and survival, and that her accomplishments as a mother afforded her a certain domestic integrity. The physical and psychological hardships of this role, as well as the cloud of wifely submission that hung over a married woman's head, undoubtedly made the status of wife and mother bittersweet. In cases where her subordination was interpreted by her husband or father as licence to abuse and violate, a woman would have experienced marriage as only bitter, even while love for her children brought joy to family life. Women who, for whatever personal or political reasons, lived on the edges of what public Mennonite ideology presented as the ideal and normal family conversely struggled to find that sense of belonging and place within their communities. For them, the idea of family became flexible, and the relationships that constituted family were many-faceted and often changing. Their lives as 'others' possibly foreshadowed the notions of diversity in family forms that increasingly characterize the imagination and reality of family life in the twenty-first century.

CHAPTER THREE

Preachers, Prophets, and Missionaries: Women in the Church

Barbara Bowman Shuh (1857–1937) was a religious leader amongst Ontario Mennonites at the turn of the twentieth century, exercising her gifts and abilities in both sanctioned and unconventional spheres of spiritual activity. When Mennonite women of Kitchener, Ontario, formally organized a sewing circle in 1908, officially called the Sister's Aid of the Berlin Mennonite Church, Barbara was elected as the first 'chairman' of the organization, which had as its purpose "to aid the poor and distressed, and to do general mission and charitable work." The initiative of the Kitchener women, alongside their counterparts in Waterloo who simultaneously formed the Waterloo Charity Circle, represented the beginning of Mennonite women's formal organizational work in Ontario. Recognized as a capable leader for this endeavour, Barbara was also well known as a midwife and one who had inherited the gift of charming, a traditional spiritual healing art, which she used primarily to treat bleeding, burns, and scalds.[1]

Agatha Loewen Schmidt (1927–) was among thousands of Mennonite refugees who fled their homes in Ukraine during the Second World War, arriving in Canada with her mother and sisters in 1948. Having grown up during the Stalinist era, she had minimal experience of formal church life and, given the arrest and exile or death of almost all male ministers in their

Mennonite community, she looked to her mother and other women for the sustenance of religious belief as expressed in prayer, Bible reading, and hymn singing. Once established and remarried in Canada (her first husband went missing in the war), she felt called to be an occasional preacher in her Mennonite congregation, well before Mennonites in Canada officially sanctioned women as ministers and preachers.[2]

In December 1919, Helen Loewen Warkentin (1887–1975) of Winkler, Manitoba, left North America for her first term as an ordained missionary in Deverakonda, India. She would remain there for almost four decades, working as a teacher and school principal, as well as "dietician, supervisor of gardening, well digging, and carpentry." She also led Bible studies and offered religious meditations (sermons) in the community. After her death, the "Leena Orphanage" was established in her memory and one of her former students reflected, "But for your color, you are bone of our bone and pain of our pain." Though she considered India her home, the mission board that paid her salary asked her to return to Canada in 1957, ironically in the same year that her particular denominational group, the Mennonite Brethren, decided to discontinue its practice of formal ordination for female missionaries.[3]

All three women sought out or were called to exercise religious leadership in the Mennonite church. While none was formally appointed to a clerical office, a designation that was frequently equated with the concept of church leadership and thus historically limited to men, all three actively participated in and shaped various sectors of church life that were crucial to the religious functioning of Mennonite institutions and communities. Until the mid- to late twentieth century, and in certain subgroups still today, Mennonite women were explicitly excluded from important aspects of church organizational life and expression. In their literal understanding of female subordination and silence before man and God, Mennonites differed little from other Christian denominations. Women accepted, chafed, or rebelled against this man-made spiritual order, yet all the while they engaged in organizational and leadership activities that were fundamental to the mandate of their churches, and indeed foundational to the beliefs and ethos of their church. For the three women described above, these activities included sewing-circle involvement, charming, informal worship leading and occasional preaching, and overseas missionary work.

In her important exploration of the 'underside' of history, Elise Boulding asserted that early Anabaptists "practised complete equality of women and men in every respect, including preaching."[4] Indeed, there are many examples like that of Elisabeth Dirks, who was accused of being a preacher for her teaching and missionary activities and was drowned in 1549. If there is evidence for female leadership in the early decades of the Anabaptist movement, it is also clear that the cessation of persecution and the increasing formalization of church life resulted in fewer allowances for women particularly in such positions of leadership as preaching and recognized theologizing. As observed in the introduction to this book, religion can be either oppressive or empowering in women's lives but, and this is more likely, can be both simultaneously and also somewhere in between. The complex interplay between gender and religious structures is huge; as Ursula King has observed, "religions have created and legitimated gender, enforced, oppressed, and warped it, but also subverted, transgressed, transformed, and liberated it."[5] Mennonite women experienced this complicated and many-layered dichotomy first-hand, as they heard church leaders make pronouncements about female subordination and silence in formal church life, yet at the same time felt their own spiritual lives thrive and personal sense of ministry develop in the context of their own organizations, informal ministries, and personally created spiritual lives. This chapter will explore the historic roles of women as 'preachers, prophets, and missionaries' within Mennonite church life.

MINISTERS AND MINISTERS' WIVES

Throughout most of the near 500-year history of the Mennonites, women were barred from assuming formal leadership roles within Mennonite religious institutions. Within the most conservative Old Order Mennonite and other traditionalist church groups, the few formal leadership roles that exist—bishop, minister, deacon—are still today held exclusively by men. Similar lines of leadership and authority based on gender also persist in a range of moderately conservative groups. It was only in the last two decades of the twentieth century that Mennonite women became leading ministers in Canadian Mennonite churches. In the United States, Ann J. Allebach, a teacher, mission worker, and suffragist, was formally ordained as a Mennonite minister in a Philadelphia church in 1911.[6] This example would not be a precedent, however. Whatever call to 'prophesy' was granted to sixteenth-century women, the biblical admonition that women be 'silent' became dominant in Mennonite church life for the centuries that followed. Roles such as bishop, minister, and deacon could be held only by men, either through selection or election. And although the practice varied, and still varies, widely from one congregation to another and between subgroups, until late in the twentieth century women were not allowed to add their voices to formal decision-making processes in the church. Sixty years would pass after Allebach's ordination before another woman was formally ordained to pastoral ministry in North America.[7]

For most of Mennonite history, at least that which is recorded or passed on, there was limited discussion on the pros and cons of women as ministers. That women did not carry church leadership was considered natural, related to their biological and social characteristics as females, and also biblical, clearly ruled out in relevant scriptural passages. By the mid- to late nineteenth century, however, Protestant religious revivals and awakenings, coupled with first-wave feminism, saw women assume new public roles and called into question hitherto unmovable notions about women's role in church and society.[8] And, in response, Mennonites began also to debate the issue, albeit in limited ways, and to make doctrinal statements on the question. For instance, in 1879 the Mennonite Brethren passed a formal resolution stating, "That sisters may take part in church activities as the Holy Spirit leads. However, they should not preach nor take part in discussion in business meetings of the church."[9] The reasons given for women's lack of access to church ministry relied heavily on the scriptural writings of the apostle Paul, especially in the first books of Corinthians and Timothy. But frequently his commands that women keep silent in church were taken further by Mennonite leaders who sought social justification for their position.

Prominent Mennonite Brethren preacher H.H. Janzen rested his argument against women teaching in the church on specifically gendered attributes. He said: "A woman [teaching] within the church is most dangerous. First, women are more open to emotional influences. Emotions have a very little part, rather, none in biblical teaching. Secondly, wherever a woman teaches, especially a mixed audience, she must be aware of the fact that she carries with her the so-called sexual appeal, which will ... influence ... those who listen."[10] Janzen's views were echoed in perhaps less explicit language by others. Positions against women in church leadership were also grounded in ideas about religious and social hierarchy, extrapolated from scripture but reinforced by particular theological movements like fundamentalism. From the perspective of both church leaders and members, there seemed little more to be said on the issue of women in ministerial leadership for many decades, until changes in society gave rise to a spirit of critical questioning by Mennonite women themselves.

The 1963 Mennonite General Conference Confession of Faith included an article on "symbols of Christian order." While acknowledging that "in Christ there is neither male nor female," it qualified spiritual equality by stating that "in the order of creation God has fitted man and woman for differing functions; man has been given a primary leadership role, while the woman is especially fitted for nurture and service."[11] Recognizing that "Attitudes toward the woman's place in the church of today appear to be changing," Canadian church leader David Ewert published a paper on the topic in 1966. After examining a variety of New Testament scriptures, he concluded that "women should not lead in any way in public worship, whether in preaching or praying. This would not rule out the teaching of children, or of other women; it would not rule out the ministry in song and music...."[12] Among a range of opinions on the subject of women in church leadership was the view expressed at a 1967 ministers and deacons conference that "Women in the pulpit would be a sign of men shirking their responsibility."[13] And, indeed, women on occasion justified their entrance into pulpit ministry by pointing to the lack of men willing to take on the task or even the inadequacy of some laymen preachers.

It is no coincidence that these strongly worded statements were made during the tumultuous decade of the 1960s. At the beginning of the decade, Mennonites were starting to taste what lay ahead as perhaps the most divisive and ardent issue to be debated in the last quarter of the twentieth century. Canadian Mennonites may have been shaken up when the Mennonite World Conference met at Kitchener, Ontario, in 1962 and they learned that among Dutch Mennonites, 25 of 109 pastors were women. They would soon realize that the issue of women in ministry would enter their churches, schools, media, and homes in full force by the 1970s. The women's movement and second-wave feminism undoubtedly spurred Mennonite churches and their female members to question prohibitions against women in senior ministry and other leadership positions in church bureaucracies. The reinterpretation by feminist theologians of biblical passages regarding women's right to 'preach and prophesy' reinforced this development for certain liberal Mennonite groups; of course, literalist readings of scripture also buttressed the opposition to female ministry. Another reason that more openness to women in ministry developed in the 1970s and beyond was that ordination itself was being 'dethroned.' It was losing its sacredness and significance as a symbol of authority and divinely granted leadership. And even while some women and men expended considerable energy making a case for women's right to ministerial ordination, other individuals and groups were drawn to create non-hierarchical congregational models with non-ordained lay leadership, in which men and women had equal access to all church roles. Women's opportunities for leadership involvement increased with the development of non-traditional church congregations that were often informal and experimental and born out of dissatisfaction with traditional church forms; their discontent was manifest in the rejection of many long-held practices, including prohibitions against female leadership. These churches sometimes emphasized volunteerism as opposed to paid ministerial leadership and thus oriented their total congregational life around a model that had been used in women's church work for years already.

As the debate over women in ministry intensified, resistance to change was met with increasing impatience by those who advocated for gender equality in the church. For example, in the early 1980s, apparently buttons were worn on the campus of Mennonite Brethren Bible College in Winnipeg bearing the slogan: "Ordain women ... or stop baptizing them!"[14] Some women 'slipped' into a ministerial role within mainstream churches even though their denominational subgroup was still either resistant or in the midst of debate on the issue. Ardith Frey became pastor of an urban church within the Evangelical Mennonite Conference, informally accepted "even [while] there were official policy questions to be worked out."[15] Similarly, Karen Heidebrecht Thiessen took on ministerial leadership at River East Mennonite Brethren Church in Winnipeg in the early 1990s, even while the denomination continued to defeat resolutions that permitted women to take on those roles. In Ontario and eastern Canada, several of the regional conferences led the way in opening up senior ministry positions to women; that there was no official debate within these groups on the issue suggests, on the one hand, that there was easy acceptance of the transition, but on the other hand, it could leave women feeling slightly insecure when there was no clear statement of policy one way or the other.

Sometimes women moved into leadership roles in situations of sheer exigency. For instance, when the Waterloo–Kitchener United Mennonite Church was left without a minister after Henry H. Epp's resignation in 1965, Hedy Sawadsky, the church secretary for ten years, stepped into the void. For several years, she provided "leadership and direction, especially in spiritual matters, and was also able to provide for the necessary Sunday pulpit service."[16] That such a move was possible for these women reflects the localized church polity of Mennonites whereby decisions about numerous church practices and expressions of doctrine are made at the level of individual congregations. Yet congregations that acted contrary to the official stance of their denomination risked alienation and scolding from the leadership of their Mennonite subgroup. In fact, it is surprising, given the latitude that most Mennonite subgroups allow for a localized ethos to develop within individual congregations, that more Mennonite churches did not permit women in leadership positions much earlier.

The first woman in Canada to be ordained to ministry in a Mennonite congregation was Doris Weber, who was simultaneously 'commissioned' and ordained at Avon Mennonite Church in Stratford, Ontario, in 1979, although prior to this, Alma Coffman was a non-ordained pastor at the Ottawa Mennonite Church.[17] A number of the early female pastors had already worked in leadership positions for years prior to ordination. For instance, Martha Smith Good was ordained at Stirling Avenue Mennonite church in Kitchener in 1982 after serving in senior ministry for eight years. Like many women of that early era of women in ministry, Smith Good had many doubts about the 'nudges' she felt towards ministry in the Mennonite church: "I said No repeatedly and with strong persistence because I am a woman. This role seemed forbidden territory to me and I was not prepared to face the difficulties I knew I would encounter. Trail blazing is always hard work."[18] Smith Good's personal doubts were undoubtedly exacerbated by the initial denial of her request for ordination by her regional Mennonite conference. After "many painful conversations with conference leadership," ordination eventually went ahead, though "no clear reasons [for the initial refusal] were ever articulated."[19] Smith Good's personal situation demonstrated that even when women were granted the right to enter pastoral ministry, their roles as wives and mothers could sometimes subsume their professional life in the eyes of their community. Smith Good entered the ministry as a single woman; after marrying another Mennonite pastor—a widower with four children—she soon found that she was viewed primarily as the 'pastor's wife' and not the 'pastor.' She reflected that her vocational training was viewed as an asset mainly because it qualified her eminently to 'assist' in her husband's ministry.[20] That women pastors usually *added* to their roles, as opposed to giving up any of their gendered domestic responsibilities, is indicated by one woman's question—a "tricky issue" for her—whether women pastors were expected to bring a dish to the church potluck supper.[21]

Despite the increase in the number of women being ordained in Mennonite churches in the late twentieth century, "pockets of strongly ingrained resistance to women preachers endure."[22] One of the largest of the 'modern' Mennonite subgroups, the Mennonite Brethren—with 36,000 members in Canada in 2005—at the end of the twentieth century still did not sanction the ordination of women, though, remarkably, their denominational counterparts in the Democratic Republic of Congo had taken this step. In 2003, even while North American Mennonite Brethren conferences still held to the position that "women be encouraged to minister in the church in every function other than the lead pastorate," the Congolese Mennonite Brethren Church moved ahead. Having "discerned the biblical texts in their own context," the Congolese church became the first of twenty national Mennonite Brethren conferences around the globe to ordain women as pastors.[23] In 2006, the Canadian Mennonite Brethren Church passed a resolution, but by only 77 percent, that would allow congregations to set their own direction, based on their particular interpretive approach, regarding women in ministry leadership.

Even in the Mennonite conferences where affirmation of women in church leadership was given early on, the actual presence of women as senior pastors in churches was slow to take hold. In 1988 the Conference of Mennonites in Canada passed a resolution aimed at "helping congregations move in the direction of including women in leadership," motivated in part by the fact that an increasing number of women were completing seminary studies but were not finding jobs as pastors in Mennonite institutions.[24] For women who personally felt drawn to enter ministry as a vocation, rejection could be devastating. Renee Sauder said that she shared an interest in a ministry career with two young men in her congregation. She recalled the church's response as follows: "I remember the disappointment of being told the invitation to preach would not be extended to me because the congregation, my pastor felt, was not yet ready to hear a woman preach. It was a moment of feeling exiled from the place that had been so life giving."[25] Women themselves offered a range of rationales for their desire to 'preach and prophesy.' Sometimes women who felt an inner call to preach or were asked to do so by others explained their motivations by factors other than an 'equal rights' argument. Agatha Janzen, for instance, justified her Sunday preaching by pointing out that she was just "following in the footsteps" of her father, who was a minister.[26] Others would disavow their own ego by saying that they were only responding to God's call. As Pamela E. Klassen observed, when women relinquish their own aspirations to God's will, they transform "a potentially controversial act of speech into an act of obedience."[27] Thus even while stepping outside traditional gender roles vocationally, women could in their demeanour and rationale conform to normative gender constructions of submission and obedience.

When Martha Smith Good obtained her seminary degree and was thus qualified to be an ordained minister in the Mennonite Conference of Ontario, she first utilized her skills and training in the capacity of minister's spouse. In the many decades before women were allowed into formal ministry itself, social and spiritual prominence in their communities often came by virtue of marriage to a minister. And sometimes ministers' wives have been more visible than other women in history simply because of their marital ties. For instance, in the 1986 biographical collection *Encircled: Stories of Mennonite Women*, more than half the women profiled are wives of ministers. Editor Ruth Unrau observed that the minister's wife "was expected to be the spiritual leader of the women of the congregation, a model in dress and deportment.... "[28] Women who were wives of church leaders had important, if only inferred, roles within their churches and communities. While there were no overt expectations of a minister's wife, it was generally assumed that a minister would come with a wife, if not immediately, then eventually. It was rare for a minister to remain unmarried throughout his career. While his job description may have been more clearly delineated, a minister's wife also had implicit roles as teacher (of women and children), counsellor, host, and even more so as moral and spiritual example. Mennonite periodicals frequently carried articles about the roles and challenges of being a minister's wife.

A 1957 article on the topic emphasized that it was important for the minister's wife to also feel a "call" to her role in order that she rise above any criticism directed towards her or her husband, but also, a sense of call would help her to "attain the right tension between being [her husband's] servant on the one hand or his promotional manager on the other."[29] Indeed, being a minister's wife was a vocation unto itself; at the Mennonite seminary in Illinois in the 1950s, there was even a 'Pastor's Wife' course specifically for ministers' wives, where assignments included essays on the tasks and demeanour demanded of such a role. In a paper written for the course, one participant commented that perhaps no profession demanded more of a woman, as her job demanded that she be "an efficient homemaker, an adequate mother, an expert economist, a gracious hostess, a loyal church worker, and ... an expert in the fine art of inter-personal relationships."[30] Another essayist painted a picture in which the primary job of the minister's wife was to create a "serene and peaceful" environment that was both solace and protection for her husband, whose own vocation could be "difficult and trying" and who was "constantly dealing with men's souls and their relationship to God and one another." While advice from the wife was occasionally warranted, the writer suggested that "most of the time she will be silent and listen sympathetically."[31] Hildegard Neufeld, described in her obituary as "a pastor's right hand," wasn't always silent but "as a wise woman, who walked with God, she often had excellent advice for her husband."[32]

Women who were married to ordained men were expected to share the vocation, even if they hadn't chosen ministry as a family profession, nor been chosen by God, in the case of men who were called by the lot to a position of leadership in the church. The counsel given to Ada Ramseyer Litwiller at her husband's 1925 ordination that she could be "either wings or ... weight" to her preacher-husband must have created a daunting sense for Ada of the responsibility she would carry.[33] When her husband was ordained as a deacon in the Markham Mennonite church in the early 1950s, "Lizzy" had many questions about the potential impact on her life, even though it was assumed that she shared her husband's aspiration:

> I knew my husband felt God's call, but how was this going to change my life? ... Was I going to like sharing my husband with the church? Could I handle seeing my husband struggle as he tries to deal with conflict in the church? ... I had to sit with all the ordained men's wives. I had to entertain people from the [United] States. I had to go to all the ordinations and many funerals—all long services. I felt I had to be and live the way I thought I should live as a deacon's wife. I always worried about what people thought and would think.[34]

Ruth Reesor similarly described the impact on a woman of her husband being chosen by lot to become a minister: "She will have no official status, but will suddenly find herself under scrutiny, because people are people after all and ministers' wives must immediately be just a little more perfect."[35] For Tina Thiessen, wife of a prominent church leader in western Canada, to depart from an "ideal" of "meekness, self-sacrifice and long-suffering endurance" would have been "tantamount to one of the children smoking or frequenting the movies."[36] The fact that at the ordination of three men in Winnipeg in 1927, their wives all sat on the platform and wore black was an indication of both the shared nature of the vocation and the sobriety of the women's new role.[37]

In earlier eras, ordained men carried a myriad of community roles and were away from home frequently and for long periods. In the time period before the ministry was professionalized, about the 1960s, ministers were normally unpaid but were expected to generate an income from another vocation such as farming, supplemented by donations from their congregations. Not only did a minister's wife then have to maintain a busy household in her husband's absence, on minimal household earnings, but she often had to ensure the stability of farm or business at the same time. Ella Mann Coffman, married to Ontario bishop, evangelist, and Bible teacher S.F. Coffman, was able to get by with the produce she grew on their large property, by keeping a cow for milk and pigs for butchering, and with infrequent and unpredictable cash donations. An early indication of what life as a minister's wife would be like came to Ella when, on the eve of their 1901 wedding, S.F. gave his savings of $100 to the Mennonite Church Evangelizing Committee, thinking the money should not be "sitting in the bank doing nothing."[38]

Anna Warkentin Toews was married to Kleine Gemeinde bishop Peter P. Toews and was among the earliest immigrants to Manitoba from Russia in the 1870s. In the latter years in Russia, while Peter was promoted in the church and was deeply involved in church politics, including planning for emigration, Anna gave birth to four children, all of whom died very young. While Peter was assisting the first emigrant group to depart for Canada, Anna was at home giving birth to their fifth child. In Canada, Anna lost three more babies in infancy but four more lived to adulthood. Thus, of twelve children born, she lost seven. While Anna was absorbed in the emotional upheavals of birth and death, Peter was absorbed in church upheavals. In 1882 he left his position in the Kleine Gemeinde to join American evangelist John Holdeman in establishing the Church of God in Christ, Mennonite denomination in Canada (known as the Holdeman church).[39] Similarly, Tina Schulz, whose husband was an elder in the church and especially involved in negotiations regarding military exemption for Mennonite men during the Second World War, noted in an understated way that "my responsibility then was to keep everything organized at home."[40] Gertrude Lepp was described as "a widow to the needs of the settlers" when her husband became the sole minister at the 1920s immigrant settlement at Reesor in northern Ontario.[41] Sometimes the minister's wife stood in for her husband, such as when Tina Thiessen paid pastoral visits to needy families in her husband's absence, usually bringing a "pot of soup" with her. She also performed necessary tasks like decorating the church bulletin with her own sketchings, baking the "thimble-sized" bread for communion, and preparing the white linens for that service.[42]

Ministers' wives also carried extra hospitality duties, as they were often expected to host visiting ministers and missionaries, as well as to have an open-door policy towards their own church's members. An article of advice to ministers' wives observed that, "Her home must be ready for any emergency that may arise—always tidy, always ready." A minister's wife was admonished to learn housekeeping shortcuts in order "to have her house looking presentable even though there may be a speck of dirt here, or a dusty curtain there."[43] Anna Reimer Dyck noted the surprising visits she sometimes received because her home was located right next to the church where her husband Willy was pastor. On one Sunday, she returned home to fetch an item, only to find someone sleeping in each of her bedrooms, and hair lying on the kitchen floor, evidence that someone had snuck in for a quick haircut before church. And in one entire year, she had hosted guests for Sunday dinner on all but two Sundays.[44] As Ruth Unrau has observed, ministers' wives were veritable hotel keepers.[45]

Not only were they to be model housekeepers, but they were also to be exemplary Christian mothers and the deportment and piety of their children were to reflect this. The minister's wife was to "keep the family altar on a high spiritual level" and maintain vitality in family devotions, especially on Sunday evenings when her husband was tired of preaching all day.[46] Many family histories include reminiscences by daughters of ministers regarding the extra constraints of dress and behaviour placed upon them. Not only were ministers' wives expected to have exemplary homes and children, but sometimes they were called upon to chide others to meet their standards. According to her granddaughter, Margaret Loewen Isaac was once asked by her minister husband to chasten a woman at their church for her slovenly housekeeping. To which Margaret responded that "she didn't want to hurt anybody's feelings."[47] Even if a minister's wife had a career of her own, she was still expected to give almost as many hours to the church as her husband. Doris North came to First Mennonite Church at Vineland, Ontario, with her minister-husband Wayne in the mid-1950s. Although she worked full-time as a nurse, she said: "I attended all the functions of the church ... I was expected to teach Summer

Bible School. I sang in the church choir which Wayne directed.... In the evening I was to quilt with the women."[48]

Some wives of church workers viewed the loneliness and extra household demands that were exacted from them as their own contribution to 'the work of the Lord.' For instance, Anna Sawatzky, wife of a Manitoba evangelist, said, "I enjoyed taking care of the farm [in her husband's absence]. Then I felt I had a part in the kingdom work as well." Others, like Susan Hoeppner, resented especially the financial difficulties faced by families during the era when ministers were unpaid. To keep her nine children and husband clothed on their meagre income, she mended endlessly, sometimes into the night, adding patch onto patch until there was little left of the garment being fixed.[49] Susan Klassen, wife to a busy Manitoba minister and mother to fifteen children, commented that her marriage was a "good marriage until David became a minister."[50] In a family history, many of Susan's fifteen children reflected on the heavy workload carried by their mother while their father was often away and involved in church work. One daughter observed that "Mother was expected to be a quiet helpmate, staying in the background but supporting her man. Lip service was paid to the role of the wife in the ministry, but mostly her role was to keep quiet and not hinder the work of the Lord."[51]

If 'Lizzy,' Susan, and others chafed at their role as wife of a clergyman, some women heralded their husband's new status because their own identity was enhanced accordingly. For instance, Katie Funk Wiebe recalled that when her husband was ordained, she was pleased to now call herself "Mrs. Reverend Walter Wiebe," and said, "we young wives secretly gloated when our husbands got elected to key positions. We lived our lives through them because there was no opportunity to live them any other way. We couldn't clamber to the top branches of the tree after our husbands, but we could point them out swinging on the top branches to passersby."[52] The biographer of Mennonite church leader Jacob J. Thiessen observed that his wife Tina also obtained status "simply because she was 'Mrs. J.J. Thiessen.'"[53] In 1949, Barbara Coffman of Vineland, Ontario, in an article about her grandfather, evangelist John S. Coffman, recommended that the church's historic and publishing committees urge ministers' wives to keep diaries, "just in case their husbands might some day be famous."[54] Reinforcing the notion that a minister's wife should reflect his clerical position like a mirror, women whose husbands held leadership posts were also more likely than others to be appointed to comparable titles within women's organizations. For instance, Meta Regier Bahnmann, wife of

British Columbia minister and elder Nicolai Bahnmann, became the first president of the BC Mennonite Women in Mission in 1939, a post she held for twenty years.[55]

DECISION MAKING IN THE CHURCH

Women who were neither ministers nor ministers' wives had to find other ways to participate in the regular life of the church. For the Ontario Swiss, the introduction of Sunday schools in the latter half of the nineteenth century, while controversial and opposed by certain Mennonite subgroups, gave women an opportunity to take an active teaching role in the church and undermine traditional prescriptions regarding women's silence in the church. They were, of course, expected and allowed to teach only children and other women, not adult men. For women with children, Sunday school teaching could be viewed as an extension of their maternal roles, while women who were not mothers could find in Sunday school teaching an outlet for caring for children and thus 'mother' vicariously.[56] While Sunday school teaching was considered a lesser role, one that garnered women no real religious power or influence, it was likely in the Sunday school classroom—with its Bible story felt boards, its Christmas pageant preparations, and at least in some eras its introduction of concepts of damnation and salvation—that Mennonite men and women gained their formative experience of being Christian and Mennonite. Indeed, in the early 1970s, one woman argued that, "by receiving almost total responsibility for young children, women ... possess the positions of greatest possible influence in the church. Preaching to adults may be more prestigious, but pre-schoolers are more impressionable."[57] Youth programs, such as the *Jugendvereine* (young people societies) or Christian Endeavour in Russian Mennonite churches or the Literary Societies in Ontario Swiss Mennonite churches that emerged in the late nineteenth century, also provided a setting in which young women could play a prominent role. Gradually over the course of the twentieth century, women were allowed to take on other designated roles in the church, such as choir director, Sunday school superintendent, or perhaps deacon.

The deaconate had a fairly long history in Mennonite congregations, the deacon being the appointed or elected individual (or group of persons) who assisted the minister (and bishop within groups that held to this three-fold clerical hierarchy). Canadian Mennonites did not follow the precedent set in

Russia and later in the United States, where Mennonites established deaconess institutes in which single women trained and worked primarily as nurses in church-run hospital settings.[58] Deacons were traditionally responsible for looking after the needs of the 'poor and needy' within the congregation and would also assist at such church rites as baptism, footwashing, and communion. When the latter was observed, often at Thanksgiving and Easter, the deacon's wife might have the important role of baking the bread or small buns that were used in the communion service. When a man was appointed as a deacon in the church, it was assumed that his wife would serve equally in that capacity, and in some churches a couple was 'ordained' to the deaconate together. When Catherine Klassen's husband became a deacon in 1952, she believed that the assignment included her as well, saying, "I thanked God for this opportunity to serve him, because I felt, this would be my responsibility as well. . . . I enjoyed the work, we did everything together, except go to deacon's meetings." When her husband died, Catherine continued to perform the deacon's role of "visiting the sick and the widows" on her own volition, but on "an unofficial basis." She undoubtedly recognized the value of a female presence in the work of visitation especially, saying, "A deaconess and deacon's wife can sometimes be more helpful in certain situations."[59]

Probably well aware of the gendered aspects of home visitation, in 1947 one Ontario congregation formally appointed Louida Bauman, a single woman, to "do personal work and in general assist the Pastor," although only the church minister referred to her as deaconess, Louida herself spurning the title and the stature that it connoted.[60] Once the deaconate ceased to be an ordained office, the door was opened for women to be appointed to the task. In 1966 Katie Hooge became the first woman to serve as a deacon at First Mennonite Church in Saskatoon. Her contribution was obviously successful, since, in 1972, a new clause was added to the church constitution, stating, "At least one of the deacons shall be a woman."[61] Even though there was both a biblical and historic precedent for women as deacons in the church, when the practice was reintroduced in the 1960s, there was opposition in some quarters. A 1967 recommendation that women be installed as deacons at the Altona (Manitoba) Bergthaler church passed by a narrow margin of fifty-eight to forty-six, but the decision was rescinded the next day.[62]

Despite their presence in important and formative settings such as Sunday school and the deaconate, for most of their history in Canada, Mennonite women had almost no opportunity to be publicly and formally involved in shaping the church customs and rituals that reflected their congregation's interpretation of religious doctrine. They sat in the pews, sang aloud, and prayed silently with the congregation, but had no formal voice. Women who were ardent about their religious beliefs struggled sometimes outwardly but mostly within themselves over a spiritual culture that expected female silence. In her religious testimony, Catherine Klassen wrote: "I loved to go to church. When the preacher would ask a question which I thought I understood, I would raise my hand, but to my chagrin he always answered it himself."[63]

Women like Catherine, of a generation that didn't experience second-wave feminism in the church, spent their lives looking for venues in which they could give expression to their theological and practical ideas. While questions and debate surrounding women as ordained ministers seemed clear-cut, there was also opposition at times to women in non-ministerial roles. Though the practice varied widely, many congregations imposed restrictions on women's official activities within the organizational structure, sometimes based on formal understandings of church governance but more often on informal rationales about a woman's proper place vis-à-vis positions of authority. And in a familiar pattern of history, women were frequently given access to positions only when there was a lack of willing men. For instance, by the 1950s, Sunday schools were commonplace among the Saskatchewan Bergthaler Mennonites. However, it had become difficult to find enough teachers, who had always been men. At a 1957 leadership conference amongst conservative groups in Manitoba and Saskatchewan, it was decided that in cases where there were not enough male teachers, then women should be encouraged to teach.[64] In such cases, exigency triumphed over ideological position.

Frieda Esau Klippenstein, reflecting on the community of Coaldale, Alberta, in which she grew up, wondered how most women could feel like full members in Mennonitism, when they were "systematically restrained from entering" those aspects of public life—the church and its connected institutions—that defined a Mennonite identity.[65] Ruth Nighswander, who grew up in a conservative Ontario Mennonite conference, chafed at the limits on women's involvement in making decisions within the church. This included women's exclusion from choosing ministers, bishops, and deacons by lot, and also prohibition against women's attending important decision-making church conferences. Ruth felt it ironic and unjust when reports from those conferences were often aimed at women and focused on such issues as dress regulations when women had no formal voice or access to the opinions expressed, except through the men in their families.[66] Patriarchal dominance in church life could extend to the ridiculous. At one Saskatchewan church, the annual Sunday school picnic, purportedly an event for children, remembered as "a nightmare" by one child, saw the men eating first while their wives served, and the children ate last.[67] While most women did not agitate for formal leadership, accepting the biblical rendering of the gender hierarchy, many were less satisfied with their exclusion from general decision-making processes within the church.

Although the practice varied widely from one Mennonite group to the next and also between congregations, until the latter half of the twentieth century, most churches denied women direct participation in the major decision-making bodies of the church administrative structure. Generally, the rationale for this was biblical injunctions that women keep silent in the church and be submissive before men and God. But there was also a social perception that women had neither interest nor proclivity for the business of the church, being created for the domestic enterprise of home and children. The traditional *Bruderschaft* (brotherhood) meetings, as they were called in Russian Mennonite congregations, at which most church business was discussed and significant decisions made, were restricted to men for many years. Even if allowed to attend membership or congregational meetings, women were not allowed to speak or cast a vote. As one woman recalled, "Women didn't come to church business meetings for a long time and then when they did, they kept quiet."[68] Conference bodies dealt very little with this issue in a formal way, and, as a result, individual congregations developed their own customs and procedures. Thus attitudes and practice could vary considerably depending on the leadership, power brokers, and family dynamics in particular churches. For example, at the Vineland (Ontario) United Mennonite Church, women received the right to vote on all matters in 1936, whereas at the nearby Niagara United Mennonite Church (within the same conference), women did not gain those rights until 1962.[69] The disparity that existed reflected the congregational nature of Mennonite church polity generally. The records of many churches simply do not record a debate or pivotal moment when women were granted the franchise and rights of participation in church decision making. In a few locales, they may have exercised those rights from the very beginning. In others, change did not occur without painful and contentious debate, nor without strong resistance that was met with equally strong demands.

During the 1930s and 1940s, the Altona local of the Manitoba-based Bergthaler group was the only congregation within that conference to allow women to vote at annual meetings and to hold committee positions.[70] These privileges were withdrawn, however, when constitutional revisions in the late 1950s meant that Altona had to defer to the majority of Bergthaler congregations that refused to accept such a level of female participation. The historian of one Bergthaler congregation, reflecting on the church in the year 1931, stated that "women had no vote in the church [and] were excluded from the Brotherhood. . . . " She noted the 1929, now famous, Persons Case, whereby the British courts had decreed that women in Canada were also 'persons,' but observed that "the message had not yet reached all areas of the social fabric of Canada."[71] The issue did not rest there, however, and in 1966 women in the entire Bergthaler conference received voting rights, and soon after 'brotherhood' meetings became 'membership' meetings. One prominent minister in the Bergthaler group, David D. Klassen, advised against giving women the vote, as this would cause "conflict and division." Though he was considered a "risk taker" on many other church issues, Klassen "distrusted and feared women in church work," according to one of his daughters. When the decision in favour of a nomenclature shift from brotherhood to membership meeting passed by only two votes, Klassen suggested postponing the change, though his recommendation was defeated.[72] According to historian Anna Ens, the Conference of Mennonites in Manitoba, of which the Bergthaler group was a part, saw most congregations grant women a vote during the late 1950s to early 1970s, though at least one church did so as late as 1988. At the Morden, Manitoba, Bergthaler church in 1969, a motion favouring women was defeated when it failed to receive the necessary two-thirds majority. One female member argued the following: "The Lord seems to have endowed our church women with a special quality of love, patience and dedication. Surely he has also given them the attribute of spiritual intelligence and wisdom needed in the consideration of church policy."[73] The national Mennonite newspaper reported on the Morden decision with the headline "Women Still in the Cold."[74]

In some churches, the decision over the female franchise was divisive, involved substantial struggle, and required several attempts before a majority reached agreement. At West Abbotsford Mennonite Church in British Columbia, a church split was narrowly avoided in 1951, one of the issues of controversy being the authority of the *Gemeindeberatung* (congregational meeting), at which women participated, vis-à-vis the *Bruderschaft*, which was the domain of men. My grandfather, the Reverend Heinrich M. Epp, was supportive of women's involvement, saying that a woman's presence could have a positive influence on an "impetuous" husband, and furthermore, "the participation of the sisters was also especially helpful for the many immigrant women in the raising of their older children." The opposition of some members to women voting and a call for a return to "brotherhood" meetings nearly cost Epp his job. The dissenting group held that the matter could be decided only in a brotherhood meeting without women present, but the rest of the congregation felt otherwise. By a vote of 200 to 97, the church decided in favour of the congregational meeting; Epp was also affirmed in his position. Lacking a unanimous outcome and with such a large number of opponents, both women and men, it is likely that women were hesitant to exercise their new-found voice in the church very loudly.

Home Street Mennonite Church in Winnipeg had a similarly rocky time with the issue, paradoxically having at the same time a female church treasurer while not allowing women to vote on church business. In that congregation in 1964, the 'Brotherhood' recommended "that men are to take the greater responsibility in the work of the church and the women bear out the attitude of submission and cooperation in principle." When the treasurer resigned the next year, the leadership attempted to clarify its position by suggesting that women were restricted from voting only in Brotherhood meetings, but could vote when they were part of a committee or delegation, or held church office.[75] The obvious inconsistency in practice here made the issue of power very transparent and the biblical foundations only a subterfuge for the enforcement of a social hierarchy. Indecision and disagreement also reflected many anomalies in practice, whereby some churches allowed women to vote in ministerial elections but not on other business, while in other churches exactly the reverse was true; in some churches the *Bruderschaft* carried greater weight than the membership meeting while elsewhere the opposite was the case.

In many congregations, there was a large gap between the time when the issue was first raised officially and the point at which an inclusive decision was made. At the Eden Mennonite Church in Chilliwack, BC, for instance, a 1947 motion that women be allowed to vote in congregational meetings was tabled for ten years. When the constitution of the Westheimer Mennonite Church at Rosemary, Alberta, was first printed in 1947, it included the stipulation that only men could vote at brotherhood meetings and indeed that women were not even allowed to attend. These prohibitions were not officially reversed in the constitution until 1970.[76] Similar constitutional changes were made at the Vauxhall, Alberta, church in the late 1960s.[77] At the Crystal City (Manitoba) Mennonite Church, five women attended the 'brotherhood' meeting in 1954, but reportedly "someone took offence to their presence" and so they did not appear again until 1970, when sixteen women attended, at which point the nomenclature changed to 'annual' or 'membership' meeting. The next year the first woman was elected to a church committee.[78]

Debates over the female franchise became even more acrimonious when other current church conflicts existed simultaneously, as happened at Winkler Mennonite Brethren Church in the early 1960s. In this historic congregation (the first Mennonite Brethren church in Canada), the question of whether women should vote on key congregational decisions became intertwined with deep differences over which language—English or German—would be used predominantly in church worship and business. With male leaders split over the issue of language transition, women's vote on the question was perceived, in the end incorrectly, as having the potential to shift the outcome in important ways. First introduced in 1959, the contentious issue of the female franchise was repeatedly voted down, deferred, or "buried" until 1966, when, after a "series of motions, counter motions, and secret ballots," the decision was finally made to grant the vote to all members eighteen years of age and older. Along the way, the gender issue became a pawn in personal and ideological conflicts amongst a small group of men; in 1962, the church council vote on the question of allowing women to vote was six against, five in favour, and one abstention, within a congregation of more than 350 members. In the end, the battle between progressives and conservatives left the congregation "deeply wounded," according to historian Gerald C. Ediger, and an obvious women's vote did not "tip the scales" on the language question.[79]

The wide difference of opinion that existed among Mennonites was noted by minister N.N. Fransen of Vineland, Ontario, in a talk given in 1959 on the question of women's franchise in the church. On the one extreme, he pointed out, were Mennonites in the Netherlands, where women not only voted but actually had been appointed as ministers. On the other end of the spectrum were churches where women did not vote and where all questions of church life were determined by men in brotherhood meetings. The matter was complicated, Fransen went on to say, by the fact that the Bible could be used to support both sides. While I Corinthians called women to be silent in the church, other passages told of women who had prophesied. He argued that the current practice in the church, whereby women taught Sunday school, expounded on the Bible among the 'heathen' overseas, and brought reports from the mission field, already was inconsistent with the prescription to be silent. A questionnaire that was distributed to seventy churches showed an almost even split between those who allowed women the franchise and those who did not.[80] Indeed, the level of divisiveness over this issue is evidenced in the narrow margins of acceptance or rejection that resulted when votes were cast on the question. At the Rosthern (Saskatchewan) Mennonite Church in 1960, a motion to extend voting privileges to women at the annual meeting was approved by a vote of twenty-six to twenty-three; half a year later, the question of allowing women to vote at business meetings was defeated twenty-three to seventeen.[81] Since such decisions were made solely by male members (as women could not vote), this was clearly a debate that was divided not only on gender lines. At another church, a 1968 decision to extend voting rights to all church members passed by only one vote, after the meeting chairperson broke a tie.[82] The lack of formal channels by which women could participate in church discussions and decision making resulted in some rather ludicrous situations where all-male committees were making policy on such topics as birth control, women's dress codes, food to be served at conferences, and women's mission projects, as well as other matters relating to female culture.

The obstacles to women's formal voice in church decision making became especially discomfiting when female members comprised significant majorities in individual congregations, or for self-supporting widows who contributed to church budgets. Two widows in the Eigenheim church in Saskatchewan were vocal about their frustration that they had to learn about "what went on" at congregational meetings through their sons. One of the women, Katharina Siemens, simply began attending brotherhood meetings in the early 1950s, even though she did not have a vote.[83] This anomaly was acutely the case for churches that received large numbers of post-Second World War refugees from the Soviet Union and eastern Europe. A demographic imbalance in this migration, whereby the ratio of women to men (aged thirty and up) was almost three to one, meant a sudden bulge in female members for churches that received these refugee families. For instance, at the Sargent Avenue Mennonite Church in Winnipeg in 1952, there were thirty-six adult men and sixty-three women; and at the Niagara United Mennonite Church, during the years 1947 to 1950, there were seventy-eight new female members, versus thirty-seven male. The Sargent Avenue congregation gave women full rights from its inception in 1949, mainly because of "the fact that we had so many women who had lost their husbands in the Second World War necessitated such an attitude."[84]

First Mennonite Church in Saskatoon faced the dilemma of other urban Russian Mennonite churches that received a large number of post-war immigrants. The presence of numerous widows and single women amongst this group meant that the question of women's vote in church matters became acute during the 1950s. The situation here highlighted a contradiction that had existed in some churches for many years whereby a single woman who was financially independent was required to pay full church dues, yet had no voice in the decision-making process. In 1947, the suggestion of a male member at First Mennonite that women be allowed to attend brotherhood meetings was not considered; the issue had been raised already in 1939. The following year, after serving supper to the brotherhood, women were permitted to sit in for the giving of reports. In 1949 the concern was again raised that widowed and single women who were members had no one to speak for them. The only concession made at this point was that women could attend the annual reporting session, so long as there was no discussion or decision making.

Thus, the 1950s saw a division of annual meetings into two sessions: a first evening of reporting to which all members were invited, and a second evening to set the budget and make decisions, at which only men were present. The issue continued to appear on the agenda of brotherhood meetings, but in 1960 the female franchise was again defeated when a secret vote failed to obtain the necessary two-thirds majority. A 1962 petition from the women's society pressed the church's leadership further, pointing out that "50 women ... had no knowledge of church affairs."[85] It wasn't until 1964, however, that the constitution was amended to allow women to attend and vote at congregational meetings. When one considers that out of a membership of 478, there were 198 men and 280 women, of whom 113 were single or widowed, one can begin to understand the source of the resistance and also the need to push forward on this issue.[86] According to one historian's analysis, most of the opposition came from older men in the congregation, who often quoted biblical passages on female silence to buttress their position. One man purportedly asserted that "if in the barnyard the goose followed the gander, surely that was a sign that women should not have the same rights as men."[87]

The influx of female-headed families into churches such as First in Saskatoon was one factor that spurred the debate, but there were other reasons as well. By the 1960s the laity were increasingly involved in church decision making, and at both conference and congregational levels, there was an enormous growth in bureaucracy—committees and councils that shared both the authority and the work that had previously gone mainly to a three-fold clergy of bishop, ministers, and deacons. As opportunities increased for the average lay member to participate in church administration, it seemed less reasonable to keep women out of those activities. Furthermore, the visibility that women were attaining in secular society made the situation in the church seem all the more unrealistic. Esther Patkau, in her 2002 history of *Canadian Women in Mission*, also remarked on the dissonance that existed into the 1970s between women's financial obligations to the church and their official voice in church decision making.[88]

The mid-1960s were a turning point on this issue in many church groups. Within the Blumenorter church in Manitoba, women had exercised the right to vote for elders, ministers, and deacons since 1928, but had no franchise at brotherhood meetings. In 1963, after a visit with Blumenorter students in Winnipeg, a minister and deacon of the church returned to their home congregation, having observed "the professionally independent women who constituted a bloc of the church's most loyal supporters, who paid their dues and channelled their funds into projects of the church and yet had no voice in its councils." A study paper presented to an all-male brotherhood meeting in 1965 failed to sway the status quo, yet three years later women received full rights of participation.[89] Among Mennonite churches with Swiss/Pennsylvania roots, the practice also varied, but the arguments for and against the female franchise were similar, as was the era of transition. At Stirling Avenue Mennonite in Kitchener, Ontario, women had been vocal participants when the congregation had split from First Mennonite in 1924, and they were included on the church board by the late 1920s. In Ontario Mennonite churches with Amish roots, the change came much later. For instance, at the East Zorra congregation, business meetings were all-male until the 1950s. Until 1952, men would even read and adopt the report of the sewing circle. One woman, commenting on this in retrospect, said: "No wonder women started kicking up their heels and voices. I never saw men flock to the sewing circle."[90] At the Steinmann Mennonite Church, women began attending the annual meeting in the 1950s but didn't have a vote until 1968.[91] At Floradale Mennonite Church, women began attending the annual business meetings in 1959.[92]

In certain conservative groups of both Swiss and Russian background, church polity that included women's full participation often did not come into effect until the 1970s and 1980s. In 1972, for instance, the Reinland (Manitoba) Evangelical Mennonite Mission Church (EMMC) received a rather benign motion "that ladies be invited to the annual meeting," a motion that was passed once it was amended to read "that ladies be given equal rights with men at the annual meeting."[93] Within the closely related Evangelical Mennonite Conference, the question of "Women Suffrage" was also dealt with in the late 1970s. In the midst of "vigorous discussion" and "diverseness in thought and practice," the conference leadership found it difficult to arrive at a definitive statement at its council meetings in late 1977 and so chose to defer the issue.[94]

The pace of progress towards women's greater involvement in decision making was also slow within the 'modern' Mennonite Brethren (MB) denomination. In 1975 the Canadian MB conference for the first time provided food service and childcare so that women were freed to attend all sessions. That same year women became eligible for election to some boards and committees, a resolution that passed by a vote of 339 to 20 and reportedly elicited more discussion than any other issue. The divergent opinions that existed on the question of 'women's place' became evident when a seminar titled "Fascinating Womanhood," which "stressed woman's role as wife and mother," was held concurrent to the conference business sessions.[95] Katy Penner, a career missionary in Congo, experienced this process first-hand. At the 1975 Canadian MB conference, she had been asked to let her name stand for the Board of Christian Education, a task she viewed with enthusiasm as a stimulating challenge. At the conference, a "deep rift" developed over the question of whether women could serve on national conference boards, and, after much discussion, the leadership decided to defer further discussion on women's eligibility until after elections were held the next day. Katy opted to withdraw her name from the slate for the education board because, in her words, "How can I let my name stand if it has not been decided whether I am eligible?" Only a month later, Katy was elected to the North American conference body's Board of Christian Service after being nominated, ironically, by the same conference leader who had opposed women's election to boards at the Canadian conference.[96]

The fear that women might represent a 'gender force to be reckoned with' if they received the vote in the local congregation was echoed in a reluctance to give them a representation or voice at large church gatherings, as was the case for Katy Penner above. In 1954, the presence of two Saskatchewan women as congregational delegates to the annual Conference of Mennonites in Canada sessions aroused some debate on the floor. The two were not officially recognized that year, but a decision was made to allow women as delegates the following year. The first female delegate to the Mennonite Conference of Ontario attended in 1959. In one recollection, a Saskatchewan woman attended the annual sessions of the Canadian Mennonite Brethren Conference as a delegate during the 1960s, but apparently the conference executive asked that she not be counted and so the tally of women delegates remained at zero that year.[97] As this anecdote suggests, the entrance of women into formerly all-male realms of church bureaucracy did not come without pain and irony. One woman, the first to participate in a particular all-male conference meeting, felt "whipped across the face" when it was announced at the noon break that the men should make use of all the washrooms in the building so as to reduce the lineups. When the meeting chair was confronted with this awkward situation, he replied that she should fend for herself.[98] For some women, however, trail-blazing was empowering and effected change in institutions. When Eleanor High of Ontario became the first woman delegate at a North American Mennonite conference gathering in 1969, she "obviously did not go to ... champion women's rights," yet her speech from the floor that chastised the church for not utilizing the gifts of "women with capability, imagination, insight and dedication" resulted in general applause and a formal resolution on "Using Gifts in the Church."[99]

A numerical tabulation of gender balance (or imbalance) on congregational committees and boards, or within conference delegate sessions, does help us to understand the transition in the acceptability of women's presence and formal participation in official Mennonite church institutions. It does not, however, reveal the breadth or depth of women's participation, nor does quantifying women's involvement address the qualitative change, if any, in women's presence within these structures. Were they called on to speak as often as men were? Did they want to speak? Were their suggestions and opinions recognized? Even when institutions began to change their policies on women in leadership positions, or when churches began to grant women an official voice in congregational decision making, this did not necessarily mean all women were ready or eager for that involvement. A psychology of subordination and silence, which for some women was quite deep-rooted, inhibited many individuals from taking on new roles without reservation. As one woman said: "The image of women being unfit to speak in public lingers long after the rules change. Silence has been bred into many generations of women."[100] Some women later in life expressed bitterness over the fact that they had no voice in the church, yet contributed so much to the sustenance of the institution. Anne Enns Braun recalled little difference amongst Mennonite churches with respect to women: "The *Bruderschaft* [men] always decided everything in both churches. Women, stay at home and sew your clothes.... They [men] were very domineering and when it came to churches they were the ones who said how it should be done and yet the women did all the planning and the working, sales, and teaching."[101]

While some women grumbled amongst themselves, and others expressed resentment only in retrospect, a few resisted women's exclusion by making their opinions heard and their skills and abilities felt. Helene Toews of Niagara-on-the-Lake, Ontario, attended as many Mennonite conference meetings as she could, at provincial, national, and bi-national levels, paying all her own expenses at a time when women were not sponsored as official delegates.[102] Agatha Klassen, a schoolteacher with an equal love for church work, often swam against the tide as she tried to contribute her opinions and skills at Yarrow Mennonite Brethren Church in British Columbia. As her own self-confidence grew, she "was no longer content to serve quietly and unobtrusively while less-qualified people made the decisions." She became frustrated by the limits placed on female authority, exemplified in one case by the need for a male member on all church committees who could report to the all-male church council, something women were not allowed to do. In the early 1970s Agatha chose to challenge the system; when nominated to be church education director, Agatha indicated that her acceptance was conditional on her simultaneous appointment to church council. After a vote by council with one dissenting voice, she became the first female church council member at Yarrow MB.[103]

MISSIONARIES AND MISSION SOCIETIES

If Agatha Klassen chose to stay close to home and, by sheer persistence, eventually be included in the leadership structures of her church, other women realized they would have to leave home to exercise their vocational goals and leadership skills within the church. Indeed, long before the shroud of silence was lifted from women in their churches in Canada, Mennonite women were 'preaching and prophesying' in very audible ways in the context of mission work far from home. In the late nineteenth century, as overseas and city missions were introduced to the program of Mennonite churches, women found a way in which they could effectively function as religious leaders but far away from the watchful eye of church authorities. Initially it was mainly unmarried women who seized the opportunity to travel to distant places like Africa and India to preach, teach, and in other ways minister. Indeed, some women from Mennonite churches were so eager to express their faith in concrete vocational ways that they accepted overseas assignments from other denominations well before their own church developed a missions program. Mission work in 'foreign fields' over an extended period of time also offered (especially single) women an escape from insular Mennonite communities that placed severe limits on the scope of activity for multi-talented women. Especially for adventuresome women with a zeal for a church vocation, missions offered "more status and excitement, and more opportunity for reaching people with the gospel than teaching, nursing, or maid's work at home."[104]

Historian Peter Penner has said, "It is widely acknowledged that without the work of single women (who outnumbered men on almost any field by two to one or close to that) the history of evangelical missions from 1850 to 1950 would look quite different."[105] The number of women who chose mission work as a vocation increased dramatically in the years after the Second World War, when a new spirit and mandate of relief work and 'active pacifism' (as opposed to passive nonresistance) pervaded Mennonite churches and induced an unprecedented interest in volunteerism, especially in international settings. Beth Graybill, in her study of women missionaries in Puerto Rico, also notes that a post-war shift in mission work from primarily one of evangelism and preaching—traditional men's work—to more interest in social programs such as teaching and health care—traditional women's work—made it easier for women and mission organizations alike to include female missionaries in their program.[106]

Especially in the early years, mission projects offered particularly single women career opportunities in church work that were inaccessible to them in their home communities. For unmarried women who felt called into church work, overseas missions offered both an escape from limited vocational opportunities at home and the pitying glances of those who deemed marriage a woman's highest purpose, as well as the opportunity to exercise their

independence in a way that was not possible at home. One of these was Margarete Siemens, who did housework when her family immigrated from Russia in
1927, but "had no satisfaction" in that type of work and so went to study at
Winkler Bible Institute. In 1936 she went to Africa as a nurse and midwife and
later to Colombia, where she spent another five years before returning home
to care for her mother.[107] Many women missionaries completed significant
tenures in their positions, effectively turning their service assignments into
long-term careers. These include Anne Penner and Helen Kornelsen, who
worked in India for thirty-five and thirty-six years, respectively; Anna Dyck,
who worked in Japan for thirty-nine years, and Helen Willms in Taiwan for
thirty-four years. One Ontario church supported two 'lifetime' missionaries:
Alice Bachert in Colombia, and Leona Cressman in India. The number of
single men choosing a missionary career was always noticeably fewer. Indeed,
in 1955 Helen Kornelsen, on leave from her work in India, asked the question,
"Women are responding to the call, but where are the men?"[108] Male missionaries were either quick to marry before they left for the 'field' or found a
partner in one of the missionaries already at work overseas.

There was also a certain exoticism that surrounded women who bravely
travelled alone to faraway southern hemisphere places where the climate,
language, food, dress, and culture were so unfamiliar to Canadian Mennonites
of northern European ancestry. Beth Graybill describes how women missionaries in Puerto Rico thrilled their North American audiences with tales of "ford-
ing streams on horseback [and] encountering machete-wielding farmers."[109]
One of my own most vivid childhood memories is of a missionary to India who
visited my church girls' club. We were enthralled with the many beautiful saris
she showed us and even more thrilled when we were each allowed to don one
for a special missions program at the church.

Embarking on a career in missions was advantageous and attractive for
women, because they were able to "sidestep" normative gender roles, as Beth
E. Graybill suggests.[110] The prohibitions against women in leadership positions in Canadian churches, especially related to preaching the gospel, were
frequently overlooked in faraway places like Central America and Africa, and
even in city missions in urban Canada. When the male superintendent of the
Mennonite mission in Toronto resigned in 1914, his co-worker Elizabeth
Brown was asked to be "in charge" and so she then carried leadership for
the next year, although she wasn't given the title of superintendent. During
Elizabeth's tenure of leadership, Simon M. Kanagy of Pennsylvania arrived

and was given responsibility for pastoral work at the mission. In 1915 he was appointed superintendent and the next year Simon and Elizabeth were married. Elizabeth was now "wife of" the superintendent.[111]

Sidestepping normative gender roles included assuming the kind of authoritative preaching and teaching roles traditionally reserved for senior male ministers. Helen L. Warkentin's collection of papers includes references to, and notes on, many sermon-like presentations Helen gave. Lorraine Roth, missionary in Central America in the late 1950s, recalled that when the ordained men at the mission returned home on furlough, it was often missionary women such as herself who gave a 'message' at worship services. When questioned about this practice by a male missionary, Roth told him that "the men 'preach'; we women 'speak.'"[112] It seemed that the semantics of church leadership—sermon versus message, or preaching versus speaking—were important indicators that the tradition of female silence in the church was being upheld and thus mission board leaders and Mennonite constituents in North America could maintain the pretense that women missionaries were not women ministers.

When female missionaries returned home on furlough, they were expected to visit Canadian churches and tell of their work and the needs at their particular mission project. These presentations created a dilemma for churches, which had to discern whether the woman was 'preaching' (done behind the pulpit with spiritual authority) or 'reporting' (performed beside the pulpit in a factual manner). If a husband-and-wife missionary couple was speaking in a church, it was self-evident who would bring the message, the wife perhaps speaking to the children's Sunday school or the women's organization. There was plenty of evidence, however, that female missionaries were equally articulate about the church's mission program. At a 1917 missions festival in Langham, Saskatchewan, the featured guests were P.W. and Mrs. Penner, missionaries in India. When P.W. ended up in the hospital with an appendectomy, his wife took his place and held the audience "spell-bound" for three sessions throughout the day, leaving "a powerful impact on the listeners" and an offering of $1184.[113] Once again, exigency won the day. During her two-year furlough in the mid-1950s, Margaret Willems gave up to 240 talks about her work in India.[114] As churches gradually became more flexible towards the idea of 'women preachers,' it was often female missionaries who were first granted the privilege of speaking directly from the pulpit. However, one 1972 reflection noted that "missionary ladies" were still speaking beside the pulpit, "with one hand resting lightly on it."[115]

In the earlier years of overseas missions, women would sometimes be 'ordained' for such service, an indication of spiritual status in the church that was later removed by at least one Mennonite subgroup, likely because it may have given women the sense that they also had access to formal ministry in the local church. The discrepancy between what women could do at home in North America versus across the ocean in a foreign country was described by Katie Funk Wiebe as one aspect of the "ambivalent theology" that some Mennonites had towards women.[116] Helen Loewen Warkentin of Winkler, Manitoba, profiled at the outset of the chapter, was ordained as an overseas missionary in 1919 and was teacher and principal at a school in India for thirty-six years.[117] In that same church, four more women were ordained in the 1940s and 1950s for missionary service in Africa and South America.[118] Susie Brucks was ordained in 1944 by the Mennonite Brethren Church at Yarrow, British Columbia, for mission service in the Belgian Congo. Between the years 1919 and 1956, thirty-seven women, nineteen of whom were single, were ordained in the Mennonite Brethren Church in Canada in a procedure that was the same for men and women.[119]

In 1957, however, the Mennonite Brethren church changed its written policy on ordination of women, stating, "That in view of the fact that we as an M.B. Church, on the basis of clearly conceived Scriptural convictions, do not admit sisters to the public Gospel preaching ministry on par with brethren, we as a Conference designate the fact of setting aside sisters to missionary work a 'commissioning' rather than an 'ordination.'"[120] This most obvious shift in semantics would quickly disavow women workers from any sense that they were being granted a status comparable to an ordained (male) minister or missionary. And the change in status may well have represented an effort to reduce the spiritual authority that single women especially held within their particular mission work. An indication of this shift is Mennonite Brethren leader David Ewert's 1966 statement, in the context of an essay on women in the church, that "we recognize that we do not live in an ideal world and it happens, at times, where men fail to do the work of the church, single women rise to the challenge in home and foreign fields. But even in such situations Christian women should be instructed to permit men to assume leadership in the church, even where they have trained them."[121] The General Conference Mennonite Church also ordained women for overseas mission work at one time, but was ambivalent about whether such an ordination afforded a woman the same rights and privileges in Canadian churches as at 'foreign' mission stations.

Single women were also often the pioneers in opening inner-city missions in urban centres like Chicago and Toronto at the turn of the past century. When Ontario Mennonites opened a city mission in downtown Toronto in 1907, among the first volunteers were Lena Weber from Waterloo and Bernice Devitt from Breslau, Ontario. The women engaged in such activities as teaching Sunday school, running a girls' sewing and cooking school, and general neighbourhood visitation. Because of a furniture shortage at the mission station, the two women initially slept on the kitchen table. Women were key to the success of urban mission work because the targets of such efforts were mainly impoverished children who, it was hoped, would influence their parents with their newly gained understandings of Christianity. Because women, whether single or married, were considered by nature to be nurturers of children, they were crucial to the success of Mennonite efforts to guide new Christians towards conversion. When Elizabeth Brown was temporarily put in charge of the mission, as noted above, three other women workers took over some of Elizabeth's housework. Etta Perry, converted at the Toronto Mennonite Mission and baptized at the age of twelve, later became a worker herself at the mission, teaching Bible classes to children and helping with boys' and girls' clubs. And numerous other women workers served for short or longer stints at the mission, sometimes supplementing their income (if they received any at all) by domestic service positions in Toronto.

In addition to their work with children, the women workers were responsible for the domestic caretaking of the mission, in particular the preparation of food to feed the workers themselves, but also the many guests who were regularly at the table. And quite often, the women had to be extremely resourceful in stretching their already meagre supplies to feed an unpredictable number of hungry visitors. In one year, the Toronto mission reportedly served more than 1000 guest meals, a statistic that was presented as "almost a footnote" to the number of converts. Extra work came to the women during such events as the annual picnic (attended mainly by city children and sometimes their mothers) on Centre Island and the Christmas food and gift hamper distribution. It was clear that young single women were crucial to the daily functioning of the mission in Toronto, which included an array of tasks, both ministerial and domestic. Mission worker Viola Good described the routine

that included "visiting Sunday school pupils or hospitals, distributing literature door-to-door, preparing for or attending Bible studies, prayer meetings,
club meetings and Sunday events [as well as] shopping, entertaining, painting,
canning, gardening and ... janitor work at the church.[122]

Indeed, the workload may well have been a factor in the physical and
mental health problems experienced by several women workers at the Toronto
mission; reacting to the health breakdown of one decade-long female worker,
one male church worker wrote the following to a mission board official: "Do
we demand too much? Has a study ever been done of such cases ...?" On the
situation of single women workers generally, he wrote, "How long a vacation
should they have? Since they are busy on Sundays, should they drop their
duties on a week day? Is financing a disadvantage? Are there any plans for
welfare when they can no longer serve? Should a rest home be established?"[123]
If a few individuals showed concern, there is no evidence that church institutions or officials moved to rectify the conditions for workers such as the women
at the Toronto mission. Since their female nature was assumed to include a
propensity towards serving others, the multi-faceted work of women missionaries, whether married or single, could be construed within a framework of
self-denying service, rather than vocational labour.

The overall construct of service extended to the realm of financial support.
Mission work for single women was a challenge, not least of all because they
were expected to cover their own expenses, or solicit donations from their
home congregations. This had the effect of limiting the amount of time a
woman might spend in mission work, or might create a situation of depen-
dence on her own congregation. In the early years of the Toronto mission,
women workers were paid only five dollars per month, in addition to receiving
room and board. Another urban mission worker, Barbara Sherk of Preston,
Ontario, left her station at the Chicago Home Mission after less than a year
and the suggestion is made by Carol Penner that perhaps she wasn't receiving
support from her home church. The correspondence between Helen L.
Warkentin, missionary in India, and the Mennonite mission board that
employed her contains ongoing discussion of salary and it would appear that
there was little consistency in either the amount of her monthly stipend or
other mission expenses. Letters to her sister in Manitoba inquiring about the
status of her bank account and asking that money be sent suggest that Helen
was also drawing on her own funds to support her school in India.

Alice Bachert of Kitchener, Ontario, was another woman who, at the age of twenty-seven, found her vocational calling by training as a nurse-midwife and entering mission work first in Costa Rica and later Colombia. Alice, with financial support of $600 per year solely from her home congregation, spent most of fifty-three years working in Latin America, combining her nursing skills with efforts to spread the message of Christianity. Like many female missionaries, she was often frustrated when her own zealous desire to 'preach' was impeded by notions held both at home and in the mission field regarding gospel preaching as a male domain. She said at one point that "it seems a pity that there is not a man working in this district, as there is such a demand for preaching." Alice was reportedly "reluctant to take furloughs," so zealous was she about her evangelistic work and comfortable in her Colombian home. Alice's dependence on her home congregation became apparent when, despite her own wishes to retire in Colombia, it was deemed necessary to bring her back to Canada.[124]

The alienation and loneliness Alice experienced away from her 'home' in Colombia was felt by many returning missionaries, especially single women, who had been free to use a range of their talents and fill a multitude of roles overseas, but, once back in North America, were limited by gender-stratified roles within Mennonite churches. One British Columbia woman passionately described her state of being at "loose ends" when she returned from overseas mission work.

> [T]o top it all off, the pastor of your home church completely ignores you.... That is heartbreaking. No briefing, no word of comfort, no encouragement except from some dear ladies that come and say that they have been praying for you for years.... Your frustration grows. Don't they want to know what's going on, or are you ignored because you are a woman? ... Financially you're not faring much better.[125]

Alice Bachert was not the only missionary to experience a quick and unexpected end to her overseas career. Ontario sisters Una and Mabel Cressman, who were both working as missionaries in Paraguay, were sent home on "permanent furlough" in 1959, after it was deemed unsafe for single women to be travelling to remote areas to visit indigenous settlements in the country.[126] Helen L. Warkentin was also "involuntarily retired" after thirty-six years of service in India.[127] In July 1957 she and her co-workers received a visit from several representatives of the Mennonite Brethren mission board that oversaw her mission project. They spent four weeks reviewing the work and then advised Helen that, "Since our visit with you the judgment of our brethren at home and our own impressions have brought the question of the terminating of your ministry of the field into a fuller focuse [sic]."[128] In a letter to her family in Manitoba, Helen reported with some dismay on the decision that was made: "before they left there was a meeting of all the single sisters with them.... There they told us that we should come home in October. It seemed a bit hard, we had been working here quite a while and were yet healthy and strong and willing to go on for at least a year—but we said we wanted to obey.... I really don't know who could take my place here now." A month later, she repeated, "It was too sudden, that call to come home and there are no free missionaries to take up our work either." That she was perplexed by the order to terminate her work is suggested in her use of words like "unexpected" and "surprise" in her letters home; she also wondered whether her age—close to seventy years—was a factor when she says, "I did not feel quite old enough to leave the work yet. So that is what sometimes takes away the peace of mind." Clearly at a loss for what the future would hold for her, she wrote, "I really don't know where I am at now."[129]

Her resentment did not quickly go away upon arrival in Canada. In December 1957 Helen received a letter from the mission board's executive secretary, welcoming her home and inquiring about outstanding expenses owed to her. On the back of the typed letter, Helen scrawled the following few sentences, likely the draft of a letter she hoped to send in return: "It was hard to leave the work, the place, the people, the children, hard to leave so suddenly the school year almost finished. It would not have felt so hard if it had been at the end of the school year, but now. I ask why had it to be like this? But it is finished."[130] In response, the mission board secretary wrote to Helen that "We fully agree with you that it must have been difficult for you to leave the work in India ... ," though no rationale or explanation is given.[131]

Whatever the reasons for her termination, it is clear that Helen's work in India was nevertheless appreciated by people in that country since, after her departure, a village and orphanage were named after her and a school holiday declared on her birthday. In the case of both Alice and Helen, more detailed investigation of their missionary careers is needed to discern the exact reasons why church personnel in North America pressured the women to discontinue their work when the women themselves felt able and willing to stay. It is possible that churches and mission boards did not fully understand that for single women in particular, perhaps more than for missionary couples, their mission work had become their career and the mission locale had become their home. For them, ending their lives in retirement at the mission seemed quite possible and indeed perhaps desirable. Single women probably knew full well that their status would decline significantly once resident again in their home communities in Canada. Not only would they be unable to teach, preach, and evangelize with the kind of spiritual and social authority they had enjoyed overseas, but as unmarried women they would also be considered dependent and viewed with pity, as single women so often were. Similar abrupt terminations faced single women doing 'home' mission work in Canada. Ilda Bauman had "managed" an inner-city mission in Kitchener, Ontario, for ten years when, after a new director was hired, she was "released" from the mission in 1949 on the advice of a doctor and given half her salary for two months. According to one account, she "admitted disappointment" over her termination.[132]

Despite the unique challenges presented by a church career in mission work, many Mennonite women, single and married, found fulfilment in such a vocation. By the mid-twentieth century, as more Mennonite women obtained post-secondary education and entered the workforce, church leaders were beginning to recognize the skills women had to offer outside the household and perhaps began to fear the possible loss of talented and educated women to the work of church institutions. And, so long as women were barred from senior administrative and ministerial posts, it was possibly deemed in the church's best interests to create an alternative sector in which they could labour. In the mid-1950s, a program called Women in Church Vocations was established to provide church-related training and employment for single women. The program, which lasted only a few years, was compared to the deaconess orders that existed within some American Mennonite conferences earlier in the century and that were more common in other Christian denominations. Recognizing that single and married women in unprecedented numbers had worked for various church organizations during the Second World War both overseas and on the home front, and that Mennonite women were increasingly obtaining professional qualifications, the Board of Christian Service of the General Conference Mennonite Church pointed out that "we have increasingly used them" but "we have made no provision to train, guide and place women where they are best fitted and most needed." The program provided training and placement for women in a variety of church-related vocations and was novel in that it was not exclusive to single women, even though unmarried women were its main focus.

The first general assumption of the program proposal was that it not be seen to "discourage marriage," undoubtedly an important point for those who feared that the 'working woman' was a 'non-marrying woman.' In fact, married women could remain in the program only if they were available for full-time service, presumably meaning before they had children. Participants were required to "possess emotional and physical health, have a wholesome personality, be under thirty-six years of age when accepted, and be desirous of growing spiritually in her chosen vocation."[133] The proposal was also forward-thinking in its assumption that participants would receive a regular income as well as benefits similar to those offered to Mennonite ministers. The program, while having fairly clearly defined parameters, nevertheless represented an important step on the road to women's right to pastoral ministry in Mennonite churches. The organizing committee also decided to ask certain Mennonite colleges that offered special scholarship privileges to male ministerial candidates to extend the same rewards to 'girls' who were committed to church work within the Women in Church Vocations program.[134] Canadian women were participants and Ontario Mennonite Hedy Sawadsky was director for several years. Advocates of the Women in Church Vocations program noted that one reason such a program was needed was to address a demographic issue that saw many talented Mennonite women never marry. As Elaine Sommers Rich described it, "men tend to marry women who are slightly less intelligent than they are" and, thus, "the unmarried in our society tend to be the most capable women and the least capable men."[135] Women entering church vocations were thus the cream of the crop!

For women who did not assume church-related vocations, women's organizations offered a specifically female venue for women to express themselves within church life. It has in fact been said that women's organizations—variously called sewing circles, mission societies, ladies auxiliaries—within the Mennonite church functioned as a "parallel church" in which women could exercise leadership in performing some of the roles that were historically unavailable to them in the main institution.[136] While women themselves, in an earlier era, might not have viewed their gender-specific organizations within such a framework, they did on occasion put forward justifications for their work. In a 1944 report, the leader of one women's organization compared the role of the "ladies aid," as it was sometimes called, in the overall life of the church to the respective roles of women and men in the home: "Even though the women work separately from the rest of the congregation, we still feel that we are very much a part of the whole. It is the same as in the home, the wife goes after her own work while the husband also follows his own work; it is a distribution of responsibility in the family."[137] In a sense, women's organizational work offered them autonomy, if not authority. Indeed, the sewing circle was described as a "veritable battleground for the emancipation of Mennonite women"[138] in an era when women were to be 'seen and not heard' in the more public settings of church life. Elsie Neufeld, in a strongly worded defence of women's organizations in 1958, noted that when husbands objected to their wives' participation in sewing-circle work, they were "robbing [the women] of a much needed outlet for their pent-up spiritual emotions."[139] However, especially from the 1970s onward, distinct women's organizations were also criticized as a way of channelling women's energies away from the centre of church activity and developing what was sometimes described as the 'auxiliary syndrome': on the periphery rather than at the centre of the church, supportive but not decisive.

Because Mennonite religious values included the maintenance of social boundaries between believers and the 'outside' world, women were historically discouraged, and sometimes prohibited, from participating in the activities of women's organizations in wider society. Thus, beginning in the late nineteenth century, they began to carve out a space for themselves under the umbrella of male-run Mennonite church institutions. In the context of their own organizations, women sewed and knitted for charitable causes, raised funds in support of their own congregation and its projects, and also engaged in Bible study, prayer, and devotional discussion. Mennonite women never organized on the kind of scale that Jewish women did, for instance, into large, national, activist organizations like the National Council of Jewish Women, which lobbied government and other constituencies on issues related to labour, education, and social conditions. The factors that motivated Mennonite women to organize in groups were varied but revolved mainly around a growing interest in missions and charitable work, both at home and abroad. Reflecting and reinforcing ideal notions of gender within their families and church communities, women's organizations were primarily oriented around goals of service, an ethos that was demonstrated in the biblical texts chosen by many groups to represent their mandate. In her study of Mennonite women's organizations, Gloria Neufeld Redekop found that approximately 74 percent of women's societies used texts that had a service orientation or linked service to working for God.[140]

In the first years of organized women's work, the purposes and outcomes were clear and minimalist. The leader of one society that began in 1926 in Ontario stated its purpose as follows: "The purpose of a *Verein* [society] was to make craft items. These we sold among each other. The money went to help our men fulfill their obligations to the mission board." The first craft items were things such as pillowcases and tea towels that were created from bleached flour and sugar sacks.[141] Initially, women's groups did handwork and raised funds for mission projects, both local and overseas. The desperate need of war sufferers in the First World War, followed by the disease and famine that Mennonites living in the Soviet Union experienced during the subsequent civil war, provided further impetus for women in Canada to organize and work collectively on relief projects. As the economic Depression intensified in the 1930s, women's groups were called upon to raise money and donate clothing to needy families, Mennonites and others, especially on the prairies. Even while women worked from dawn until dusk, there seemed to be time, mostly in the winter months, to engage in relief work. The women of Yarrow, BC, United Mennonite Church organized into a sewing circle in 1929. Although they were poor, and new immigrants themselves, they were compelled to help those in need. Thirteen women met to form a "Maria Martha Verein." They collected two dollars in the first two offerings, and were "ecstatic" when the Eaton's Company sent ten dollars' worth of fabric.[142] The sewed items that resulted were sold at an auction that raised $140, which was then used to purchase relief parcels for Mennonite families in the Soviet Union. This first group dissolved because of "hardship circumstances and poverty," though a new group was begun later when more families began settling in Yarrow.[143]

Of course, throughout history, women had performed these charitable material tasks individually, as an extension of their everyday domestic work, outside any organizational framework. Women of the conservative Anabaptist groups, such as the Old Order Mennonites and the Amish, did not have formally constituted organizations. But they nevertheless met, and continue to meet, in each other's homes to quilt and sew for themselves, for sale to 'outsiders,' and for charitable causes.

In most areas, women organized themselves into work groups well before official church bodies recognized them or included them within organizational structures. Amongst Mennonites from Russia, the first women's organization formed in Manitoba about 1895 and called itself a 'charity organization.' Their main purpose initially was to generate support, material and financial, for the new Mennonite high school at Gretna. A 'mission society' began in Rosthern, Saskatchewan, in 1907 and, by 1938, there were reportedly ninety-five General Conference women's societies in Canada. Despite efforts at centralization from the US-based General Conference office, women's societies functioned informally and with minimal structure and organization. Amongst Swiss Mennonites, the first women's 'sewing circle' had thirty-five members and was organized in Ontario in 1908 as the Waterloo Charity Circle to sew clothing for poor children in the city. But it wasn't until 1917, at which time twenty circles had been formed, that the Mennonite Conference of Ontario recognized and "encouraged" their work, recommending that they affiliate with the wider North American body, soon to be called the Mennonite Women's Missionary Society.[144]

This relatively autonomous women's activity did not progress without opposition. In the late 1920s, the Mennonite Women's Missionary Society, based in Ohio and led by Clara Eby Steiner, was effectively 'taken over' by the church's mission board and its male leaders, who were threatened by women's success in raising funds and supporting overseas missionaries. They may have feared the potential influence this would have given women in the area of missions overall, a growing area of interest and activity within Mennonite bureaucracies in the early twentieth century. Though these developments unfolded mainly south of the border, Canadian Mennonite women were aware of what was happening and may well have been grateful that they were somewhat removed from the geographical centre, and thus some of the control, of Mennonite denominational life. Mennonite women were not alone in this loss of organizational autonomy, as the 1920s saw a trend in other Protestant denominations whereby "formerly independent women's missionary organizations were merged into denominational missionary bodies ... often against the better judgment of the women."[145]

As women organized, named themselves and worked together in separate yet clearly identifiable women's organizations, men gradually took notice, sometimes offering supportive gestures and at other times presenting obstacles to women's self-sufficiency. For instance, following an acrimonious church split in 1924, men reportedly intervened to separate the women's organizations of Stirling Avenue and First Mennonite churches in Kitchener, Ontario, which had continued to meet together. In some congregations, church business was conducted in such a manner that the female sewing-circle leadership was elected by male church members at their annual meetings, with women sometimes in attendance but not voting. While women's autonomy was clearly limited in such a scenario, the work of the women's organization was nevertheless recognized as existing within the overall mandate of the entire congregation. At one Alberta church, during the early years, the president of the women's society was the minister's wife, with the minister opening the meetings and the church secretary handling the finances.[146] In other cases, women resisted efforts on the part of their denominational leaders to consolidate their efforts within church structures, perhaps fearing a loss of independence and authority over their own activities. Unity, of course, had its benefits but the words of one leader in a Mennonite newspaper may have instilled some worry for local, self-determining women's groups: Benjamin Ewert said, "Our sewing societies are being considered branches of the congregations and thus also as branches of our conference.... It is desirable that they unite in each province...."[147]

Lorna Shantz Bergey recalled that men often attended the annual meetings of the Ontario women's sewing circles, sometimes to provide a devotional or meditation—a gender-specific task—or to drive women who did not yet have their licences, also apparently a gender-specific function. In the case of women who did drive, male car-parkers were deemed necessary to assist women to maximize the space in the church parking lot.[148] In the earlier years, it was not uncommon for men to drive their wives to the meetings and remain amongst themselves while the women did their work. According to one report, the men spent their time in discussions that "solved many economic and church problems."[149] The leader of one local women's group in fact suggested that the men might be jealous of the women's biweekly get-togethers and she expressed the hope that "our husbands do not begrudge us this pleasure."[150]

The assistance of men could be a mixed blessing, however. One woman, in recalling the 1940s when men drove women to their meetings, remarked: "The fathers would, or so we thought, look after the little ones while we ladies sewed. Most of the time, though, the men became so involved in their games and conversations that they forgot all about the children and we mothers ended up with several little ones at our feet."[151] "Several" might be an understatement, given the size of Mennonite families at least in the early years of women's organizations; writing about the history of the mission society at Morden Bergthaler Mennonite Church, Susan Hiebert points out that the fourteen women who started the society in 1931 had ninety children between them.[152] The "Willing Helpers Ladies Aid" in Alberta considered themselves "liberated" when they moved their meetings to evenings so that their husbands could stay home and "babysit," and in Leamington, Ontario, Wednesday evenings came to be called "Ladies Night Out" because that was when the women's societies met and men were expected to stay at home.[153] Of course, leaving the men at home while women went out, a reversal of space for both genders, might also have been a deterrent for women to organize. At the sewing circle established in the Markham area in 1917, it was customary for older girls and young married women to stay home in order to ensure that husbands and fathers were fed, while the older women gathered elsewhere to sew. The president of the circle, Ida Reesor Hoover, however, took her daughter along with her since "They set out Father's dinner for him, and he could fry potatoes."[154]

In the early years, women often had to defend their right to organize, as if there was something inherently subversive about it, even if the subversion was limited to expecting men to take on minimal domestic responsibilities in their absence. Reporting on the beginnings of women's work in the Evangelical Mennonite Conference in 1925, Gladys Isaac Fast reported, "Possibly this was looked upon with some skepticism by a number of people in our conference at that time." She went on to say that some years later two women were "stalking" through their village, canvassing for members for a local sewing circle, and carried with them a written statement from a leading minister granting the group liberty to engage in material support for Mennonite Central Committee.[155] Katie Funk Wiebe remarked that while "men's activities in the church have always been self-justifying," women have always had to appeal to notions of the greater social good or Christian service in order to justify their work.[156] In actual fact, the act of meeting together as women was perhaps the greatest motivation for women to organize, particularly in the era when women lived substantial distances from one another in rural areas.

For most women, participating in women's organizations was a spiritual activity as much as a material one. As Maria Vogt Derksen commented, "the danger is there that the woman in the hum-drum of her everyday tasks and mundane duties from early morning till night, becomes spiritually famished." The "Ladies' Aid," she continued, provided women the recreation and relief that were of "great personal value."[157] In the days before mass-circulation magazines and other media inundated women with advice and instruction, the sewing circle created a context in which women could share recipes and remedies, discuss parenting issues, and exchange expertise in household management. As members of the same congregation, undoubtedly women also discussed church issues and politics at their meetings, thus finding a venue in which they could voice opinions and share ideas on matters about which they were officially supposed to be silent.

For women in rural, isolated communities, the impetus to begin meeting arose from the need to do material mutual aid, but it was also a social outlet for women with few other opportunities to communicate with one another. The gatherings, however infrequent, were "a necessary social outlet for ... hard-working farm wives" and were "even therapeutic."[158] When a sewing circle was organized at Port Rowan, Ontario, in 1926, its explicit purpose was to create 'fellowship' among new immigrants. As a chronicler of the church's history stated: "a feeling of loneliness is often experienced when one moves to a new country with a foreign language, and as a result of this a deep need for fellowship with those of your own kind develops."[159] To the extent that older and younger women interacted in the groups, they also represented a training ground in domestic skills, according to this comment: "A beautiful and clean piece of handwork by a young girl is like a letter of recommendation. She will later also keep her husband's clothes and her household neat and clean."[160] Sex-specific organizations thus also served to reinforce clearly delineated gender roles and, as such, were less threatening for both women and men.

Women's organizations were sometimes criticized as 'gossip centres' or 'coffee klatsches' by those who believed that any endeavour that drew women away from their homes was a threat to the social order. In response to the amount of time women were spending to raise money for a new church roof in the late 1940s, one male member penned a poem that contained these lines: "Why do they sew so much? / It's just to pass the time, / They only gossip and turn their heads."[161] One woman countered such accusations by (sarcastically) noting that modern conveniences like the telephone gave women a sufficient outlet for discussing the latest scandals without having to create organized meetings to do so. Her 1958 protest went on: "We seem to become knit together in one large female family as we participate in the devotions. As our fingers stich [sic] love, and sympathy into the quilts and garments our tongues are certainly not idle, but our talks consist largely of wholesome, friendly interest in our neighbours."[162] And the women indeed viewed their work as crucial and central to the life of the church, even if it was trivialized as an auxiliary or 'gossip centre.' This is evident in the descriptions of obstacles overcome and hardships confronted in carrying out their work, as the following impassioned comment by the leader of a Steinbach, Manitoba, women's group indicates: "Sometimes we have difficulties and problems to overcome—cold north winds blow so that we freeze, or sometimes we become wary, especially when health fails. But as we cast our eyes upon Jesus we will not sink in the waves of the sea. Everything will again be fine."[163] For this woman, her women's society was a dramatic bulwark against competing forces, such as household labour that might have compelled her to stay at home, or the suspicions of church leaders that women were furthering the work of the church outside the institutional reins of control.

Indeed, as has been argued by Gloria Neufeld Redekop and others, the identity of the women's organization as a "parallel" church, in which women carried leadership and authority, meant that women could envision their material labour and social interaction within a discourse of 'ministry.' For Leah Weber Cressman, for example, her sewing machine was described as "her altar and pulpit."[164] One woman wrote in the women's newsletter of Mennonite Central Committee that "Our faithful women who toil and sacrifice in the home or in a sewing circle group have the opportunity of giving the Master's touch of love through the garments they send forth."[165] For women who wanted to be central participants in the ministry of the church, sewing and sending clothing to the needy was not just a material act, but also a gesture of love and redemption, at least so it was perceived by women themselves. Some women interpreted the spiritual ministry mandate of their organizations quite directly: at Stirling Avenue Mennonite Church in Kitchener, the women made lists of people they thought the pastor should visit and themselves paid visits to individuals who were spiritually and not just materially in need.[166] While the devotional aspects of women's meetings closely paralleled the features of worship in their churches—hymn singing, Bible reading, spoken meditation, prayer—as Redekop notes, unlike in a formal church setting, the women's society "became a context in which women could determine how their spiritual needs would be met. They could study the Bible for themselves, decide which songs they would sing, and choose which religious books they would read." In essence, they "conducted their own church."[167]

Women's church organizations received a boost during the Second World War and after. Indeed, the wartime and post-war era was described as a "golden age" for Mennonite women's societies.[168] Though sewing circles had functioned in individual churches for years already, it was at the mid-twentieth century that many began to consolidate within the structures of provincial and national conference bodies, once individuals at the helm of those structures recognized that women's societies were not a threat and, indeed, were a significant resource for the church's charitable mandate during a time when worldwide needs were great. As an example, provincial women's societies of the Conference of Mennonites in Canada first met all together in 1941. They subsequently organized under a national umbrella as Canadian Women in Mission in 1952. Women's groups in BC organized as British Columbia Women's Conference in 1939 while the Manitoba Provincial Women's Conference officially organized in 1944 after a meeting two years earlier of forty women from ten congregations. Simultaneously, many local groups emerged during the war and post-war period. The need for material relief for war sufferers, for Mennonite refugees from the Soviet Union and eastern Europe who went to South America and Canada, and the growth of both foreign and home missions meant that the financial and material offerings of women's groups were in high demand. Impatient for their own denominational relief structures to kick into gear when war broke out, many women's groups began generating wartime relief supplies under the auspices of the Red Cross already in 1939, before Canada even entered the war. During the war itself, women's groups generated thousands of dollars' worth of goods and funds that Mennonite volunteer relief workers distributed in Europe and England.

After the war, the sheer number of women in many urban congregations increased as a result of post-war immigration, meaning that entirely new groups were formed, composed almost exclusively of the German-speaking newcomers. The older congregations found that one circle couldn't possibly meet all the interests and needs of an ever-widening span of ages among the women. So in addition to the traditional *naehverein*, or sewing society, groups with new mandates and formats appeared during the 1950s and 1960s. Organizational names such as 'Willing Helpers,' 'Mary-Martha,' and 'Dorcas Circle' were popular, and groups were increasingly known as mission societies or ladies auxiliaries rather than sewing circles. As well, organizations were formed for girls in their teens and younger, who did many of the same types of activities as their mothers.

In the post-war years, the activities of women's organizations comprised a dizzying array of fundraising for local social service projects, overseas mission and relief work, and individual congregational needs. For instance, in 1957 the Ontario Women's Mission and Service Auxiliary projects included the following: "Ontario Hebrew Mission, Fairview Mennonite Home, Rockway Mennonite School, Ailsa Craig Boys Farm, Mennonite Central Committee, Milk for Korea, Newfoundland, Nursing Education, Foreign Literature, Government surplus food, and many missionary projects such as India, South America and Bragado Bible School, Voluntary Service, Navaho Indians, Puerto Rico, Brazil Mission Home, London, England, Japan."[169] Along with the breadth of projects and activities, the reports of women's organizations were usually very detailed numerically, as if the sheer quantity of output legitimized the existence of the societies. The 1958 report of the Dorcas Mission Circle of Vancouver was typical: "Contributions to the Mennonite Central Committee include: sixty-six rolls of bandages, several hundred white squares for the leper mission, four large blankets, seventy-three diapers and thirty-two nighties. Articles of clothing for Hungarian refugees totalled 193. Twenty-one layettes were sent to the mission field in Africa. Quilt squares for the native women on the Arizona mission field totalled 1,694."[170] Pride also increased when women's groups could quantify their activity, materially and financially. In 1965 the Sewing Circles of the Evangelical Mennonite Conference reported that there were approximately forty-six different groups, which each generated about $315 annually, resulting in a total of $14,000. "This is quite a responsibility for the weaker sex!" said the female reporter.[171]

Though the work of women in the context of their organizations was central to the functioning of Mennonite churches right from the beginning, most church histories have treated their activities as a separate, even incidental, aspect of congregational life. For instance, while the women's society of the Rosenorter church group began its work in Saskatchewan in 1907, no mention of this group is made in the church's official history written in 1950. Historian Lucille Marr observes that in photographs in the newspaper *The Canadian Mennonite* during the 1950s, women sewing for relief are "faceless and nameless" whereas male leaders are identified and "shown in a variety of policy-making tasks."[172] Yet, frequently, it was women's organizational work and economic activity that undergirded the successful functioning of local churches, larger denominational institutions, and mission boards.

While much of the output of women's societies was directed to charitable causes outside their particular church communities, when there was an identifiable financial need within their own congregation, women were quick to generate funds through the sale of their domestic labour. For instance, women's groups were sometimes the ones to generate the seed money, and provide ongoing capital, towards church building projects. In her history of *Canadian Women in Mission*, Esther Patkau reports that it was two women at Sardis, British Columbia, who had the idea to begin raising money for a church building in 1931, so that the new settlers could stop meeting in each other's homes. The project began when a group of twelve women met, each contributing twenty-five cents with the promise to give five cents at each subsequent meeting. The initial fund purchased fabric from Eaton's department store for sewing into items that were auctioned, along with fruit and vegetables, for a total of $108. The proceeds were divided between missions ($35), the church building fund ($96), and seed money ($8) for new projects.[173] The church building at Aldergrove, BC, received a similar start from the women in that settlement group.

Urgent material needs in churches were frequently addressed by immediate practical action on the part of women. When the women's society at Carrot River (Saskatchewan) Mennonite Church held their first quilt raffle, they used the proceeds to purchase a new suit for the church's minister, apparently a high priority![174] When an engaged couple wished to be married in the newly constructed Steinbach (Manitoba) Mennonite Church, the Ebenezer Sewing Circle sewed and raffled a quilt "in record time" in order to raise funds for the church floor so that the couple "could walk down a shiny, brand new aisle to the marriage alter."[175] After the formation of Stirling Avenue Mennonite Church in Kitchener, Ontario, in 1924, it was the newly organized Women's Missionary Society that funded shrubbery for the church grounds, and dishes, cupboard, and stove for the kitchen; several years later they helped to pay down the mortgage.[176] Many churches relied, perhaps subconsciously, on the volunteerism of women to keep their activities going. The response of one church leader to his local conference's plea for funds is revealing: "I think I can promise the money for our congregation. The ladies' aid will not leave me in the lurch."[177] For the thirty years of its existence (1937 to 1967), the Menno Bible Institute at Didsbury, Alberta, was supported by women's groups who spent "countless hours ... canning, cleaning, painting, baking, cooking."[178]

Sometimes male leadership, for whatever reason, feared or resented the autonomy or power that this activity accorded women. In the late 1940s and early 1950s, a women's support group was responsible for cleaning, painting, and raising significant funds towards the operating costs of the Mennonite Brethren Collegiate Institute, a denominational high school in Winnipeg. They did this in part through their successful fall suppers, whereby city women cooked chickens that were donated by country women. One year some local ministers called an abrupt halt to the chicken suppers, wanting instead for a more "controlled, institutional approach" towards finances that included raising tuition and hiring cleaning and maintenance staff. Commenting on this situation, historian Frieda Esau Klippenstein says, "The differences in thinking and approach are striking. The men were getting position, policy and doctrine straight and expressing their power, while the women were quietly expressing through action what they really cared about."[179] Not all leaders were so quick to brush off the work of women in the church. Western Canadian church leader J.J. Thiessen publicly observed that "If it were not for the zeal of the women, their sacrificial service and generous giving, many projects would never have started and others would have died on the way long ago."[180]

If the public voice of the church was noticeably silent in recognizing the foundational nature of women's work, occasionally women pointed this out themselves, as in the following observation: "No congregation would manage without its women. In all of the great relief services thousands of women are active.... For the aid we received in Russia after World War I, we must probably thank women who had warm hearts and open hands."[181] One woman expressed this notion rather bitterly: "I think the women in our community have always done all the work in the churches as far as church work goes. They start out with their *Frauenverein* [women's auxiliary]. They do this or that. Anything to try and drum up some business. At first just to build the church itself, to help pay for things that are needed at the church. In fact, I think of the hours. Yet they had no say in it."[182] In 1963, in an article questioning the role of women's organizations in the church, Katie Funk Wiebe asked whether they were "merely a crutch under the arm of men?"[183] Another woman eschewed participation in the mission society at her church, partly because she disliked quilting but also she "believ[ed] that women work very hard for various Mennonite organizations without receiving the recognition that they deserve."[184] Without question, the grassroots material work and fundraising of women's organizations have provided the foundation on which a wide range of Mennonite institutions and organizations have been built.

The activities of women's organizations that involved money management, such as overseas material relief projects or local church building projects, inevitably developed the financial acumen of women individually and collectively. The first project of the consolidated women's groups in Alberta was to assist Mennonite refugee widows in Paraguay by sending $835, an undertaking that required "ingenuity" on the part of "Mrs. H.L. Sawatzky," who needed to establish "favourable rapport" with the local bank before the money could be sent.[185] In some cases, such initiative was viewed as a surprising aberration to the naïveté that women were presumed to have about money matters. As an example, during the Second World War, Ontario Mennonite women established a Cutting Room to centralize and standardize the clothing and bedding that would be sent overseas. In 1942, a specialized pattern-cutting machine was purchased, a machine operator was hired, and a large inventory of fabric maintained. Ready-to-sew cut cloth was then distributed to women's groups who would produce finished clothing for war sufferers in Europe. The first cutter, Barbara Eby, was paid two cents per garment, and the sewing circles were charged two and a half cents per cut garment purchased. The small half-cent profit thus generated went into the coffers of the district women's organization.[186]

In order to establish a sizeable inventory, the women received several interest-free loans from the Non-Resistant Relief Organization (NRRO), an all-male inter-Mennonite organization established in 1917. While the loans may have undermined the women's autonomy over decisions regarding the project, the financial boost allowed the Cutting Room to move its operations from a farmhouse to a Mennonite-run relief depot in Kitchener and meant that operator Alice Snyder (who succeeded Eby) could run the machine for an eight-hour day. Despite ups and downs, financially and in terms of personnel, by the 1950s the Cutting Room began generating a profit and in 1957 was able to purchase $21,000 worth of materials.[187] The women in charge saw little point in maintaining the $3300 loan on their books while revenues accumulated, and so repaid the loan, much to the surprise of the NRRO, who never expected to see their money again. A short time later the Cutting Room in turn provided an interest-free loan of $2000 when Mennonite Central Committee (MCC) built its Kitchener headquarters and took over the work of the NRRO.[188]

Despite the success and longevity of the Cutting Room—still in existence today—it never received an equal visibility or reporting status with the other relief programs of the NRRO and MCC. In the decades that followed the post-war expansion of female volunteerism in the church, the funds that women's organizations contributed to larger institutional coffers grew to the point that the denomination could no longer ignore or overlook the significance of their labour. In a 1972 newspaper article entitled "Women's Conference More than Peripheral," it was noted that Canadian Women in Mission (a national coalition of Mennonite women's groups from one historic stream) had raised $245,000 for that year, an amount that represented two-thirds of the total budget for the related denominational body, Conference of Mennonites in Canada.[189]

Women indeed learned administrative and bureaucratic skills through their work in societies. At the same time, they may have also resisted the bureaucratizing of their own structures. In 1950, when a vote was taken by the Leamington, Ontario, society on the question of amalgamating all the women's societies in Ontario, the minutes recorded that "the majority voted for a quiet, withdrawn, continuous performance as it had been until then."[190] In 1957 the same group resisted the registration of each individual society by number, with the remark that "this is not at all romantic nor appealing," yet rationalized this administrative move by saying "in Revelation we read that at the end of the world the visible signs will be numbers."[191]

The existence of separate women's organizations has sometimes been derided as confining women within gender-limiting, domestic roles. Yet many of the projects supported by women directly and indirectly affirmed the professional and educational roles of women outside the home. For instance, in 1942 the Manitoba sewing circles collectively agreed to support a scholarship fund that would enable capable but financially needy young women to further their education at the Mennonite high school in Gretna.[192] Other examples of this include significant interest and support that went towards single women opting for a career in mission work. The memoirs and correspondence of numerous female Mennonite missionaries offer evidence and appreciation of the ongoing letters and financial donations received from local women's groups. Undoubtedly, the hard-working women who formed the core of labour at the Toronto Mennonite Mission in the early twentieth century were delighted to receive an electric washing machine from a Mennonite women's mission auxiliary in 1923;[193] only other women would have understood the significance of lightening the effort of laundry. Helen Willms and Mary Janzen, who worked as nurses for Mennonite Pioneer Mission at an Aboriginal community in northern Manitoba in the 1950s, were the recipients of numerous letters of support, cash donations, and material aid. For instance, in 1955 a "Mission Club" of ten-year-old girls sent a parcel of unspecified handwork to the nurses, writing, "will you please tell us when you are in need because we will be willing to help you out if possible," and that same year, the Flying Needles Sewing Circle from Steinbach, Manitoba, sent a money order for $10.[194]

In the 1970s and onwards, the need for church organizations specific to women was called into question. Some Mennonite feminists asked whether women's 'auxiliaries' existed as separate entities because of choice or because of segregation. And if the latter, they said, it was time that sex-specific organizations ended.[195] The decline in interest and activity of women's organizations reflected the busyness of women's lives and the fact that many married women were now working at part-time or full-time jobs. One woman said, "There are so many more interesting things which attract our attention, like taking some night classes at the university, joining a community choir, going to the 'Y'...." Rather than wanting "to get out for an evening, ... we are now looking for an evening where we can stay home with the family."[196] A different concern was raised in 1963 by an Ontario Mennonite minister who admonished the women of his church "not to exchange [their] knitting bags for briefcases,"[197] fearing, correctly so, that the waning of women's organizations was also a reflection of women's resistance to the placing of gender limitations on their activities and involvements.

In her study of Mennonite women's organizations within two Russian Mennonite subgroups, Gloria Neufeld Redekop notes that while 102 new societies were founded during the period of "flowering" in the 1950s and 1960s, only twenty-six new groups were established during the period of "decline" between 1970 and 1987.[198] Even while the membership of women's organizations within churches was declining, calls were made for the ongoing validity and need for those organizations. To oblige the growing number of women in the workforce, many congregations formed new groups that met in the evenings. Other new groups sought to accommodate women with young children by finding meeting times when the latter could be left at home with their fathers. One woman argued that for housewives, "ladies' aid" was comparable to work outside the home, and called it her second "job."[199]

The shift in agenda and decline in material output of women's organizations also came about when relief organizations began asking for more financial and fewer material donations. While such an approach was viewed as a positive reinforcement for indigenous control over overseas and local mission and development programs, it minimized the important role of actually collecting and producing material goods that was central to women's work in the church. While some women mourned the loss of activity, others decried the traditional purpose of sex-specific women's organizations exactly because of that emphasis. For instance, one woman rejected the 'sewing circle' philosophy: "It was all wrong. Men gave only money. Why shouldn't women also only give? Why all that work to raise money? The whole thing had to do with position. Women were being obedient, serving, making men comfortable. I rebelled against it."[200] Needless to say, difference of opinion among women on the mandate of their organizations was mainly a generational issue. Older women accustomed to the practical and material aspect of quilting, sewing, and mending were less comfortable in organizations that were oriented towards fundraising and self-education. Gradual name changes, from 'sewing circle' or 'mission society' to 'women's auxiliary,' 'fellowship,' or 'friendship circle,' were indicative of transition, as were developments that saw one large women's organization in a congregation or district split into groups according to age and/or interest.[201] Towards the end of the twentieth century, women's organizations increasingly focused their goals on spiritual and social issues—child abuse, pornography, alcoholism, for instance—more than material production. And in some locales, the activity shifted away from fundraising and outreach to Bible and other book study and personal development.

Among the reasons for questioning the purpose of Mennonite women's organizations, or at least their shift away from sewing circles or fundraising mission societies, was the fact that by the 1970s women were slowly finding their way into elected or appointed positions on church committees and boards—at least in some churches—and also as employees in Mennonite organizations. The pace at which women entered decision-making circles within church-related organizations was somewhat slower than the evolution of their voice within actual congregations, however. For instance, the Mennonite Benevolent Society of British Columbia, a church-related association that operated homes for seniors and whose employees were primarily women, had only men on its board of directors from its inception in 1953 until 1993. This deficiency was not for a lack of qualified women; in 1982 a woman with extensive experience on hospital boards and auxiliaries and who was also an accountant was not elected.[202]

Yet, by the early 1970s, women were beginning to publicly voice a concern over their lack of representation in the higher levels of church and related institutions. For instance, a 1972 study of Mennonite Central Committee—probably the largest inter-Mennonite organization—found a decided imbalance in the number of women in top administrative positions. There were forty-eight men as full-time administrators compared to three women, and the latter all at material aid centres, where women traditionally had a prominent role. Conversely, in clerical positions—defined as secretaries, bookkeepers, receptionists, filing clerks—there were six women, zero men in the Canadian office, and twelve women and one man in the Akron, Pennsylvania, headquarters. At the board level, MCC Canada had twenty-eight members, one of whom was female.[203] Similar statistics applied to the General Conference Mennonite Church office in 1972; although women outnumbered men thirty-five to twenty-two, all clerical employees were women and only nine of thirty administrators were women. Discrepancies were also noticed in salaries, whereby most men received a 'head of household' allowance on top of their base pay while women did not.[204] A follow-up survey in 1973 of overall structures in the Mennonite Church found a ratio of men to women of 7.8:1; if the sixteen women working in specifically women's programs were excluded, the ratio rose to about twelve to one.[205] As for women in other labour sectors of Canadian society, Mennonite women had hit a glass ceiling within their church organizations, one that would begin to crack open only nearer to the end of the twentieth century.

RELIGIOUS LIFE AND SPIRITUALITY

The privilege and right to speak, vote, and be elected or employed in Mennonite congregations and organizations are not, of course, an indication of Mennonite women's personal religiosity. As noted earlier, aside from the material, concrete activities of women's organizations, most groups also functioned as venues for the expression and nurture of women's spiritual lives. One woman recalled that her mother's "ladies fellowship" was "all about ... studying the word of God ... something to guide their life."[206] Yet institutions, be they congregations, missions, or women's organizations, were certainly not the only settings in which religious faith was experienced or expressed. For instance, the written word, whether in private journals, letters, and diaries, or published articles and poems in Mennonite periodicals, was an important and sanctioned channel for women to communicate and express religious beliefs. Selma Redekopp was one woman for whom private journal writing was an outlet for intense—some called her fanatical—religious ideas and convictions. Born in Russia in 1887, she migrated to Canada in the 1920s and, while already very pious as a young woman, at mid-life she felt she was called by God to prophesy the second coming of Christ. Her zealous testimonies, both verbal and written, were viewed by members of her family and community as extremely eccentric, and eventually her family had her sign a contract that she would desist from her aggressive preaching and evangelism in public and in church.

Selma was caught between what she felt was a personal call from God to be a prophet and community norms that expected a quiet piety of women demonstrated in physical labour and works of charity. She urged women to respond to calls to prophesy, even while she recognized that her "greatest problem" was her husband's difficulty in accepting "all this writing of mine."[207] Despite his disfavour, he bought ink and paper for her writings, which were "meticulously [bound] ... with glue, yarn, and her sewing machine into large folders made of brown wrapping paper or bags."[208] Selma's emphatic forms of expression and extreme religious beliefs, while acceptable in many male evangelists —often praised for their ability to rouse an audience of restrained Mennonites into emotional religious fervour—were considered inappropriate when displayed by a woman. Contributing to the gendered perception of Selma as eccentric were her interest in world affairs and regular reading of the newspaper, "quite unusual for a Mennonite woman of her age."[209] Not surprisingly, Selma questioned the practice of the Mennonite Brethren church, of which she was a member, of allowing women missionaries to preach overseas but forbidding women to do so in North American churches.[210] Prevented from the public preaching and prophesying that she felt compelled to do, Selma channelled her mental creativity and spiritual thoughts into writing.

The individuals who likely experienced Selma's religious tutelage most closely were her six stepchildren. Informal religious training and faith development most often occurred in the household and in family circles, where mothers and grandmothers had greater freedom—indeed, were expected—to act in a teaching capacity. Helena Penner recalled that her mother was "the custodian of faith" in their home, regularly reading sermons and singing hymns with the family. For Helena, the theological meaning of the sermons was less important than the enjoyment of hearing her mother "reading any kind of story."[211] Emphasizing the importance of religious teaching in the home was a way of finding a place for female spiritual influence outside a public sphere. As one congregational history noted, "The teaching of grace at table was only one of the many ways in which women put into action the preaching from the pulpit, which would have been empty indeed if the tenets of the faith had not been present in the church community, through the family."[212] Because they were more accustomed to leading religious practice in domestic space, women may have viewed the home in more sacred terms, and, indeed, may have more readily fostered a private and unstructured religious life.

The centrality of the household and family to religious formation was especially true in settings in which formalized church life was geographically distant, infrequent, or disrupted by circumstances of political repression, war, or migration. In pioneer settings, while immigrants expended all their energies at building homes and working the land, home-based ritual became central in perpetuating religious life before the structures, physical and organizational, of Mennonite churches could be established. Pamela E. Klassen suggests that women who grew up in Ukraine under the Stalin regime, during which religion was outlawed and most preachers were exiled, developed a "domestic religion" based on the personal and private rituals of prayer, song, and Bible reading, rather than on formal institutional practice.[213] For this group of Mennonites, not only were ministers and men generally more scarce in the decade of the 1930s, but some sources suggest that women were at less risk in performing religious rites and rituals. For example, Justina D. Neufeld recalled that, at her uncle's funeral, one of the women read from the Bible because "men would not risk reading from the Bible for fear of being reported and arrested."[214]

During the brief period of German occupation of western Ukraine in 1941 to 1943, when religious practice was restored, women challenged conventionality and took unprecedented roles in public worship. But when they fled their homes in the fall of 1943 and spent years as refugees moving westward across Europe, religious expression was once again privatized and maintained as mothers and grandmothers led their children in prayer, hymns, and Bible reading as signposts of hope for the future in the midst of despair. Katie Friesen, whose father disappeared during the Stalin purges, recalled her mother's informal transmission of religious belief:

> My brother and I had a devoted Christian mother, who by her example and instruction radiated the love of Christ. She passed her faith on to us. She taught us to love and pray and gave us her very best. I can still see her standing in the corner of the room by the shelf on which a kerosene lamp stood, reading from the bible and her book of meditations. After blowing

out the light, she would kneel and pray at length and then join me in bed. She instructed us concerning the special celebrations of the church: Christmas, Easter, Pentecost, and Thanksgiving.[215]

Families—indeed, entire village communities—that became accustomed to privatized female-led religious ritual during this era experienced a sharp disjuncture when a process of "religious rehabilitation" in European refugee camps and later in Canada undermined the value of the spiritual guidance and teaching of mothers and grandmothers.[216] Even while female refugees experienced a deconstruction and reconstitution of their religious gender roles through the process of trauma, displacement, and migration, their ties to a faith-based collection of symbols and relationships strengthened and empowered them to deal with the incredible hardships they faced.

A somewhat similar pattern occurred much later in the twentieth century, when small numbers of new Canadians, mostly refugees from wartorn parts of the world such as southeast Asia and Central America, established Mennonite congregations with new ethnic identities. In one of these churches in Kitchener, Ontario—whose Hispanic members were mainly from Central America—women predominated for a time in the 1990s in both leadership and numbers; of about fifty adults and children who were regularly involved, there were only about five adult men. In this case, the physical and psychological dislocation of the migration experience, which also, typically, disrupted gender roles, combined with the circumstances that surrounded new church formation, nurtured a female religious culture.[217] In the same city, a Mennonite congregation of Hmong refugees from Laos formed in the early 1980s. According to sociologist Daphne Winland, religious beliefs and practices—both Christian and indigenous Hmong—enabled Hmong Mennonite women to negotiate the challenges of migration and settlement in significant ways. Although Hmong women were reportedly "slow to take an interest in the church" at first because they "saw it primarily as a male domain," as they were drawn into the programs of the church as well as the perception of a strong family orientation in Mennonite culture, women came to dominate in numbers in this group as well.[218] For Hmong women, church involvement offered "the chance to socialize ... share information and make use of educational facilities and other services...."[219] The social network available within the church community as well as a clearly defined relationship with a supportive and protecting God offered refugee women, whether mid-century Soviet Mennonite or late-century Hmong, a sense of belonging and knowledge that they weren't alone as they struggled with the hardships of settlement and memories of the past.

Women's spiritual authority (albeit limited) within their households could also be undermined by the infiltration of outside theological trends into Mennonite religious thinking. Historian Delbert Plett remarked that it was the 'matriarchs' in Mennonite communities who clung most strongly to the "tried and proven traditions" of their culture, and were also the ones with the most to lose when new religious cultures entered their church communities and threatened to undo those traditions. He noted that influential senior women frequently lost their "relative power and prestige" when forces such as evangelical fundamentalism entered Mennonite communities at the mid-twentieth century.[220] As traditional home-based religious rituals and practices were threatened by modernism and new theological trends, a woman-centred domestic spirituality that was a central, if unacknowledged, aspect of being Mennonite may have suffered a decline.

If women perceived the home as a space where they could enact their religion in equal if different ways from those at church, then staying away from church altogether may have been easy to justify. In the case of some farm women, Sunday was valued as a day's rest from the gruelling week of work. Such was the motivation of Maria Heinrichs, who initially stopped attending church because of exhaustion, but later in life (1940s) continued the habit of staying away. Her rationale? "I'll read my Bible and religious papers at home. The people sit in church but do they hear anything that is said? Is church the only place where God can be found?" she said.[221] Maria's daughter Susan Klassen was also remembered as being frequently absent for Sunday morning service; though ostensibly her excuse had been to prepare the noon meal for her large family and potential company, on later reflection her son had wondered whether there was a "deeper root" for his mother's behaviour.[222] In other communities, during agricultural harvest season, it was not unusual for women to stay home on Sunday to prepare a week's worth of food required for a team of workers, in addition to their own families. Even when religious practice was formalized in designated church buildings, it was common and acceptable in some groups, such as the Kleine Gemeinde, for women with young children to remain at home rather than attend church.[223] In such cases, family devotional rituals within the home were crucial for the proper religious upbringing of children.

Certain church ordinances that had highly gendered overtones may have also served on occasion to keep women away from church on a Sunday. Foot washing was a ritual practised by many, though not all, Mennonites churches until it began to decline in the 1960s and 1970s (though recently it has experienced an upsurge in some congregations). Normally twice a year, members of a congregation would wash each other's feet as a re-enactment of Jesus washing the disciples' feet and also as a symbol of humility and service to one another. Because it was deemed inappropriate for a man to wash the feet of a woman other than his wife, and vice versa, the ceremony was segregated. Inevitably the necessary disrobing created more challenges for women than for men. Katie Funk Wiebe recalled that in her rural Saskatchewan church, "The women went downstairs for this because taking off stockings held up by homemade circles of elastic (maybe even canning jar rubbers) or girdle garters might be embarrassing."[224] Foot washing posed peculiar problems in light of the emphasis on female modesty, as Ruth Reesor recalled: "I don't know how the women protected their modesty while removing their stockings. I know the communion table had a table cloth that reached the floor and I also know that not a single inch of the skin on the legs of any of the women were seen by anyone except the woman who was washing a sister's feet."[225] For women who spent much of their time cleaning up after and serving others—in continuous foot-washing mode, one might suggest—the ritual may have seemed like an extension of their domestic roles as opposed to the completely humble and selfless act that it was meant to be and was in fact for the men of the congregation. Of course, one might quickly point out that in some other Christian denominations, women were excluded from foot washing altogether.

In many religious traditions, such as Hinduism, Judaism, and indigenous tribal religions, women are predominant in organizing and performing religious rituals in the home. This is perhaps even more the case when women are not active in the public realms of church. As participants in an iconoclastic denomination not given to ritual performance, Mennonite women perhaps had less opportunity to formally enact religious practice, even within the home, than did, for instance, Jewish women who presided over such home-based religious observances as the Seder meal. Mennonite women had fewer opportunities to be explicitly central in maintaining religious traditions. One could argue nevertheless that certain domestic tasks in themselves became akin to religious ritual. The baking of Ukrainian paska bread at Easter, by Mennonite women of Russian background, marked a religious event, the resurrection of Christ; the baking of peppernuts at Christmas was also a culinary ritual specifically tied to events in the church calendar. As noted earlier, wives of ministers and deacons in particular had the important function of baking the communion wafers or bread. This particular custom was one way in which women crossed the boundaries between private household and public church ritual. Maria Martens Klassen, whose husband was a non-ordained church leader in rural Saskatchewan in the mid-twentieth century, described it thus: "On the Saturday before our communion service, I bake fresh bread. Carefully, I shaped several loaves of suitable size and hope that at least one will come out perfectly. Before taking it to church, I trim the crusts. Just as in the old country, we pluck a piece off the loaf as we partake of the elements."[226]

Lacking formal church rituals in which women played significant parts, Mennonite women themselves may have, perhaps subconsciously, generated their own religious customs. Art historian Nancy-Lou Patterson described a set of aprons made by Katherine Suderman Wiens in 1974 for women and girls serving at the Russian Mennonite church in Waterloo, Ontario. Patterson observed that the aprons, decorated with crocheted medallions, "are a kind of ceremonial garb; some have even been decorated in black ribbons (for funerals) and green ribbons (for weddings) to make their ceremonial and symbolic significance clear."[227] Patterson's observations lead one to speculate that women who served meals in church may have viewed their labour in a certain sacramental way.

Even less conventional manifestations of spiritual authority existed in some rural Swiss Mennonite communities. Charming—also called *brauche*, or pow-powing—was a form of healing with early modern European origins that was deeply imbued with spiritualism. Because of its associations with the supernatural and even witchcraft, it was not sanctioned by the church but was widely accepted among Swiss Mennonite and Amish communities in Ontario. An example of the vagueness with which charming is referred to in historical accounts is found in a biographical account of Magdalena Reschly Nafziger, a midwife and healer in early twentieth-century Ontario; when asked if she "charmed" as well, people responded, "I am almost sure she did," or "I think so, but I don't know for what."[228] Often it was women, like Barbara Bowman Shuh, mentioned at the outset of the chapter, who received the 'gift' of charming and were thus sought out for their healing abilities. To the extent that the incantations recited and gestures performed in the act of charming had spiritual connotations, such women were also exercising a certain informal and domestic religious role.

While certain women were respected for their abilities, some women came under suspicion for this. This may have been the case for a 'Miss Metzger' who, along with several men from a conservative Mennonite community in Ontario, was excommunicated from the church in the 1900s for an alleged affair with her employer. According to one historian, the situation, which involved a court case and accusations of libel between several Mennonite ministers, could have been complicated by Miss Metzger's "charming (witch-craft) abilities." Apparently her reputation included stories like that of an individual whose buggy wheel stopped going around when he drove past her place.[229] The co-existence of Mennonite-Christian beliefs and practices with non-Christian spiritual traditions would be embodied (in the same Ontario community) close to a century later when Hmong refugee women migrated from Laos to Canada, where they joined the Mennonite church. Among these newcomers was Blia Yang, who was simultaneously deeply involved in her Mennonite congregation and described as a "model of Christian devotion and service," and also was a shaman who drew on Lao Hmong indigenous religious practices for healing purposes.[230]

As self-identified or externally labelled Mennonites, the women of this study were, by virtue of the Mennonite label, religious individuals. Yet, over their 200-year presence in Canada, Mennonite women expressed this religiosity in multiple and varied ways. Women like Selma Redekopp or 'Miss Metzger' possessed religious feelings and gifts that were considered peculiar, and perhaps dangerous, by their families and communities. Most women, on the other hand, functioned within their churches, at least outwardly, in a manner appropriate and acceptable to the official gender constructs of the Mennonite denomination, as decreed in various ways by different subgroups. They were publicly silent, visibly pious, socially submissive, and industrious in their material support of Mennonite congregations and institutions. Even so, they gained inward satisfaction in the power they possessed to create a sacred environment within their homes and, also, in the opportunity to create parallel, female-centred religious cultures in the context of women's organizations.

It was in the realm of church life that the situational nature of socially created gender norms is most clearly revealed. Women could be leaders in churches, but only when men were temporarily unavailable. Women could preach and prophesy on the mission field, but only because they were well out of sight, and when male missionaries were fewer in number. Women could provide the most foundational basis for an individual's ongoing religious development, but only if that teaching was to children or other women. Women refugees and immigrants could lead group worship, but only when men were exiled, missing, or dead. Exigency was, in many respects, then, the primary condition that allowed women to give audible voice to their internally held religious beliefs and ideas, before the onset of an era in which external pressures unsettled the gender inequality in Mennonite church life. Beginning in the 1950s, it was the reality of women's increased activity outside the home, be it in the workforce, in higher education, or in volunteer labour, that pressed forward the debate on women's voice in the church. And it was the feminist movement of the 1970s and onward that ultimately pushed open the door to women in official church ministry positions.

Mennonite women, southern Manitoba, 1910s. (MHC—Peter G. Hamm Collection)

"Sunshine Girls" postcard of Ontario Mennonite women at the beach, 1905. (MAO)

Ontario wedding before 'plain' dress era, 1902. (MAO)

Wedding photo, Manitoba, early 20th century. (MHC)

Wedding photo of Ontario bishop Oscar Burkholder and Laura May Shantz, 1913. (MAO)

Wedding photo, Manitoba, 1920. (CMBS)

Informal funeral photo, Manitoba, early 20th century. (MHC—Peter G. Hamm Collection)

Gender imbalance in class of 1946 at Ontario Mennonite Bible School, Kitchener. (MAO)

Ontario women on their day off while working as domestics in California, 1911. (MAO)

Helen Loewen Warkentin, missionary to India,
c1920s. (CMBS)

Helen Willms, long time missionary nurse in
northern Manitoba and Taiwan, c1950s. (MHC)

Gathering at Mary Martha girls' home for Mennonite women workers in the city, Winnipeg, 1920s. (CMBS)

Helena Penner (second row left), first Mennonite woman graduate of University of Manitoba, with classmates, 1895. (MHC)

City missionary Anna Thiessen and sewing class, Winnipeg, 1916. (CMBS)

Women's society, North End Mennonite Brethren Church, Winnipeg, c1930. (CMBS)

Women's sewing circle, Erb Street Mennonite Church, Waterloo, 1932. (MAO)

Sorting material aid bundles at Mennonite Central Committee relief depot, Ontario, 1955. (MAO)

Fraktur painting by Ontario artist Anna Weber, 1873. (MAO)

Old Order Mennonite women quilting, 1978. (Waterloo Region Record, Ontario Canada)

Susie Reddekopp, packing for return trip to Mexico from Ontario, 2000. (Waterloo Region Record, Ontario Canada)

Hmong Mennonite women in traditional dress. (Chung Vang)

Ontario Mennonite woman who enlisted
in the Canadian Women's Army Corps,
1942. (EKMHA)

Midwife Frieda Isaak on her way to a
delivery, northern Ontario, 1930s. (EKMHA)

Mennonite women domestics in uniform, 1930s. (CMBS)

Making teaballs for Ontario Mennonite Relief Sale, 1970. (MAO)

Selling eggs at Kitchener Farmers' Market, 1948. (David Hunsberger)

Mennonite woman picking raspberries in the Fraser Valley, British Columbia, 1948. (Anne Funk)

CHAPTER FOUR

Nonconformists, Nonresistors, and Citizens: Women Living in the World

Malinda Bricker (dates unknown), an Ontario resident, was a convert to the Mennonite Church in 1895. Though initially inclined to join the Methodists, she could not reconcile herself to their practice of infant baptism and the swearing of oaths, religious customs that were rejected by Mennonites. At the time, Mennonites of some subgroups were just beginning to enforce a dress code of 'plain' attire, including a head covering, cape dress, and bonnet, that was part of church membership. That Malinda was reluctant to adopt the dress code is evident in a letter to her mentor, Mennonite evangelist John S. Coffman. She wrote, "I made a cap for myself and I want to go to Berlin [Kitchener] tomorrow if I can to get a bonnet. If I would live to please men or even myself I would never join the Mennonite Church as you well know, but I want to live for Christ and for this reason I join this church...."[1] After her baptism into the church, Malinda's plain dress set her apart from surrounding society and identified her clearly as a Mennonite, as it would for many other women in the decades that followed.

Helen Erb (1918–2005), a young Ontario woman, married her boyfriend Clayton Burkholder at Christmas 1943, during his second leave from Alternative Service camp in British Columbia. As a Mennonite conscientious objector (CO) to war, Clayton Burkholder earned fifty cents a day, first working on road construction in northern Ontario and later as a forestry worker on the west coast. After a full year apart, and with no prospects in sight for Clayton's return home, Helen chose to relocate to Vancouver Island in British Columbia, where she found employment doing housework in Victoria, earning fifty cents an hour. Like other Canadian women during the Second World War, she participated in a reversal of gender roles that saw her become the primary breadwinner, even while she also maintained a more traditional female role of caretaker and nurturer by bringing with her to BC a steamer trunk full of home canning that nourished the stomachs and spirits of the CO men in nearby camps.[2]

In 1948 Elfrieda Klassen Dyck (1917–2004) led approximately 750 Mennonite refugees away from the war-ravaged European continent to new homes in South America. The nearly two-month cross-Atlantic voyage on the ill-fated *Charlton Monarch* was beset with difficulties that included many sick passengers, most of whom were women and children, numerous ship break-downs, a mutiny by the crew, and various other obstacles and delays. This journey, about which Elfrieda would years later remark, "I can't believe I did this," was one of numerous courageous and ingenious acts that she performed during her years as a wartime relief worker in Europe. As a young, newly trained nurse from Saskatchewan, Elfrieda first went to England in 1942 to work with children war sufferers. Later she operated, together with her new husband, a Mennonite refugee camp in the dangerous and provision-scarce Allied sector of Berlin. For Elfrieda, raised in a household and church that resisted warfare, helping those who suffered from the impact of war was her way of being a peacemaker.[3]

These three women lived out, in some manner, the distinctive religious beliefs and cultural traditions of the Mennonites. Within many other religious traditions, women frequently were the ones who bore the cultural markers— be it customs such as food or dress or dance, or the rituals associated with religious expression—and were in a sense the physical signposts that differen-tiated and separated their sectarian group from the rest of society. For some women, such ethno-religious attributes enriched their lives and propelled them into vocational endeavours and activities that might otherwise not have been options for them. Other women chafed against the restrictions of behaviour and ideals of demeanour and thought that were part of a Mennonite identity. Mennonite religious doctrines and the practices that reflected those doctrines have varied in emphasis over time and also between subgroups and across locale. The history of Mennonites in Canada in the nineteenth and twentieth centuries was shaped in significant ways by their group responses to the two world wars and also to the momentous changes in society that resulted from industrialization, urbanization, and other facets of a modernizing world. Beliefs that had uniquely gendered manifestations were nonconformity and nonresistance, distinct principles of faith based on a literal reading of the Bible that was characteristic of the Mennonite tradition. Nonconformity reflected the desire of the Mennonites to live differently, or separately, from surrounding society, a belief that historically had outward expressions in such things as dress. The Mennonite objection to war and military involvement, today most commonly called pacifism or nonviolence, was known as nonresistance. This chapter will explore the gendered way in which Mennonite women lived out and experienced the impact of these beliefs.

A DOUBLE STANDARD OF NONCONFORMITY

The pattern of some Mennonite groups to migrate and resettle in order to escape persecution and obtain a degree of isolation has been accompanied by a general orientation of separation from the outside world; that is, from the behaviour and thought outside the church of believers. For some groups, that has meant geographic separation; for others, it has been manifest in nonconformity or disassociation from trends of the world. Mennonites believed that they should follow a lifestyle that was 'nonconformed' to the rest of the world, based on their reading of Romans 12:2. A popular descriptive phrase for this stance was "separation from the world," a position deemed necessary for a truly holy and Christian life. This view manifested itself, for example, in abstinence from voting in political elections or refusal to swear an oath in a court of law, in establishing separate schools, in insisting upon the maintenance of the German language or related dialects, in disallowing marriage with people of other denominations, and in objections to the use of musical instruments, electricity, and motorized transportation, for example. Today the majority of Mennonites, except for those in Old Order and some other conservative groups, do not adhere to these obvious and outward forms of separation. Of course, living in a manner that is explicitly nonconformed to the 'outside' world demands a certain degree of conformity 'inside' the community. As a result, efforts of Mennonite leaders to encourage and enforce behaviour of nonconformity vis-à-vis secular society also meant that standards of uniformity within the group, or subgroup, of Mennonites were also applied.

Separation from the world, or being nonconformed to the world, had disparate implications for men and women. Women, especially in ethnically distinct communities, have often been viewed as cultural carriers, with responsibility for maintaining traditions, customs, language, and other group distinctives across generations. Within Mennonite communities that valued internal conformity alongside nonconformity with the outside world, women frequently bore the signs of social boundaries most visibly. As Katie Funk Wiebe observed, "Long after men had moved in other directions, women were expected to be the social conservators of Mennonite culture, presumably based on Scripture, particularly clothing and hairstyles."[4] And outsiders indeed took more note of Mennonite women than of men. An American physician travelling through Lancaster, Pennsylvania, in 1924 commented that "the thing that made the most impression upon me was the Mennonite women with their becoming bonnets and their clear skins unmarred by cosmetics.... I never found a group of women anywhere with such clean complexions."[5] Somehow, their very physical beings—all the way to their skin tone—marked them as different. In a sense, women carried the markers of nonconformity, but also were physical symbols of church purity.

Throughout history, as Mennonites in varying degrees sought to buttress their distinct beliefs and traditions from modernization—however that was interpreted in a given era—they had to reinvent their ethnicity; indeed, even their religiosity. Particularly the more conservative, nonconformist groups repeatedly found new patterns of behaviour, sometimes stringently enforced in rules and faith statements, that more clearly set them apart from, and indicated their rejection of, societal trends. In her study of the River Brethren, Margaret C. Reynolds proposes that in the ritual of bread making at communion services, women become the "instruments of change, accommodation, and resistance to the host society," and are co-opted in the transformation of a home-based activity of food preparation to a church-located symbol that "affirms group ethnicity, separation, and world denial" as well as female subordination.[6]

Cultural rituals, modes of behaviour, and deportment all become akin to church doctrine when they are part of an ethno-religious system developed to uphold a group identity standing apart from the world. R. Marie Griffith points out, "Systems that sustain particular ideas about gender roles and social distinctions exert pressures that are not always tangibly felt by participants but that help secure conformity by seeming to attain the status of religious truth. In this way, standards of behaviour and appearance are reinforced at multiple levels, with little resistance, beyond jokes, to what may be seen as rigid prescriptions for ideal Christian womanhood."[7] Throughout much of their history in Canada, Mennonite women were the carriers and preservers of cultural symbols and rituals that reinforced a shared ethnic and religious sensibility within the group and that also presented images of difference to the world looking in on the group. While such symbols also included food and folk art traditions, it was oftentimes the physical appearance of women that was the focus of efforts to uphold Mennonite sectarianism.

Given the different ways in which Mennonite men and women interacted with, and were consumers in, society around them, and also given the inequities of power in church and community decision making throughout much of the past, what developed was a sometimes blatant and ludicrous double standard with respect to the sexes. Many women and girls experienced the double standard of behavioural expectations that were placed on them. Writing about his sister in a family history, one Saskatchewan man observed that "Boys were permitted many of the freedoms and exploits of their Canadian counterparts, but it seems that girls were often still subject to many of the same restrictions as in a Mennonite village in Russia."[8] Similarly, Leonard Neufeldt recalled the everyday way in which people reported on one another's misdemeanours in the (then) isolated community of Yarrow, British Columbia, where Mennonites settled in the late 1920s. He also notes that, "Generally speaking, girls and young women felt the community's regulatory hand on their shoulders more than young males did."[9]

DRESS

The double standard of nonconformity was particularly gender-specific when it came to the issue of dress. At different points in history, and to varying degrees for different groups today, Mennonites adopted distinctive dress forms that were applied with particular intensity and inflexibility towards women. In essence, women's bodies became public markers of Mennonitism. Pamela E. Klassen has argued that Mennonite teachings on women's dress has deep roots in the Judeo-Christian story of Eve and Adam in the garden of Eden. Their transgression, followed by the clothing of their naked bodies, she says, "has ever since linked women's bodies and clothing with shame and sexual temptation." Dress that was perceived to be too fashionable or immodest was linked to the biblical Fall and to Satanic temptation. Mennonite clergy used this interpretation of scripture to "convey their own symbolic messages about women's and men's roles in the social order."[10] Elsewhere, she suggests that the church deliberately drew boundaries between things of the world and the church in order to guard "against the effluviatic effects of women's bodiliness." And so, Klassen points out, the lines of worldliness were "arbitrarily but meticulously drawn in the contours of women's bodies" and focused on such things as covered heads, closed-toed shoes, and prohibitions against lipstick.[11] As a range of scholars writing about diverse groups have noted, dress offers an important symbolic message regarding gender roles, whether prescribed by the group or chosen by the individual. Women's reactions, to the imposition of regulations and pronouncements regarding what they wore, varied: while some women "rested in the security of the uniform conformity ... others wrestled deeply with wrenching bitterness."[12] As they chose what to wear, women were also thereby choosing what they wished to portray about themselves as women.[13] As Linda B. Arthur proposes, for ethno-religious groups in particular, dress was and is a key method of maintaining patriarchal authority as well as social control over women within a community.[14]

The question of dress became a significant point of contention for Mennonite women, their families, and their churches especially during the first half of the twentieth century. Towards the end of the nineteenth century and at least up until the Second World War, Mennonites of Swiss/Pennsylvania background developed dress codes that for women included the wearing of a cape dress (a kerchief or cape-like attachment to the bodice of a dress) as well as a prayer covering and bonnet for the head. The head covering, also called a prayer veiling or cap, was to be worn by all baptized women, following a literal application of I Corinthians 11, in which the apostle Paul commands that women have their heads covered during worship in recognition of their subordinate place in the universal order. The head covering was essentially a cap, varying in size over time, made of lightweight white fabric or netting and tied under the chin. These dress forms were encoded in church statutes and constitutions and, to a widely varying degree, were made a test of membership. These regulations caused considerable conflict in some congregations when local ministers or groups of individuals, seeing no justifiable grounds for such rigidity, chose to defy them. Resistance to 'plain' dress, as it was called, was particularly acute when it was apparent that standards were applied more rigorously to women than to men.

The dress issue, especially in Ontario where Swiss Mennonites predominated, arose in the context of liberalizing fashion styles at the turn of the twentieth century, but also as a response by conservative evangelicals and fundamentalists to the so-called 'new woman' making her appearance in public life. The entry of women into higher education and the professions, the struggle for the vote by first-wave feminists, and the declining birth rate were all cause for concern among those who decried women's departure from traditional roles. Mennonite women were assuming new roles as Sunday school teachers, missionaries, and writers for religious periodicals, and also training as nurses and teachers. The growing range of activities in which women were involved was accompanied by a more natural dress style, replacing the heavily corseted, bustled, and restrictive forms of dress dominant for much of the nineteenth century. Distinct dress as a reaction to the trends of modernism served to emphasize Mennonite nonconformity to the world at a time when more Mennonites were losing other aspects of their historic separation by using English, engaging in missions, moving to the cities, and entering non-farming occupations.[15] The uniformity that resulted from adherence to a dress code also promoted group unity, identity, and sameness and, as Beth E. Graybill argues, "enable[d] the group to exert authority over its members."[16] As dress regulations began to appear in the late nineteenth century, wives of clergymen were usually the first ones called to comply with new standards of conformity. For instance, at Shantz Mennonite Church (Ontario) in 1898, "Mrs. Wismer" was told that she must wear plain dress and not wear "her beads and jewellery," or her newly ordained husband would not be allowed to preach.[17]

Importantly, the emphasis on dress also reflected the influence of fundamentalism, a theological movement that gripped many Mennonite individuals and institutions in the first half of the twentieth century. Fundamentalists shared a "general horror" over the "new woman" who had appeared in the twentieth century and were increasingly skeptical about the hitherto accepted belief in woman's moral superiority. Some apocalyptic thinkers believed that the growing social freedom of women was a sign of the end times. The perceived bad influence created by the "cigarette-smoking, knicker-clad flappers" was countered by a legalism that one scholar of fundamentalism

suggests was manifest especially in "strict adherence to modest dress standards."[18] Evangelical theology of the time also had a "penchant for order"
which meant "a prescribed place for everything and everything in its place—
especially in the case of women."[19] With respect to headgear, dress regulations
also defined woman's role as subordinate in the creation order of God-Christ-
Man-Woman, and also within the human order.

While women had historically covered their heads as a matter of custom,
by the late nineteenth century, Mennonite church leaders began to define the
head covering in theological terms, using I Corinthians as their primary
defence. American leader Daniel Kauffman, whose 1898 manual of Bible
doctrines placed the head covering on a list of seven Christian ordinances,
argued that a covering was necessary to visibly define the relation between
man and woman. As the doctrinal significance of the covering was highlighted,
the frequency of wearing increased. At first it was customary in some districts
for women to leave their coverings hanging on pegs at the church and not even
bring them home after the service. However, many promoters of the ordinance argued that the covering should be worn at all times if a woman was to
"pray without ceasing," as instructed in scripture. Gradually, women began to
wear their coverings at mealtime, during family devotions, and finally at all
times. Beyond their association with the act of prayer was the belief that her
covering offered a woman physical protection from molestation and that
constant wear served as a Christian witness to society. For instance, Ontario
Mennonite women serving lunch at an International Ploughing Match were
"encouraged to wear their devotional coverings" as part of an "emphatic evangelistic effort."[20] Not only was the head covering thought to offer protection
to the wearer, it was also imagined to encourage virtuous behaviour and remind
women "who they are" morally and ethically.[21]

The fact that the argument was made for wearing the covering during
all daily activities suggests an interest in enforcing the lesson of woman's
submission to man beyond the sphere of her formal religious life and that the
question was, in fact, also a social one. This is confirmed by the words of
American Mennonite church leader and professor Harold S. Bender, who
offered one of the most orthodox justifications for the practice: "The entire
question is not one of moral or religious nature, but social. The covering of
the head is not a necessity to make God hear the woman's prayers, or to recognize as valid her contribution to the religious life of the community—it is a
necessity to preserve the divinely ordained social order from disruption and to

enforce the lesson of woman's submission to man."[22] One Canadian minister argued that the head covering was a sign to the angels that a woman was serving in her proper spiritual sphere—a sphere different from man's. A woman required the "power of angels," he said, first of all for physical reasons—because of her responsibility in procreation. Second, she needed extra power spiritually because she was more easily led astray, as epitomized in Eve's transgression in the Garden.[23] Ontario bishop Oscar Burkholder argued that women who refused to wear the head covering were "usurping man's position and power" and "scorning her God-given position of motherhood." This same minister decried the "physical freedom" offered by the fashions of the 1920s, which was contrary to woman's recognition, through the clothing she wore, of her subordinate relationship to man.[24]

Closely related to the head covering was the bonnet, which, because it did not carry the same doctrinal significance, became the focus for much of the friction surrounding the dress issue. Nineteenth-century changes in fashion included the gradual demise of the Victorian-style bonnet that enclosed the back of a woman's head and tied under her chin, to be replaced by the modern hat, often highly decorative with feathers and flowers, that sat directly on top of the head. In addition to being somewhat 'mannish' and thus associated with the world in which men operated, hats were thought to be symbolic of women's emancipation.[25] The bonnet was prescribed partly because it preserved a plainness of dress in opposition to the sometimes outlandish modern turn-of-the-century hat. But it was also promoted because it was worn more easily over the prayer covering; church leaders feared that should women discard their bonnets, the covering was sure to go next. Like the head covering, the outmoded plain bonnet set a woman apart and served as a testimonial to her religious beliefs and social separation.

A third aspect of women's dress that became part of the Mennonite 'uniform' was the cape dress, essentially a plainly styled dress with a square or v-shaped piece of fabric covering the bodice. Arguments for the cape dress followed the emphasis on scriptural simplicity as well as uniformity in light of drastically changing secular fashion. Modesty was also a consideration, since the cape functioned to hide or at last de-emphasize the female form. While it was highly favoured, the cape dress did not become part of dress regulations, as did the prescribed form of headgear. These dress prescriptions were enforced quite stringently in some locales and women who chose not to wear the covering and bonnet in particular might lose their church membership. For

instance, in 1923, the Swiss-origin Alberta–Saskatchewan Mennonite Conference passed a resolution that included a statement of disapproval of "women
wearing men's head dress" and the threat that women who disregarded the
official position were "liable to Church censure."[26] Although certain dress
guidelines were established for men—a suit jacket without lapels called a 'plain
coat'—for the most part, only clergymen adhered to them.

Following a trend occurring somewhat earlier and even more rigidly in
American Mennonite churches, and under the influence of visiting American
Mennonite evangelists, Ontario Mennonite leaders gradually moved towards
enforcing standards of dress that were tied to church membership. The years
of the First World War, during which Mennonites sought clear forms of separation to contrast the militarism of society around them and simultaneously
witnessed more single Mennonite women filling factory jobs vacated by men
in military service,[27] saw an increase in sermons and admonitions regarding
distinct dress. During the decade of the 1920s, with fundamentalist-style
theology and language finding a sympathetic base among Mennonites, the
mood was right for a further entrenchment of dress regulations. Much of the
prevailing sentiment was clearly a reaction against changing fashions. One
article reprinted in a Canadian Mennonite periodical blamed women for what
was seen as evil in female fashion trends: "It would seem that the woman is still
bent on dragging man down; she was the one who first tempted man, and she
is still at the same old game."[28]

Eventually, the enforcement of, and reaction to, plain dress regulations
caused acrimonious debate and conflict, especially within Swiss Mennonite-
origin communities in Ontario. At the root of the struggle were differing
interpretations of scripture and, sometimes, divergent views about woman's
place in relation to God and man. In the early 1920s, one of the most
outstanding and bitter struggles was occurring at First Mennonite Church in
Kitchener, Ontario, a conflict that culminated in a church split and the formation of a new Mennonite congregation, Stirling Avenue Mennonite Church.[29]
Reacting to the fact that a large number of women at First had ceased wearing
bonnets (and possibly also coverings) in favour of hats to their factory jobs in
town, the district meeting of ministers and deacons passed a resolution in 1921
that made the wearing of the bonnet a test of church membership for women.
On one occasion, the district bishop refused to serve communion to any
church members who did not offer assent to the conference resolution. A
committee charged to investigate the situation at First was presented with a

number of issues, not least of which was the double standard that existed between men and women regarding dress. Many of the men and women interviewed by the committee also pointed to the fact that thirty years earlier, dress standards within the Ontario Mennonite conference did not follow a particular uniform, but were about overall simplicity. The official church position was shown to be untenable when women could easily refute arguments about custom and tradition by pointing to the attire of their nineteenth-century mothers and grandmothers, which did not differ to any great extent from that of the rest of society. A few older women also pointed out that in earlier years they had been explicitly given permission to wear hats to work. The collective and individual voices of "articulate and thoughtful women leaders" in the congregation were key to the strength of the dissenting group.[30] Those who resisted the bonnet regulation were supported by the liberal-minded minister of First, who argued that "making a certain cut of head gear the test of discipleship was ... not borne out by the teaching of Jesus."[31]

That the issue was a consuming one for several years is indicated in numerous diary entries by Susannah Cressman, a member at First. Already in 1915 she wrote: "went to church. Jacob Schmidt preached sermon on bonnet question, took vote on same. ... " Three years later, she reported on a "meeting at our church to consider bonnet question and some other minor troubles. ... " In 1922 she noted that "Ministers and bishops met at the church to thresh out the Bonnet trouble here—had a three day session." A year later, on her birthday, Cressman wrote that she "Went to conference all day—discussion on bonnet question," and finally, on 3 August 1924, she recorded the following: "This is one of the most memorable Sundays in the history of the [F]irst Mennonite church at Kitchener, there being three ordained ministers excommunicated, among them Urias Weber our resident minister. ... "[32] The tensions within the congregation and between the congregation and the district conference had climaxed that year when, after the Conference bishop refused to serve communion to members at First unwilling to abide by the bonnet regulation, about one-third of the members broke away to form an independent congregation, ironically located just around the block from First.

Stirling Avenue Mennonite Church quickly developed a reputation as a liberal church, in which women were allowed to be members of the church council and participate equally with men in church decision making. In fact, in what was probably at that time unprecedented in Canadian Mennonite churches, the church 'board' included two representatives of the Women's Missionary Society local of the congregation. Also unique to the new congregation was the significant number of female members, over 60 percent in 1925, and that 11 percent of the congregation consisted of single working women between the ages of twenty-five and sixty.[33] Clearly, gender played a significant role in the emergence of this new liberal congregation. Five years after its inception, Stirling had its own internal debate on dress, this time focused on the head covering, or prayer covering, as it was sometimes called. As an independent congregation that was not part of the Mennonite Conference of Ontario, it seemed that Stirling Avenue needed to decide whether the head covering should be a gauge as to how 'Mennonite' the church was. After "lively discussion," the decision was reached to make the covering optional, but to encourage overall simplicity of dress.[34] Here again, women's bodies were the mechanism for inventing and conveying group identity.

While individual churches and regional conferences struggled through conflicts over the dress issue, with women sometimes pawns, sometimes protagonists, the dress code also presented particular dilemmas for women and men working at missions, overseas and within North America. Especially at mission stations, where Mennonite ministers and volunteers were attempting to evangelize individuals with no background in the Mennonite church, newcomers to the church, like Malinda Bricker, mentioned at the outset, sometimes found it difficult to connect spiritual renewal with the symbols of separation held by Mennonites. At the Toronto Mennonite Mission, established in 1907, dress was a problem right from the beginning. Nelson Martin, superintendent of the mission, wanted the church restrictions relaxed, especially those pertaining to the wearing of the bonnet, since mission participants were "constantly subjected to criticism and misunderstanding" when wearing bonnets. Tensions between workers at the mission and the Ontario Mennonite Conference culminated in Martin's resignation in 1923.[35]

Just two years earlier, a worker at a rural Mennonite mission west of London, Ontario, wrote to a senior minister that "the largest problem that faces us to get the members in line I fear is not anything very much save the Bonnet question." In order to be persuasive, he felt it necessary to take his wife with him "to help out on the dress question."[36] Women often had the special and difficult task of teaching converts the importance and nuances of dress codes, especially the wearing of a head covering. As noted in the previous chapter, however, a distant mission setting also afforded women some freedom from the codes of conduct at home, including adherence to dress regulations. Well-known is the story of two American Mennonite women who purportedly tossed their bonnets overboard while en route by ship to mission work in Turkey. Lorraine Roth, an Ontario woman who was a missionary in Honduras from 1954 to 1962, recalled the problems posed by the "strict dress code" imposed by the US-based mission board through which she worked. In this case, the difference between what the mission board expected and the conventions of her Ontario conference was merely the existence of strings on her head covering. The elimination of strings tied under the chin was, for some conservatives, a first step towards discarding the head covering altogether. Roth was apparently instructed by a senior male leader to reply to criticisms of her stringless covering by saying simply that she was "thinking about it."[37]

The wearing of the bonnet had declined significantly by the 1940s, despite the fact that the bonnet regulation was, for the first time, officially enshrined in the constitution of the Ontario Mennonite Conference in 1943. It may well be that signs of the bonnet's impending demise was the impetus to a last-ditch effort to enforce it. Yet, it simply could not be enforced, given the lack of biblical foundations for the practice. The head covering remained a sign of a woman's church membership well into the 1960s, but it too was subject to ongoing debate and enforcement that varied widely between congregations, districts, and families. In fact, in the late 1950s, another acrimonious split occurred in Ontario, whereby half a dozen conservative Swiss Mennonite clergymen left the larger conference to form a new subgroup that was more explicitly nonconformist in such external practices as uncut hair and head coverings for women, non-wearing of jewellery, and non-involvement in politics, among some other practices.[38]

During the years of the Second World War and after, as other forms of nonconformity in lifestyle seemed to be slipping away, the head covering received renewed attention in some Swiss Mennonite districts. Bishop Oscar Burkholder, a conservative but powerful voice amongst Ontario Mennonites at mid-century, wrote the following, seeming to suggest that the ordinance of the head covering required especial attention in light of the current behaviour of the female sex:

> Woman, because of her disposition, her place in creation, her suffering in the great issues of life and death, should give herself much to prayer. And in order that she may, she is admonished to refrain from fussing with the fashions of the world in her personal adornment, to keep her place of

scriptural relationships to the man in the affairs of the church, and especially, not to evade her responsibility in child-bearing. We are living in a
time when all three of these exhortations are sadly unheeded and disobeyed
by modern women.[39]

Burkholder's voice was increasingly an isolated one, however, and by 1965 the
Mennonite Conference of Ontario decreed that the head-covering ordinance
had neither scriptural nor historical foundations.

For women growing up in the mid-twentieth century within Swiss-
background Mennonite churches, the dress issue shaped their experience of
church in defining ways. Ruth Nighswander grew up in the conservative
Markham–Waterloo Conference in a community just north of Toronto,
Ontario. She knew that baptism into her church meant, for women, adhering
to a dress code that included cape dresses, head coverings, and black shoes and
stockings. When her father-minister responded to her questions about the
purpose of the dress code with scriptural admonitions about modesty, Ruth
replied that surely one could be modest without a cape dress, and, since God
had created her with light-coloured legs, why should she cover them up with
dark stockings?[40] Naomi Martin, married to an Ontario Mennonite bishop,
said she "just hated that old bonnet" and chose to wear a hat to high school in
the US, even if it meant being excommunicated from the church. Aside from
the way in which dress codes 'marked' them, Mennonite women were resentful
(expressed mainly in later years) over the double standard. One woman said: "I
always thought there was a differentiation that wasn't quite fair. The men ...
could have the best kind of cloth in their suits and be very well-dressed. But
the women were supposed to abide by a pattern, a very plain pattern of dress—
and of course a headdress that matched. A Mennonite woman was very easily
recognized as a Mennonite."[41] Similarly, Ruth Reesor observed that, for
Mennonite women of her generation, church membership "meant the girls
now had to wear cape dresses and white head coverings, black shoes and stockings at all times and all non plain clothes were given away." For their part, she
noted, boys continued to wear "ordinary clothes" during the work week, and
only on Sunday made a concession to plain dress by wearing suits without ties
and black hats.[42]

Because of this double standard of nonconformity, men were able to
interact more inconspicuously with non-Mennonites as a result. The most
extreme consequence of this was that, according to some recollections, men
began dating non-Mennonite women and marrying out of the church, leaving

behind the 'plain' Mennonite women. However, women did not always unquestioningly absorb the admonitions and guidelines of their church with respect to dress. Some women chose to hold up their special role as 'ambassadors for Christ' in their physical depictions of Mennonitism. The head covering in particular bestowed upon women a certain public depiction of purity and piety that was important during an era of rapid social change and assimilation. While some women, wearing their coverings proudly, exalted their position as 'brides of Christ,' others resisted what they saw as a clear double standard whereby they were expected to carry the banner of nonconformity for the entire church.

Opposing responses to the dress regulations were sometimes exhibited within the same family. For example, when sisters Elvina and Saloma Habermehl attended family reunions in the late 1920s, people assumed that Elvina was "a little more rebellious," since she wore a "contemporary and colourful dress" and "dared to wear makeup, ever so faintly, but still visible," while her older sister Saloma "wore dark clothes and devotional bonnet in Mennonite fashion."[43] Some women rejected the social control inherent in dress regulations and left the Mennonite church altogether. In Ontario, a late nineteenth-century split that spawned a new denomination called the Mennonite Brethren in Christ (later Missionary Church) initially attracted Mennonite women who resisted wearing the Mennonite 'uniform' and who were keen about the apparently greater opportunities for women in the evangelical program of the break-off group. Other women may have felt like Vera Hallman, who, though raised in a Mennonite home, delayed her spiritual commitment to join the Mennonite church because of its dress regulations. When her younger sister was baptized, Vera was the only woman in her family left wearing a hat.[44]

Those women who wanted to maintain membership in their Mennonite congregation, but who chafed at wearing outmoded dress styles and at the gender roles they represented, often subverted dress prescriptions through small acts of rebellion. Resistance to the head covering was expressed by leaving the strings dangling or removing them altogether, and gradually shrinking the size of the cap. Many working women opted to wear their coverings and bonnets to church but not to their non-farm workplaces. Indeed, as Kimberly D. Schmidt has demonstrated, for one American Mennonite congregation, the enforcement of dress regulations and resistance to those rules was especially intense during historic periods when women were entering non-farm occupations. Wage-earning, modern-dressing women out 'in the world' were a threat to Mennonite ideals of separation and also to the norms of humility and submission that were expected of women.[45] A female missionary, who in her own mind questioned the hierarchy implied by the doctrine, nevertheless used the teaching about the covering to her own advantage. When approached by a minister to reprimand a female song leader for wearing a blouse he considered inappropriate, the missionary refused. She insisted that "If we didn't have the authority to teach, neither did we have the authority to correct."[46]

Some women found ways of modifying their bonnets to render them less unfashionable: Ontario women became known for their 'hat-bonnets,' a type of headgear that tied under the chin like a bonnet but had the shape of a hat. When three young Mennonite women from Ontario travelled to California in 1908 (the trip itself stretched the boundaries of what was acceptable) and returned with a photograph of themselves, one perched on an ostrich and all three wearing large, elaborate hats, they were asked to confess their sin before the congregation. Eva Bergey, one of the three, felt that "a confession would be hypocritical, since she wasn't really sorry for what she had done" and so she and her sister Ida were disallowed from participating in communion, although they continued to attend church.[47] In another case, a minister's wife had a bonnet custom-made of pink straw for her eleven-year-old daughter, who was told to wear one even though she wasn't yet a church member.[48] Stretching the official boundaries was not only the purview of women in modernizing groups. One Old Order Mennonite woman wore a pale mauve flowered dress when her son married a woman coming into the Mennonite church from a different church tradition; she "figured everyone else would be in light colors" and wanted to fit in, but later dyed the dress royal blue in order to fit in amongst her own church people.[49]

The degree to which individual congregations enforced dress regulations varied and so in some churches women frequently found a middle road between conference regulations and current fashion. Margaret White Cressman became a Mennonite church member upon her marriage, and while she did begin wearing a head covering at that point, she chose to wear a hat instead of a bonnet, and did wear a wedding ring, a practice proscribed by the Ontario district conference but allowed within her husband's more liberal congregation.[50] Similarly, at the First Mennonite Church in Vineland, Ontario, in the 1950s, women were expected to wear hats, suggesting that most were no longer wearing bonnets or coverings. In fact, Doris North, who arrived at First in 1954 with her husband, the church's new pastor, was surprised at this practice, since hats were considered worldly in Ohio, from where they had come.[51] Some women, like Leah Weber Cressman, were able to turn the bonnet regulation to economic advantage by developing home-based bonnet-making businesses when no other clothing stores still carried the out-of-fashion bonnet style prescribed by the Mennonite conference.[52] Sisters Florence and Salina Shantz ran a cottage industry in downtown Kitchener, Ontario, in the 1930s that specialized in bonnet making—"a difficult skill to master"—and, ironically, also sewed "fancy wedding dresses" for non-Mennonite women.[53] For these women, servicing women who adhered to the bonnet regulation paradoxically also enhanced their own financial independence as urban working women.

Women who grew up during the era of strict dress regulations frequently carried feelings of bitterness after the period had passed. Mary Martin, who grew up in a conservative Ontario Mennonite group, remarked that "the earlier teachings and how I interpreted them affected how I felt about myself as a woman and as a sexual woman. The part of me that loved color and creativity was stifled for a long time."[54] Aside from the onus for displaying sectarian boundaries that dress regulations placed on women, some women took exception to the underlying views of women that were reflected in the symbols of attire. Dress codes taught that women were to be humble and submissive but also that they were easily led astray morally. It wasn't coincidental that strict dress codes for women arose during an era when Mennonites generally were interacting with the world more than ever before and when women in particular were departing from traditional behaviour by working in urban workplaces, by enrolling in higher education, and by volunteering at mission projects, both near and far from home. The dress question, as manifested among Swiss Mennonite groups, demonstrated that Mennonite women were expected to carry the badge of nonconformity for the entire church community. To the extent that the head covering and bonnet also served as symbols of woman's subordination, the mechanisms used to express Mennonite nonconformity also served to define woman's role by defining her dress. Furthermore, the efforts on the part of Mennonite church leaders to enforce the wearing of bonnets, rather than hats (a practice with no religious basis), was simply an exertion of male power over women who were increasingly self-sufficient and autonomous and interacting with 'the world' on their own terms.

If dress regulations became more strictly encoded in certain Swiss Mennonite churches, Mennonites of Russian background also had dress forms that varied over time and place. In Russia, baptized women usually wore a prayer covering in black silk or rayon, sometimes decorated with elaborate black embroidery. One recollection described the replacement, on the wedding day, of a bride's head-wreath and veil with a black bow as a "sign of responsibility" and the new role the married woman was taking on. The switch in headgear occurred during a wedding ritual that included singing the following verse: "The bridal wreathe you have no more, For duties weight you by the score."[55] The *Haube* (the German term for a married woman's head covering) was almost always black and varied in style, size, and plainness from one denominational group to another and between local congregations. More conservative groups had coverings that tied under the chin and others had a lace veil that hung down to the shoulders. The ornateness of some *Haube*, trimmed with ruffles, ribbons, rosettes, and lace, was a source of pride and even competition amongst women.

The Mennonite Brethren group issued a resolution in 1878 that instructed women to wear head coverings in church and family worship. The Manitoba-based Evangelical Mennonite Conference called for the use of a head covering by women, though not of a regulation style, as a sign of humility. In 1952, at a joint meeting of several conservative groups of Russian Mennonite origin, it was agreed that in keeping with I Corinthians 2 and Genesis 20, married women should keep their heads covered with a dark kerchief.[56] Variances in regional enforcement of rules regarding head coverings, as well as inconsistency of application, aroused no small amount of resentment in women. In one northern Saskatchewan congregation, practice on women's dress, as well as other issues in the late 1920s, was determined by a demanding and rigid minister. One woman was resentful when, unable to afford a "decent hat or a 24-inch ribbon to make a bow," she was compelled to pull apart a lace cap that she had brought from Russia as a keepsake. She wore the resulting head bow only once, and undoubtedly was hurt and angry that this "work of art" was ruined.[57]

By the 1930s, hats of various styles had more or less replaced a black bow as a head covering in the majority of Russian Mennonite groups. During historic moments when hats were fashionable, women could simultaneously be in vogue and act in accordance with overt or implicit commands to cover their heads in submission. At the 1962 annual meeting of Canadian Women in Mission, for instance, the sanctuary was described as "a sea of pastel-colored hats like a garden of bright flowers."[58] A hat had multiple symbols that varied slightly between churches; in some congregations a hat might indicate that a woman was a church member after having undergone the ritual of baptism, while in others a hat indicated that a woman was married, and thus the biblical submission inferred by a woman's covered head clearly extended to her social relationship with a husband. In one family history, an incident is related of a Mennonite preacher who remonstrated with the married women in his congregation to wear bonnets, after a young man had fallen in love with a married woman in the church, thinking that her uncovered head was a sign of her availability.[59] Lina Wohlgemut, a young widow with three children, came to Canada as a refugee from eastern Europe in 1949. The day after her arrival on a Friday, her sister-in-law, who had immigrated one year earlier, took Lina shopping for a hat, since it was very important that, as a married woman, she "conform to the church's expected dress code and have her head covered for church the next day."[60]

While the most urbanized and assimilated of Mennonite groups gradually gave up distinctive dress practices after the Second World War, numerous conservative groups still maintain certain aspects of separatism in dress. Usually, some form of head covering, because of its biblical foundation, is for such groups a symbol of both nonconformity and female subordination. The Old Order Mennonites and Amish exhibit the greatest uniformity and traditionalism in dress, with women dressed in dark- or plain-coloured long dresses and aprons and with nineteenth-century-style bonnets and shawls. However, in these very conservative groups, men also adhere to church-prescribed dress standards, and thus one might propose that a certain gender equality is obtained in that both sexes are standard-bearers for nonconformity. With respect to head coverings, however, conservative groups adhere to the religious principle of headship, whereby women cover their heads in deference to the hierarchical order of God-Christ-man-woman.[61]

Closely related to the issue of what Mennonite women should wear *on* their heads was the question of what grew *out of* their heads. Debates and exhortations on long or short hair, straight or curly hair, consumed some families and communities with nearly the same intensity as did the bonnet and head covering issue in Ontario in the early twentieth century. With the same zeal with which Mennonite leaders preached that women should keep their heads covered, many also demanded that women's hair remain uncut. As with other issues of nonconformity, concerns over cut hair arose from literal readings of scripture. Many Mennonites who took strict positions on women's hairstyles pointed to I Corinthians 11:1–16 as a clear guideline: "But every woman that prays or prophesies with her head uncovered dishonours her head; for that is even as if she were shaven. For it is a shame for a woman to be shorn or shaven, let her be covered." Along with warnings against cut hair was a concern over 'permed,' that is, artificially curled, hair, since the latter almost inevitably followed the former.

Mennonites were also influenced by their reading of such vitriolic tracts as fundamentalist John R. Rice's *Bobbed Hair, Bossy Wives and Women Preachers*, in which cut hair was associated with all manner of unbiblical and unbecoming behaviour for women.[62] By the 1920s and 1930s, Canadian women were increasingly abandoning long, uncut hair that was braided, wound, and bundled on their heads. And by the mid-twentieth century, beauty parlours were proliferating as shorter hairstyles required ongoing professional attention.[63] As we saw earlier, cut hair was less accommodating for just about any form of head covering, except the modern hat, which sat clearly on top of one's head. Resisting cut and curled hair, then, was for church leaders an issue of biblical interpretation, combined with dissension from a modernizing world, as well as an attempt to keep female independence and autonomy in check.

At its 1952 annual meeting, the Mennonite Conference of Ontario resolved to emphasize the practice of "uncut hair from early childhood" according to their interpretation of I Corinthians. An additional fear was that a woman who cut her hair would probably discard the head covering as well. In a 1958 statement, the same group decreed, "Women should wear their hair long, arranged neatly, with becoming head dress and avoid current fashions."[64] The concern with hair spread across ethnic Swiss/Russian and subgroup boundaries. Short hair on women, along with "the practice of sisters working in Ontario," were among moral dangers noted by the Manitoba-based, Russian Mennonite-origin, Evangelical Mennonite Conference in the 1950s.[65] One woman was told by her aunt in the 1940s that she wouldn't go to heaven after she cut her hair.[66] For some of the women who immigrated to Canada from the Soviet Union and eastern Europe after the Second World War, the concerns about haircutting may have caused some confusion. Katie Dirks, who spent time as a refugee in the Netherlands before coming to Canada, had her hair cut and permed on the insistence of her Dutch hostess, who felt Katie's long hair in a bun made her "look too German," which, in Europe at the time, was a serious liability.[67] As well, many refugee women were compelled to cut their hair because they were plagued with lice, following months of emergency travel in filthy transport trains and living in crowded, substandard housing. The issue of cut hair extended well into the 1960s (and for some groups continues today). In 1961 two members of Home Street Mennonite Church in Winnipeg wrote to their pastor asking whether it was permissible for women to cut their hair or get a permanent.[68]

The two women at Home Street Church asked permission, while refugee women cut their hair for practical reasons, but many others rebelled or at least expressed resistance to religious dictates about women's hairstyles in a variety of ways. The opening of a beauty salon in the predominantly Mennonite community of Yarrow, British Columbia, in the 1950s by resident barber Hank Giesbrecht was a radical signal that worldly culture had entered the community. Yet Giesbrecht's first female customer wore a shawl to and from the shop so that passersby would not see her new 'cut and curl' while another woman requested an appointment after-hours and entered through a side door.[69] Similar suspicions must have faced entrepreneur Agnes Toews when she opened Steinbach, Manitoba's, first beauty salon fifteen years earlier in 1935. It didn't take long before haircuts and perms were commonplace on Main Street in that town.[70]

In the Klassen family of Manitoba, with six girls, rebellion against their minister-father's dictates on the biblical importance of uncut hair included dismantling their long braids before arriving at school each day or cutting their long hair so gradually that the shortened length was almost imperceptible—"they would never appear with a radically shorter hair-do, yet their hair never grew long either."[71] According to one daughter, "Hair seemed to be central to the issue of authority" in this family.[72] Frustrated that she was the only one in her class at school in the north end of Winnipeg with pigtails, while all the others had "lovely curly hair," Selma Enns began dipping the end of each braid in the inkwell. She explained this to her mother by blaming the boy sitting behind her, and so her mother took pity on her and allowed her hair to be cut short. Selma recalled: "I had short hair just like movie stars."[73]

Rebellion exerted by mothers on behalf of their daughters was also not uncommon. My own mother tells how her mother-in-law, married to a rigid and conservative minister, asked my mother to go ahead and perm one of her daughter's hair, despite my grandfather's resistance to it. Marie Klassen was permitted to get her first hair permanent in 1945, but only after "years of trying to wear [her father] down."[74] But it wasn't always fathers who were resistant. Johan Klassen was the one to insist that his two teenage daughters get a professional permanent hair wave, instead of rolling their hair in pincurls and rag rollers, on the occasion of their elder sister's wedding in 1946.[75] That fathers could have such control over a young woman's hairstyle preferences, whether to encourage or disallow, is indicative of the lines of authority that existed in patriarchal Mennonite families. As with most other issues related to fashionable adornment, the pressures against modernism and nonconformity began to disappear by the 1960s. When Susan Klassen, wife of a leading minister and mother to the six sisters mentioned above, had her hair cut and permed when she was over the age of fifty, the opposition to cut hair, at least in that family, "was doomed."[76]

Similar proscriptions as were applied to cut or curled hair also applied to jewellery or cosmetics. But if a girl didn't purchase commercial makeup products, either because they were prohibited or unaffordable, there were nevertheless ways to work at the same results. For instance, girls in the Edenburg community in southern Manitoba, anticipating the regular young people's meetings, applied cornstarch to reduce the shininess of their faces and create a "velvety powdered appearance," and also rubbed their cheeks with red crepe paper "to create that harvest apple blush."[77] Sometimes women simply rejected the expected norms and then braced themselves for outrage and responded with equal vehemence. Anne Konrad recalls that her cousins, described as "city people," wore lipstick to the local Mennonite Brethren church when they moved to the Fraser Valley of British Columbia. When faced with continual stares from churchwomen, Anne's aunt approached a group and asked why they wore Sunday hats with sprigs of ornamental flowers. When they simply said, "to look nice," the mother of the "cherry-red lipped daughters" replied by boldly saying that was also why the girls wore lipstick.[78]

Even in subgroups where no explicit regulations or 'uniform' existed, women were expected to dress and present themselves in simple and modest ways that resisted acculturation to the ways of the world, however that was defined in a given era. (Of course, men also were called to maintain standards of simplicity and separation from the world as far as their physical beings went, but admonitions were much less frequent and less specific.) For women, cut and permed hair, cosmetics, short sleeves and short skirts, pants instead of skirts, high-heeled or open-toed shoes: all these were signs of following modern and secular trends, and were indications of a lack of humility and modesty on the part of the wearer. The issue of fashion was perhaps even more problematic for those groups that had few specific rules but yet demonstrated strict vigilance and general condemnation of what young women were wearing, frequently marking boundaries arbitrarily. Sometimes, crossing the boundaries of what was acceptable, even if it was not encoded in rules, could jeopardize a woman's church membership. Hildegard Peters Isaak recalled a baptismal ceremony at her Mennonite Brethren church at which her friend was asked whether she intended to wear slacks as a church member, though Hildegard was not questioned in this way at her baptism the next year.[79] In such churches and families, women were always pushing at the edges to determine what might pass and what would not.

Magdalene Redekop, daughter of a conservative bishop, made the important observation that prescriptions that defined Mennonite identity could vary a great deal between Mennonite families, depending on the degree to which the rules were enforced by either mother or father. She recalled about her own experience: "My sisters and I had to live according to the rules set by an exceptionally strict father. Being a Mennonite in the larger society of 'Englaenders' [English] paled before the immediate horror of the specific ways in which we were different from all the other girls. They wore pants; we wore skirts. They had their hair cut and curled; we were taught that this was sinful. They went on skating and baseball excursions; at such times we stayed behind in the empty schoolroom."[80] Elsa Klassen, also a minister's daughter, recalled with indignation a confrontation with her father over newly purchased high-heeled shoes that she bought for "the enormous sum of $18" at the age of eighteen. When she brought them home, her father promptly picked one up and tossed it in the air: "It landed in a tree and the side of my first real-leather brand-name shoe was punctured."[81] Elsa and her sisters chafed under their father's demands that they not wear pants, even for such activities as "gardening, milking, painting, and field work," nor were they allowed to wear swimsuits; girls were "not tolerated" in the swimming pond anyway. One sister recalled that the "silent conflict over clothes" with her father "was broken by door-slamming and temper outbursts on my part whenever I tried to break the code." Appeals to older brothers for support met with no response.[82]

A renewed emphasis on nonconformity during the 1950s meant that the regulations on dress and other 'externals' continued to be a priority. The move of Mennonites to the cities and into spheres of employment in which they were a minority also brought them into greater contact with the influences of secular and non-Mennonite society. Particularly the older church leadership feared an erosion of Mennonite distinctiveness as a result and reacted by renewing their campaign against conformity to the world in faith and practice. Rigid controls aimed at maintaining sectarian boundaries between Mennonites and 'the world' were reinforced by the theological influences of evangelical fundamentalism and piety that were once again attractive to Mennonite preachers in the 1950s. One post-war newcomer to Canada recalled frequent preaching on such things as dress codes, hair length, silk stockings, and makeup—described as "the preacher's harping on women's behaviour"—and felt that the proscriptions of the day pertained to women more than to men.[83] To the extent that behavioural standards did exhibit a double standard, this position was perhaps a gendered reaction to the liberalization of women's roles that had occurred in Canada during wartime. Harvey Neufeldt, analyzing the Mennonite community at Yarrow, also suggests that, as a way of regulating sexual behaviour, in their codes of piety "church leaders, all male, paid special attention to women."[84] Women, and some men, in return acquiesced to such regulation, defied them outright by leaving the Mennonite church, or, as scholar Pamela Klassen suggests, offered "sartorial challenges" to implied taboos.[85] Some individuals knew that if they were patient and waited out the resistance on the part of a culturally conservative leadership, eventually they would "[catch] up with the fashion about two years later."[86]

The general emphasis on simplicity in most Mennonite subgroups was frequently offset by particular contradictions in what was expected of women. Even while churches and families were resisting modern fashion, based on religious principles and also their cultural conservatism, they nevertheless on occasion exhibited ironic and amusing inconsistencies as they obsessed about the female form. For instance, in early twentieth-century rural Manitoba, Susan Heinrichs and her sisters were expected by both parents to wear binding corsets under their dresses—a clothing item intended to emphasize the female shape—even in hot summer weather while helping with harvest. Apparently the sisters would take off and hide the corsets as soon as they reached the fields, but then had a hard time finding them behind the sheaves; sometimes they panicked with fear that the lingerie would go through the threshing machine![87] In Yarrow, church leaders were concerned to prevent the exhibition of distracting feminine features, yet the predominantly Mennonite community seemed willing to follow societal norms with respect to the 'beauty myth.' In 1942, they celebrated the annual crowning of the May Queen by crowning Hilda Neufeldt, who took over from Selma Fast, both of them Mennonite women.[88]

The degree to which communities, churches, and families varied in their interpretation of dress as a symbol of separation could be seen even in the perceived contradictions that existed in the personal lives of church leaders. For instance, prominent western Canadian Mennonite minister J.J. Thiessen received a scolding letter from a fellow minister when a photo of J.J. and his wife Tina in a Mennonite newspaper showed Tina wearing earrings.[89] And when First Mennonite Church in Kitchener lost one-third of its members, including the minister, in a church split over the dress issue (discussed above), the new leader at First, Clayton F. Derstine, portrayed a real enigma with regard to appearance. While he preached, especially to women, on the importance of uniformity and modesty, his own 'plain' coat (suit coat without lapels worn by clergy) was often a beige or tan colour, rather than the sober black or dark blue worn by other ministers.

It is not coincidental that it was during the two world wars of the twentieth century that the issue of nonconformity as it pertained to women's dress became more pressing. It was during the wars that Mennonites were simultaneously trying to portray their 'difference' from the world around them, yet it was circumstances and consequences of the war that also drew them into greater contact with a modernizing society. As they struggled to shoulder the burden of nonconformity for their church community, Mennonite women were simultaneously excluded from another central tenet of their religion, one that rose to prominence when Canada was at war.

NONRESISTANT WOMEN

Mennonites set themselves apart from the mainstream not only by establishing social boundaries of nonconformity, but also by rooting their religious values in the doctrines of nonresistance. Again, they took their cues directly from New Testament scriptures, believing that warfare is wrong because it is contrary to Jesus's command to love one's enemies. Historically, the most concrete expression of this belief was an unwillingness to participate in secular warfare, and thus much effort was expended in securing exemptions from military service and alternate status as 'conscientious objectors' (cos) for

Mennonite men. The fact that women were not conscripted into the military, however, meant that women from the historic peace church traditions have by and large been left out of the great stories of nonresistant expression. As one woman said: "Because the destiny of the Mennonites revolved around the way sons were involved in [conscientious objection] and not the way the women experienced the truth of scripture, women's contribution was not as significant."[90] Similarly, historian M.J. Heisey offered, "Nonresistance, then, reflected not only the goal of living in a new kingdom but also unequal power among the people pursuing it."[91] It would seem that Mennonite women had to live by, even if they didn't help define, certain Mennonite ideologies. Magdalene Redekop expressed the dilemma in this way: "It was not women who had to think about being conscientious objectors to war. My father did not quiz prospective daughters-in-law on their attitudes to pacifism. In what sense, then, can a woman be a Mennonite?"[92] In many respects, women were historically excluded from participating, except in a gendered supportive manner, in discourse regarding possibly the primary signifier over time of what it meant to be a Mennonite.

Women from historic peace churches, such as the Mennonites, experienced a wartime shift in gender roles that closely paralleled the experience of their mainstream counterparts. Indeed, especially in the Second World War, CO women found themselves supporting the 'peace effort' in much the same way that other Canadian women were supporting the 'war effort.' On the one hand, wars often meant economic difficulty for women because their menfolk might spend significant periods of time away from the household, either to perform public service work or to spend time in prison. During both world wars, many women took responsibility for managing family farms or took the unprecedented step of entering the paid workforce. Unlike wives and mothers of soldiers, however, CO women who lived in urban settings especially, and those whose plain dress identified their religious affiliation, frequently felt public censure because their menfolk were perceived to be shirking their duty to the country. The female relatives of conscientious objectors stepped outside traditional gender roles for a short time, yet without the kind of propagandistic or material support lent to Canadian women who supported the war effort.

At the same time, challenges to the church's position also presented women with the opportunity to increase activity deemed appropriate to their particular gender sphere. Mennonite women, and others from historic peace churches, expressed their nonresistance primarily by providing material relief, both to their own men in work camps for conscientious objectors at home and to war sufferers overseas. Not unlike women with men in the forces, pacifist women prepared care packages with writing paper, envelopes, socks and gloves, and home baking for their own men in co camps. In the United States, a church-administered work program for cos called Civilian Public Service (CPS) also drew women into supportive labour as nutritionists, nurses, cooks, and in other roles within the 151 CPS camps established across the country. Wives and girlfriends of cos also uprooted themselves to be nearer their menfolk in CPS camps, and, together with those employed at the camps, were ▸ seen as morale-boosters and nurturers. Those involved with CPS developed vocational aspirations and also a "sense of purpose and usefulness in time of war."[93] In her analysis of nonresistance in the history of the Brethren in Christ, a related peace church, M.J. Heisey observed that for some women, the belief was "not so much proclaimed as expressed in the massive work of nurturing those under [their] care ... reflecting old and ongoing gender expectations."[94]

In Canada, the Alternative Service (AS) work program for cos was government-run and so women were not as involved in the actual program as were American women with CPS. Yet, they supported and encouraged conscientious objection in a variety of other ways. Following the passage of conscription laws in Canada in 1940 and negotiation with various Mennonite lobby groups, in 1941 the Canadian government established an Alternative Service program to put cos to work on non-military projects of 'national importance.' Conscientious objectors in western Canada were initially sent to national parks at Banff, Jasper, Prince Albert, and Riding Mountain, where they cleared forests of dead timber, built trails and roads, planted trees, and dug ditches. Most Ontario men were sent to a camp at Montreal River north of Sault Ste. Marie, where they cleared rock and bush for road building. In 1942, a significant number of men were sent to the west coast mainland and Vancouver Island to fulfill their Alternative Service in forestry and firefighting work. At the same time, AS terms were extended from their initial four months to the duration of the war. As labour needs in agriculture and other sectors increased during the war, some of the 7500 Mennonite men who received co status were able to fulfill their work obligations mainly on family farms and in essential industries nearer to their homes.[95]

In keeping with their gendered roles of nurturing and caring, women declared a non-verbal pacifist stance by regularly sending care packages and letters to their own sons and husbands in Alternative Service camps during the Second World War. For instance, Nancy Nahrgang Snyder, an Ontario woman who "thrived on giving reports," corresponded regularly with men who were in AS camps and then read letters and offered reports to her home congregation as a way of maintaining awareness of the distant COs.[96] And while most of the official advocacy for military exemption came from male leaders, on occasion women spoke out on behalf of their church's peace stance. For instance, when the war broke out in 1939, Elizabeth B. Toews, who had sons of conscription age, wrote to the federal government reminding it of its promises of military exemption. Apparently her letter was returned with the request that it be written in English.[97] A 1945 women's conference, held concurrently with the Conference of Mennonites in Canada sessions, featured a "timely paper" on nonresistance by Mrs. P.P. Rempel, who stressed "that it was an issue not only for men but also for girls." Among a number of recommendations that emphasized teaching peace principles, Rempel suggested that the General Conference peace committee include at least one woman.[98] In one family, it was apparently the mother who counselled her son, not yet a church member, that his only grounds for seeking military exemption were that he was German and couldn't join the army and fight his German brothers.[99]

Women's cultural customs were also used as explicit statements of nonresistance. Marie Shantz was a teacher in a one-room schoolhouse in Wilmot Township in Ontario during the Second World War. While other schoolchildren were being encouraged to buy war stamps to assist the war effort, Marie felt this inappropriate when 90 percent of her students were nonresistant Mennonites and so she found other means for them to be involved. Over a four-year period, her students—boys and girls—made four quilts that were donated or sold for war relief purposes. "The children embroidered the squares and their mothers did most of the quilting.... Nearly every girl and boy, from grade three to eight, had some stitches in it," she said.[100] That women wanted to construct a discourse on nonresistance and conscientious objection that included them is reflected in an article by an American Mennonite woman whose sentiments were likely shared by her Canadian sisters. After listing twenty different methods by which women could contribute to the CO cause, she said, "Have you ever wished that you could prove your convictions on peace and war as your boy friend, husband, brother, or son has? ... Girls and women of the Mennonite church groups! Our Christian responsibility, to our God, the world, the church, our boys in [alternative service] is tremendous.

The challenge is before us; the projects await us; the question is, do we as girls and women want to serve?"[101]

For Mennonite women, the Alternative Service program presented the opportunity to affirm nonresistant beliefs by supporting their menfolk in camps and other work placements, but it also exacted an emotional toll and created economic hardships for some. Women whose husbands or sons were 'conchies,' as they were sometimes described, had to deal with animosity from the public and in the media (in some regions and districts of the country more so than in others) towards men who were perceived as 'shirkers,' 'yellow-bellies,' and 'cowards.'

One Manitoba man who was a CO in Alberta seemed to feel that his wife had a more difficult time than he during his alternative service term; three decades after the war he wrote: "My wife of four months had to manage the farm while expecting our first child. She carried a greater load by being alone and having farm responsibilities ... while we were with friends and could engage in fellowship and sight-seeing."[102] Some families experienced financial difficulties as they struggled to maintain themselves on the small remuneration paid to COs—fifty cents a day—in an era when normative gender roles placed the burden of family income on the male 'head' of the household. Letters to Mennonite ministers and to government officials included pleas of chagrin from COs who worried about the financial situation of their mothers, wives, and children at home. The extra burden carried by married COs was noted in the CO newspaper, *The Beacon*, congratulating three fathers of "handsome baby boy[s]." The writer wondered "how these fellows are able to keep so cheerful, realizing they are confronted by a financial difficulty greater than our own."[103] Dire need, combined with disenchantment with the Alternative Service program, compelled some COs to join the military, such as Sheldon Martin, who left his AS camp in British Columbia and joined the army in order to pay for costly medical treatments for his new wife Mary Ann.[104]

Recognizing the growing dilemma facing their members, some Mennonite churches did establish funds for COs with dependents. In most cases, however, these were not monies divided equitably but were more akin to welfare funds, which put the onus on individual families to prove their own need. A Mennonite minister from Kitchener, Ontario, expressed the church's own ambiguous position with respect to the problem of support for families of COs. Stating that the most preferable and "normal" option for CO wives would be to "return to their own parents," he nevertheless recognized that some

women had taken on work "in a shop, office, or factory." Although he advocated financial assistance for CO families, the minister expressed the fear that
support for younger women (those under sixty) could cause them to become
"idle, busybodies, tattlers, and wanderers from house to house."[105] Once again,
Mennonite officials were speaking in contradictions, as they simultaneously
expressed skepticism about financial support for women while decrying the
growing presence of women in the paid workforce.

A small number of women dealt with both emotional loneliness and
economic hardship by moving temporarily to British Columbia, where they
found housing and employment near the Alternative Service camps where
their husbands were stationed. Like Helen Erb Burkholder, profiled at the
outset of this chapter, most of these were young married women, some
bringing along small children and a few giving birth to their first child while
on the west coast. Martha Rempel "found it very difficult to be separated"
from her husband during his CO service on the west coast and so moved from
Manitoba with her infant daughter to be near him. First she picked hops for
three weeks, then shared a rented cabin with other CO wives.[106] Clara Lebold
Roth was pregnant with her first child and only two weeks short of her due
date when her husband Ken was sent into Alternative Service in BC. Without
her husband's income as a truck driver, Clara could not afford the rent on their
apartment and so moved in with her parents. After seven months, Clara moved
out on her own, supporting herself and her infant son by sewing lingerie at
home for a nearby clothing factory but loneliness overcame her. She took a
"big step" and travelled to BC to be near her husband, despite opposition from
her mother-in-law and even though her church "wasn't much for it either."[107]

Helen and Clara both found work as housekeepers, but other women
worked in factories, as salesclerks, and picked hops. Annie Martin from Ontario
stumbled somewhat unintentionally into what would become a lifetime vocation during her two-year sojourn in BC. While working as a housekeeper for a
family in Victoria, she was unexpectedly left with the care of two young children when her employers (their parents) abruptly separated and the children
were left with the local Children's Aid Society. Over the next months, Annie
took in five more foster children, a responsibility she resumed after returning
to Ontario and continued well past the age of retirement. The stipend she
received for the children's care, as well as money earned providing room and
board for sailors stationed in the city, created a good income for her and her
CO husband Sylvester.[108]

Those women who took the bold step to accompany their CO husbands to the west coast experienced a shift in gender roles that typifies wartime exigency. For the first, and perhaps only, time in their marriages they were the primary income earners for their household. Their sojourn thousands of kilometres from home was also an adventure and allowed them certain limited freedom from the rigid constraints that characterized their sectarian communities. One woman, who was excommunicated for marrying outside her Old Order Mennonite church community, chose to accompany her husband west because there was no support for her at home and, in her words, "it was easier to be among strangers."[109] For women from those Mennonite subgroups that maintained dress prescriptions as discussed earlier, the distance from home may have afforded them the opportunity to discard the head coverings and outdated bonnets that were part of their church's 'uniform.' One woman from a conservative branch of the Mennonite church who, in the 1990s, was still wearing her head covering and cape dress, said that she had not worn her covering while living in Victoria, since it would have been unfamiliar to the general public. Another continued to wear her bonnet but dressed it up with ribbons to make it more fashionable.

While Mennonite men entered alternative service assignments or the military, as several thousand did, women found expanded opportunities in the paid workforce, as the experience of the BC women described above indicates, and as historians have documented for Canadian women generally. Increasing labour shortages, wartime production needs, and a massive government-advertising campaign summoning women to work meant that in 1944, the peak of wartime employment, one-third of all Canadian women over the age of fifteen were in the paid labour force.[110] Married women and women with children, in particular, represented a new working cohort. Wartime industry and labour demands definitely meant that Mennonite women, like other Canadian women, entered the urban and rural workforce as never before. Furthermore, they could be found in traditionally male sectors of labour, such as in agriculture and heavy industry. Doug Millar of Kitchener, who did a stint of Alternative Service at Montreal River, recalled that by the summer of 1940, his office at the Mutual Life Insurance Company was "reduced to girls and old men."[111] One Winnipeg woman remembered that when the war began, women became streetcar conductors and, "No matter where you walked, women took over. They had to."[112]

The activity at the Mennonite-run girls' homes for city domestic workers fell off during the war as young women either stayed home to replace their brothers' labour on the family farm, or found better paying work in offices and factories that allowed them to live in their own apartments. In a style that echoed much of the propaganda surrounding women's wartime roles, a 1942 article in a Toronto newspaper featured a Mennonite-owned farm north of the city where the Wideman sisters were helping to run the farm in the absence of male hands. Entitled "Girls Man the Farm Front," the article described how Anna alone ploughed 120 acres while her sister Ella "did a man's job daily."[113] The profile of one man in the CO newsletter also noted that "his wife now operates his large farm" in Saskatchewan (ironically, it is still 'his' farm).[114] In cities like Kitchener, Ontario, with a large population of Mennonites and a significant rubber industry, it was inevitable that Mennonite women would thus find themselves working in jobs that assisted the war effort. This irony, although rarely addressed at the time, was not lost on Erma Cressman, wife of a conscientious objector, who obtained a job at B.F. Goodrich, making aviation boots during the war. Erma's reasoning was that she couldn't live on the fifty cents a day that her husband earned as a CO, though she recalled that "there was a lot of criticism at the plant" and people asked her "How could I work on war material when my husband was a CO?" To which she responded, "I had no other support and no Mennonite offered me an alternate job."[115] Even those women who did not work in factories or offices sought out opportunities to earn extra dollars, such as taking in boarders, or doing laundry and sewing in their homes. Like other Canadian women, they had to manage households with many product shortages, especially foodstuffs. One woman recalled that they managed better than some families because their larger family meant they received more food coupons.[116] Another woman similarly recalled that when her younger sister was born in 1944, her mother sent her to register for additional meat and sugar on their ration book.[117]

The absence of men, performing either alternative or military service, also created vacancies in non-labour sectors that shifted normative gender roles during wartime. In educational institutions, for instance, there was a dramatic flip-flop in the sex ratio. For instance, at the Ontario Mennonite Bible School in Kitchener, the enrolment for the first week of January 1944 was ninety-two, with about "fives times as many sisters as brethren."[118] Elim Bible School in Altona, Manitoba, "virtually became a girls' school" with the departure of men for Alternative Service camps, as did the Pniel Bible School in Winkler.

According to one memoir, this imbalance was rationalized by one minister, who stated that "training women was important so that when the men returned they would have good life partners to choose from."[119] Following the 1943–44 school year at Rosthern Junior College, a teacher training school in Saskatchewan, the principal observed that most of the 129 students had been girls. From this he concluded that the majority of Saskatchewan's Mennonite teachers would in the future be women. He also pointed out that during the war, women had a better chance to acquire higher education because the male university students, refusing to sign a waiver disclaiming their conscientious objection to war, had to discontinue their studies.[120] A similar scenario was occurring at the Mennonite teacher training institute in Gretna, Manitoba. This trend also happened at other educational institutions and, indeed, some schools would not have survived the war years had it not been for their willingness to allow more women to enroll. Another wartime development that gave women vocational training was the creation and increase in church-run voluntary service programs, alongside the government-run alternative service program, that saw both young women and men gain experience working especially in agriculture and health-care fields. The Saskatchewan Youth Farm, started in 1943, became a place where "especially ... young women ... had opportunities for careers they may not have had otherwise."[121]

The lack of menfolk placed other kinds of demands on women, and nurtured independence regarding other skills. For instance, with fewer men in their households, more women learned to drive. One minister observed that in Leamington, Ontario, a woman sitting behind the steering wheel of a car was practically unheard-of before 1940, since "driving a car was clearly a masculine function."[122] But this changed during the war, as women headed households and needed to get to jobs, and accelerated after the war as roads improved and the price of cars declined. In Altona, Manitoba, Rhineland Car offered an auto mechanics course for women during the war.[123] For rural women, these changes meant that women "gained the unprecedented ability to leave the farm house at will."[124] The possibility of jumping into one's car and in little time driving to town or to one's neighbour's had the effect of reducing the isolation and loneliness of farm living. It also offered opportunities for involvement in community activities and, more importantly, probably contributed to the flourishing of Mennonite women's organizations during the 1950s and following. With a car at her disposal, a woman could easily leave her husband at home with the children for an evening and, on her own, attend her church's women's meeting or sewing circle.

In entering the paid workforce, relocating themselves and their children across the country, and having greater access to education and other opportunities during the Second World War, Mennonite women were departing from normative gender roles in a number of ways. Their deconstructed roles were, however, for the most part reconstituted after the war, as was the case for other Canadian women. Most left the paid workforce and stayed at home fully engaged in child rearing and housekeeping. In Canada's post-war economy of prosperity, jobs for men were plentiful and a second income provided by women's labour was usually not needed to maintain the middle-class family. The "gender-stratified household" containing the "production-oriented husband and the domestic-centered wife" that characterized one Mennonite community in the post-war era probably held true for other similar communities.[125]

Even while Mennonite women remained mostly loyal to the pacifist cause, they also extended their works of assistance to men and women in the forces. Women, probably more than men, were in a position to walk the fine line between patriotism and pacifism. Mennonite women offered material support to soldiers in almost the same amount as they offered it to COs. In Yarrow, BC, for instance, the women lined the streets handing *Zwieback* (buns), apples, and dill pickles to soldiers on their way back to the base.[126] One Mennonite sewing circle in Ontario reportedly sent mouthwash to soldiers overseas, "a relatively nonviolent gesture," notes historian Lorraine Roth.[127] Mennonite women were also aware of men in their community who were in military service overseas. An October 1918 diary entry by Laura Shantz notes the death "in Action" overseas of a certain Private Elgin Eby.[128] Similarly, Susannah Cressman wrote several entries in her diary in November 1917 that noted male acquaintances who were killed in action, or prayers offered on behalf of men going to war, or instruction to "our young men about the war."[129]

A small number of women even joined the military. One such woman, Mary Faust from Leamington, Ontario, joined the Canadian Women's Army Corps (CWAC) in 1942 and was discharged in 1946 at the rank of sergeant. A year after enlisting, she wrote to N.N. Driedger, the pastor of her home church, wanting to inquire after rumours that her church membership had been discontinued. Driedger responded that she was indeed still a member of the church and, in regard to her CWAC service, he said, "Hope you will do well and bear a good testimony to our Christian faith."[130] At least one woman from Stirling Avenue Mennonite Church in Kitchener entered active military service.[131] A Saskatchewan woman, Helena Kasdorf, joined the air force in 1942 and, before long, attained the rank of corporal. While stationed in Ontario, she sent occasional donations to her home congregation, First Mennonite Church in Saskatoon, and maintained a correspondence with the minister there. Although the minister continued to be supportive of male church members who joined the military—his own daughter married a soldier in full military uniform—Helena's name was removed from the membership list in 1944. The exact reasons for her dismissal from church are not clear, but historian Esther Epp-Tiessen speculates that because "double standards for men and women were common . . . it may have seemed much more abhorrent for a woman to join the military than a man, particularly since there was no conscription of women."[132]

Women's nonresistant activity during the two world wars was displayed most prominently in their relief efforts on behalf of war sufferers. During the Second World War, many Canadian women left the confines of home and threw their hearts and hands into voluntary organizations such as the Red Cross, International Order of the Daughters of the Empire, the Salvation Army, and Women's Institutes across the country. Whether it was to campaign for Victory Bond contributions, to organize blood banks for the Red Cross, to coordinate the collection of waste products for wartime recycling, or to individually sew and knit for relief of soldiers and civilians, the volunteer effort of Canadian women was perhaps their greatest contribution to the country during wartime. Mennonite women's organizations also received a boost during the wars as women gathered to prepare clothing, bandages, and other relief goods to be sent directly overseas, or held sales and other events to raise money to support the activities of Mennonite organizations engaged in wartime relief.

While some churches formally cautioned their female members against involvement in non-Mennonite organizations such as the Red Cross, sources suggest that women were, either individually or within their societies, making wartime contributions outside their own denomination. Women's support of Red Cross efforts, in particular, frequently saw them acting patriotically more than in opposition to the military campaign. For instance, in a 15 March 1917 entry in her diary, Susannah Cressman wrote: "Caller Red Cross lady to collect for whirlwind campaign to raise $150,000 for Patriotic purposes, gave $2.00."[133]

For the most part, however, Mennonite women were eager to cooperate with Red Cross work that was relief-oriented; for instance, at Coaldale Mennonite Brethren Church in Alberta, a committee of four women was elected already in 1939 to coordinate sewing and knitting for the Red Cross.[134]

For many Mennonite women, collecting used, and sewing new, clothing and quilts, and knitting socks and bandages became their unique contribution to their country. In 1939 women in Ontario organized local sewing circles into the Nonresistant Relief Sewing Organization, an indication that they themselves viewed their material labour in the context of a faith principle. In describing the material assistance and moral support given to conscientious objectors in camps and war sufferers overseas, Clara Snider, the secretary of this organization, said: "We are representing a common cause and stand for the same principles.... United we stand, divided we fall."[134] Between the years 1941 and 1944, approximately $71,000 worth of clothing was sent under the auspices of Mennonite Central Committee from Canada to England, the main destination for relief supplies during the actual war years. Mennonite relief workers in England suggested that women in North America adopt the slogan "Non-Resistant Needles Knitting for the Needy" to underscore the "magnificent opportunity" that their work represented.[136]

Not only did women prepare and send material aid overseas, but quite a few Canadian Mennonite women, in addition to Elfrieda Klassen Dyck, profiled at the outset of the chapter, themselves crossed the ocean to work at clothing distribution, in orphans' homes, and in other volunteer capacities. One of these workers, Arlene Sitler, compared the situation of women in England with that of Mennonite women at home in Canada. Writing in the *Women's Activities Letter*, a paper distributed from Kitchener, Ontario, to women's groups beginning in 1944, Arlene observed that during the war, English women had taken over many occupations previously occupied by men such as embassy staff, subway ticket agents, and bus conductors. Though Mennonite women in Canada had not undergone the trauma experienced by European women, nevertheless each of them had "had to adapt herself to war conditions." Arlene affirmed the material relief provided by Canadian Mennonite women, suggesting that through their giving, "the bonds of peace and Christian fellowship may become stronger throughout the world."[137] Alice Snyder of Kitchener, Ontario, was another woman who volunteered in Germany for two years beginning in 1947, acting as hostess for the voluntary service units where she was stationed, distributing food and clothing, and supporting child-feeding programs.[138] Dorothy Swartzentruber offered her volunteer labour at Mennonite Central Committee's German headquarters for five years, beginning in 1949, when she was only twenty-four years old. Her tasks varied widely regarding the post-war relief agenda, from distributing food and clothing to providing secretarial services to teaching Sunday school and running sewing clubs for Mennonite refugees. Upon her return to Canada, Dorothy's talent for writing and public speaking was utilized as she educated an interested audience regarding the situation in post-war Europe: she spoke to "women's groups, ministers [sic] groups, in morning church services, and in afternoon meetings to groups of women and men and at times at conferences." She was also an entrepreneur, establishing her own business, the Golden Rule Secretarial Service, which had the job (among many other contracts) of registering 12,000 delegates and billeting 6000 visitors to the Mennonite World Conference assembly in 1962.[139]

Women who volunteered for overseas post-war relief work, or who offered material assistance to conscientious objectors, or who entered the workforce to support their families during the war, were living out Mennonite beliefs in nonresistance in gender-specific ways. Outside wartime circumstances, however, the gendered meanings of pacifism have only begun to be explored. Feminist analyses of Mennonite nonresistant/pacifist beliefs have drawn attention to the ways in which notions of peace and nonviolence, espoused as key markers of Mennonites past and present, have overlapped with gendered character traits such as submission, humility, and service. In an analysis of proverbs and sayings embroidered on a quilt made by young Mennonite women working as domestics in Vancouver, Ruth Derksen Siemens proposes that sayings like "Strive to live at peace with everyone," "Submit to those in authority over you," and "Love seeks no evil against another" were understood in a very gender-specific manner. While for Mennonite men, such phrases meant "refusing military service [and] not provoking any violent physical attack or invasion," for the quilt makers and domestic servants, the proverbs "were experienced as a passive response to any aggressive act...." and an "unquestioning acceptance of a parent's, matron's or church elder's authority."[140] In Derksen Siemens's interpretation, these statements encouraged a woman to be obedient to her employers, even when their behaviour towards her was exploitative and abusive, and to Mennonite church authorities who monitored her behaviour in the city away from parental control.

RELATING TO OUTSIDERS

A further manifestation of both nonconformity and nonresistance, in the context of their overall belief system, was Mennonite guardedness towards political involvement, be that direct engagement in the structures of state and government, or the more oblique participation in organizations and public activities that were not explicitly under the auspices of Mennonite church or community. An assumed, but little studied, understanding of pre-Second World War Mennonites is that they, for the most part, eschewed political involvement, defined mainly in terms of holding political office or voting in elections.[141] However, actual practice in this regard varied according to the degree of separation from the world held by a particular branch of Mennonites, the more conservative groups being more likely to avoid even the franchise, while the most acculturated groups had members who held local and national political office.

It is probable that practice was also dictated by gender, whereby men were the ones most likely to demonstrate involvement in the public political sphere. In this regard, it is interesting to see in a 1908 diary entry of Ontario resident Barbara Shuh that "Men all went voting. (William L.M.) King was elected."[142] Of course, in that year Canadian women did not yet have the vote, and one can hardly speculate, given a lack of direct evidence in sources from that era, to what extent the suffrage movement affected Mennonite women. The connections between suffrage and the war effort may have generated some suspicion, at least during these years. The Mennonite diffidence towards matters of the state meant that possibly a majority of men did not even vote until the second half of the twentieth century, although again, there has been minimal analysis of Mennonite voting patterns. Mennonites who immigrated from the Soviet Union in the 1920s and after did not obtain citizenship immediately, so this would have precluded both men and women from voting. Olga Dyck Regehr, a 1920s immigrant, recalls that she couldn't recall her mother ever going out to vote.[143] This doesn't mean they were not interested, especially those Mennonites living in urban areas. For instance, Susannah Cressman noted in her diary that she went to hear famous Canadian suffragist Nellie McClung when she visited Kitchener in January 1932.[144] A number of years earlier, in a 1915 diary entry, she noted that the Mennonite Young People's Literary had a "large meeting" that debated women's suffrage.[145]

One aspect of indirect political involvement was the extent to which Mennonites accepted or rejected government social programs that became familiar parts of Canadian lives in the post-Second World War era. Ideals of separation were behind the church's past rejection of various government social programs, some of which were crucial in helping widows and single mothers out of financial straits. For example, in Canada, family allowance cheques were issued to all Canadian families, beginning in 1944. While many other Canadian women hailed this program as a gesture towards greater autonomy in managing their households, some Mennonite churches feared potential government intervention in family life and warned their members not to accept the cheques. Under this program, a monthly sum was paid to all families with children under age sixteen attending school. The first universal welfare program in Canada, the family allowance cheque was considered income for a mother's use for child and income maintenance. For many Canadian families, Mennonite and otherwise, who had barely made it through the Depression, this government assistance was welcome and crucial to keep them out of poverty. This appeared to be the case for a group of Mennonite families that left Saskatchewan in the early 1940s and settled at the remote community of Vanderhoof in northern British Columbia. When a BC social worker visited the Mennonites in 1945, he reported that all but two of the families were receiving family allowance cheques. He went on to note that many of the children were wearing new footwear and clothing and said, "For this reason we believe it is safe to assume that the money is generally being spent for its intended purposes."[146]

Though the cheque undoubtedly went into the general family coffer in many cases and wasn't necessarily designated for special needs, some women held on to their small sum as their sole bit of financial independence. As was the case for other Canadian women, the government cheques gave Mennonite mothers often the only household cash they felt they could dispense according to their own priorities. In the David and Susan Klassen household, one daughter recalled that whenever the subject of a new purchase for the household came up, "our brothers quickly reminded us (sisters) of a family which had gone bankrupt shortly after the woman of the house had bought new drapes." Seemingly, women's upgrades for the house were considered extravagant and frivolous. Yet, when family allowance cheques began arriving at the Klassen house, mother Susan finally had "an opportunity to make some decisions with her own money."[147] In this family, when successive door-to-door salesmen raised the choice between a set of encyclopaedia or a vacuum cleaner, the latter won out at mother Susan's urging. According to one daughter, their mother's "financial emancipation reached a high point with the arrival of her Old Age Pension cheque."[148]

Yet, despite the boost in income that universal social programs gave to some households, Mennonites leaders felt bound, on the grounds of nonconformity, to object to the family allowance program. A special committee, all male, of the Mennonite Conference of Ontario, in 1945 advised members against the acceptance of family allowances, though subsequently the conference passed a motion allowing individuals to be guided by their consciences.[149] Selma Schwartzentruber Bender became a widow in 1945 after only six years of marriage, and, with three young children and "no financial assets," she would have probably benefited from government assistance in the form of widow's allowance, but her Amish Mennonite church group did not allow members to accept such aid. Instead, she supported her family by helping on her sister's dairy farm, selling garden produce at the market, raising baby chicks in her basement, sewing slips for a nearby lingerie factory, and also making coverings and bonnets for other Mennonite women.[150] Similarly, a Manitoba woman who was a member of a conservative Mennonite subgroup was anxious to apply for family allowance benefits to help feed and clothe her four children, but her husband had promised his father that they would never accept aid from the government and so she was compelled to run the household with "severe austerity."[151]

Mennonite diffidence towards political involvement extended to involvement in most other public organizations, religious and secular, that were not Mennonite. By cautioning their members against such involvements, church leaders could uphold nonconformist beliefs as well as keep out ideas and influences that might threaten Mennonite uniqueness and internal conformity. This was difficult and sometimes well-nigh impossible for Mennonites, both women and men, whose occupations and avocational activities drew them into contact with such organizations. For men, connections might have been made with agricultural or rural marketing associations, while, for women, common interest was often found with non-Mennonite social and charitable activity. Laureen Harder, historian of one liberal urban congregation in Kitchener, Ontario, remarks that despite the fact that taking interest in "solving social ills outside the fellowship went against the Mennonite doctrine of separation from the world," many women of that church were actively involved in non-Mennonite women's work at mid-twentieth century. This included the Local

Council of Women, Women's Institutes, the Women's Christian Temperance Union (WCTU), and the Young Women's Christian Association (YWCA).[152]

The popular Women's Institutes that sprang up across the country early in the twentieth century, beginning in Ontario in 1897, saw many Mennonite women become active members. Local Institutes taught homemaking skills and also performed charitable service in local communities. In Ontario, many women joined up, including Ida Bergey Millar, who was president of the Women's Institute in New Dundee, and Lillian Snyder, who was president of the Maple Grove Women's Institute for three years in the 1930s, also convening the Peace Committee in 1938.[153] A number of Mennonite women were on the first board of directors of the Altona, Manitoba, Institute, formed in 1936, but, as Esther Epp-Tiessen has suggested, local Mennonite church leaders initially put forth substantial opposition to their work on the grounds that the Institute was not explicitly motivated by Christian principles and that it had English and Jewish as well as Mennonite members. Some women whose husbands were important figures in the church in fact gave up their membership in the Institute, because of the pressure. Epp-Tiessen notes that a similar standard of non-fraternization was not applied to Altona Mennonite men who frequently joined secular agricultural associations and also ran for local politics.[154] Mennonite women in Manitoba were also involved with the Women's Co-operative Guild movement, founded in 1951, which focused on "the teaching and practise of the co-operative way of life" and "to work for world peace by seeking understanding of the problems and thinking of women of other countries." Tina Wiens of Lowe Farm became secretary of her local chapter, signing her letters "Yours co-operatively."[155]

Single women who were at the forefront of Mennonite urbanization in the early twentieth century were often the first to encounter and participate in many events and organizations that were likely considered worldly by their church leaders. In her diaries written in the years 1911 to 1946, Susannah Cressman commented frequently on political events. For instance, when her home town of Berlin (later Kitchener), Ontario, became a city in July 1912, she described the celebrations in several diary entries; on 17 July, the "Aeroplane flights," "Midway," "military tattoo," and "fireworks" all made for a delightful day. She also noted the passage of bylaws allowing for the construction of a "monster rubber tire factory"[156] and, in 1919 (year of the famous Winnipeg General Strike), commented on the "unusual number of strikes and troubles all over the Dominion."[157] On 19 June 1914 she commented on the

"Great election, hard fight of temperance people against Whitney Government, C.H. Mills gained a majority of over 1,500."[158] In May 1916, she wrote that two ladies from town had called at her home to solicit her vote regarding a name change for the city of Berlin. In the following day's entry she noted that the vote to change the city's name from Berlin to Kitchener had passed by a majority of 80 percent, "the greatest nonsense the city has ever committed."[159]

Nor did she and her counterparts eschew involvement in public events and activities, whether religious or not, that were outside the boundaries of her Mennonite church life. Susannah regularly attended meetings and went to hear guest speakers that included travelling evangelists, Chautauqua meetings, a lecture on Mormonism in 1922, a performance of the *Messiah* at a Methodist church in 1926, and the Dionne quintuplets when they were in town in 1936. Her diary entries indicate that she also regularly attended various parades in the city that celebrated dignitaries such as the governor general, or various members of the royal family. She noted Agnes McPhail (Canada's first female Member of Parliament) speaking in early 1933, with a "monster attendance, 5,000 being turned away," though it isn't clear whether Susannah herself attended.[160] Susannah also reported attending a national gathering of Women's Institutes, with 4000 to 5000 in attendance.[161] Though a member and regular participant in the oldest and most established Mennonite church in the area, she nevertheless also was attuned to and interested in the goings on of the nation and community outside her religious enclave.

Another important way in which Mennonite women encountered the 'outside' world and incorporated its influences into their lives was through regular encounters and interaction with their neighbours. Early Mennonite settlement patterns, whether it was block purchases of land by the Swiss Mennonites in the early nineteenth century, or street-village formations within reserves by the Russian Mennonite immigrants, enhanced Mennonite isolation and self-sufficiency. It also reinforced social boundaries and meant that especially women, who 'went to town' less than men, related mainly to family and co-religionists. However, for those Mennonites who resided on rural homesteads that were not within Mennonite concentrations or those who moved into larger towns and cities, it was likely that one's closest neighbour was not Mennonite. Newly arrived Mennonite women often looked to their neighbours for information and advice about gardening, for help with children, or even assistance in childbirth when no Mennonite midwife was available.

The initial Mennonite settlers in southwest Ontario and southern Manitoba looked to the Native peoples for information about the climate, soil, and environment to which they came. Irmgard Dyck Regehr recalled that in the early 1930s, when Mennonites began settling in an area north of the city of Winnipeg now known as North Kildonan, they received a lot of help from their Jewish neighbours.[162] In that community, Maria Janzen Koehn recalled that Mennonites were able to receive credit "all winter" for groceries, wood, and coal purchased at one of the several Jewish stores, because "they trusted us."[163] In these interactions with 'outsiders,' Mennonite women undoubtedly absorbed information, ideas, and traditions that transformed, however subtly, their own cultural patterns of thinking and doing.

Whether they moved nearer to diverse population centres or farther out to more isolated locales, there were, of course, many other aspects to living in Canada that tested Mennonite separatism. Throughout the twentieth century, an abundance of inventions, discoveries, and technological advances made life easier for Canadians in certain respects, but also made it challenging for sectarian groups to maintain a sense of self-sufficiency and isolation. Such innovations and trends included the improvement of roads and increase in car production, media inventions such as radio and television, and gradual introduction of hydro and plumbing to towns and rural areas. Most of these developments had a dramatic impact on the lives of Canadian Mennonite women. As historian Royden Loewen wrote about the improvement of roads in southern Manitoba, "With first a gravel and then a paved corridor to Steinbach and to Winnipeg, the distance to the market-place shrank. Women learned to drive the smooth, dependable post-war motor cars and gained the unprecedented ability to leave the farm house at will."[164] Driving a car, while today a mundane part of daily life for both men and women, was transformative in the lives of women in the second half of the last century. Not having access to a car or good roads meant isolation especially for women. Katie Funk Wiebe recalled her frustration over not having a driver's licence when her husband was hospitalized repeatedly and she was on her own with four young children. She regretted that driving was "a skill never encouraged for women in the small rural communities of Saskatchewan" where she had previously lived. Newly moved to Kitchener, Ontario, in 1959, and without a licence, "it was difficult to get the children to their various appointments and destinations, and even to visit Walter [her husband] at the hospital."[165]

Restrictions for women on driving, because they were so gendered in application, reflected a perception about the appropriate places and spaces that women were to occupy. They also reflected nonconformist ideals about avoiding modernism and its evils. This is suggested in the observation by concert pianist Irmgard Braun Baerg: "I remember distinctly as a child, when we played games we desperately avoided playing the part of the woman.... I didn't think that it would be a whole lot of fun because the man got to drive out with a car. He got to get around. He had that opportunity while the woman was at home."[166] Yet, with respect to driving an automobile, some aspects of Mennonite nonconformity could have unusual results for women. For instance, as a Mennonite minister in early twentieth-century Ontario, Thomas Reesor was expected to hold higher standards of nonconformist practice than his church members. This included not driving a car even when the automobile became increasingly prevalent in his community. Thomas addressed this dilemma by purchasing a car and having his youngest daughter chauffeur him wherever he needed to go.[167] Once again, situational applications of normative gender understandings prevailed with respect to women's roles.

Until late in the twentieth century, few analyses of Mennonite doctrine or theology considered the gendered implications of living out religious beliefs in daily life. Yet, ideals and practices that were conceptualized and articulated exclusively by male church leaders over several hundreds of years inevitably had different meanings and import for women. Principles of nonconformity and nonresistance were particularly gendered in their impact because they revolved around how Mennonites interacted with Canadian society, which itself experienced dramatic changes regarding the prescribed and actual roles of women from the late nineteenth century onwards. As Mennonite churches and communities discerned how to respond to a modernizing society, greater acculturation by their members, and decreasing isolation from Canadian political structures and socio-economic trends throughout the twentieth century, women faced particular opportunities and dilemmas with regard to living in the world.

As participants in a community that felt called to be separate even while it was drawn to some social and technological aspects of modernity, women became the carriers of Mennonite efforts at nonconformity through admonitions and regulations regarding their physical appearance. During particular eras that compelled church leaders to respond in radical ways to social phenomena around them, women's bodies became symbolic of what set Mennonites apart from the world. However, during wartime, when Mennonite beliefs in nonresistance were tested most acutely, men were the focus of efforts to reinforce church doctrine. For their part, women were largely ignored in the sense that they weren't perceived as having a unique role to play in presenting to Canada and the rest of the world an alternative to military involvement. In the meantime, individual women responded to the negative financial consequences of conscientious objection by stepping outside traditional gender roles and running family farms or even working in factories geared towards war production. Collectively they thrived as they responded zealously to the needs of war sufferers in Europe and elsewhere.

CHAPTER FIVE

Quilters, Canners, and Writers: Women in the Material World

Anna Weber (1814–1888), an Ontario Mennonite woman, was considered to be "unbrilliant," yet became the most "prolific and outstanding" *Fraktur* artist in Ontario.[1] *Fraktur*—meaning 'fragmented' or 'broken'—is a form of calligraphic writing combined with pen and wash drawings of particular motifs such as hearts, birds, trees, and flowers. It originated in European folk cultures and was brought to Ontario by Pennsylvania German immigrants. Anna, who never married, was considered 'queer' and 'strange' with a rebellious, individualistic nature. After both her parents died, Anna apparently lived with up to nine different families over the next twenty-four years until her death. It was said that "People got along better with Anna if she didn't stay too long at the same place."[2] It seemed that Anna's artistic talents and inclinations were viewed as a hindrance to her homemaking abilities and responsibilities and so some families viewed her as a burden. People sometimes tried to direct her energies into more 'useful' handwork like knitting or hooking mats, but Anna resisted this. As a nonconformist within a community that expected internal conformity, Anna was considered unusual. Spurning normative gender expectations that she marry and apply herself to household skills, Anna instead chose to give expression to the creativity within herself. Anna's artistic work was never sold but was preserved in many family Bibles.

Elizabeth "Isby" Bergen (1908–2001), born in Saskatchewan, became a well-known journalist and local historian in southern Manitoba, writing a regular column for the *Red River Valley Echo*, a community newspaper, for many years, beginning in 1940. She was also involved in the Altona, Manitoba, Women's Institute, through which she helped establish the first community hospital and United Way branch. Her numerous contributions to the betterment of her community earned her a Citizen of the Year award in Altona in 1997. A gifted writer with an inquisitive mind, Isby channelled her gifts into a form of expression that was acceptable for women of her day. Like some other women, her non-married status allowed her the kind of time and independence she needed to pursue her many interests and activities.

Esther Hiebert Horch (1909–1994) moved to Winnipeg with her family when her minister father was appointed to pastor a church in that city. Following high school, she obtained teachers' training and taught for two years but, after her marriage in 1932, was compelled to quit teaching. Instead, she started a kindergarten in the church basement in order to earn income during the difficult years of the Depression, while continuing studies in English at the University of Manitoba. When her husband was invited to chair the music department of a newly formed Mennonite college in Winnipeg in 1944, Esther also began teaching English and music at the college, though she was never listed as faculty. In the 1960s, she was in charge of women's programming at a Mennonite-run radio station in Manitoba and also hosted a weekly program called *The Story of Our Hymns* for six years. Turning her energies to pen and paper, she then wrote a biography of her father, which was published in 1979. Esther was among a growing number of Mennonite women who, at the mid-twentieth century, received post-secondary education and went on to develop a multi-faceted career while homemaking and accompanying her husband as his own work evolved. She accomplished this while dealing with personal challenges that included the tragic death of her only child, and a physical disability following the amputation of an arm.[3]

All these Mennonite women used their gifts and skills in material and productive activity that enriched their households, communities, and society around them. Their zealous desire for self-expression was channelled into forms of creativity and output that were allowed for Mennonite women within a church and societal context that often circumscribed female behaviour and activity in rigid ways. While some women were lauded within their communities for productive activity that clearly reinforced both normative gender and ethno-religious characteristics, others exercised their creativity on the margins of, or slightly beyond, the boundaries of what was acceptable within many Mennonite families and communities of an earlier era.

One of the early theoretical assumptions of women's historians focused on the 'separate spheres' within which women and men acted out their respective gender roles. The sphere of men was the public world of the marketplace, the political realm, and the institutions of society. Women's sphere was, conversely, the private world of household and family. Speaking about the Mennonites, Katie Funk Wiebe articulated the separate spheres model that characterized gender roles for much of the past two centuries:

> Women's place was not with the men. Not with thinking. Not with dreaming, declaring, determining sin, disciplining, deciding to stay or leave Russia. Her place was at home kneading the soft dough with strong hands, stripping milk from soft, warm udders, serving Prips and Schinkefleisch to tired men when they came home from the fields. Her place was cradling children into quietness; loving deeply without open words; praying silently with head covered.[4]

As for others of their sex, Mennonite women were often associated with the material world, in contrast to men, who were connected with the intellectual, the spiritual, and the divine. In reflecting on her family story—one that included a minister-father, an outspoken overworked mother, and fourteen siblings—Katherine Martens observed that "the spiritual domain was male, the physical was female," and the former "more highly valued both at home and in church."[5] It is clear that in the memories of both these authors, men and women functioned in opposite, sometimes opposing, realms. More recently, scholars have questioned the sharp dichotomy assumed to exist between the public and private spheres, nuancing this paradigm with the awareness that male and female worlds of activity were never mutually exclusive but, rather, dependent on and in constant relation with each other. Yet, within a community that already maintained an ethos of dualities and separations—between believers and the world, good and evil, worldly and otherworldly, spiritual and material—a separation of gender spheres was also fitting.

If value was measured in economic success, financial return, title and formal respect given, and in particular historical veneration, then the activity of men was indeed more important. Yet Mennonites generally have tended towards a pattern of self-evaluation and also judgment of others based on 'works'; that is, what is contributed towards the community and society in terms of labour productivity and 'good deeds.' Because they were historically recognized for neither intellectual nor spiritual abilities, women received extra appraisal for their material output. As has been said about Jewish women, their "works praised them."[6] Mennonite women have been described as "women of the earth,"[7] closely associated with the material, rather than the spiritual, world, because of their practicality, hard-working natures, and connectedness to production and reproduction. While they were praised and valued for their material productivity, it was precisely because of their exclusion from the realm of intellectual authority within their ethno-religious communities that they individually and collectively became known for their functional artistry and culinary output. The quintessential homemakers, one might say. And indeed, it was (and is) such activity that served as cultural symbols and signifiers and enabled Mennonites to maintain their distinctiveness vis-à-vis the world around them. In current parlance, one might say that Mennonite women had a key role in 'marketing' the Mennonite 'brand.' Literature professor Magdalene Redekop has argued that the very identity of women as Mennonite was more related to their preservation and production of material ethnic tradition than it was to their religious beliefs. Speaking about her mother's early twentieth-century generation, she said,

> The women were Mennonite, not because they held passionate opinions, but because they made the quilts, they made the borscht, they made the varenike. It was my father who made the decision to offer hospitality to the Indians, but it was my mother, my sisters, and I who served the food and made the beds. While the *Bruderschaft* [brotherhood] was making the important decisions in the main body of the church, the *Frauenverein* [women's society] was in the basement, getting the food ready. They might be talking, but they did not have a voice.... Mennonite identity, as defined upstairs by the men, may be built on the bodies of the women who offer their labors in the basement.[8]

One might choose to view Mennonite women's linkage with material culture as pejorative and limiting to women as a group, but more especially to individual women who did not fit an image in which women were known by the work of their hands. Or, one might examine the ways in which women did exercise creativity and experience fulfilment in the context of roles that, while confining in some respects, allowed some opportunity for self-expression and through which they gained some renown.

This chapter will explore the material culture, historically so closely associated with Mennonite women, exemplified mainly in their handwork and cooking. All this, of course, took place within the overall art of homemaking, which was the vocation of almost all married Mennonite women prior to the late twentieth century. However, beyond the traditional domestic arts, Mennonite women also expressed themselves as artists, writers, and musicians. Single women, and others who eschewed homemaking as their primary occupation, also pursued education and developed careers that took them down different productive paths, sometimes away from the Mennonite church and community altogether. This, of course, did not occur without debate.

ARTISTIC AND DOMESTIC CREATIVITY

In 1967, the Mennonites in southwestern Ontario held their first annual Relief Sale, a weekend event that raises thousands of dollars each year for Mennonite Central Committee, an international relief and development organization. At the heart of the Relief Sale is the auction or sale of work created by the hands of Mennonite women, most notably quilts and other craftwork, and an array of foodstuffs representing different Mennonite ethnic traditions. Though men have always played key roles as fundraisers, auctioneers, and organizers, and more recently have been seen deep-frying doughnuts and flipping pancakes (and also generating a few stitches on a bed quilt), the material production of Mennonite women has been foundational to the invention and sustainability of this event. From the beginnings of Mennonites' presence in Canada, this production has included weaving blankets and quilting bed covers, embroidering towels and other linens for show and use, crocheting and knitting items for warmth and decoration, hooking and knotting floor mats, creating *Fraktur* and other painted items, and baking and cooking an abundance of foods from a variety of historic cultural traditions.

Mennonite women have long been stereotyped for their ability to sew and cook, skills that allowed for a degree of individuality and creativity, but yet were also a mundane and everyday part of household maintenance. Created items were fundamentally functional in meaning, though the creator might bring additional aesthetics to the item to the extent that her talent, interest, and community standards allowed. The Mennonites have a history of iconoclasm and emphasis on simplicity that historically undermined artistic endeavours and decorative approaches to material output. Indeed, for some church leaders, artistic expression that lacked a pragmatic purpose was akin to sin. As poet Di Brandt observed, "beauty was altogether a disturbing category for Mennonites no one knew quite what to do with it even though God must have put it there for a reason if only we could know what it was."[9]

In spite of this, and because of limited chances to put themselves forward in their churches and communities, Mennonite women found solace and a sense of accomplishment in bringing beauty to the mundane. Or, as one woman observed, "they infused a world often bordering on drabness and drudgery with order and beauty...."[10] For "Lizzy," a conservative Mennonite woman, gardening and quilting offered an outlet for expression that was limited in other contexts.

> I ... find pleasure in my talents. My clothes may be plain, my husband may be head over me and many times I am not able to express who I really am. I cannot express my own beauty. But you know, I find beauty in my roses and my glads [gladioli].... When I give my roses or sell my glads or when I present my grandchildren with my quilts, see the joy and take in their smiles, I know then that I have expressed my creative and beautiful self.[11]

For this woman, and undoubtedly for others, gardening was a way in which women expressed creativity—in the precision of the rows, the variety and arrangement of plantings—and also was a source of pride and measure of comparison with neighbours and relatives. Today, when one drives past or flies over the farmyards of conservative Mennonites in Ontario, one is struck by the amazing beauty and artistry in a 'simple' country garden.

Susanna Kehler Wiebe was able to offset the hardships of her life—memories of violence, hunger, and illness in the Soviet Union, and Depression-era farming as an immigrant in Saskatchewan—by imbuing her daily labours with a sense of beauty and refinement. Her daughter Hilda described her mother thus: "She planted flowers, kept her linens immaculate, and ironed innumerable white shirts to perfection. Her handwriting was small and precise, and her handstitching was neat and tiny. She crocheted delicate and beautiful lace edgings as well as table runners and doilies, and created elegant embroidered pieces."[12] Eleanor Martens observed that her mother's artistry was evident in a household task as apparently mundane as food preservation: "the way she lined up the fruit—apricots, cherries and plums ... the jars stood there gleaming on the basement shelves, straight and sparkling in their newly-preserved perfection, pleasing to the eye as well as to the palate."[13]

Creativity sometimes took the form of extreme functionalism and frugality and thus was not recognized as artistic endeavour at all. One Manitoba pioneer woman made scatter rugs from wool socks that were beyond mending by cutting them into strips, curling up the open edge, and then arranging them in layers for a shingle effect. The same woman decorated her house with bird ornaments made from stiffened rye dough and feathers from the birds shot by her husband.[14] Elsie Burkhardt Frey, who "always liked art," began to paint flowers and birds on ordinary household objects and furniture such as kitchen canisters, cookie tins, chair backs, and the baby's playpen when she was a teen-ager in the mid-1940s. She matter-of-factly stated, "I thought I'd like to paint, and got some [paints]."[15] Artistic expression in the everyday was also manifest in such things as butter sculpture and pie crusts patterned with birds and flowers. Art at a very basic level also entered the homes of early pioneer women, who used white sawdust to create artistic designs on dirt floors in the living and guest rooms of log houses.

Artistic expression that was clearly related to domestic skills was more acceptable and garnered women social approval within their communities. Her disdain of domestic art forms in favour of *Fraktur* and calligraphy was one reason Anna Weber, profiled at the chapter's outset, was considered odd by her community. Other women justified their artistic endeavours by pointing out that their creative pursuits did not impinge on their domestic responsibilities. For instance, Margaretha Wiebe, a Manitoba woman who developed a "special hobby" of making cloth dolls, of which she completed close to 100, stated that it took her about three days to make a doll, "but my household tasks do not suffer on account of this. My husband likes well-prepared meals and pretty well on time...."[16] Quilting, hooked-rug making, and embroidery, for example, required skills in sewing and needlework that were part of a woman's overall job of homemaking. Some of this domestic creativity derived from the sense that women's hands must never be idle. Ruth Reesor recalled that her mother had purchased a loom for weaving rugs from torn rags in order "to keep her teenage daughters occupied.... [Mother] was sometimes driven to unusual lengths to keep us busy, for doing nothing during the day was unacceptable."[17]

Besides keeping young women occupied, encouraging domestic creativity also reinforced appropriate gender roles for young women, and kept them mindful of their vocational goal as wives and mothers. For this reason also, many of the domestic art forms corresponded to particular rites of passage, such as births, marriages, and deaths. That women were destined for a career of homemaking after marriage was made apparent particularly in the rituals surrounding wedding preparations. A young woman preparing for marriage would usually make quilts, show towels, and other handcrafted functional items as part of her 'trousseau' or 'hope chest.' For example, Elvina Wideman Shantz made a set of decorative painted canisters when she knew she had a "husband-to-be."[18] Mary Konrad's early 1940s 'hope' chest included tea towels embroidered by her younger sisters, one for each day of the week, decorated with "ever so cuddly cats doing their full week of duties, Monday a clothes-washing kitten, Tuesday an ironing kitten and so on."[19]

The show towel, an embroidered linen cloth used only for decorative purposes but with a functional form, was done by Swiss Mennonite girls for their hope chest. The show towel, as an intricate work of embroidery requiring skill and practice, was also "proof of feminine value"[20] and was a way in which a young woman could demonstrate her domestic worthiness. The show towel, as a social and artistic custom, had more or less disappeared by the twentieth century. Unlike quilts, which were often done by a group of women and thus had a kind of communal authorship, show towels were individual creations and the artist would almost always embroider her name on it. Sometimes she would add a motto, such as the following: "Fanny Bricker is my name/Upper Canada is my station/Waterloo is my Dwelling place/and Christ is my Salvation."[21] Gender norms and religious values thus received expression and were reinforced in the creation of show towels and similar items.

Perhaps the quintessential hope chest item was the quilt, an item that still today symbolizes functional artistry, female busyness and productivity, and domestic concerns. In Waterloo County early in the twentieth century, Mennonite women became known for their distinctive quilt making, which used "bold shapes, large forms and brilliant colours of striking contrast." Yet, quilt making was a craft not unique to the Mennonites, but one that evolved from the influence of imported textiles and British settlers in the mid-nineteenth century.[22] Prior to this, Mennonite women with Pennsylvania German culture were known for woven bed coverings (often using red and black as the main colours) rather than sewn quilts. Mennonite women also followed changing styles of quilt making that evolved throughout the twentieth century. Quilt making in particular may have been taken up by Mennonite women because it could be done as a group, in the context of quilting 'bees,' and thus a quilt became the product of a collective effort as opposed to an individualistic endeavour that might generate personal pridefulness, a quality that went against Mennonite ideals of humility and self-denial. As Susan D. Shantz said: "In the Mennonite culture ... where individuality and pride are discouraged, quiltmaking is nevertheless regarded as a socially acceptable outlet for personal expression because it does not undermine a woman's role within her home or church."[23] The bees also provided a setting in which visiting occurred while women worked, and so their work ethic was not undermined by socializing.

The transformation of scrap fabric into functional objects of beauty also reflected Mennonite ideals of thriftiness and simplicity; one woman expressed guilt when she began using newly purchased fabric rather than scraps. The argument has also been made that the 'piecework' nature of quilting corresponds to the fragmented nature of women's daily lives as they care for children whilst performing a myriad of household tasks. And to the extent that quilts became family heirlooms and that mothers passed on to daughters their quilt-making knowledge, the craft reinforced nuclear and extended family ties. Quilts were an important part of Mennonite dowries in the early twentieth century: one Waterloo County woman, in recalling her mother's marriage in 1923, commented: "each boy got three quilts when he married. The girls had five, naturally, because they made their own."[24] Quilt making was also a necessary life skill for females to learn as young girls; Mary Ann Cressman Bowman began quilting when she was twelve years old and crafted over 600 quilts in her lifetime.[25]

In cases where a woman worked independently, quilting was one of the primary forms of artistic expression for Mennonite women; the quilt was a functional item, yet one that allowed for an almost endless imagination of pattern and colour. A woman's "joy, sadness, hope, expectations and memories of loved ones were reflected in her choices and effort."[26] Quilting also allowed for a subtle individualism within a prescribed structure. Though a woman adhered to a patchwork pattern handed down through generations, her choice of fabric colour and design and the arrangement of her own stitches made the finished production her own original creation. Thus, quilting as an art form allowed women to incorporate both thriftiness (by using fabric scraps) and beauty, humility, and individuality. Quilting was also an acceptable escape, allowing women to express ideas and emotions in fabric and colour that they couldn't otherwise utter. About her Amish grandmother, Louise Stoltzfus said:

"She spent hours behind a closed door, stitching quilts and braiding rag rugs which became masterpieces of colour, reflecting an inner life quite unlike the reality of her everyday existence."[27] Like the show towels with religious verses embroidered on them, or *Fraktur* with similar text in decorative calligraphy, collectively made quilts with embroidered images and text could also reinforce religious ideals and values. In her analysis of a quilt made by young Mennonite women working as domestic servants in Vancouver in the early 1940s, Ruth Derksen Siemens observes that the proverbs and sayings stitched onto the quilt blocks reinforced multiple levels of meaning and self-understanding—service, purity, submission, for instance—that enabled the women to cope with their often difficult situation as immigrant domestics.[28]

The material production of household items served to reinforce female roles and goals as homemakers, wives, and mothers, and allowed women to exercise creativity and artistic inclination in functional ways. Artistic production was also an important aspect of women's work for relief and mission endeavours. Even in poor immigrant and settlement communities, where most of their time was absorbed in sheer subsistence, women created "[b]eautifully embroidered articles done on white bleached flour bags, white crocheted borders on pillow slips and tablecloths and knitted articles," which were then sold to raise funds for relief and mission work overseas or closer to home.[29] For some women, such activity also served more personal economic purposes. For instance, women turned quilting into entrepreneurial activity, and especially Old Order Mennonite women have contributed to the family income, and in some cases become self-supporting, through quilt production. In 1964, three Old Order Mennonite sisters moved off the family farm and into a nearby town where they supported themselves by working five to six days per week making and selling quilts; the first quilt sold that year for $65 but by the late 1980s they collected $500 per quilt and received orders from as far away as Europe and Australia.[30] Today, these small businesses are thriving and are undoubtedly crucial to the total income of a farming household. Just a few kilometres from my home, on the edge of Waterloo city limits, is an Old Order Mennonite farm; a separate addition with its own entrance built onto the house contains the quilting business of the Martin family women.

Other forms of material creativity grew out of financial need and became a form of income generation to sustain a woman's household. For instance, in the 1920s frontier settlement at Reesor in northeastern Ontario, where immigrant Mennonite families were desperately poor, Mathilde Friesen transformed her knitting abilities into a small business. Recognizing the need for warm mittens and socks for men working in the northern Ontario bush in winter, she regularly supplied the local storekeeper with these knitted items in exchange for food and other supplies.[31] As a newly married woman who, with her husband, had left the Old Order Mennonite community—and probably its social supports—in 1936, Salome Buehler Martin supplemented her husband's Depression-era wages by selling craft items made from driftwood, artificial flowers, and also baked goods.[32]

The creation of distinctive decorative items for the household was also an important site for ethnic interaction and exchanges. Their notable migratory history meant that Mennonites frequently found themselves in geographic locales where they were introduced to new and unfamiliar cultural traditions and where they, in turn, brought their own ethnic influence to bear on neighbouring peoples. The artistic handwork and culinary traditions practised by Mennonite women were often adopted from the ethnic cultures that existed amongst their neighbours. This was particularly true for Mennonite women in Russia, who incorporated Ukrainian foods like borscht and perogies into their culinary canon, often learned from Russian women who worked in their homes. Mennonites who migrated from Switzerland and south Germany to Pennsylvania in the seventeenth and eighteenth centuries absorbed and contributed to a new Pennsylvania German culture that was an amalgam of traditions brought to a shared locale in the new world by a variety of Germanic peoples. Pennsylvania German culinary and artistic forms were then transported north by Mennonites moving to then Upper Canada in the nineteenth century. Museum curator Susan M. Burke has remarked that it is "surprising, even startling" that women in early nineteenth-century Mennonite settlements would have had the time to continue the decorative needlework traditions brought from Pennsylvania. She goes on to suggest that it indicated "a conscious, even deliberate attempt to perpetuate a meaningful tradition ... [and] create a tangible bridge to the past. ... " The embroidered show towel, in particular, experienced a "rebirth" in Canada.[33]

In Canada, cultural transmission and exchanges continued. As noted earlier, Mennonite women immigrants who worked as domestics for other Canadians learned a range of English, Jewish, and other ethnic and national household customs, which they brought back to their own Mennonite homes. Ella Mann Coffman learned "refined ways of housekeeping" while working for a "wealthier class of people" in Chicago in the late nineteenth century, which apparently helped prepare her for her role as a Mennonite bishop's wife in Ontario.[34] Furthermore, when women of Swiss and Russian Mennonite backgrounds came together in Canada, they exchanged both domestic and artistic skills. For instance, when some Mennonite families from Ukraine lived with or worked for Swiss Mennonites in Waterloo County in the 1920s, the female newcomers, many of them bereft of their own handwork supplies and materials, learned the quilting arts of the Mennonites in southwest Ontario, who themselves had incorporated Pennsylvania German cultural forms into their handwork. Conversely, two Ontario Swiss sisters did a particular form of intricate red and black embroidery they had learned from Russian women who worked in the Mennonite family's household.[35] Women, in the household context, were the primary channels through which cultural traditions such as domestic art and cooking were exchanged and developed, customs that in some circumstances became key markers of Mennonite identity.

While most Mennonite women exercised their material creativity in the production of beautiful handwork and household items, a few others chose to exercise their artistic abilities through what one might call non-functional media, such as painting, sculpture, musical performance, or composition. Anna Weber, profiled at the outset of this chapter, was one of the earliest artists in the Swiss Mennonite community in Ontario. Born 100 years later and immigrating to Canada from Ukraine in the 1920s, Mary Klassen shared Anna's zeal and talent for watercolours. One of her earliest paintings is of the family's first home, about which Klassen said the following: "Because I was deprived so suddenly and absolutely of my childhood home in Russia, a home means more to me than to many who have not gone through this pain. Sometimes a dream of our first Canadian home still returns—the warmth, the safety, so close to and surrounded by the good earth, the vast dome overhead, the frogs and hoot-owls, the smell of wood burning raising the hope of supper."[36] At the age of eighteen in 1936, Mary left the family farm in the small community at Mayfair and went to Saskatoon to study painting, a rather unconventional thing for a rural Mennonite woman to do during the Depression. Not only was she drawn to a form of expression deemed frivolous and even sinful by many Mennonites, but she was departing from acceptable life choices for Mennonite women. In the city she lived with her brother, who was studying engineering, where she did housecleaning, babysitting, and ironing to help support the two of them.

Yet Mary did marry in 1940 and it is said that her best paintings date from the time in which she was primarily engaged in homemaking and child rearing. At the same time, the demands of marriage and family impinged first of all on her freedom to paint. And so she accepted full responsibility for the care of two young sons, and painted less, even while the family schedule seemed to make room for her husband's church work as Sunday school teacher and youth leader, and for his participation on the university boxing team, along with his own work and graduate studies. Like many women of her generation, her avocations were sidelined, if only temporarily, in favour of her husband's interests.[37] Yet, when her husband died suddenly at the age of forty-five, Mary turned to painting not only for solace but for economic support. When the Edmonton Art Gallery turned down her application to be an art instructor, saying she was 'overqualified,' Mary decided to open an art studio in her home, which she ran successfully for nine years.

Sometimes a woman's creativity and boldness in expressing that creativity were condemned by communities that were fearful and suspicious of such expression. One Mennonite composer commented that while Mennonites had a special respect for the 'helping' professions—"They seem so obviously 'Christian' with their emphasis on caring and healing"—the arts were perceived as "decorative, non-essential" and "self-indulgent."[38] Erika Koop, who was artistically inclined as a child growing up in Russia, observed that, "The neighbours wondered how I would ever get a husband, so it didn't do to encourage me too much.... The main thing for a girl was how to cook and how to clean and how to sew." But once in Canada, Erika exercised her creativity in a myriad of ways, including raising six daughters, most of whom became professional artists.[39]

Margaretha Schaefer was one southern Manitoba woman far ahead of her time and one who appeared indifferent to judgment by her Mennonite neighbours. Musically gifted, she was the only person in the village of Gnadenthal to own a piano, which she used not only for personal enjoyment, but also for instruction. One of her admirers recalled, "musically and culturally, Mrs. Schaefer was far ahead of the Gnadenthal of that time [1930s]. She was therefore often misunderstood. Many of her fine endeavors met with opposition. Such was the case when her presentation of Schiller's 'Das Lied von der Glocke' with some young people was denounced as not being of the Holy Ghost." She was also an accomplished seamstress; the dresses of lace and velvet that her daughters wore were the envy of all around.[40]

HOSTING AND HOMEMAKING

The friends, family, and acquaintances who visited the homes of Mary Klassen and Margaretha Schaefer were fortunate to see the watercolour paintings of Mary on the wall and hear Margaretha play the piano. But undoubtedly Mary and Margaretha also were obliged to have a clean house and serve at least tea and sweets when company came. While both women broke new ground by pursuing artistic vocations, during the era in which they lived they likely would have considered their roles as homemakers to be most important. Indeed, essentialist understandings of women placed homemaking alongside child bearing as a role only the female sex could perform. Women took on homemaking as a destiny and there was a general belief that women were by nature homemakers. For instance, in his 1942 manual of sex education, Ontario minister Clayton F. Derstine observed, "Women's bodies are formed to be homemakers, live indoors, and do the lighter tasks of life; hence they are not built so strong as men."[41] Most homemakers, especially farm-based women and nineteenth-century settlers, would hardly have considered their tasks "light" and knew that their biceps bulged from kneading endless batches of dough and that varicose veins resulted from too much time spent on their feet. Yet, in an era when married women with children did not 'work out'— that is, were not employed for wages outside the home—except in situations of acute financial crisis, her assumed vocation was to be a homemaker.

A community's assessment of a woman and often her own self-perception (however much this engendered contradictions within herself) were directly related to her accomplishments as a homemaker, from the cleanliness of her house, to the quality of her baked goods, to the productivity of her garden, to the small size of her quilting stitches. Memories of "Grandmother Snider" observe. "A thrifty housewife prided herself on her collection of hundreds of jars of colourful fruits and vegetables temptingly arranged in neat rows on sturdy shelves...."[42] One family matriarch, even though she managed a farm and raised five children alone after her husband's early death, was remembered for the following motto: "white wash, a clean floor, and homemade bread is the sign of a good housewife."[43] Even laundry was a site at which women's domestic abilities were tested, whether it was the early hour at which her newly washed clothes were hung outdoors for passers-by to see, or whether it was the whiteness of her husband's shirts, or whether they were "as smoothly pressed as a page in the Bible." And while laundry of the twenty-first century is a minimalist task, it was an all-day, all-consuming task for several people until the arrival of wringer washers and later automatic washers and dryers.

Katherine Martens recalls, "On laundry day when I was growing up Mother had time for nothing else from sunrise to sunset."[44] The process involved maintaining a fire hot enough to boil several iron cauldrons full of water, then pouring the water with shavings of lye soap into the hand-cranked washer, which was manually agitated until the laundry was clean. After rinsing and wringing, the clothes were hung outdoors, though whites were also put through a process of bleaching and bluing to ensure they were "as white as freshly fallen snow in the late afternoon" and items like shirts, blouses, and doilies were also starched. The day after laundry day was ironing day, another time-consuming affair in a pre-polyester era.[45] The task was made more arduous by the fact that in the 1920s, at least on the prairies, most rural homes still did not have running water, and the nearest well was on average sixty metres away.[46] Wringer-washer machines were a welcome improvement, but the hand-powered ones required significant physical strength to operate and so the process could be just as exhausting. Of course, the degree of difficulty of the laundry process could vary between households, depending on the nature of equipment and number of helpers that any one woman might have. Like other households tasks, the drudgery of laundry sometimes abated briefly and women experienced moments, large and small, of satisfaction and even pleasure. Susan Klassen, for instance, told her daughters that she enjoyed washing diapers by hand "because she found the feel of the Ivory Flakes suds in her hands so pleasant."[47]

The homemaking skills and talents of Mennonite women were displayed most explicitly when they hosted guests, a frequent occurrence in Mennonite households, at least during the era when visiting was the predominant leisure pastime. According to Janet Mancini Billson, the custom of visiting "symbolizes women's traditional role of keeping the community and the culture together" and, for the Mennonites especially, "across rural distances."[48] Today, after-church visiting is common amongst Old Order Mennonites and, given that visits are rarely pre-arranged, a woman is assumed and expected to have plenty of baking and other foods prepared in anticipation of any number of adults and children at her Sunday dinner table. One Old Order woman said that on any given Sunday she might have twenty people for dinner and ten for supper, and commented, "You really have to be prepared; that means cooking and cleaning the entire place the day before."[49]

In the early settlement years, it wasn't just friends and family who came to visit, but also the travelling peddler or transient worker who stopped in for a meal and sometimes a bed for night. As hosts to travellers and others, women frequently had close contact with so-called 'outsiders.' For instance, Judith Klassen Neufeld's 1922 diary entries often refer to hosting a Jewish peddler for meals and overnight, as in "The Jew came for lunch" or "The Jew again came for the night."[50] Early Ontario houses were constructed with a designated 'beggar's' or 'tramp's' room and oral lore tells of Native people also being hosted in this way. Hosting company was a key component to the vocation of minister's wife. Needless to say, some women cringed (then and now) at the daunting prospect of 'entertaining,' which meant a clean, nicely decorated home and a delectable meal, but fulfilled this expected aspect of their domestic role nevertheless. Other women relished their role as host and thrived within the parameters of such a gendered function. For instance, in her printed memoir, Maria Martens Klassen Loepp states in large bold letters "Cooking and Company is my Delight!"[51] Gathering together friends and family for food and visiting on special and ordinary occasions, while revolving around seemingly mundane tasks, was fundamentally the "work of kinship."[52]

In a rural community, especially in a pre-telephone era, guests were always expected and so women knew they had to be prepared to serve a meal to any number of people. The daughter of a minister homesteading in northern Saskatchewan recalled that her mother hosted many people in their home and "some summers we had so many visitors that Mom could hardly keep up washing the sheets, drying them on the line, and getting them back on the bed for the next company." When unexpected guests arrived near mealtime,

> Mom had to scramble to find something to feed everyone. Maybe there was a smoked ham kept out in the summer kitchen. She could cut slices of ham and fry it, or she could fry sausages. If we had no ham or sausage left, Mom could get jars of canned beef or chicken from the cellar and heat that up. There were always potatoes to boil, and canned vegetables, and home-made pickles to add to the meal, not to mention homemade bread and butter. If there was nothing ready to serve for dessert, Mom could always open a quart or two of her canned fruit. The men and the kids got the best of the visit. The women had to do quite a bit of their visiting while cooking the meal and washing dishes.[53]

Women's culinary and other homemaking talents were tested most acutely during such occasions as family gatherings or harvest time. In fact, one community history plainly states that "the culinary reputation of every house-wife on the threshing circuit was at stake each season."[54] According to one Manitoba memoir, although women enjoyed family gatherings at Easter and Christmas mainly because of the social and kinship aspect, such events "meant no holiday for the women." In this recollection, as the women bustled about preparing the meal, men would sit in the living room, visiting and smoking, and "on occasion, one of the men popped his head into the kitchen, reminding his wife that their baby's diaper still needed changing." When the meal was ready, the men would eat first, while the women hovered about refilling platters and serving coffee, then the women would eat—sometimes off their husband's unwashed plate—and then the children.[55] The hierarchy was very clear.

Serving a meal to a large group of family and friends gave a Mennonite woman an opportunity to present her skill at a task that was perhaps only second to child bearing in its place as an intrinsic aspect of being a Mennonite woman. As for some other ethnic and religious groups, food and cooking have been central to Mennonite cultural identity, as externally perceived but also internally understood. While Mennonites disdained many other forms of entertainment and cultural endeavour as being 'worldly,' food production and consumption, as an activity closely related to the land and necessary for sustenance, did not come under scrutiny as something that would induce pridefulness or excess. As such, women could receive much affirmation and encouragement, in essence, as culinary artists.

To the extent that food preparation was traditionally a very gendered activity, Mennonite women have often been portrayed foremost as preparers and conveyors of food. In her memoir, Katie Funk Wiebe noted that in her understanding, growing up and becoming a woman "in essence meant learning to cook."[56] Pamela Klassen stated it well when she observed that, "Because of the Mennonite romance with food, women's roles as the traditional makers of shoofly pie, varenike, portzelky, zwiebach, and all the other relishes, breads, and sweets clustered on the table have been a source of power used by women and against them."[57] The linkage between Mennonite women and food has been perpetuated in Mennonite folklore and also academic scholarship. In 1954 John Hostetler, an American sociologist of Mennonites, wrote the following about "Things Feminine" in a popular booklet describing all aspects of Mennonite life and belief: "[Mennonite women's] social life is a satisfying blend of work and church life. Not being afraid of hard work, they eat well. They cook, can, stock their whitewashed fruit cellars, and provide well for their household. They probably pay less attention to their waistline than do most American women.... "[58] Hostetler's depiction of Mennonite women as jolly, plump workhorses perpetually in the kitchen, a picture that seems ridiculous today, fit not only the domestic ideal prevalent in the 1950s but also reflected a Mennonite ideological framework that enclosed women securely in the kitchen. More recent popular depictions of Mennonite foods that "schmeck" [taste good] reinforce stereotypical linkages between Mennonite women and food/eating, though many of these portrayals are mainly about conservative and Old Order groups, a small minority of Canadian Mennonites, and ones who have retained rural practices of food self-sufficiency much longer.[59]

The linkage between Mennonite women and food is reinforced in the memories, oral and written, of Mennonites about their mothers. In reminiscing about their mother, the children of Susanna Kehler Wiebe all gave much space to their mother's culinary abilities, describing fondly the Russian Mennonite foods that she prepared for her husband and ten children, but also noting that she often cried while she cooked, and was always the one to eat last and to take the smallest helping. Her son Henry recalled, "At mealtimes she was the last to sit down, and constantly up again—to bring things from stove to table, to put more *gereischtit Brot* (toasted bread) on the plate, or potatoes, or to re-fill our bowls with *Borscht*, or our coffee cups." Susanna's daughter Tina echoed her brother: "Mother serves everyone before she herself sits down to eat her own small helping, half-crying because she is thinking of the children who are no longer at home, and whom she misses very much."[60] L. Marie Enns also recalled that her mother was the last to eat at the end of a long day of constant food preparation for the team of men harvesting their crop in northern Saskatchewan in the 1940s. The day's menu included fried potatoes and bacon and eggs for breakfast; freshly baked cake with coffee for mid-morning break; roasted chicken with dressing, vegetables, and potatoes, and homemade pudding for dinner at noon; cookies straight from the oven in mid-afternoon; and for supper, fried ham, potatoes with cream gravy, canned corn, dill pickles, bread and buns, and blueberry pie baked that day. Of course, everything was home-grown and home-preserved. "It was late when the men had eaten, later when we had eaten, and even later when Mom had everything under control and could go to bed.... This frenzy of harvest work and cooking would continue until the threshing was done...."[61] Edward Giesbrecht of Yarrow, British Columbia, similarly recalled the mammoth task his mother had in baking weekly for eleven people: "On Saturday she bakes six pans of zwieback, 12 loaves of bread, butterhorns, cinnamon buns, and pies. Except for the bread, most of these are consumed by Sunday night. Often she bakes biscuits on Monday and pancakes on Tuesday to tide us over until Wednesday, when she bakes another eight loaves of bread. Her baking requires over 200 pounds of flour every month."[62]

The above reminiscences are common; memory sources are replete with reflections on the cooking and baking of mothers. Though my own mother has on many occasions avowed her dislike of kitchen labour, among my sharpest childhood memories is the aroma of the curly butterhorn rolls that she regularly baked on Saturday afternoons. And among the few images I have of my grandmother is her slow shuffling back and forth between kitchen and dining room table; I don't have a mental picture of her situated in any other room. Anne Konrad's family memoir echoes this: "Imagine keeping eleven persons clean and fed. Mother cooked many soups and baked brown and white bread every week. On Saturdays she baked *Zwieback* buns and perhaps (if she anticipated guests) raisin bread (*Stretzel*) or *Pljushky*, a sweet roll brushed with egg white to a shiny brown top.... Saturday suppers always consisted of fresh *Zwieback* buns, boiled eggs and tea."[63]

Women themselves viewed cooking as one of their primary roles in adulthood. Margaret Heinrichs Groening recalled that her goals as a wife were to be "kind, cheerful, a good cook, ... to be neat, have the house clean, meals on time."[64] An example of how closely women were tied to the kitchen in reality and in memory is indicated by a special Mennonite heritage event in the year 2000 devoted to the Mennonite woman's apron as a symbol. The writer of a newspaper article giving an account of this event said, "Definitely one of my clearest memories of my mom when I was a child is of her stirring a pot of soup or kneading bread on the kitchen cabinet ... wearing a turquoise blue checkered apron with cross-stitch along the bottom."[65]

Even amidst the gender-limiting and undervalued realm of domestic labour, many women found their greatest creative outlet in caring for homes and families. For generations of Mennonite women, the preparation of food and its distribution within the household was historically an activity over which they had an important measure of control: "women's ability to prepare and serve food gives them direct influence over others, both material and magical."[66] Food preparation has long been a means for women to express creativity within the parameters of gender. Furthermore, women were the primary conveyors of ethnic culinary traditions, passing their knowledge through generations of daughters. As mentioned already, for the first generation of immigrants in Canada, foodways were often the site at which the old and new worlds met. The preparation of ethnic foods was one means for newcomer Mennonites to "survive psychologically"[67] as they made other difficult transitions in climate, language, and host society environments. Their capacity for food production also nurtured women's entrepreneurial initiatives that were sometimes spurred on by economic necessity. The economic hardship created by a husband who was an unpaid church worker during the Depression prompted Lydia Bauman Martin to begin a market gardening business. In addition to selling fruits and vegetables at the local farmers' market, she baked up to 200 dozen cookies and eighty loaves of bread weekly.[68] This business approach to food production is evident today in the modest signs advertising foodstuffs for sale—'no Sunday sales'—at the end of laneways of Old Order Mennonite women in Ontario. Or the tiny, tucked-away but locally famous Sittler Bakery, run by several conservative Mennonite women in Conestogo, Ontario.

Lydia may have sometimes enjoyed the task of food production, which, for her, amounted to a small culinary industry. But preparing and serving food for family, guests, and workers could be a burdensome, labour-intensive, and seemingly never-ending activity, as many memories attest. During difficult economic times, as in the years of early settlement or during the Depression, women were severely tested in the role of feeding their families according to Mennonite custom and expectation. For instance, during the Depression years, with six children to feed and clothe, Mary Neufeld offered meals consisting mainly of "bread with lard (or shortening) with a sprinkling of sugar and for dessert, bread dunked in the juice of preserves."[69] Women who arrived as refugees from Ukraine after the Second World War, many of whom came to adulthood during years of food shortages and famine, felt inadequate when their abilities to 'cook Mennonite' were found wanting in Canada. While women were praised for their culinary skill, food preparation and presentation were also a site at which women were tested for their worthiness. Furthermore, competition could easily develop between women as they judged amongst themselves and were judged by their menfolk on such pivotal things as whose pie crust was flakiest and whose *zwieback* were the shapeliest. Hence, women's authority in or confinement to the kitchen could both empower and oppress.

One way in which Mennonite women capitalized on their reputation for kitchen production was in the creation and publication of cookbooks. Cookbooks, as possibly the best-selling genre of books, have consistently been produced by Mennonite women as a means to raise funds and to celebrate a long history of food production. Analysts of community-based cookbooks suggest that in such volumes, women tell of their "lives and beliefs" and "present their values."[70] Cookbooks, associated with the mundane, with the material, and with women's work, have rarely, as Matthew Bailey-Dick argues in a 2005 article, been regarded "as having any serious historical value."[71] This may be considered ironic, given that *The Mennonite Treasury of Recipes*, produced by women's groups in Canada, is among the best-selling 'Mennonite' books of all time. First published in 1961, by the mid-1980s the book had gone through thirteen printings and sold 42,000 copies. The inspiration for the book came at the 1960 annual Conference of Mennonites in Canada sessions at Steinbach, Manitoba, when, after cooking meals for several hundred delegates, women agreed that it would be a good idea to write down recipes for mass cooking for future reference. When the project committee learned that the printer wanted to produce 3000 copies to start, one woman expressed deep skepticism that such an amount would ever be sold.[72] The 1962 edition that I possess begins with a poem entitled "The Housewife" that exalts the "small affairs," "trifling worries," and "little cares" that consume the life of a homemaker, among which was "A hungry husband to be fed...." Reflective of its particular social era, the cookbook's individual recipe authors are named according to their husbands, as in "Mrs. John Rempel," or "Mrs. F.E. Reimer," while the single women contributors are labelled as "Miss."

The editors of another best-selling Mennonite cookbook recognized the importance of food preparation to arenas well outside the home. The *Canadian Mennonite Cookbook*, first published in 1965, claimed that "throughout centuries of recorded history, food has played a leading role as a force behind many great events. This has included conferences, banquets, dinners or other occasions where important decisions have been made."[73] These women knew how fundamental their food offerings were to the functioning of the more 'public' institutions of church and community. As Bailey-Dick has argued, the discourse in cookbooks is about more than the material act of food preparation. Using examples such as the immensely popular *More with Less* cookbook, which first appeared in 1976 and twenty-five years later had sold 840,000 copies in forty-seven printings, he argues that cookbooks—at least this one—in fact moulded a Mennonite identity based on principles of discipleship and simple living, and thus were extremely important as shapers of ideology and values. Other cookbooks have served to heighten interest in Mennonite heritage or raised global awareness.[74] If understood in terms of their wider goals and impact, cookbooks have served as a female voice in the otherwise male-dominated discourse on Mennonite beliefs and identity. Cookbooks, initiated and produced by women, shaped both Mennonite cultural self-understanding and generated external perceptions and knowledge about Mennonite historical development and sociological identity.[75]

That cooking and baking were part of the overall vocation of homemaking is also indicated by the inclusion, in many Mennonite cookbooks like *The Mennonite Treasury of Recipes*, of a section devoted to a range of non-culinary 'household hints.' The *Treasury*, for instance, offers advice on how to hang pictures, how to clean bathroom fixtures and shower curtains, how to pick up slivers of broken glass off a rug, and how to re-cover an ironing board. The 'hints' are indicative of a mid-twentieth-century ethos of domesticity that placed a great deal of emphasis on perfectionism in homemaking on the part of women, Mennonites not excepted. Standards of exactitude increased as the time and effort associated with the labour of homemaking eased.

The material nature of homemaking changed dramatically over the course of the twentieth century, even if the meaning of it did not. The daughters and granddaughters of turn-of-the-century pioneers and rural women certainly did not labour over tasks such as laundry and meal preparation with the same physical intensity and arduousness as their foremothers. But for rural Canadian women in particular, maintaining a household remained very laborious until well after the Second World War. For instance, in 1941, only 20.2 percent of farm areas had electric lighting, 12.2 percent had inside running water, 29.3 percent had telephones, 22.2 percent refrigeration, and only 8.1 percent had flush toilets.[76] The fact that 87 percent of Mennonites at this time lived in rural areas meant that household technology was for most women still in a relatively primitive state.

Housework changed qualitatively, if not really in amount, in the modern era. Much of this difference was owing to the introduction of hydroelectricity in the 1940s to most rural communities. In Blumenort, Manitoba, the advent of hydro in 1948 and, thus, electrical appliances, revolutionized the Mennonite home. According to the community's historian, "Electricity ended the need to pump water by hand, maintain an outdoor toilet, burn firewood and kerosene, and wash by hand. The electric stoves, fridges, freezers, lights, washing machines, clothes dryers, vacuum cleaners, sewing machines, hot water tanks, furnaces and indoor plumbing which were taken for granted in 1960 had been unknown only fifteen years before."[77] Anna Reimer Dyck recalled that when Niverville, Manitoba, obtained electricity in 1939, she received an electric washer, "the greatest Christmas gift I ever received, for now the tiring task of washing by hand was over."[78]

Many memoirs speak with notable delight about the arrival of a vacuum cleaner in the home: Maria Martens Klassen was surprised when her husband used their 1950 berry cheque to purchase a vacuum cleaner, justifying the seeming extravagance by saying it was the only way he could get rid of the salesman. Maria recalled, "The girls find the Electrolux very handy to keep this big house clean."[79] However, in many households, 'conveniences' such as washing machines and vacuum cleaners—the tools of women's work—were a lesser purchasing priority than was new equipment for the farm, since improving agricultural productivity was considered more important to the overall household economy. According to one family memoir, "Household conveniences took second place to the luxuries of potato diggers, a spanking new McCormick tractor in 1939 . . . and other assorted outdoor toys."[80]

For Mennonites, who, until after the Second World War, lived mainly in rural areas, the 1950s really represented a transitional time in the nature of homemaking. On the one hand, increased access to utilities in rural areas, and the appliances that depended on them, dramatically changed the time and physical effort spent in such chores as laundry, cleaning, and food preparation. The arduous tasks of pumping and hauling water, chopping wood, and building fires, which were the daily fare of their grandmothers, began to disappear even for rural women. On the other hand, more and more Mennonites were now living in cities, in which household labour was lessened somewhat by the absence of care for huge farmstead gardens and livestock. Although certain tasks became quicker because of new technology, the overall time expended in housework may have lessened only slightly. Instead, standards increased and the home now had to be not only cleaner but also colour-coordinated, and show evidence of 'home decor.' Children had to be brighter and given more attention, husbands had to be well-fed and nurtured, and, on top of this, a woman had to give plenty of time to her own appearance and femininity in order to complete the picture of the perfect home. One historian has described the 1950s as a period when "homemaking was magnified so that it appeared to demand a woman's entire waking attention."[81] This trend did not change much, even while household technology continued to modernize. In 1971, LaVerna Klippenstein wrote that even though "modern appliances have taken over long, arduous household tasks, ... women now spend hours polishing already shining floors, baking rich dainties for dieting friends, and sewing yet another garment to add to a bulging closet."[82]

While Mennonites frequently resisted modernization with appeals to simplicity and separation from the world, women were not immune from the lure of convenience and marketing campaigns that called them to perfectionism as wives, mothers, and homemakers. Of course, Old Order and some other conservative Mennonite women whose communities spurned modern household and farm technology, or at least 'modernized' at a much slower pace, continued to perform the daily chores of a rural household in a manner similar to that of their great-grandmothers in late nineteenth-century Ontario. The gradual advent of electricity and telephones beginning in the 1980s, first installed in farm buildings such as barns, and later into houses, changed the nature of housework for conservative women as well, although there was, and is, much internal debate regarding the extent to which modern 'conveniences' undermine Old Order beliefs in separation from the world. One contemporary Old Order Mennonite woman, a mother of nine, enjoyed a refrigerator in her kitchen after electricity was hooked up in their home; when her husband was ordained a deacon in the church in the 1990s, however, they removed the fridge and she went back to using an ice box and cellar. As the wife of a church leader, she was to set an example of simplicity, purity, and humility.[83]

It is important to recognize that some women thrived as homemakers, enjoying the feel and smell of freshly laundered clothes, the productivity of a kitchen counter covered in fresh baking, and the beauty of a garden in full flower. Others, who were not naturally inclined to homemaking, or simply chafed at the expectations that this was the only vocation open to them, may have secretly carried other aspirations. Erica Epp Koop observed that when her mother began doing clerical work—answering phones and addressing envelopes—at their church later in life in the 1960s, she "just blossomed." At the end of the twentieth century, Koop reflected, "If mother had lived now, I think she would have been a very different woman. I think she would have been basically happier because she would have a little more to concentrate on than just sweeping and cleaning and cooking and sweeping and cleaning and cooking" [repetition from original].[84] Koop herself, as a Mennonite woman coming into adulthood in the 1960s, certainly had more vocational choices than her mother had. The increased interest in and presence of Mennonite women in higher education and the paid workforce outside the home during this decade and following meant that, like other Canadians, Mennonites found themselves debating what woman's true nature and role were indeed.

WORKERS AND PROFESSIONALS

Canadian women's relationship to paid labour went through dramatic changes, especially over the course of the twentieth century. Until the 1930s, young women generally left the workforce upon marriage, but, during the Second World War, married women were drawn into the workforce to buttress the war effort and to fill the male labour shortage. After the war, overall female participation in the workforce dropped, but the proportion of married women remained higher than at pre-war levels and women increasingly stopped working only with their first pregnancy. By the late 1950s and 1960s, it became more common for women to return to paid employment, most often in service sectors like clerical, nursing, and teaching, once their youngest child began school. By the 1970s, more and more women were maintaining their involvement in paid labour, at some level, through the stages of marriage, child bearing, and child rearing. Mennonites, who, like other Canadian groups, viewed the primary vocational goal of married women to be that of child rearing and homemaking, became concerned with the post-war trend of women 'working out,' that is, women choosing to work for pay outside the home. To church leaders and others who spoke out on the topic, the phenomenon of 'working women' undermined separate sphere ideals about woman's place in the home, a role that was considered both biblical and 'natural.' Much of the official thinking reflected essentialist notions of female physical and mental capacity, as in Clayton F. Derstine's statement on homemaking mentioned earlier, and also doctrinally based perceptions of the proper relational roles of men and women.

The ideological debates and statements about woman's roles of course failed to recognize that women had always 'worked' in ways that supported Mennonite households well beyond the housekeeping and child-care tasks that most narrowly defined household management. Prior to a significant wave of urbanization on the part of Mennonites after the mid-twentieth century, women's primary setting for work was the rural household, which encompassed both 'indoor' domestic labour and 'outdoor' farm and garden labour. There has been some debate among scholars regarding the 'status' of farm women vis-à-vis their male partners. Some have argued that a subsistence-based rural household created an equalization between men and women based on the labour and management required of both to ensure the success of the family farm enterprise, and that the move to towns and cities and its accompanying separation between workplace and home led to a decline in the perceived value of women's labour. Such an interpretation is also reflected in some first-person reflections. In her autobiographical account of growing up Mennonite in Ontario, Ruth Reesor observed,

> Country wives actually had a better chance of equality between the sexes than their city counterparts. The raising of chickens was entirely a woman's job, for men often refused to have anything to do with raising chickens or gathering eggs. The women often helped with the morning and evening chores, milking cows or feeding pigs. They drove tractors in the fields and most were very well informed in the art of animal husbandry.... The country men were home all day and there is greater opportunity to discuss mutual problems and financial affairs if your three meals a day were spent at home.[85]

A writer to a Mennonite periodical in the 1950s echoed this observation, pointing out that in the city, a father spent less time at home and thus the homemaking demands on a woman were greater than ever. Certainly women and men both worked hard from dawn until dusk on farm enterprises, especially before mechanization and modern agricultural techniques became commonplace. And so it is difficult, and perhaps futile, to sort out questions of which sex worked more or harder, or which work was valued more. What does seem clear, however, is that however much women participated in the farm labour of milking cows or bringing in the harvest, they also carried the large portion of the household labour and certainly the primary care of children and other dependent relatives. As the daughter of Sara Wiebe, a rural woman in early twentieth-century Manitoba, recalled about her mother: "She was a woman who walked and worked beside her husband in the fields and on the farmyard and still found time to perform the multitudinous tasks that were expected of a Mennonite homemaker on the farm."[86]

Women had long generated income for their households, either informally or professionally, but especially in the years prior to the separation of spheres of paid work and home, and the professionalization of occupations, women combined various types of income-earning labour with a multitude of household tasks. Barbara Bowman Shuh, for instance, combined her involvement in the family cheese-making business in Ontario with her own midwifery and healing practice.[87] Like many turn-of-the-century community midwives, Barbara also attended at deathbeds and prepared bodies for burial, thus also adding the vocation of informal undertaker to her many-faceted work roles. Katherina Born Thiessen, who received formal training in midwifery, bone setting, and other healings arts in Germany, continued her practice after settling in Manitoba in the late nineteenth century. Once they could afford it, she and her husband built a large house designed for her busy practice: a reception room, operating room, and pharmacy on the main floor and individual patient rooms on the upper floor. One end of the house was reserved for the Thiessen family's living quarters. One account of Thiessen's life suggests that the residence-cum-hospital was built to allow Katherine to do her work while remaining at home, "which was the proper place for a woman according to the church elders." Other strategies for combining her profession and her domestic life included closing the pharmacy and clinic on Thursdays, which was her washday.[88]

Many other Mennonite women, throughout the nineteenth and twentieth centuries, sold farm produce and handwork at local markets, sewed and tailored clothing for friends and neighbours, and contributed to the family coffers through fees charged for a whole range of services, many of which were entrepreneurial extensions of their own domestic labour. Today, Old Order women in particular produce goods for sale at the end of the lane or in urban marketplaces. Other women worked alongside their husbands or other relatives in family businesses while also carrying primary responsibility for the household, though historical sources rarely acknowledge the centrality of women's involvement in such enterprises. One of these was Gertrude Martens, who was known to assist in her husband's garage in Lowe Farm, Manitoba; a community history says the following about her: "What she did was not a woman's job but she turned her hand at running the drill press, sharpening scythes, putting spokes in buggy wheels, and sewing up a buggy or car top, or repairing car seats."[89]

Single women were frequently important income earners for their families, especially during economic downturns in the male labour market. Single young women working in the cities were the most employable among immigrants from the Soviet Union in the 1920s, and during the decade of the 1930s as well, there often seemed to be jobs for young women when their brothers and fathers were without work. Hildegard Neufeld, who immigrated to Manitoba with her family in 1925, left her parents three months after arrival, on her seventeenth birthday, for domestic work in Winnipeg. Later she sewed men's shirts in a factory, and then worked at Eaton's for thirteen years. She recalled, "For many years I was the only breadwinner in the family."[90] Nora Brubacher spent "the greater part" of her working life as a domestic, typically cleaning ten houses per week, and was described in the Kitchener–Waterloo daily newspaper as "The greatest cleaning woman in the world."[91] Other women who never married typically entered gender-specific professions such as teaching, nursing, or other parts of the caregiving sector. A few who carved out professional spaces in work sectors that were non-traditional for Mennonites, never mind women, often functioned independently and on the margins of Mennonite communities. For instance, Ann Neufeld was the second female bank manager in the Niagara Peninsula and only the thirteenth in Canada when she became manager of the Canadian Imperial Bank of Commerce in St. Catharines in 1968. She had begun her career as a bank teller in 1941.[92]

Mennonite families that moved to remote parts of the country in search of economic opportunity as well as greater cultural isolation were able to employ their sons on farms and farm-based businesses, but daughters frequently found employment outside their households and sometimes outside the community as a means of generating more income. When about twenty-five Mennonite families left Saskatchewan in the early 1940s and moved to Vanderhoof in northern British Columbia, it was young women who were "employed as maids and waitresses in hospitals and hotels and as domestics in private homes while most of the young men [were] working along side their fathers on the farms."[93] One Yarrow, British Columbia, resident, Susie Giesbrecht, considered herself fortunate that after high school she had found employment as a store clerk in Chilliwack, rather than having to work as a domestic in Vancouver, as her sisters had done. Despite the felt discrimination towards Mennonites in the Fraser Valley, Susie's wages were increased to $12.95 per week, as much as longer term employees.[94] Like most other unmarried women, she gave most of her wages to her parents.

Women often found themselves doing waged labour during economic and political cycles in which male labour was insufficient to support a family, such as during the Depression of the 1930s, or when men themselves were absent, such as during the two world wars, or following the death or disability of a spouse. One example of this is described by Kimberly D. Schmidt, who studied a conservative Mennonite community in New York state that, when confronted by financial crises on family farms in the 1970s and 1980s, saw married women with children enter the waged workforce, a practice outside the ideological norms of the church.[95] And, as we have seen, periods of immigration and settlement in all time periods saw women working for wages as domestic help. During the 1930s, with four young children at home and her husband "often without work," Louise Martens Fehderau was able to earn between $3 to $5 per week doing the washing and ironing for three families. She had to fetch and return the laundry on foot, carrying the bundles for up to six blocks. Her earnings from this and sewing, she recalled, enabled her to clothe the children and buy groceries and meat.[96] Mary Regehr recalls that during the Depression, her mother went out to work and left her, at the age of ten, at home caring for three younger brothers.[97] Similarly, between the years 1929 and 1936, Katherine Friesen held three different positions as a domestic worker in Saskatoon to ease the financial hardships for her rural farming family. For her, the motivation was not just to earn money, but a "desire for adventure" that led her to the city.[98] After a move from Saskatchewan to Ontario in 1935, Violet Koch eagerly took up domestic work in Kitchener–Waterloo, since she could earn $5 per week, which was $2 more than the going rate for farm labour.[99]

The death of a father or husband—the family 'breadwinner'—created another scenario that defied prescriptive roles for men and women. The death of her father when she was nine years old meant that Salome Buehler, like her siblings, had to work to contribute to family finances; her jobs included seasonal work at a Niagara canning factory, and live-in domestic service for a bank manager.[100] And Lorna Shantz Bergey, whose husband was disabled from a farm accident and then died young, took over the family cheese business and over time became a successful businesswoman. Though she had, in her own words, "no business experience or training," in the days after her husband's accident she realized she was in a "sink-or-swim" situation and would have to keep their market stand running to pay the mounting medical bills.[101]

The pattern whereby women, both married and single, stepped outside traditional gender roles to enter the paid workforce was repeated in the 1980s when Hmong refugee women from Laos migrated to Canada, where they joined the Mennonite church in Ontario. Women in this community were able to secure employment, even if menial and low-paying, at a greater rate than could their menfolk. Households in which women thereby became the primary breadwinner experienced no small amount of conflict as families tried to reconcile the new economic realities with traditional gender hierarchies in which men were dominant and women dependent.[102] During these periods of economic exigency, debates over women's appropriate work roles tended to subside in the face of family want and reflected a common historical pattern whereby situations of particular need had always broken down rigid ideological boundaries that defined a woman's proper place. When Mennonite women from their communities opted for roles that were normatively outside what was acceptable to the church, but were nevertheless useful to promote the socio-economic security or theological goals of the church, then leaders created a discourse to transform these roles into the 'work' or 'mission' of the church. For instance, when Mennonite girls and young women were working as domestic servants in cities in an era when urban life and all its perceived evils were anathema to Mennonites, church leaders and women workers themselves recast this type of labour activity into a mission activity.[103] And, as noted earlier, when single Mennonite women, prohibited from exercising preaching and teaching gifts in their local congregations, went into urban or overseas missions to follow their vocational aspirations, some church leaders described their work as irregular but nevertheless crucial to the saving of heathen souls.

During the Second World War, Mennonite women began 'working out' in significant numbers. The expansion of Mennonite factories and other enterprises provided job opportunities for women in environments that were specifically Mennonite, sometimes within their own family businesses. In such industries as food canning, the unskilled, temporary nature of the jobs made women the ideal employees. At the Mennonite-owned Niagara Canning Company in Virgil, Ontario, 80 percent of employees were women during the latter years of the war. In order to reach their production capacity, the company advertised in Mennonite papers and imported women workers from western Canada for six-week periods. The company provided room and board for $5 per week and paid thirty-seven cents an hour for girls under sixteen years of age and forty-two cents for those over sixteen. As well, one-half of a return ticket was paid to those who worked the minimum of six weeks. Despite the fact that the workday was ten hours and sometimes longer, an advertisement for women in a Mennonite newspaper offered "a good opportunity for anyone to come rather cheaply to beautiful Ontario and to view and to enjoy the gorgeous fruit region."[104] Boese Foods in St. Catharines also recruited Mennonite women from the west to work during the heaviest six weeks of the canning season, although at least one Mennonite group in Manitoba issued warnings against "the practice of sisters working in Ontario."[105] Jobs in Mennonite-owned factories sometimes brought young women to membership in Mennonite churches. For instance, a Scottish-born woman working as a maid in Toronto went to work for Bishop S.F. Coffman and family in Vineland. She recalled that in the summer, "girls came down from 'upcountry' to work in the canning factory" and "there were fourteen people at the dinner table." This woman eventually joined First Mennonite Church in Vineland.[106]

As happened for many other Canadian women, the decades following the war, characterized by social upheaval on many fronts, brought the issue of women and work to the agenda of Mennonites. Within families, churches, and denominational structures, the question of woman's role as paid labourer or homemaker became one of the most pressing debates in the post-war decades. The introduction of the Women in Church Vocations program, alongside radio programs and newspaper columns with such titles as "Conversation with Mothers," "Kitchen Kathedral," "Just Around the House," and simply "Homemakers," represented the dichotomy that existed for women especially from the 1950s through the 1970s. On the one hand, the church-sponsored vocational program recognized that women were attending post-secondary educational institutions and entering a variety of professions at an unprecedented rate. Canadian society—including Mennonites—was recognizing and for the most part affirming women's presence in the public workforce.

Yet, at the same time, popular thinking was denying the reality of women as workers and focusing on a domestic ideal of women as homemakers, wives, and mothers. As housekeeping was being transformed by modernization at mid-century, it appeared that homemaking as a vocation required renewed attention. In order to keep up with (and also offer a counterpoint to) women's entry into the workforce outside the home, homemaking required legitimization as an occupation unto itself. Mennonite newspapers ran articles entitled "Homemaking—A Challenging Vocation" and "Occupation: Housewife." The common argument in these articles was that good homemaking, which included care of a household and its occupants, was essential to building a good society. As one author concluded, "Good homemaking has far-reaching consequences and sufficient challenge so that it can be the most meaningful occupation a woman could enter."[107]

For women who chose to marry and bear children, homemaking was portrayed as their primary vocation and domesticity their sphere of authority.

The home was often idealized by writers and leaders, who rarely addressed the isolation and lack of self-esteem that frequently accompanied a homemaker's career. One Mennonite church history described women's roles as follows: "It was expected that women should create a warm centre, where all family members could retreat to from the hard knocks of life."[108] As if to encourage women at home and probably to stall the societal trend that saw women rejecting homemaking as their primary career, Mennonite media launched gender-specific radio shows and newspaper columns directed to women. The content of these often rested on the assumption that women were at home and able to take time out from their chores to listen to the radio. For instance, the Mennonite-operated radio station CFAM had several radio features for women during the 1950s, among them *Homemaker's Chat* and *Afternoon at Home* with Esther Horch. In 1957 the station also began airing the popular American Mennonite show *Heart to Heart*; its mandate was to "bring Christian inspiration to mothers and homemakers in the midst of everyday tasks."[109] Interestingly, twenty-five years later, pamphlets from *Heart to Heart* broadcasts were included in a compilation by some non-Mennonite women in Saskatchewan of "church literature [that] perpetuates sexism."[110]

The *Canadian Mennonite*, a national weekly paper, carried columns entitled "Kitchen Kathedral," "Conversation with Mothers," and "Conversation with Wives" in the 1950s. In her first article, columnist Anne Bargen exalted the role of housewife: "To be a capable housewife is a wondrous feat, which taxes the personality of a woman."[111] At a more mundane level, she offered tips on how to get the smell out of dill pickle jars, how to correctly position a corsage, and how to prevent eyeglasses from steaming up. Bargen's emphasis was on women as wives and mothers, as if to counter an obvious trend taking place around her. Indeed, in response to a debate by the Association of Mennonite University Students on women's greater social involvement, she remarked that woman's greatest purpose remained that of making a house into a home.[112] Another Canadian magazine, the *Mennonite Brethren Herald*, ran a column simply titled "Homemakers" that "presented ideas on keeping baby books, conquering holiday blues, writing cheerful letters, getting to church on time, and planning children's birthday parties."[113]

The somewhat contradictory ideas and ideals of womanhood during the post-war era in turn influenced each other. While homemaking took on the proportions of a career, higher education and work outside the home were considered useful mainly as preparation for marriage and motherhood. For instance, one Mennonite writer remarked that women who attended college "will probably become homemakers after they leave school," yet college women would make the best homemakers since "they have learned to think, to make intelligent choices, and to be creative."[114] The fusing of the ideal and the reality was epitomized in such individuals as "Aunt Olly" Penner who hosted *Children's Party* and a variety of women's radio programs on Manitoba's CFAM beginning in the late 1950s.[115] While her radio features such as *Hints for the Homemaker* and *For the Ladies* were aimed at women in the home and affirmed that role, Olly was herself a mother working outside the home. Similarly, some skeptics may have wondered who was cleaning out Anne Bargen's pickle jars while she was exercising her writing talents. Ruth Brunk Stoltzfus, host of the program *Heart to Heart*, maintained a fairly traditional stance on women's roles, yet on one occasion suggested that women's work in the home was worth a wage. Perhaps somewhat ahead of her time, Stoltzfus chose to focus her first broadcast in 1950 on the importance of fathers in family life. When she resigned in 1958, she said she wanted to spend more time with her family and be an example of what she had been telling mothers for years.[116] Yet, thirty-one years later, Stoltzfus rocked the Mennonite church by asking for and receiving ordination as a minister from the Virginia district conference in the United States.

The women mentioned above were examples of an issue—homemaking and domesticity—that increased in prominence ideologically in response to its decline in actuality. One history of Canadian women suggests that the media image of the "happy homemaker" promoted particularly during the 1950s was a reaction to exactly the opposite trend in society.[117] The truth was that women were increasingly involved publicly outside the home. Though immediately after the war many women left jobs created for them by the exigencies of war, the overall trend was towards an increase of women in the workforce. The industrial and factory jobs that had opened up to women during the war were replaced by an escalating number of positions in the clerical and service sectors. Furthermore, the wartime scenario created an acceptable precedent for married women in the workforce. In 1941 approximately 10 percent of employed women in Canada were married. By 1961 this had risen to almost half. That Mennonite women were also a growing presence in the public workforce is evident in the debates that surfaced especially in Mennonite periodicals. On the pages of denominational newspapers, and likely even more so in less public settings, Mennonites debated the pros and cons of married women entering the salaried workforce and generally following career aspirations beyond homemaking. Helene Toews, a leader in Canadian women's organizations, criticized the trend towards married women's employment outside the home in a 1945 presentation on "The True Role of Woman." Among other points, she echoed societal myths that blamed unemployment levels on working women and mentioned non-Christian women who "push the man aside and take his place."[118]

The naysayers on this issue rarely pointed to economic need or self-fulfilment as reasons for women to seek employment. For instance, one writer in *Christian Living* suggested in 1961 that if a woman was motivated to seek outside employment because of boredom as a homemaker, perhaps she should bring a more creative approach to homemaking that would stimulate her imagination.[119] In the same magazine, Anna L. Schroeder wrote vehemently in favour of women working outside the home: "So let us be feminists. Let us ask, seriously, whether making a home for our families is enough, or whether the Lord might not have other 'spheres of action' waiting for us. I think every woman should work—not for the money, not for 'fulfilment' but simply because there is so very much to do."[120] Aside from diatribes made publicly, individual women also felt criticism personally when they chose to pursue a career and have a family. Iva Sherk Taves, who entered medical school in Toronto in the late 1940s and later became the chief pathologist at a large Ontario hospital, heard talk amongst male classmates that she and other women were taking places that rightfully belonged to returning servicemen.[121] And when concert pianist and college professor Irmgard Braun Baerg sought to place an advertisement for domestic help in a Mennonite newspaper in the 1960s, she was told that "they'd rather not run the ad, I should probably look after my own children."[122]

Some voices cautiously affirmed the trend in women's paid employment outside the home. Paul Erb, editor of the Mennonite denominational magazine *Gospel Herald*, in 1959 offered that "confining a woman to the four walls of a home, even to the additional opportunities of Sunday school and the Missionary and Service Auxiliary, does not provide every outlet needed for our women."[123] More conservative thinkers, like Ontario Bishop Oscar Burkholder, were less optimistic about the trend. He argued that when Christian men and women departed from their God-assigned roles, as found in scripture, only trouble could come to the realm of human relations. He was accordingly quite puzzled by the desire of Christian women to leave their homes and husbands and enter the workforce when the Bible clearly stated that woman's place was "Kirche, Küche und Kinder" (church, kitchen, and family). Burkholder implied that educational institutions were partly to blame for the trend, citing the case of a married, trained nurse who worked in order to have economic security after marriage, should she need it. The bishop also implied that the economic arguments for the second income only played into the acquisitive and materialist leanings in modern society.[124]

Few women would have said that they worked outside the home in order to increase their purchasing power, unless the financial circumstances of their households demanded it. Yet the desire to be employed outside the home and garner a wage or salary reflected women's resistance, however subconsciously, to what in some households was their severely limited access to financial resources and thus economic control. While Burkholder considered women's desire for economic security a negative impulse, women who were without that security knew only too well the hardships that could result. In some households women had little control over the family income and were painfully limited in self-sufficiency as a result. Ruth Reesor recalled that her husband Lorne had given her spending money for a trip to Australia and, upon their return home, had asked her to return the unspent cash. Having seen "fairly lavish spending" on the part of Lorne during the trip, Ruth refused to return what she had frugally saved and instead spent it on a new set of dishes, "twelve of everything, including glasses."[125] When her husband was hospitalized in 1966, Mary Neufeld experienced a financial crisis because she didn't have access to the bank account that was only in her husband's name. As a result, she didn't have funds to buy groceries or pay the bills and so it was up to her son to approach his father's employer and request that his father's paycheques be made payable to Mary.[126]

There were other factors that propelled women, especially those who were married with children, to 'work out.' One of these was the increased longevity of women and, more importantly, their declining rate of child bearing. By the 1960s, not only did women have approximately forty years ahead of them after their youngest child went to school, but they also had several decades to live after all their children had left home. This was a far cry from a previous era, when women spent nearly their entire adult lives in child rearing. As well, the urban woman's work as homemaker was not valued as part of the general family economy like her rural counterpart. And furthermore, with a rapidly increasing number of young men attending university and college beginning in the 1950s, many women took on paid employment in order to put their husbands through school. One Mennonite woman, married in 1957, reflected on what was expected of young women of her era: "Men came first and it was a woman's job to catch and then to support her man. In the fifties and sixties ... young wives could work to support their husbands achieve high profile careers, but once these husbands got their degrees or placements, wives were expected to stay home, have families, and become expert homemakers, hostesses and volunteers in church or community service."[127]

In the midst of public and private debates in the 1950s and 1960s over whether married women with children should work outside the home, individual women struggled personally between their own aspirations and economic needs and the prescriptive dictates of church and society. Hedy Durksen, a columnist in a Mennonite newspaper, in 1962 reflected on the quandary women were facing: "The trouble seems to be that we women are no longer quite sure whether we belong in the home, whether we should be out getting more education so as to keep up with our well-educated husbands, or maybe have a career outside the home.... Just where do we go from here?"[128]

Responding to the many mixed messages they received, individual women tried to find a balance between what they 'wanted' to do and what they felt they 'ought' to do. Agnes Eby of Kitchener, Ontario, graduated with a nursing degree in 1952 and nursed for a while after marrying in order to pay her school debts and to save for a house down payment. When her first child was born, the uniform went into "the attic" since, she recalled, "after all, every Mother's Day sermon glorified mother as the 'keeper of the home.'" During her years at home she "was not bored or frustrated, but I felt a part of me was dying." When she made the decision to return to her nursing career, she dealt with feelings of guilt and overcompensated by trying to be a "super" parent and wife. Agnes was well aware of the judgments placed on her choices: "Too many people seemed to view my career as purely monetary, or as an escape from homemaking. They did not seem to understand that beyond the advantages of extra money and a stimulating diversion, nursing was my call to serve God and others."[129] Sometimes it wasn't just societal norms, but straightforward rules that compelled women to make a choice between marriage and career. Tena Klassen of British Columbia was twice accepted into nurses' training in the early 1950s and even measured for her uniform. But because the school dictated that a woman couldn't marry in the first three years of training, Tena decided not to go, since she didn't "want to risk losing [her boyfriend]."[130]

Both Agnes and Tena entered a career that was among the few professional work sectors deemed acceptable for middle-class women, Mennonite and otherwise, through much of the twentieth century. Nursing, and teaching as well, were occupations that were considered feminine and service-oriented and thus suitable for Mennonite women, and offered workplace experience that would hold women in good stead for marriage and parenting; as such, they were professions that were often entered into with the understanding that once a woman married, she would 'stop working.' Nursing had long been an acceptable career for women, and particularly single women trained as nurses were often trailblazers at mission stations within North America and overseas. While Mennonites in the United States established several church-run nurses' training institutions in the early twentieth century, this did not occur in Canada, and so Canadian Mennonite women trained at schools linked to urban hospitals.[131]

Agnes Fast left her home in southern Manitoba in the early twentieth century and went to Minneapolis to study nursing, even though Winnipeg had a nursing school at the time. According to one recollection, churches were encouraged to send young women to that city for a six-week midwifery course because so many babies were dying in childbirth. Agnes later "rose to fame" in Steinbach when she ran a makeshift hospital for victims of the 1918 influenza epidemic.[132] Agatha Wiebe, who received a nursing degree in Missouri in 1914, was perhaps the first Canadian Mennonite woman to graduate as a registered nurse.[133] Writer Anne Konrad observed that nursing was "highly placed" among the "limited number of Mennonite community-sanctioned professions for young women." Growing up in the Fraser Valley of British Columbia, she recalled that "many Mennonite girls" entered nurses' training at Vancouver General Hospital.[134] Hildi Lohrenz Bergen had given some thought to becoming a medical doctor until her father had said such a choice would mean "foregoing marriage and children." She then planned to enter nurses' training but changed her mind again when she learned of Manitoba's teacher shortage and the fact that she could train as a teacher at age seventeen, a year ahead of the age requirement to train as a nurse. But after one year of teaching, she entered nurses' training in 1946.[135]

Recognizing that many female members were training and working as nurses, Mennonite denominational bodies initiated the formation of professional associations within which Mennonite nurses could establish common ground and make connections between their work and faith; such organizational endeavours also undoubtedly provided some church legitimacy for Mennonite women in the workforce. The Mennonite Nurses Association of Ontario held its first annual meeting in 1944 with ten women present. By 1955 the association had a total of eighty-three members and associate members. The name of the association's official periodical, *Mennonursing*, was changed to *The Christian Nurse* in 1947 because the earlier name was thought to be "too masculine."[136] The organizational structure offered by the Nurses Association allowed Mennonite nurses to speak collectively on issues of concern to them, which included a 1946 resolution sent to the Mennonite Conference of Ontario, calling on the conference to encourage senior matriculation for Mennonite young people. Their concern to promote high school education, the resolution said, arose "from the new demands made upon nurses in almost every field of service."[137]

Teaching was also a profession that single women initially were encouraged to pursue, and later also sanctioned for married women, at least until they had children of their own at home. Maria Friesen is listed as the first female Mennonite teacher licensed with the Protestant School Board of Manitoba in the year 1879. Maria, who had likely begun her teaching career in south Russia, immigrated to Canada with her parents in 1874.[138] Anna Vogt, an immigrant of 1923, started Steinbach's first nursery school/kindergarten in the 1920s. When asked to begin using English in the school, Anna refused and instead moved to Winnipeg, where she continued her German-language teaching.[139] Mennonites in Canada had in fact established several teacher training institutes near the turn of the century in order to train teachers who would then teach in the public school system but offer education with a Mennonite ethos particularly in locales with a significant population of Mennonites. These teaching academies—one founded in 1889 in Gretna, Manitoba, and the other in 1905 in Rosthern, Saskatchewan—provided a safe and familiar learning environment for women, but were also places where they could obtain provincially recognized teaching credentials.

Though Mennonite women had been small-scale entrepreneurs since first settling in rural Canada, a few became professional businesswomen during the post-Second World War economic boom in Canada. While rarely getting the credit that male businessmen did, many Mennonite women put their entrepreneurial skills to work in creative and successful ways. Nellie Kinsie, a daughter of Ontario Bishop Oscar Burkholder, who was well known for his conservative views on women's roles, opened her own wool and knitting store in the mid-1960s. By the early 1980s, Kinsie Wool Ltd. was a family business with twenty-one outlets across Canada and annual sales of nearly $4 million. She recalled that the early years of business were difficult ones, when "Businessmen and salesmen did not take her seriously as many were unsympathetic to a woman-run business."[140] Numerous other women continued the long-standing practice of operating small-scale, home-based cottage industries that nurtured their entrepreneurial skills and fed the household coffers.

LEARNING AND WRITING

In the post-war era, in addition to increasing their presence in the paid work-force, Mennonite women, along with their male peers, were attending high school and post-secondary educational institutions in record numbers. In this, they were reflecting Canadian trends that saw enrolments in all levels of public education increase dramatically in the late 1940s and through the 1950s. One of the trailblazers in higher education was Helena Penner Hiebert, the first Mennonite woman to graduate with a university degree in Manitoba in 1899 and the first Mennonite, man or woman, to teach at a university in Manitoba.[141] While she was a first, many would follow half a century later.

The trend towards higher education was reinforced by the increase in the number of Mennonite parochial schools—nine high schools and two colleges were established in the 1940s—that created a controlled and value-specific venue for educating Mennonite young people. The high schools that were established in Ontario and all provinces west provided an alternative to the public schools that, with their cadet training and militarist patriotism, had been hostile environments for Mennonite pacifist young people during the Second World War. Two post-secondary Bible colleges were established in Winnipeg to provide professional training for Mennonites who were preparing for careers in church work.[142] While these were mainly men at first, women also chose to expand their educational horizons in these sanctioned settings, and it wasn't long until the amusing descriptor 'bridal (as opposed to Bible) college' was applied. Indeed, my adventurous mother was the first young woman to leave her Ontario community to enrol at Canadian Mennonite Bible College in Winnipeg, where she met and became engaged to my father.

Recognizing the presence of the "opposite sex" in universities and colleges, the Association of Mennonite University Students decided to admit women to its membership in 1956. The decision followed a debate at the same meeting on the topic, "Resolved that Mennonite women assume a more active role in society." The affirmative argument focused on the gifts and talents of women other than homemaking that could be utilized, whereas the negative believed that married women with children did not have time for activities outside the home.[143] Once again, however, while their menfolk were debating women's roles within public settings and in print, women were making choices for themselves that reflected their individual aspirations, interests, and abilities. Women who chose to further their education and train for careers likely did so without first consulting the Association or other such bodies.

Though Mennonites as a people had historically accorded high value to education, particularly to private education that was imbued with Mennonite religious values and practices, schooling for girls was generally of lesser importance. In her memoir, Maria Martens Klassen tells how her husband always checked over the letters she wrote because he had more education; Maria had attended school for only six years "like most of the other village girls."[144] That a socially constructed religious and gender demeanour of humility and self-deprecation had also shaped women's perception of themselves as learners is suggested by one woman's statement in a Mennonite newspaper in 1961. In an article advocating separate Sunday school classes for women as a way of involving them in discussion, Hedy Durksen stated that "granted ... our thoughts and expressions are not as profound and deep as those of our men, but I dare think that we are perhaps more practical and down-to-earth in our approach."[145] Efforts to educate girls and women were limited by both community expectation of how much learning was necessary for women, and also the perception that many females had of their own potential. However, as with women's involvement in the church or in the workplace, expediency frequently took precedence over ideological notions. More often than not, the educational aspirations of Mennonite women were thwarted by wartime upheaval, by financial need, by community social boundaries, and by prescriptive gender roles.

Education for girls was a lesser priority in most families for a number of reasons, but primarily because daughters were needed at home to assist their mothers with household labour and care of younger siblings. And, given that, until the latter twentieth-century decades, women were destined to be homemakers with limited roles in the church and minimal contact with public sectors, specific training was not considered necessary or valuable. While boys were needed to help on the farm, because agricultural labour was partly seasonal, sons were freer to attend school in the winter months, after fall harvest and before spring seeding. The labour of females in the home abated only a little in the winter. Mary Konrad Epp wrote that during the 1930s in rural Saskatchewan, she and her sister often had to stay home from school to help their mother with the heavy and time-consuming task of doing laundry: "We helped as Mama melted snow, heated water on the cookstove, scrubbed the clothes on the corrugated washboard, wrung them out, rinsed and then hung up the gangly long johns and flapping bed sheets on a wash line. How I longed rather to be in school." Mary and her sister, as "Mama's helpers," also missed a lot of school when their mother gave birth to twins when the youngest child was only thirteen months old.[146] As her friend Mary recalled, Kaethe Friesen arrived at school one day during the 1930s, packed up her books and other school supplies, and, "sobbing away," left school during grade six, "never to darken the door of the schoolhouse again." Kaethe's mother had just had a new baby and Kaethe was now expected to stay home and help.[147]

Another prairie woman, Katherine Friesen, used some of her wages earned as a domestic to attend Bethany Bible School in Saskatchewan. She did not graduate, however, and gave up her dreams of becoming a pastor in order to help her younger brothers with their schooling.[148] Similarly, in the early 1950s, Erma Martin Bauman had a "strong desire" to attend the Ontario Mennonite Bible School in Kitchener but, since she was expected to serve as her sister's "hired girl" after the arrival of a new baby, those educational goals remained unfulfilled.[149] For rural families, the challenges of transportation and the distances between home and school could also be a deterrent to the attendance of both boys and girls. Mennonite families living in La Glace, Alberta, for instance, could send their children to the La Glace High School up to grade eleven, but grade twelve was available only forty-nine kilometres away in Grande Prairie. Because some parents worried that "their good Mennonite girls would get into 'bad company' if they attended a public high school in town," they opted to send their older daughters instead to a Bible school connected to their local church.[150] Bible schools, especially those run by local Mennonite churches, were viewed as places at which women could "learn how to tell Bible stories to children and to meet 'Mr. Right.'"[151]

Yet, in their early years, some post-secondary schools relied on female enrolments to be viable, even though they were not specifically mandated to educate women. For instance, initially most of the students at a Mennonite Bible school established in Winnipeg in 1932 were rural women working as domestic help in the city. While men predominated in the daytime classes, the evening classes were especially appealing to working women; in 1937 to 1938, there were fifteen students (nine men and six women) enrolled in the daytime classes, and twenty-five women enrolled in evening classes. The curriculum included classes in biblical studies, Mennonite history, German language, and choral singing.[152] The gender balance in Mennonite-run schools was also affected by economic and political circumstances that had an impact on Mennonite families and communities. In its first few years, the Elim Bible School at Yarrow, British Columbia, established in 1929, had only male students, since most of the older girls and young women in the community were working as domestic help in Vancouver.[153] This imbalance was almost reversed fifteen years later; in the class of 1944 there were sixty-two women and thirty-two young men, the five instructors being male. This shift was due to the absence of young men in wartime military or alternative service, and the return to Yarrow of young women who had been working in Vancouver. This wartime demographic shift also occurred in other Mennonite Bible schools across the country.

A small minority of Mennonite women, like Helena Penner Hiebert, had already attended high school, Bible school, or college/university in the late nineteenth century. Many women who enrolled in post-secondary institutions—mainly Mennonite-run colleges in the United States—in the early years were motivated by their eagerness to make a contribution to growing initiatives in mission work, both local and overseas. Most of these were unmarried, but there were exceptions, such as Ontario's Lydia Bauman Martin, who took her two-year-old daughter with her to classes while she and her husband were both enrolled at Eastern Mennonite School in Virginia.[154] But in the years following the Second World War, interest in higher education on the part of both men and women increased exponentially. Partly in response to this activity, but also identifying a new need for professionally trained church workers, Mennonite denominational bodies established two post-secondary Bible colleges in Winnipeg in the late 1940s. Whether church leaders even expected women to attend is not known, but that women did demonstrate interest is clear. At Canadian Mennonite Bible College, established in 1947, there were two women in the first graduating class of twelve, but the first-year class of that year was half women. According to Katie Funk Wiebe, women enrolled at Mennonite Brethren Bible College in Winnipeg in the late 1940s were advised not to take theology classes, but instead focus on such areas as Christian education, the former necessary for church ministers, the latter for Sunday school teachers. This gender-streaming, she felt, was a manifestation of perceptions of men as thinkers and women as doers. In her words, spoken tongue-in-cheek: "Obviously, to study theology required a higher mentality than what we women as a group had received."[155] When the college opened in 1944, Esther Hiebert Horch, profiled at the outset of the chapter, was among the first teachers and certainly the first woman teacher, although she wasn't listed as 'faculty.' Even so, that first year she taught an English class with three students. Her status at the college over the years was listed in varying ways, from assistant registrar to dean of women, though it appears she was always teaching in some capacity as well.[156]

Women's interest in pursuing formal education indicated the need for training for various sectors of the workforce, but it also reflected their desire for self-improvement and self-expression. As members of a church that at least formally prescribed silence and submission on the part of females, women may have found in Bible school and college training a venue in which they could give voice to their ideas and opinions, if only in limited ways. Another way they sought and found a channel for expression was through the medium of writing and, indeed, it is notable how eagerly Mennonite women in all centuries and decades found an outlet in literary pastimes—diaries, letters, articles, memoirs, essays, and sometimes fiction. Writing, while not quite as acceptable for women as the domestic art forms discussed at the outset of this chapter, was nevertheless an act of creativity that was not explicitly prohibited for either sex. Furthermore, given the limitations to expression placed on women in the formal church setting, many women turned to writing as a way of articulating ideas, thoughts, and feelings that they were either prevented by prescription from vocalizing or hesitant to do so because of their strong sense of humility, even low self-esteem. Their propensity for the written word was also in keeping with a generally high valuation of literacy and historical preservation amongst most Mennonite groups. Literacy was, according to historian Royden Loewen, a means for Mennonites to "create a common set of understandings," and indeed reinforce their ethnic and religious sectarianism,[157] but for women it may conversely have been a means to speak about that which wasn't held in common, at least across gender lines. Writing about their daily activities, especially in the context of letters and diaries, served to validate, for themselves and for others, the significance of women's domestic tasks, which were often-times seen as mundane and not worth reporting on.

Letter writing was one of the primary venues through which women were authorities on information giving, and was central to maintaining, across vast distances, those kinship ties that were so important to Mennonites. Private diaries, by both men and women, provided an outlet for personal self-expression in a community where both publicly presented individuality and pride were frowned upon. Historian Delbert Plett commented on the many women among the early Mennonite pioneers on the prairies who kept diaries, primarily as a way of passing on their heritage and stories to their children. One of these, Elizabeth Esau Plett, reportedly kept a diary for eighty years, noting daily temperatures, events in the community, and important stages in the farming cycle.[158] The prevalence of daily diary writing amongst pioneer women is especially noteworthy, given the endless hours they spent in childcare and labour to maintain the household. On the other hand, writing in their diaries gave women a medium, however minimal, to reflect on their lives and some-times to be self-expressive, not to mention that it gave them the chance to sit quietly and rest, but not be seen as idle.

For Mary Eidse Friesen, diary writing was given the same meticulous attention she gave to other daily household tasks; she drafted a rough copy of each day's entry and then carefully transcribed it into a pocket-size book, even-tually filling a total of sixteen books.[159] Some women, like Marie Schroeder, used their diaries as a channel for wider literary applications; in a 1926 diary entry, she wrote about her "secret hope that I may write things that have a real worth someday; things that are worth printing, and things that other folks would love to read and pay for."[160] Others found in diary keeping a means to fill gaps or respond to losses in their lives. For instance, Susannah Betzner Cressman began a diary in 1911 when she was widowed at the age of fifty-five with four daughters. And Agatha Martens began writing journals when she was housebound with illness and became very depressed. For her, writing was better therapy then "running to people, or running to my minister ... it seemed to help me, it was my way of coping."[161]

Many other women, willing to give public voice to their thoughts, wrote for community newspapers or religious periodicals, or other localized venues. For instance, Alma Barkman wrote a weekly column for eight years in the *Carillon News* (Steinbach) and the *Saskatchewan Valley News* (Rosthern), both community newspapers in Mennonite-populated areas. Elizabeth "Isby"

Bergen wrote regularly in the *Red River Valley Echo* (Altona) for several decades. As journalists, these women carried significant influence in shaping local community consciousness by publishing their particular viewpoints on what they deemed important and newsworthy. A few women developed community reputations and female followings as a result of their 'women's columns' in Mennonite newspapers in the 1950s and 1960s, described earlier. If women were barred from formal theological expression behind the pulpit, church periodicals provided a venue for women to preach, admonish, and reflect. Mabel Groh published for close to twenty-five years in at least four different Mennonite periodicals on topics that were "not typically women's subjects."[162]

Ontario woman Barbara Sherk was a prolific writer in the United States-based *Herald of Truth*. Barbara lived with her parents until her mother's death in 1894, after which she worked for a time at the Chicago Home Mission, an inner-city outreach that worked with disadvantaged people. Later she kept house for her brother, a task she considered a mission, even if "obscure or insignificant."[163] Her many articles to the *Herald* appeared mainly between the years 1895 and 1902 and were written in a "flowery and emotional style." She wrote about love of God and service to God wherever there was need. Many of her articles drew on stories of biblical women and occasionally her writings were directed specifically to women. As a woman who described herself (at least in a letter to a Mennonite evangelist) as "too decided in my views, and too pointed in my expression," she nevertheless urged other Mennonite women to "study the moral, social, and religious questions of your day until you have convictions concerning them." As has been conjectured about other women whose husbands or fathers were writers or ministers, Carol Penner suggests that Barbara Sherk may have acted as a "scribe" to her father, David Sherk, and possibly was the actual author of some writings attributed to him.[164] Even women from conservative Mennonite groups found an accepted outlet in writing for and corresponding with church periodicals; such was the case for Nancy Martin, who pursued an "active intellectual life" by reading and writing for conservative Mennonite and Amish journals on topics like folklore.[165]

Other women developed the art of 'essay' writing, whether for published purposes or for recitation in the context of church meetings that were not akin to Sunday morning preaching. Young people's meetings, and, especially in Ontario, the popular early twentieth-century literary societies offered an important forum for women to present essays, frequently of a religious or devotional nature, but also on many other themes of interest for the era. For instance, Lydia Bauman Martin wrote "Sunday evening" essays for herself and also for others, less gifted with the pen, to present; she expounded on such topics as "The Spiritual Sphere of Christian Womanhood," "The love of Christ constrains us to work at home," and "Bible Teachings Concerning War."[166] Literary societies, in fact, were one venue within Ontario churches in which there were no rigid lines drawn between men's and women's work, both sexes serving equally on executive committees and making presentations from the platform. Chronicling a church or community's history was another acceptable means for women to utilize their analytical and literary gifts, as exhibited on paper. Liese Neufeld Peters did "quite a lot" of writing according to her daughter. One of her outlets was to chronicle the historical highlights in the development of her Mennonite church in North Kildonan, Manitoba, which she referred to as "consultations."[167]

As in many other professions, women who were able to write with the productivity of Barbara Sherk or in fact turn writing into a career were frequently single. Margaret A. Epp of Waldheim, Saskatchewan, was one of the most well-known of Mennonite writers in the mid-twentieth century. Her books and short stories for children and youth were extremely popular within the genre of Christian literature. By 1956, within ten years of the start of her writing career, she had sold 40,000 books and was able to support herself by writing seven hours a day, five days a week. Epp believed that her writing filled a need for "clean Christian literature" by "substituting pure literature for the impure found on the news stands of today."[168] Yet public writing, unless it was in a diary or was purposefully spiritual in nature, was in some cases not an acceptable vocation for women to take up. Women who had a passion for writing could be seen as defiant of appropriate female forms of expression and neglectful of household responsibilities, as was the case for Selma Redekopp profiled in an earlier chapter. Katie Funk Wiebe reflected on her own childhood aspirations to be a writer:

> As a young girl I secretly wanted to write. Write? The word was foreign to my parents. Young girls married, or typed, taught or nursed until they died. Mennonites were agrarian, poking the ground, making green things grow, not producing words on paper. I could not envisage writing as a possibility for me, for I was conditioned to accept the image of the ideal Mennonite woman in Russia and the early years in Canada: silent, modest, and obedient.[169]

Though Wiebe went on to become a prolific and popular writer of many books and articles, on a wide range of themes, her success obviously didn't come without personal hardship and challenges from her Mennonite community. She reflected on the dilemma of being a woman and a writer as follows: "Writing can seldom be a first for women if they are wives and mothers. Mothers don't have a secretary. They don't have wives. They can be interrupted by most anyone. They are eased out of writing early unless they make peace between family concerns and writing."[170] Wiebe herself struggled with her choice of becoming a writer: "My Mennonite conscience told me I should find sufficient meaning in life as the wife of Rev. Walter Wiebe, without making any specific contribution of my own. Most Mennonite women had done so. My mother had never had any other aspirations. Or had she? The thought dumbfounded me. Had she buried her longings for creative expression deep inside her as she baked pan after pan of Zwieback and Platz?"[171]

In the late twentieth century, the writing of Mennonite women entered a new phase, becoming part of the Canadian literary canon, at once sophisticated, brutally honest about Mennonite families and communities, and sometimes bitter about how women were treated and depicted. Literary theorist Hildi Froese Tiessen has commented that the writing of Mennonite women is "often projections of the authors' foremothers who suffered an enforced silence throughout the official histories of their people."[172] Contemporary Canadian writers such as Sarah Klassen and Di Brandt, for instance, were deliberate in their early poetry about writing as a mechanism for breaking silences enforced on them.

If women had neither time nor inclination to be writers themselves, they may have sought spiritual and imaginative sustenance in reading. In 1954, the Association of Mennonite University Students did a survey of reading habits of Mennonite young people; 51 percent of females reported being good readers, compared to only 12 percent of males.[173] Today, the book 'club,' a phenomenon that has perhaps replaced the women's mission society or sewing circle in many Mennonite congregations, is largely composed of female readers. Olga Dyck Regehr recalled that in her community of North Kildonan in the 1930s, "Most of the women were literate." She said that "While the women were not given too much authority they nonetheless read." Much of their reading material was magazines for mothers and homemakers from Germany.[174] Another woman from the same community said about her mother that, "I don't think there was a book in the house from the first reader to when we quit school that she wouldn't read. Every book that we brought home, whether it was a school book or a book from the library … she read it all."[175] As one Mennonite woman says, books "create connections" for women who are isolated "physically, emotionally or spiritually" and "sitting down to read" allows for "an intentional act of claiming personal time amidst … many external demands."[176] If women internalized Mennonite beliefs about silence, or at least pretended to follow these prescriptions, it didn't prevent them from absorbing information and ideas through reading.

Whether reading a book, writing a diary entry, working nine to five, baking a loaf of bread, painting a canvas, or stitching a quilt, Mennonite women over the past 200 years lived productive lives that sustained themselves and their communities inwardly and contributed to Canadian society in a myriad of outward ways. Women's material labour reflected ideas, aspirations, and activity that were frequently overlooked and undervalued in the characteriza- tion and self-identity of Mennonites. In the context of a sectarian outlook that emphasized 'works and deeds' and a well-entrenched work ethic that derided idleness, productive output was encouraged and praised, insomuch as it remained within the boundaries of normative gender roles and acceptable religious sensibilities. Domestic art forms that included needlework and cooking were functional necessities of everyday life, and also symbolized and reinforced distinct Mennonite ethnicities. Where female creativity stretched the edges of communal values and ideas about functional simplicity, then women's material activity was often frowned upon.

As for most other married Canadian women, the economic labour of Mennonite women was mainly reflected in vocational homemaking, at least until the late 1960s and onwards. Until the latter decades of the twentieth century, it was primarily unmarried women who ventured into such careers as teaching or nursing or church-related mission work. The entry of women, married and single, into higher education and into the paid workforce prompted debates within Mennonite circles that reflected larger societal discussion regarding women's proper role, but that were also shaped by biblical and theological interpretations of woman's natural place in the Christian universe and in relation to men. Mennonite homemakers may have thrived or felt constrained by their destiny as caretakers of family and household, but more likely they occasionally experienced both extremes and most often felt themselves somewhere in between. As they listened to and participated in the debates regarding the appropriate setting and channel for their material labour, Mennonite women made personal choices that grew out of their own skills, interests, and needs. Furthermore, a woman's particular productive activity also reflected the degree to which she wished to acquiesce or resist the prescriptive gendered ideology directed at her.

CONCLUSION

In 1979, Doris Weber of Stratford, Ontario, became the first Mennonite woman to be ordained to ministry within her denomination in Canada. Just a year prior, Martha Smith Good of Kitchener was commissioned to this role, a status that was different more in ritual and semantics than in actual function. The ordination of a woman to formal church ministry that year represented what some considered to be "the last barrier of overt discrimination against women in the North American Mennonite churches. . . . "[1] In assuming leadership roles within Mennonite congregations, both women crossed historic barriers that had made it impossible for women to follow career and spiritual aspirations as ministers in Mennonite churches.

Also in 1979, the changing identity of Mennonite women was symbolized with the arrival of a group of Hmong people from Laos, after several years of living as refugees in Thailand following the Vietnam war. Having been sponsored by Mennonite churches in Ontario, the Hmong soon formed their own Christian church congregation and began services at the First Mennonite Church in Kitchener.[2] The presence of Mennonite women with a cultural background that was Hmong and Laotian added to the increasing ethnic diversity that would characterize Mennonite women—Mennonites generally —towards the end of the twentieth century. Today this diversity is most vividly displayed and symbolized at the annual Mennonite Relief Sale in New Hamburg, Ontario, where foodstuffs for sale include a multicultural Mennonite mix of *Rollkuchen* (Russian), tea balls (Swiss), spring rolls (Laotian), and *pupusas* (Hispanic).

That same year, Heidi Quiring, a young Mennonite woman from Manitoba, fulfilled her reign as Miss Canada of 1979, having been crowned at the annual pageant in November of the previous year. Some Mennonites questioned whether Quiring had "acculturated" beyond what was acceptable, or suggested that she was conforming to a system that was "exploitative of women." She responded that the reaction from her Winnipeg congregation to her victory in what she called a "personality pageant" was "very, very favourable," and that it was important to clear up misconceptions that Mennonites were not "progressive."[3] The national prominence achieved by Quiring was a clear sign that at least some Mennonite women were thoroughly immersed in mainstream Canadian society. Yet, coming at the end of a decade in which second-wave feminists had denounced the beauty pageant phenomenon, the scenario created somewhat of a puzzle for Mennonites who were trying to sort out what roles— 'traditional' or 'progressive'—Mennonite women should play.

The year 1979 represented in some respects a pivotal point for Mennonite women and for Canadian women generally. Beginning already after the Second World War, but especially throughout the 1970s and after, women's roles in church and society received unprecedented scrutiny. The rights movements that arose in the 1960s questioned many social and economic hierarchies, but women's historic subordination, challenged by what came to be known as the 'women's liberation movement' or second-wave feminism, affected possibly more sectors of society than did any other social movement of the late twentieth century. Significant dates for Canadian women included the launching of the government's Royal Commission on the Status of Women in 1967 and its Report in 1970, the declaration of International Women's Year for 1975 by the United Nations, and, in 1979, the founding of the Feminist Party of Canada.

Mennonites, of course, were not immune to the transformation—indeed, revolution—that was under way around them and affecting their lives directly. By the end of the 1970s Mennonites in Canada for the most part recognized— whether with disapproval, enthusiasm, or resignation—that women's roles had changed dramatically in just a few decades and that there was no turning back. The second-wave feminist movement entered Mennonite churches and communities slowly and tentatively. To be sure, only a few Mennonite women embraced the agenda of radical or socialist feminism, and, similarly, the majority did not take up one of the movement's main issues, which was abortion rights. While many women were eager to see gender discrimination end and wanted to take on positions of greater authority in church and society, only a few Mennonite women openly used the language of feminism to assert these interests. The statement "I'm not a feminist, but ... " often prefaced an avowal of affirmation for women's rights. Yet some women were quite outspoken when the ideals espoused by the feminist movement allowed them to give voice to the oppression they felt within the Mennonite community. In a 1973 newspaper article, Mary Regehr Dueck of Waterloo, Ontario, outlined the state of affairs for Mennonite women, as she saw it, rather boldly: "Our strict enforcement that women keep silent in the church has left its mark on Mennonite women. Many are timid, lack self-assurance when among men and have little confidence in the value of their own thoughts and opinions. This is the natural consequence of generations of subtle suppression in the church which has been also frequently carried over into the home."[4] For her, the time was long overdue for women to have a voice equal to men in the Mennonite church and in Mennonite households.

At the same time, women could also be the ones most publicly resistant to the principles of the feminist movement. For instance, also in 1973, Katherine Wiens of Regina, Saskatchewan, wrote that "A truly liberated person is a Christ-filled, Christ-centered person willing to be used by God for His purpose."[5] For her and others who were like-minded, the feminist movement was problematic particularly because it was secular and appeared at times to be anti-Christian in its questioning of biblical interpretation and historic church practice regarding women's roles. An anti-feminist stance among Mennonites continued to cling to beliefs that the 'headship' of men over women was divinely ordained and that biblically based submission applied to gender roles in secular and sacred realms.

Some people felt that the concern with women's limited roles in church structures was a fleeting one. At its annual meetings in 1975, the Conference of Mennonites in Canada responded to the agenda of the United Nations International Women's Year by holding a session on the role of women that included a paper on "Women and the Bible," presented by a man. Following this and other discussions at the meetings, one woman apparently "declared that she could hardly wait until this year was over so she wouldn't have to hear about women anymore!"[6] Yet another woman spoke up with a different point of view, saying, "We are men and women all in the image of God. In today's society women are more competent and better qualified to hold offices within the church."[7] Other women responded in a conciliatory manner by proposing that the movement called for the liberation of both women and men from traditional gender roles.[8]

Regardless of any one woman's stance, the 1970s represented a clear escalation of programs, discussion, and alteration to the norms of Mennonite women's roles. The decade was also a time of fervent disagreement over the value of the changes taking place. And Mennonite women could be found at either end of the 'women's lib' and anti-feminist spectrum. Some women were inspired by American Mennonite Lois Gunden Clemens's 1971 book *Woman Liberated*, radical for its time, which argued that male-female sex differences were the basis for gender equality in church and society; Clemens challenged the Mennonite church to make full use of women's gifts, including in ordained ministry. But other Mennonites were also keen readers of *The Total Woman*, by Marabel Morgan, published in 1973 and a North American best-seller, which suggested that marriages would improve if wives were submissive, obedient, and obliging to their husbands.[9]

Beginning in the 1960s and continuing through the 1970s, Mennonite media carried regular articles and series on 'women's roles' with such titles as "Equal Opportunity to Serve" or "The Role of Women in the Church" or "The Place of Women in Church and Society." Debates on the 'revolution' under way became so heated that one female writer to a Mennonite periodical declared that "the battle between the sexes is on [and] I am not a conscientious objector to this war."[10] Others cancelled their subscriptions to Mennonite newspapers in protest over numerous editorials, letters, and articles on 'women's lib.' Polarized positions arose on both ends of the ideological spectrum; on one side was the proposition that Mennonite women were "more oppressed" than women in other groups, while detractors of feminism correlated women's demands for independence with "breakdown in the home."[11] Both sides could easily draw on scripture to buttress their position, whether advocating for women's equality in church and society, or whether affirming a God-ordained gender hierarchy in which women were subordinate. Nor was the battle drawn along gender lines; some women were just as likely to speak out on "the beauty of submission" as were some men prone to declare themselves as feminist allies.

Reflecting the diverging stances of women was a 1971 article published in the Kitchener–Waterloo, Ontario, daily newspaper, which reported on women's involvement in a North American gathering of Mennonites in that city. Noting that 6 out of 450 delegates at the conference were women, the article began by stating, "Mennonite women are slowly becoming liberated." However, several women interviewed for the story had varying responses to questions about their emancipation. Lorna Bergey replied that "I have no feeling of not being liberated," while Eleanor High said "she believed Mennonite women were just as liberated as they wanted to be." A third, more definitive, stance was offered by Salome Bauman, who said, "I'm no women's lib. I much prefer the secondary role."[12]

While the debates in the media continued, various Mennonite church institutions established programs of research and advocacy on 'women's concerns' that would respond to what one commentator called "the greatest revolution of this century."[13] Perhaps the most significant institutional response came in 1973 when the Peace Section of Mennonite Central Committee (based in the United States) established a Task Force on Women in Church and Society. The mandate was to place women's interests on the agenda of the Peace Section and to bring their concerns to the attention of the Mennonite church. One of the first issues was the lack of women on boards, major committees, or the administrative hierarchy of Mennonite church and related organizations. At its ten-year anniversary, some Canadian participants lamented the lesser voice of Canadians in the task force as well as its lesser visibility in Canada generally.[14] Nevertheless, over the next two decades the task force became a vital and vibrant place for research, discussion, and advocacy for Mennonite women in North America.

In particular, the task force's regular thematic newsletter, mostly known as the *Women's Concerns Report*, offered a dynamic and provocative site for the telling of women's stories on a range of topics, such as child rearing, education, careers, church work, and finances, for example. The periodical did not shy away from controversy in dealing with issues such as domestic violence, abortion, incest, and pornography, and occasionally confronted resistance as a result. The decision to cease publication in 2004 of the thirty-year-old *Report* was based on the fact that subscriptions continued to decline and, in the words of the departing editor, "Today, in some places, women do experience more opportunities and support, so this forum may be less necessary than it was formerly."[15] Undoubtedly some of the *Report*'s readers differed on this assessment.

If Mennonite women's opinions on the feminist agenda varied widely, this reflected the diversity of women themselves in terms of background, personality, and position along the widespread continuum of Mennonite identity. After 1979, it was also true that the character of Mennonite women and their lives were increasingly diverse. Even while a few Mennonite women were assuming leadership positions in their churches and other societal sectors, women of conservative subgroups such as the Old Order or Old Colony continued to live out their lives within a religious culture that maintained a clear delineation of separate spheres and a gender hierarchy in which men were dominant and women subordinate. Within these separatist and mainly rural communities, the feminist movement, as a manifestation of 'the world,' had minimal impact. While the majority of Mennonite women still married and had children, by 1980 an increasing number were ending marriage through divorce, or choosing to be childless, or not marrying, or living in same-sex partnerships. And while historic Swiss or Russian Mennonite ethnic identities continued as important cultural ties for many women, a growing number— newcomers to Canada or the Mennonite church (or both)—brought a divergent and rich array of new ethnic and cultural traditions to Mennonite communities. All these are represented today within my own assortment of female friendships, which include the Russian-background lead minister of the oldest Mennonite church in Canada (of Swiss origin), a rural Old Order Mennonite mother of nine children, a Mennonite woman from Colombia, and a lesbian single parent with whom I attended a Mennonite high school.

From their first arrival and settlement in the late eighteenth century, Mennonite women, in all their rich variety, have played a part in shaping an ever-evolving Canada. As "keepers of the culture,"[16] as are so many women within groups defined by ethnicity or religion, Mennonite women were pivotal in maintaining the customs, traditions, beliefs, and manners of thought that were central to being Mennonite, however defined in a particular time and place. Mennonite women negotiated their identities within a social and religious community that oftentimes put forward prescriptions for how women should look, behave, believe, and think. Such dictates were inevitably modified in practice in situations of exigency that demanded that women step outside normative roles. Women's responses to community gender norms and regulations varied, but mostly women acted out of their own individual person-alities, shaped by ethnic background, family relationships, social class, church subgroup, and particular life experience.

As immigrants, refugees, and transnationals, Mennonite women, like other Canadian newcomers, brought their experience and identity from 'somewhere else' to participate in community building on Canadian soil. Whether they were adventurers seeking new opportunities that protected and reinforced their Mennonite identity, or whether they were fleeing sites of oppression and violence and felt mainly the erosion of identity, Mennonite women immi-grants made their particular mark in a national collective, the very nature of which was defined by families and communities from elsewhere. The fact that Mennonite women came from so many different places around the globe, and continue to do so, is crucial to understanding their multi-faceted representa-tions of being Mennonite.

As wives, mothers, and 'others,' Mennonite women understood their primary identity markers to be their situation within family units, at least until the closing decades of the last century. To the extent that Mennonite commu-nities have been organized around kinship and family relationships and have valorized these structures, women, at least obliquely, shaped Mennonitism in real and significant ways. Women who satisfied the expectation that they devote their lives to being wives and mothers could take pride in their function as builders of community, though the sheer amount of labour and the some-times limited creativity attached to these roles could be overwhelming. Women who were single, childless, widowed, or otherwise on the margins of accept-able family structures may have lived personally fulfilling lives, but did so with the burden of knowing that they fell short of their community's expectations. Within the realm of religious belief and practice, Mennonite women were preachers, prophets, and missionaries in the broadest definition of these terms. The principles and values of the Mennonite belief system limited the potential for women's formal religious expression, and, when applied to social realms, undermined their personhood altogether. Yet women interpreted and responded to religious expectations in different ways, and many women created spaces, sometimes subversive ones, in which they could express their spiritual notions and feelings.

Certain Mennonite beliefs were particularly gendered in their impact and so, as nonconformers, nonresistors, and citizens, Mennonite women lived in the world in ways that diverged from those of most of their Canadian counterparts. Church ideals of separation from the world at times served to reinforce women's secondary status within their families and communities, even while women were expected to be not only the 'keepers,' but also the standard-bearers for their culture. In a church that espoused non-participation in the military as part of its pacifist stance, Mennonite women were in the unique position (and perhaps one more flexible than that of their menfolk) of acting in ways both similar to and unlike other Canadian women when the country was at war. As in all things, Mennonite women had no singular response. Keeping the culture was, for Mennonite women, also about material production, and, as quilters, canners, and writers, they creatively contributed to popular understandings of what it meant to be a Mennonite within a Canadian context. As for other Canadian women, their material lives were also labouring ones, whether unpaid within the domestic space of home, or whether for wages as workers and professionals. As women participated in higher education in greater numbers and aspired to careers other than homemaking, Mennonites, like other Canadians, engaged in vigorous debate about proper female roles.

Commonalities, divergences, and dichotomies are all featured in the history of Mennonite women in Canada. My own feminist curiosity led me to peer into the low-lying fog that has hidden the complexity of women's lives in the Canadian Mennonite past. Mindful that there is much more that could yet be said, my hope is that this book will encourage others to engage in research and writing that will continue to burn away the fog that still might linger.

GLOSSARY

This glossary provides brief definitions for terms and labels used with some frequency in the book. The list does not explain all Mennonite subgroups in Canada. A comprehensive and useful guide to Mennonite groups in Canada is Margaret Loewen Reimer, *One Quilt Many Pieces: A Guide to Mennonite Groups in Canada* (Waterloo, ON; Scottsdale, PA: Herald Press,2008).

AMISH
An Anabaptist group that became differentiated from the Mennonites in the late seventeenth century in Switzerland. The Amish migrated from Europe to Upper Canada in the early to mid-nineteenth century, settling west of present-day Kitchener–Waterloo, Ontario. The modern Amish merged with Ontario Mennonites in the mid-twentieth century, while the Old Order Amish (who are similar to Old Order Mennonites) remain distinct.

BERGTHALER
A group of Manitoba Mennonites in about twenty congregations that had their origins in the Bergthal Colony in Russia, and migrated to Canada in the 1870s. The descriptor Bergthaler was dropped in the 1970s and the churches became part of the Conference of Mennonites in Canada. Another group known as Bergthaler in Saskatchewan had its origins also with the 1870s migrants from Bergthal, but retained the name while resisting modernization to a greater extent.

CHORTITZER

One of the smaller, more conservative, and separatist groups that were among the 1870s migrants from Russia, and that settled initially in Manitoba. Chortitz was the name of the village where their bishop lived.

EAST RESERVE AND WEST RESERVE

Two blocks of land, one on each side of the Red River in southern Manitoba, given to the Mennonites for their exclusive settlement when they migrated from south Russia in the 1870s.

EVANGELICAL MENNONITE CONFERENCE (EMC)

A subgroup of Mennonites known as Kleine Gemeinde (see below) until 1952. Through most of the twentieth century, EMC churches were found mainly in Manitoba, but today they are spread across Canada and in Central America.

EVANGELICAL MENNONITE MISSION CONFERENCE (EMMC)

A subgroup of Mennonites known until 1959 as Rudnerweide, the name of the village in Manitoba where a revival movement caused a split in the Sommerfelder church (see below) in 1937. The group was characterized by an emphasis on evangelism and missions.

GENERAL CONFERENCE (GC)

A twentieth-century designation for the largest Mennonite conference body with origins in the Russian Mennonite settlements, most of whom immigrated to Canada in the 1920s. Differentiated mainly from the similarly modern and acculturated Mennonite Brethren.

KANADIER

A German term translated to mean 'Canadian' that was used to designate those Mennonites who immigrated from Russia to Canada in the 1870s. The term differentiated this migrant group from the Russländer (Russians), who migrated to Canada in the 1920s.

KLEINE GEMEINDE

Translated as 'little church,' this was the name given to a group of traditionalist dissenters that split from the larger Mennonite church in Russia in the early nineteenth century. The entire group migrated to Manitoba in the 1870s and, in the mid-twentieth century, became known as the Evangelical Mennonite Church (later Conference).

MARKHAM–WATERLOO CONFERENCE

An Ontario-based group of conservative Mennonites that separated from the Old Order in 1939 and adopted the use of black cars rather than horse-drawn transportation and also allowed telephones. Women wear a distinct plain-dress uniform.

MENNONITE BRETHREN (MB)

Currently one of the largest subgroups of Mennonites in North America, the Mennonite Brethren was a renewal movement that led to a split from the dominant Mennonite church body in Russia in 1860. They were differentiated mainly by their practice of water baptism by immersion, rather than pouring, and by their emphasis on spiritual rebirth, evangelism, and missions.

MENNONITE CENTRAL COMMITTEE (MCC)

An international relief, development, and peace organization, established in 1920 by North American Mennonites with the initial purpose of providing relief to Mennonites experiencing famine in the Soviet Union. Today MCC has many projects and personnel around the world.

OLD COLONY

The most conservative of the several Mennonite groups that migrated from Russia to Manitoba in the 1870s. In an effort to preserve traditional ways and resist acculturation that included public school education, a substantial number left Canada for Mexico in the 1920s. Beginning in the late 1950s and continuing in the present, the Old Colony (and some other related groups) in Mexico began a return migration to Canada.

OLD ORDER

The most conservative (along with Old Order Amish) of Mennonite groups in Canada, based almost entirely in rural Ontario. The Old Order split from the larger Ontario Mennonite church in the late nineteenth century and rejected various aspects of modernization. Today they are identifiable mainly by their uniform plain dress and use of non-motorized transportation. They maintain a high degree of separation from society and do not participate in most government social programs.

RUSSIAN MENNONITES

A descriptor to identify Mennonites whose history of migration and settlement began in the Netherlands in the sixteenth century and led to Prussia and the Russian Empire (later the Soviet Union). The Russian Mennonites migrated to Canada in three main waves: 1870s, 1920s, and post-Second World War.

SOMMERFELDER

A small conservative subgroup of Mennonites that resulted from a split in the Manitoba-based Bergthaler group (see above) in 1894 over issues of modernization and acculturation.

SWISS MENNONITES

A descriptor to identify Mennonites with origins in Switzerland and south Germany in the sixteenth century, whose main migratory and settlement history took them to the United States, beginning in the late seventeenth century. They began moving from Pennsylvania to (then) Upper Canada (present-day Ontario) in the late eighteenth century.

NOTES

PREFACE

1. Katie Funk Wiebe, *The Storekeeper's Daughter* (Scottdale, PA: Herald Press, 1997), 37.

2. For global Mennonite population figures, see Mennonite World Conference. <http://www.mwc-cmm.org/index.htm>.

3. Term is used by Kamala Visweswaran, *Fictions of Feminist Ethnography* (Minneapolis, MN: University of Minnesota Press, 1994).

4. Franca Iacovetta, "Post-Modern Ethnography, Historical Materialism, and Decentring the (Male) Authorial Voice: A Feminist Conversation," *Histoire sociale/Social History* 32, 64 (November 1999): 275-93

5. Hasia R. Diner, "Insights and Blind Spots: Writing History from Inside and Outside," in *Strangers at Home: Amish and Mennonite Women in History*, ed. Kimberly D. Schmidt, Diane Zimmerman Umble, and Steven D. Reschly (Baltimore, MD: Johns Hopkins University Press, 2002), 29.

6. That assignment resulted in a conference presentation for the Multicultural History Society of Ontario and the following publication: Frank H. Epp and Marlene G. Epp, "The Diverse Roles of Ontario Mennonite Women," in *Looking into My Sister's Eyes: An Exploration in Women's History*, ed. Jean Burnet (Toronto: Multicultural History Society of Ontario, 1986), 223–42.

INTRODUCTION

1. Katie Funk Wiebe, "Me Tarzan, Son of Menno–You Jane, Mennonite Mama," *Journal of Mennonite Studies* 17 (1999): 10. See also Katie Funk Wiebe, "Mennonite Brethren Women: Images and Realities of the Early Years," *Direction* 24, 2 (Fall 1995): 23–35.

2. Teresa A. Meade, and Merry E. Wiesner-Hanks, "Introduction," in *A Companion to Gender History*, ed. Teresa A. Meade and Merry E. Wiesner-Hanks (Malden, MA: Blackwell Publishing, 2004), 6.

3. Lawrence Klippenstein and Julius G. Toews, eds., *Mennonite Memories: Settling in Western Canada* (Winnpeg: Centennial Publications, 1977), 163.

4. Agatha E. Klassen, ed., *Yarrow: A Portrait in Mosaic*, rev. ed. (Yarrow, BC: The Author, 1976), 27.

5. Esther Patkau, *Canadian Women in Mission, 1895–1952–2002* (Canada: Canadian Women in Mission, 2002), 31.

6. Marlene O. Martens, ed., *Returning Thanks to God: Hoffnungsfelder Mennonite Churches, 1928–2003* (Rabbit Lake, SK: Hoffnungsfelder Mennonite Churches, 2003), 58.

7. Henry Klippenstein, *Thicker than Water: The Uncensored, Unabridged and Completely Unbiased Account of the Life and Times of the Dietrich Klippenstein Family* (North Vancouver: Loon Books, 2004), 49.

8. Michael D. Driedger, *Obedient Heretics: Mennonite Identities in Lutheran Hamburg and Altona during the Confessional Age* (Aldershot, UK: Ashgate, 2002), 178.

9. Cynthia Enloe, *The Curious Feminist: Searching for Women in a New Age of Empire* (Berkeley: University of California Press, 2004).

10. "Regier Receives 'Emeritus Stole' for 40 Years in Ministry," *Canadian Mennonite.* 8, 15 (2 August 2004): 5.

11. Elise Boulding, *The Underside of History: A View of Women through Time* (Boulder, CO: Westview Press, 1976); on compensatory history, see Gerda Lerner, *The Majority Finds its Past: Placing Women in History* (New York: Oxford University Press, 1979); and *Women and History* (New York: Oxford University Press, 1986).

12. Such biographical collections include: Mary Lou Cummings, ed., *Full Circle: Stories of Mennonite Women* (Newton, KS: Faith and Life Press, 1978); Katie Funk Wiebe, ed., *Women Among the Brethren: Stories of 15 Mennonite Brethren and Krimmer Mennonite Brethren Women* (Hillsboro, KS: General Conference of Mennonite Brethren Churches, 1979); Elaine Sommers Rich, *Mennonite Women: A Story of God's Faithfulness, 1683–1983* (Scottdale, PA: Herald Press, 1983); Ruth Unrau, ed., *Encircled: Stories of Mennonite Women* (Newton, KS: Faith and Life Press, 1986).

13. Historiographical essays on Mennonite women's history include: Carol Penner, "Mennonite Women's History: A Survey," *Journal of Mennonite Studies* 9 (1991): 122-35; Kimberly D. Schmidt and Steven D. Reschly, "A Women's History for

Anabaptist Traditions: A Framework of Possibilities, Possibly Changing the Framework," *Journal of Mennonite Studies* 18 (2000): 29-46.

14. An example of a Mennonite institutional history that incorporates gender analysis throughout is Lucille Marr, *The Transforming Power of a Century: Mennonite Central Committee and its Evolution in Ontario* (Kitchener, ON: Pandora Press, 2003).

15. M.J. Heisey, *Peace and Persistence: Tracing the Brethren in Christ Peace Witness Through Three Generations* (Kent, OH: Kent State University Press, 2003), 19.

16. Some important English-language historical monographs on women and Christian religion in Canada include: Marta Danylewycz, *Taking the Veil: An Alternative to Marriage, Motherhood, and Spinsterhood in Quebec, 1840–1902* (Toronto: McClelland and Stewart, 1987); Ruth Compton Brouwer, *New Women for God: Canadian Presbyterian Women and Indian Missions, 1876–1914* (Toronto: University of Toronto Press, 1990); Rosemary R. Gagan, *A Sensitive Independence: Canadian Methodist Missionaries in Canada and the Orient, 1881–1925* (Kingston, ON and Montreal: McGill-Queen's University Press, 1992); Randi R. Warne, *Literature as Pulpit: The Christian Social Activism of Nellie L. McClung* (Waterloo, ON: Wilfrid Laurier University Press, 1987); Elizabeth Gillan Muir and Marilyn Färdig Whiteley, eds., *Changing Roles of Women within the Christian Church in Canada* (Toronto: University of Toronto Press, 1995); Lynne Marks, *Revivals and Roller Rinks: Religion, Leisure, and Identity in Late-Nineteenth-Century Small-Town Ontario* (Toronto: University of Toronto Press, 1996).

17. Linda Kerber, et al., "Beyond Roles, Beyond Spheres: Thinking about Gender in the Early Republic," *William and Mary Quarterly* 46 (July 1989): 582.

18. Ursula King, "Religion and Gender: Embedded Patterns, Interwoven Frameworks," in *A Companion to Gender History*, ed. Meade and Wiesner-Hanks, 70.

19. Lynne Marks, "Challenging Binaries: Working-Class Women and Lived Religion in North America," notes from paper presented at "Labouring Feminism and Feminist Working Class History in North America and Beyond," University of Toronto, Fall 2005. See also Ruth Compton Brouwer, "Transcending the 'Unacknowledged Quarantine': Putting Religion into English-Canadian Women's History," *Journal of Canadian Studies* 27 (Autumn 1992): 47–61; R. Marie Griffith, *God's Daughters: Evangelical Women and the Power of Submission* (Berkeley: University of California Press, 1997), 14.

20. Frieda Esau Klippenstein, "Scattered but Not Lost: Mennonite Domestic Servants in Winnipeg, 1920s–50s," in *Telling Tales: Essays in Western Women's History*, ed. Catherine A. Cavanaugh and Randi R. Warne (Vancouver: University of British Columbia Press, 2000), 200.

21. King, "Religion and Gender," 71.

22. "Introduction: Insiders and Outsiders," in *Strangers at Home: Amish and Mennonite Women in History*, ed. Kimberly D. Schmidt, Diane Zimmerman Umble, and Steven D. Reschly (Baltimore, MD: The Johns Hopkins University Press, 2002), 10.

23. Ruth Reesor, *Check Rein: A Journey of Remembrance* (Ontario: Pennsylvania German Folklore Society of Ontario, 2003); Ruth Brunk Stoltzfus, *A Way Was Opened: A Memoir* (Scottdale, PA: Herald Press, 2003).

24. Beth Light and Ruth Roach Pierson, eds., *No Easy Road: Women in Canada 1920s to 1960s* (Toronto: New Hogtown Press, 1990).

25. Frieda Esau Klippenstein, "Gender and Mennonites: A Response to Mennonites in Canada, 1939–1970: A People Transformed," *Journal of Mennonite Studies* 15 (1997): 142–49.

26. King, "Religion and Gender," 71.

27. Ruth Derksen Siemens, "Quilt as Text and Text as Quilt: The Influence of Genre in the Mennonite Girls' Home of Vancouver (1930–1960)," *Journal of Mennonite Studies* 17 (1999): 122.

28. Robert Friedmann, "Gelassenheit," *Global Anabaptist Mennonite Encyclopedia Online.* 1955. Accessed 20 January 2006: <http://www.gameo.org/encyclopedia/contents/g448.html>.

29. Carol Penner, "Mennonite Silences and Feminist Voices: Peace Theology and Violence Against Women" (PhD thesis, Toronto School of Theology, 1999). An additional resource on Mennonite peace theology from the perspective of women is *Piecework: A Women's Peace Theology* (Winnipeg: Mennonite Central Committee Canada, 1996).

30. Janis E. Nickel, "In the Name of Harmony Voices Are Lost," *MCC Women's Concerns Report* 121 (July–August 1995): 5.

31. Lydia Harder, "Discipleship Re-examined: Women in the Hermeneutical Community," in *The Church as Theological Community: Essays in Honour of David Schroeder*, ed. Harry Huebner (Winnipeg: CMBC Publications, 1990), 199–220.

32. Nickel, "In the Name of Harmony," 6.

33. Linda A. Huebert Hecht, "An Extraordinary Lay Leader: The Life and Work of Helene of Freyberg, Sixteenth-Century Noblewoman and Anabaptist from the Tirol," *Mennonite Quarterly Review* 66, 3 (July 1992): 312–41. See also Linda A. Huebert Hecht and C. Arnold Snyder, eds., *Profiles of Anabaptist Women: Sixteenth Century Reforming Pioneers* (Waterloo, ON: Wilfrid Laurier University Press, 1996); and Linda A. Huebert Hecht, "A Brief Moment in Time: Informal Leadership and Shared Authority Among Sixteenth Century Anabaptist Women," *Journal of Mennonite Studies* 17 (1999): 52–74. Earlier perspectives on women in the Anabaptist movement include: Herta Funk, ed., *Study Guide: Women in the Bible and Early Anabaptism* (Newton, KS: Faith and Life Press, 1975); Joyce L. Irwin, *Womanhood in Radical Protestantism, 1525–1675* (New York: E. Mellen Press, 1979); Keith Sprunger, "God's Powerful Army of the Weak: Anabaptist Women of the Radical Reformation," in *Triumph Over Silence: Women in Protestant History*, ed. Richard L. Greaves (Westport, CT: Greenwood Press, 1985);

Jenifer Hiett Umble, "Women and Choice: An Examination of the *Martyrs Mirror*," *Mennonite Quarterly Review* 64, 2 (April 1990): 135–45.

34. Thieleman J. van Braght, *The Bloody Theater or Martyrs Mirror of the Defenseless Christians* (Scottdale, PA, Herald Press, 1968, 8th edition, first published in 1660).

35. M. Lucille Marr, "Anabaptist Women of the North: Peers in the Faith, Subordinates in Marriage," *Mennonite Quarterly Review* 61, 4 (October 1987): 347–62. Research in the late 1990s by men's studies scholar Stephen Boyd revealed strains of Anabaptism that attempted to transform marriage and sexuality based on "an affirmation of gender equality." Boyd points to a particular south German group that fostered a new kind of marriage that emphasized a divine call directed equally at women and men and that allowed individuals to leave a 'worldly' marriage for a 'spiritual' union. See Stephen B. Boyd, "Theological Roots of Gender Reconciliation in 16th Century Anabaptism: A Prolegomenon," *Journal of Mennonite Studies* 17 (1999): 34–52.

36. Patricia Harms, "'Gott es hiea uck': Gender and Identity in an Immigrant Family from Paraguay," *Journal of Mennonite Studies* 22 (2004): 54.

37. Marion Kobelt-Groch, "'Hear My Son the Instructions of Your Mother': Children and Anabaptism," *Journal of Mennonite Studies* 17 (1999): 28.

38. "Introduction," in *Strangers at Home*, ed Schmidt, Umble, and Reschly, 3.

39. For studies of this phenomenon, see, for instance, Margaret Lamberts Bendroth, *Fundamentalism and Gender, 1875 to the Present* (New Haven, CT: Yale University Press, 1993).

40. Cynthia Cockburn, *The Space Between Us: Negotiating Gender and National Identities in Conflict* (London: Zed Books, 1998), 105.

41. Carol Penner, "Review of *She Has Done a Good Thing: Mennonite Women Leaders Tell Their Stories*," *The Conrad Grebel Review* 19, 3 (Fall 2001): 103.

42. Anne Yoder, "The Diaries of North American Mennonite Women, 1850–1950," *Mennonite Historical Bulletin* 54, 1 (January 1993): 5.

43. Quoted in Glenda Strachan, "Present at the Birth: Midwives, 'Handywomen' and Neighbours in Rural New South Wales, 1850–1900," *Labour History* 81 (2001): 16.

44. Enloe, *The Curious Feminist*, 3.

45. *Missionary Sewing Circle Monthly*, September 1952.

46. Lorraine Roth, "Use of Maiden Names—Women's Liberation in the Nineteenth Century?" *Mennonite Family History* 8, 4 (October 1989): 147.

47. Joy Parr, "Gender History and Historical Practice," *Canadian Historical Review* 76, 3 (September 1995): 355.

CHAPTER 1

1. Unpublished story of Barbara Schultz Oesch, by Lorraine Roth, used with permission. See also a version of this story in Elaine Sommers Rich, *Mennonite Women: A Story of God's Faithfulness, 1683–1983* (Scottdale, PA: Herald Press, 1983), 57–60. For background on Amish settlement in Canada, see Orland Gingerich, *The Amish of Canada* (Waterloo, ON: Conrad Press, 1972); Lorraine Roth, *The Amish and their Neighbours: The German Block, Wilmot Township, 1822–1860* (Waterloo, ON: Mennonite Historical Society of Ontario, 1998).

2. Regina Doerksen Neufeld, "Katherina Hiebert (1855-1910): Midwife," *Preservings* 10 (June 1997):14; Regina Doerksen Neufeld, "Katharina Hiebert: Manitoban Pioneer Midwife," *Mennonite Historical Bulletin* 61 (July 2000): 4. For background on Mennonite immigrants to Canada in the 1870s, see Frank H. Epp, *Mennonites in Canada, 1786–1920: The History of a Separate People* (Toronto: Macmillan, 1974), chaps. 8–9; Royden K. Loewen, *Family, Church and Market: A Mennonite Community in the Old and the New Worlds, 1850–1930* (Toronto: University of Toronto Press, 1993).

3. Susie Reddekopp's story was told in "A People Apart," *The Record* (27–28 October, 2000). See also my article, "Pioneers, Refugees, Exiles, and Transnationals: Gendering Diaspora in an Ethno-Religious Context," *Journal of the Canadian Historical Association* 12 (2001): 137–53. For background on the Old Colony Mennonites, Susie Reddekopp's denominational subgroup, see for instance, Delbert Plett, ed., *Old Colony Mennonites in Canada, 1875–2000* (Steinbach, MB: Crossway Publications, 2000); Larry Towell, *The Mennonites* (London: Phaidon, 2000); Frank H. Epp, *Mennonites in Canada, 1920–1940: A People's Struggle for Survival* (Toronto: Macmillan, 1982), chap. 3.

4. Terry R. Martin, "The Russian Mennonite Encounter with the Soviet State, 1917–1955," *The Conrad Grebel Review* 20, 1 (Winter 2002): 9; Martin does not reference his usage of the term 'mobilized diaspora.' See, for instance, John A. Armstrong, "Mobilized and Proletarian Diasporas," *American Political Science Review* 70, 2 (June 1976): 393–408; reproduced in *Migration, Diasporas and Transnationalism*, ed. Steven Vertovec and Robin Cohen (Cheltenham, UK: Edward Elgar Publishing Ltd., 1999). Frameworks of diaspora have been used by social historian Royden Loewen to analyze the movements of the Kleine Gemeinde—a small group with Russian origins. See, for instance, *Diaspora in the Countryside: Two Mennonite Communities and Mid-Twentieth Century Rural Disjuncture* (Toronto: University of Toronto Press, 2006).

5. Shirlena Huang, Peggy Teo, and Brenda S.A. Yeoh, "Diasporic Subjects and Identity Negotiation: Women in and from Asia," *Women's Studies International Forum* 23, 4 (2000): 392.

6. See my own study on the post-Second World War migration, *Women without Men: Mennonite Refugees of the Second World War* (Toronto: University of Toronto Press, 2000); and Loewen, *Family, Church, and Market* (1993).

7. Steven Vertovec and Robin Cohen, "Introduction," in *Migration, Diasporas and Transnationalism*, ed. Vertovec and Cohen, xviii.

8. Esther Epp-Tiessen, "Gains and Losses: The Experience of Mennonite Women Immigrants of Late Nineteenth Century," *Journal of Mennonite Studies* 18 (2000): 149.

9. Ibid., 148.

10. James Clifford, "Diasporas," *Cultural Anthropology* 9, 3 (1994), reproduced in *Migration, Diasporas and Transnationalism*, ed. Vertovec and Cohen, 225.

11. Epp-Tiessen, "Gains and Losses," 149.

12. Royden Loewen, ed., *From the Inside Out: The Rural Worlds of Mennonite Diarists, 1863–1929* (Winnipeg: University of Manitoba Press, 1999), 42.

13. "Helena Brandt Klassen," on-line article, <http://freepages.genealogy.rootsweb.com/~eidse/midwife.html>.

14. Linda Buhler, "Sarah Sawatzky Funk: Matriarch of Kronsgart," *Preservings* 10 (June 1997): 42.

15. Heidi Koop, comp., and Helga Dyck, ed., "The Band Plays On: Mennonite Pioneers of North Kildonan Reflect (unpublished manuscript, Mennonite Heritage Centre, 1998), 359.

16. Lester B. Shantz, *A Shantz Family in Canada, 1800–2000: Ancestors and Descendants of Samuel Y. Shantz* (Hamilton: The Author, 1997), 18.

17. Loewen, *Family, Church, and Market*, 97.

18. "Helena Jansen (1822–1897)," *Preservings* 10 (June 1997): 20.

19. Travel diary of Katherine Schroeder, cited in Patricia Harms, "'Gott es hiea uck': Gender and Identity in an Immigrant Family from Paraguay," *Journal of Mennonite Studies* 22 (2004): 50.

20. Roth, *The Amish and their Neighbours*, 55.

21. For a discussion of gender in Canadian immigration historigraphy, see for instance, Franca Iacovetta, "Manly Militants, Cohesive Communities, and Defiant Domestics: Writing about Immigrants in Canadian Historical Scholarship," *Labour/Le Travail* 36 (Fall 1995): 217–52. See also the Introduction and essays in *Sisters or Strangers? Immigrant, Ethnic, and Racialized Women in Canadian History*, ed. Marlene Epp, Franca Iacovetta, and Frances Swyripa (Toronto: University of Toronto Press, 2004).

22. Maria Klassen, "Moving to the West Reserve," in *Mennonite Memories: Settling in Western Canada*, ed. Lawrence Klippenstein and Julius G. Toews (Winnipeg: Centennial Publications, 1977), 74.

23. Loewen, *Family, Church, and Market*, 101.

24. Veronica Strong-Boag, "Pulling in Double Harness or Hauling a Double Load: Women, Work and Feminism on the Canadian Prairie," *Journal of Canadian Studies* 21, 3 (Fall 1986): 32–52. Frances Swyripa, *Wedded to the Cause: Ukrainian-Canadian Women and Ethnic Identity, 1881–1981* (Toronto: University of Toronto Press, 1992).

25. Kathryn McPherson, "Was the 'Frontier' Good for Women?: Historical Approaches to Women and Agricultural Settlement in the Prairie West, 1870–1925," *Atlantis* 25, 1 (Fall/Winter 2000): 75–86.

26. Elizabeth Bloomfield, *Waterloo Township through Two Centuries* (Waterloo, ON: Waterloo Historical Society, 1995), 116.

27. E. Reginald Good, *Anna's Art: The Fraktur Art of Anna Weber, a Waterloo County Mennonite artist, 1814–1888* (Kitchener, ON: Pochauna Publications, 1976), 13.

28. Recounted in Delbert F. Plett, *Johann Plett: A Mennonite Family Saga* (Steinbach, MB: Crossway Publications, 2003), 293.

29. Loewen, *From the Inside Out*, 261–94.

30. Sara Brooks Sundberg, "A Female Frontier: Manitoba Farm Women in 1922," *Prairie Forum* 15–16 (1990–1991): 185–204.

31. Hedy Lepp Dennis, *Memories of Reesor: The Mennonite Settlement in Northern Ontario, 1925–1948* (Leamington, ON: Essex-Kent Mennonite Historical Association, 2001), 84–86.

32. Anna Epp Ens, ed., *The House of Heinrich: The Story of Heinrich Epp (1811–1863) of Rosenort, Molotschna and His Descendants* (Winnipeg: Epp Book Committee, 1980), 163.

33. Loewen, *From the Inside Out*, 245–60.

34. Ibid., 261–94.

35. Delbert F. Plett, "Maria Koop Plett 1868–1918 Journal," *Preservings* 10 (June 1997): 33.

36. Sheila McManus, "Gender(ed) Tensions in the Work and Politics of Alberta Farm Women, 1905–29," in *Telling Tales: Essays in Western Women's History*, ed. Catherine A. Cavanaugh and Randi R. Warne (Vancouver: University of British Columbia Press, 2000), 132.

37. Unnamed woman quoted in Roselynn Steinmann, "The Marriage and Childbirth Experiences of Mennonite Women within the Context of the Amish Community" (unpublished research paper, Mennonite Heritage Centre, 1992), 3.

38. Loewen, *Family, Church, and Market*, 103.

39. Royden K. Loewen, "'The Children, the Cows, My Dear Man and My Sister': The Transplanted Lives of Mennonite Farm Women, 1874-1900," *Canadian Historical Review* 73, 3 (1992): 357.

40. Loewen, "The Transplanted Lives," 344–73.

41. Bloomfield, *Waterloo Township through Two Centuries*, appendix 3, 406.

42. Ibid., 115–16.
43. Loewen, "The Transplanted Lives," 362.
44. For analysis of bilateral partible inheritance among the Mennonites, see Royden Loewen, *Hidden Worlds: Revisiting the Mennonite Migrants of the 1870s* (Winnipeg: University of Manitoba Press, 2001).
45. Bloomfield, *Waterloo Township through Two Centuries*, 118.
46. Joseph S. Stauffer, "The Family Book," *Waterloo Historical Society* 55 (1967): 16–17.
47. Nanci Langford, "Childbirth on the Canadian Prairies, 1880–1930," in *Telling Tales*, Cavanaugh and Warne, 170.
48. See, for instance, Gupta and Ferguson, 1992, 10–11, quoted in Aparna Rayaprol, *Negotiating Identities: Women in the Indian Diaspora* (New York: Oxford University Press, 1997), 3.
49. Delbert F. Plett, "Klaas Reimer's Kjist?" *Preservings* 12 (June 1998): 92–94.
50. Reference to Georgina Taylor's article "Should I drown myself now or later? The Isolation of Rural Women in Saskatchewan" in Kathryn McPherson, "Was the 'Frontier' Good for Women?: Historical Approaches to Women and Agricultural Settlement in the Prairie West, 1870–1925," *Atlantis* 25, 1 (Fall/Winter 2000): 77.
51. Patricia Harms, "'Gott es hiea uck,'" 39–57.
52. Ruth Unrau, "Singing the Lord's Song in Foreign Lands: Anna Enns Epp, 1902–1958," in *Encircled: Stories of Mennonite Women*, ed. Ruth Unrau (Newton, KS: Faith & Life Press, 1986), 292.
53. Loewen, *Family, Church, and Market*, 187.
54. Cornelius J. Dyck and Wilma L. Dyck, eds., *A Pilgrim People* (Saskatoon: Renata and Allan Klassen, 1987), 36.
55. Bloomfield, *Waterloo Township through Two Centuries*, 116.
56. Lorraine Roth, *Willing Service: Stories of Ontario Mennonite Women* (Waterloo: Mennonite Historical Society of Ontario, 1992), 210.
57. John Dyck, "Helena Penner Hiebert (1874–1970): True Pioneer," *Preservings* 10 (June 1997): 10.
58. Margaret Klassen Neufeld, "My Grandmother was an Undertaker: A Tribute to Anganetha Dyck Bergen Baerg (1859–1942)," *Mennonite Historian* 24, 1 (March 1998): 2, 9.
59. Loewen, "The Transplanted Lives," 366. For an analysis of this case, see Hans Werner and Jenifer Waito, "'One of our own': Ethnicity Politics and the Medicalization of Childbirth in Manitoba" (unpublished paper, 2007, referenced with permission).
60. Shirley Bergen, "Dr. Katherina Born Thiessen: A Woman Who Made a Difference," *Mennonite Historian* 23, 3 (September 1997): 8.

61. Karen Bergen, "Maria Dueck Ginter (1909–1990): Chiropractor," *Preservings* 14 (June 1999): 85–7.

62. Regina Doerksen Neufeld, "Katherina Hiebert (1855–1910): Midwife," *Preservings* 10 (June 1997): 16.

63. There is extensive literature on the history of Mennonites in Russia and the Soviet Union. See, for instance, John Friesen, ed., *Mennonites in Russia, 1788–1988* (Winnipeg: CMBC Publications, 1989).

64. Ruth Derksen Siemens, "Quilt as Text and Text as Quilt: The Influence of Genre in the Mennonite Girls' Home of Vancouver (1930–1960)," *Journal of Mennonite Studies* 17 (1999): 121. The image of Mennonite household servants was in sharp contrast to Finnish women who were described as "defiant domestics." See Varpu Lindström, *Defiant Sisters: A Social History of Finnish Immigrant Women in Canada* (Toronto: Multicultural History Society of Ontario, 1988).

65. Dennis, *Memories of Reesor*, 118.

66. Margaret Thiessen Rempel, "Margaretha Frantz Enns (1892–1959)," *Preservings* 10 (June 1997): 60.

67. Frieda Esau Klippenstein, "Scattered but Not Lost: Mennonite Domestic Servants in Winnipeg, 1920s–50s," in *Telling Tales*, ed. Cavanaugh and Warne, 204.

68. Katherine Friesen, "Domestic Work in the Depression Era," *MCC Women's Concerns Report* 79 (July-August 1988): 4.

69. Koop and Dyck, "The Band Plays On," 184.

70. Esther Epp-Tiessen, *J.J. Thiessen: A Leader for His Time* (Winnipeg: CMBC Publications, 2001), 119.

71. Siemens, "Quilt as Text and Text as Quilt," 121.

72. Epp-Tiessen, *J.J. Thiessen*, 117.

73. Siemens, "Quilt as Text and Text as Quilt," 122.

74. Epp-Tiessen, *J.J. Thiessen*, 117–23.

75. Ibid., 121.

76. On Mennonite domestics, see Marlene Epp, "The Mennonite Girls' Homes of Winnipeg: A Home Away from Home," *Journal of Mennonite Studies* 6 (1988): 100–14; Frieda Esau Klippenstein, "'Doing What We Could': Mennonite Domestic Servants in Winnipeg, 1920s to 1950s," *Journal of Mennonite Studies* 7 (1989): 145–66.

77. Frieda Esau Klippenstein, "Scattered but Not Lost," 214.

78. Siemens, "Quilt as Text and Text as Quilt," 122.

79. Ibid., 124.

80. T.D. Regehr, *Mennonites in Canada, 1939–1970: A People Transformed* (Toronto: University of Toronto Press, 1996), 176. For reference, see p. 481, fn. 30.

81. Ibid., 176.

82. Klippenstein, "Scattered but Not Lost," 225.

83. Lorraine Roth, "Margaret Elizabeth Brown Kanagy: An Exemplary Life of Christian Service," *Mennonite Historical Bulletin* 54, 3 (July 1993): 1–2; Carol M. Steinman, *Refined by Fire: The Story of Hagey/Preston Mennonite Church, 1800-2000* (Kitchener, ON: Pandora Press, 2000), 57.

84. Roth, *Willing Service*, 96.

85. Ibid., 250–51.

86. Eleanor Hildebrand Chornoboy, *Faspa: A Snack of Mennonite Stories* (Winnipeg: The Author, 2003), 20–21.

87. Siemens, "Quilt as Text and Text as Quilt," 126.

88. Epp, *Women without Men*, 118.

89. Laureen Harder, *Risk and Endurance: A History of Stirling Avenue Mennonite Church* (Kitchener, ON: Stirling Avenue Mennonite Church, 2003), 30.

90. Liese Peters, in *Fiftieth Anniversary of the Mennonite Settlement in North Kildonan, 1928–1978.*

91. Koop and Dyck, "The Band Plays On," 97. See also Olga Dyck Regehr, "From Refugee to Suburbanite: The Survival and Acculturation of North Kildonan Mennonite Immigrant Women, 1927–1947" (MA thesis, University of Winnipeg, 2006).

92. Hilda J. Born, *Maria's Century: A Family Saga* (Abbotsford, BC: The Author, 1997), 75-80.

93. Carol A. Kolmerton, *Women in Utopia: The Ideology of Gender in the American Owenite Communities* (Bloomington: Indiana University Press, 1990), 2.

94. Towell, *The Mennonites,* n.p.

95. On this period of Mennonite history, see, for instance, "Mennonites in the Soviet Inferno," special issue of *Journal of Mennonite Studies* 16 (1998).

96. For a detailed study of this female-dominated migration, see Epp, *Women without Men*; also, Pamela E. Klassen, *Going by the Moon and the Stars: Stories of Two Russian Mennonite Women* (Waterloo, ON: Wilfrid Laurier University Press, 1994).

97. Miriam Ruiz, "A new breed of Mennonite women," *MCC Women's Concerns Report* 119 (March–April 1995): 9.

98. Gloria Gonzalez's story (not her real name) is from an interview with the author, Kitchener, Ontario, October 2000.

CHAPTER TWO

1. Katherine Martens, *All in a Row: The Klassens of Homewood* (Winnipeg: Mennonite Literary Society, 1988).

2. Roth, *Willing Service*, 212–14.

3. Maria Redekop Wall's story, and others like hers, is told in my book *Women without Men: Mennonite Refugees of the Second World War* (Toronto: University of Toronto Press, 2000).

4. Angus McLaren, *A History of Contraception: From Antiquity to the Present Day* (Oxford: Basil Blackwell, 1990), 242.

5. John F. Peters, "Traditional Customs of Remarriage among Some Canadian Mennonite Widow(er)s," *Journal of Mennonite Studies* 10 (1992): 119. See also, Paul Redekop, "The Mennonite Family in Tradition and Transition," *Journal of Mennonite Studies* 4 (1986): 77–93; and Alan Peters, "The Impact of the Family in Mennonite History: Some Preliminary Observations," *Direction* 1, 3 (July 1972): 74–81.

6. Royden Loewen, ed. *From the Inside Out: The Rural Worlds of Mennonite Diarists, 1863–1929* (Winnipeg: University of Manitoba Press, 1999), 262.

7. Plett, "Maria Koop Plett 1868–1918 Journal," 35.

8. Marion Kobelt-Groch, "'Hear my son the instructions of your mother': Children and Anabaptism," *Journal of Mennonite Studies* 17 (1999): 22–33.

9. Loewen, *From the Inside Out*, 50.

10. Margaret Groening, "Jugendvereins of the 1930–1965 [sic]" (unpublished manuscript, no date, shared with me by author's son, Roger Groening).

11. Anne Konrad, *And in Their Silent Beauty Speak: A Mennonite Family in Russia and Canada, 1790–1990* (Toronto: The Author, 2004), 283.

12. Thelma Reimer Kauffman, "Hop Season," in *Village of Unsettled Yearnings. Yarrow, British Columbia: Mennonite Promise*, ed. Leonard Neufeldt (Victoria: TouchWood Editions, 2002), 179.

13. Leonard N. Neufeldt, ed., *Before We Were the Land's: Yarrow, British Columbia: Mennonite Promise* (Victoria: TouchWood Editions, 2002), 173.

14. Dick H. Epp, *From Between the Tracks: 1927–1952* (Saskatoon: Eppisode Publications, 2004), 1–2. Koop, and Dyck, "The Band Plays On," 7.

15. Janet Mancini Billson, *Keepers of the Culture: The Power of Tradition in Women's Lives* (New York: Lexington Books, 1995), 229.

16. There is some evidence that within Hutterite communities, a woman was allowed to separate from a husband who didn't share her faith, though this precedent of church over marriage didn't translate into more flexible attitudes towards divorce in later years. Michael D. Driedger, *Obedient Heretics: Mennonite Identities in Lutheran Hamburg and Altona during the Confessional Age* (Aldershot, UK: Ashgate, 2002), esp. chap. 7. M. Lucille Marr, "Anabaptist Women of the North: Peers in

the Faith, Subordinates in Marriage," *Mennonite Quarterly Review* 61 (October 1987): 347–62.

17. Chornoby, *Faspa*, 155.

18. J. Howard Kauffman, "Intermarriage." *Global Anabaptist Mennonite Encyclopedia Online*. 1989. Accessed 1 Feb 2006. <http://www.gameo.org/encyclopedia/contents/i587me.html>.

19. Carol M. Steinman, *Refined by Fire: The Story of Hagey/Preston Mennonite Church, 1800-2000* (Kitchener, ON: Pandora Press, 2000), 26.

20. Driedger, *Obedient Heretics*, 167.

21. Loewen, *From the Inside Out*, 246.

22. Lorraine Roth, *The Amish and Their Neighbours: The German Block, Wilmot Township 1822–1860* (Waterloo, ON: Mennonite Historical Society of Ontario, 1998), 73.

23. John Dyck, "Helena Penner Hiebert (1874–1970): True Pioneer," *Preservings* 10 (June 1997): 9.

24. Elizabeth Peters, ed., *Gnadenthal, 1880–1980* (Winkler, MB: Gnadenthal History Book Committee, 1982), 163.

25. Konrad, *And in Their Silent Beauty Speak*, 239.

26. Chornoby, *Faspa*, 168.

27. Laureen Harder, *Risk and Endurance: A History of Stirling Avenue Mennonite Church* (Kitchener, ON: Stirling Avenue Mennonite Church, 2003), 134–35.

28. Mary Hunsberger Schiedel, *A Journey of Faith: The History of Shantz Mennonite Church, 1840–2000* (Baden, ON: Shantz Mennonite Church, 2000), 37.

29. Anna Bartsch, *The Hidden Hand in the Story of My Life* (Nelson, BC: The Author, 1987), 58.

30. Ibid., 170.

31. Pamela E. Klassen, "Practicing Conflict: Weddings as Sites of Contest and Compromise," *Mennonite Quarterly Review* 72, 2 (April 1998): 228–29.

32. Ibid., 228.

33. Pamela Klassen, "'Queen for the Day': Mennonites, Weddings, Women, and Dress" (unpublished paper, 1993).

34. Bert Friesen, *Where We Stand: An Index of Peace and Social Concerns Statements by Mennonites and Brethren in Christ in Canada, 1787–1982* (Winnipeg: Mennonite Central Committee Canada, 1986), Microfilm Page 02659.

35. Klassen, "'Queen for the Day'."

36. Klassen, "Practicing Conflict," 231–32.

37. Klassen, "'Queen for the Day'." See also "Practicing Conflict," 225–41.

38. Henry Fast, *Gruenfeld (now Kleefeld): First Mennonite Village in Western Canada, 1874–1910* (Kleefeld, MB: The Author, 2006), 288.

39. William F. Forbes, et al., *Present Faces of Waterloo Past* (Waterloo, ON: Gerontology Program of University of Waterloo, 1988), 18.

40. Agatha E. Klassen, ed., *Yarrow: A Portrait in Mosaic* (Yarrow, BC: The Author, 1976), 114.

41. Groening, "Grandmother Remembers."

42. Neufeldt, ed., *Before We Were the Land's*, 174.

43. Wiebe, *The Storekeeper's Daughter*, 35.

44. Chornoboy, *Faspa*, 124.

45. Unnamed woman quoted in Roselynn Steinmann, "The Marriage and Childbirth Experiences of Mennonite Women within the Context of the Amish Community" (unpublished research paper, Mennonite Heritage Centre, 1992), 9.

46. Chornoboy, *Faspa*, 60–1.

47. Gordon and Erma (Martin) Bauman, *Memories of Our Lives* (Tavistock, ON: The Authors, 2001), 6.

48. Epp, *From Between the Tracks*, 11.

49. Daisy Isaac Penner, "Margaret Loewen Isaac (1855–1930)," *Preservings* 12 (June 1998): 73.

50. See Figure 3, in Wendy Mitchinson, *Giving Birth in Canada, 1900–1950* (Toronto: University of Toronto Press, 2002), 263.

51. Nanci Langford, "Childbirth on the Canadian Prairies, 1880–1930," in *Telling Tales*, ed. Cavanaugh and Warne, 150.

52. Hilda Lohrenz Bergen, *Immigrants' Daughter* (Edmonton: The Author, 1997), 5.

53. Katherine Martens and Heidi Harms, eds., *In Her Own Voice: Childbirth Stories from Mennonite Women* (Winnipeg: University of Manitoba Press, 1997), viii.

54. Reesor, *Check Rein*, 161.

55. Delbert F. Plett, *Johann Plett: A Mennonite Family Saga* (Steinbach, MB: Crossway Publications, 2003), 703.

56. Katherine Martens, ed. and trans., *They Came From Wiesenfeld Ukraine to Canada: Family Stories* (Winnipeg: The Author, 2005), 52–53.

57. Mitchinson, *Giving Birth in Canada*, 92.

58. Lesley Biggs, "Rethinking the History of Midwifery in Canada," in *Reconceiving Midwifery*, Ivy Lynn Bourgeault, et al., (Montreal & Kingston: McGill-Queen's University Press, 2004), 17–45. Other useful sources on the history of midwifery in Canada include: Suzanne Buckley, "Ladies or Midwives? Efforts to Reduce Infant and Maternal Mortality," in *A Not Unreasonable Claim: Women and Reform in Canada, 1880s–1920s*, ed. Linda Kealey (Toronto: The Women's Press, 1979), 131–49; C. Lesley Biggs, "The Case of the Missing Midwives: A History of Midwifery in Ontario from 1795–1900," *Ontario History* 75, 1 (March 1983): 21–36; Jo Oppenheimer, "Childbirth in Ontario: The Transition from Home to

Hospital in the Early Twentieth Century," in *Delivering Motherhood: Maternal Ideologies and Practices in the 19th and 20th Centuries*, ed. Katherine Arnup, et al. (London & New York: Routledge, 1990); J.T.H. Connor, "'Larger Fish to Catch Here than Midwives': Midwifery and the Medical Profession in Nineteenth-Century Ontario," and Dianne Dodd, "Helen MacMurchy, Popular Midwifery and Maternity Services for Canadian Pioneer Women," in *Caring and Curing: Historical Perspectives on Women and Healing in Canada*, ed. Dianne Dodd and Deborah Gorham (Ottawa: University of Ottawa Press, 1994), 103–34, 135–62; Cecilia Benoit and Dena Carroll, "Canadian Midwifery: Blending Traditional and Modern Practices," in *On All Frontiers: Four Centuries of Canadian Nursing*, ed. Christina Bates, Dianne Dodd, and Nicole Rousseau (Ottawa: University of Ottawa Press, 2005), 27–41.

59. Irma Epp, Lillian Harms, and Lora Sawatsky, "Midwifery: A Ministry," in *Village of Unsettled Yearnings. Yarrow, British Columbia: Mennonite Promise*, ed. Leonard Neufeldt (Victoria: TouchWood Editions, 2002), 17–22.

60. Roth, *Willing Service*, 216–17.

61. Martens, *In Her Own Voice*, 27. See also Harvey Kroeker, "Aganetha Barkman Reimer," *Preservings* 6 (June 1995): 23–24; and Cathy Barkman, "Anna Toews (1868–1933): Midwife," *Preservings* 10 (June 1997): 52.

62. Lorilee G. Scharfenberg, "Helena (Klassen) Eidse (1861–1938)," *Preservings* 8 (June 1996): 51–4.

63. Lori Scharfenberg, "Helena Eidses' Medical Bag," *Preservings* 9 (December 1996): 53.

64. Neufeld, "Katherina Hiebert," 15.

65. Luann Good Gingrich, "A Mother's Garden: Planting Seeds of Hope" (unpublished manuscript, 1997), 3, 5.

66. Charlotte G. Borst, *Catching Babies: The Professionalization of Childbirth, 1870–1920* (Cambridge: Harvard University Press, 1995), 56.

67. Barkman, "Anna Toews," 51.

68. Epp, et al., "Midwifery: A Ministry," 27.

69. Hilda J. Born, *Maria's Century: A Family Saga* (Abbotsford, BC: The Author, 1997), 35.

70. Martens, *In Her Own Voice*, 98.

71. Mitchinson, *Giving Birth in Canada*, 175.

72. Martens, *In Her Own Voice*, 28.

73. Roth, *Willing Service*, 221–22.

74. LaVerna Klippenstein, "The Diary of Tina Schulz," *Mennonite Memories: Settling in Western Canada*, ed. Lawrence Klippenstein and Julius G. Toews (Winnipeg: Centennial Publications, 1977), 231; Henry Klippenstein, *Thicker than Water: The*

Uncensored, Unabridged and Completely Unbiased Account of the Life and Times of the Dietrich Klippenstein Family (North Vancouver: Loon Books, 2004), 84.

75. Linda Buhler, "The Apple Tree," *Preservings* 6 (June 1995): 27.

76. Martens, *In Her Own Voice*, 14.

77. Ibid.

78. Konrad, *And in Their Silent Beauty Speak*, 251.

79. Information from Martens, *They Came From Wiesenfeld Ukraine to Canada*, 66–67.

80. Nicholas N. Driedger, *The Leamington United Mennonite Church: Establishment and Development, 1925–1972* (Altona, MB: D.W. Friesen, 1973), 168–69.

81. Hedy Lepp Dennis, *Memories of Reesor: The Mennonite Settlement in Northern Ontario, 1925–1948* (Leamington, ON: Essex-Kent Historical Association, 2001), 131–33.

82. Eleanor Barrington, *Midwifery is Catching* (Toronto: NC Press Ltd., 1985), 93–100. It was in part because of the perceived desirability of midwife-assisted home births amongst conservative, separatist groups like the Old Order Mennonites that Canada's first birthing centre was established in the 1980s in the heart of 'Mennonite-country' in St. Jacobs, Ontario.

83. *Census of Canada*, 1941.

84. J. Howard Kauffman, "Mennonite: Family Life as Christian Community," in *Faith Traditions and the Family*, ed. Phyllis D. Airhart and Margaret Lamberts Bendroth, (Louisville, KY: Westminster John Knox Press, 1996), 40–41.

85. McLaren, *A History of Contraception*, 5.

86. Roth, *The Amish and Their Neighbours*, 44.

87. Royden K. Loewen, "'The Children, the Cows, My Dear Man and My Sister': The Transplanted Lives of Mennonite Farm Women, 1874–1900," *Canadian Historical Review* 73, 3 (1992). See also Royden K. Loewen, *Family, Church, and Market: A Mennonite Community in the Old and the New Worlds, 1850–1930* (Toronto: University of Toronto Press, 1993).

88. Loewen, *From the Inside Out*, 309–10.

89. Plett, *Johann Plett*, 543.

90. Loewen, *From the Inside Out*, 276.

91. Groening, "Reminiscences."

92. Leonard Freeman, *Up Amos Avenue: From a Path in the Woods to a Street in the City* (Waterloo, ON: The Author, 1997), 37.

93. Daphne N. Winland, "Christianity and Community: Conversion and Adaptation among Hmong Refugee Women," *Canadian Journal of Sociology* 19, 1 (1994): 34.

94. Dyck, "Helena Penner Hiebert," 9.

95. Lori Loewen Scharfenberg, "Anna Bartel Eidse, 1889–1954," *Preservings* 9 (December 1996), part 1, 30–31.

96. Henry Wiebe, ed., *Memories of Our Parents* (Kitchener, ON: Evenstone Press, 1992), 197.

97. Jacques Bernier, *Disease, Medicine and Society in Canada: A Historical Overview* (Ottawa: Canadian Historical Association, 2003), 13.

98. Elizabeth Bloomfield, *Waterloo Township through Two Centuries* (Waterloo, ON: Waterloo Historical Society, 1995), 117.

99. Marjorie Wiebe Hildebrandt, "Agatha Wiebe (1887–1979) Registered Nurse," *Preservings* 14 (1999): 80.

100. Delbert F. Plett, "Letters: Anna Klassen Goossen, 1839–1927," *Preservings* 10 (June 1997): 17.

101. Jacob G. Guenter, ed., *Osler—The Early Years and the One Room School #1238 (1905–1947)* (Osler, SK: Osler Historical Museum, 1999), 247.

102. Anna Epp Ens, ed., *The House of Heinrich: The Story of Heinrich Epp (1811–1863) of Rosenort, Molotschna and His Descendants* (Winnipeg: Epp Book Committee, 1980), 119.

103. Loewen, *From the Inside Out*, 238.

104. Bloomfield, *Waterloo Township through Two Centuries*, 117.

105. Hildebrandt, "Agatha Wiebe," 80.

106. Konrad, *And in Their Silent Beauty Speak*, 213.

107. Loewen, "'The Children, the Cows, My Dear Man and My Sister'," 352.

108. Martens, *In Her Own Voice*, 6.

109. Ruth Unrau, "Singing the Lord's Song in Foreign Lands: Anna Enns Epp, 1902–1958," in *Encircled: Stories of Mennonite Women*, ed. Ruth Unrau (Newton, KS: Faith and Life Press, 1986), 292.

110. *MCC Peace Section Task Force on Women in Church and Society*, 12 (December 1976): 6.

111. Konrad, *And in Their Silent Beauty Speak*, 293.

112. Esther Epp-Tiessen, "Gains and Losses: The Experience of Mennonite Women Immigrants of Late Nineteenth Century," *Journal of Mennonite Studies* 18 (2000): 147.

113. Konrad, *And in Their Silent Beauty Speak*, iv.

114. *MCC Peace Section Task Force on Women in Church and Society*, 12 (December 1976): 6.

115. Scharfenberg, "Anna Bartel Eidse, 1889–1954," part 1, 31.

116. Unnamed woman quoted in Steinmann, "The Marriage and Childbirth Experiences of Mennonite Women," 7.

117. Martens, *In Her Own Voice*, 19.

118. Paul Klassen, *From the Steppes to the Prairies: A History of the Agneta and David Klassen Family in Russia and Canada* (Winnipeg: City Press, 1998), 87.

119. Clayton F. Derstine, *Manual of Sex Education for Parents, Teachers and Students* (Kitchener: The Author, 1942), 122.

120. B. Charles Hostetter, "The Wife's Part in Happy Home Building," *The Canadian Mennonite* 2, (3 September 1954): 6.

121. Hilda Froese, "The Ministry of Women in the Christian Church," *Mennonite Brethren Herald* 3, 21 (22 May 1964): 13.

122. Friesen, *Where We Stand*, Microfilm page 04844.

123. "Resolutions Committee Report," *Calendar of Appointments, Mennonite Conference of Ontario (1944–1945)*, 45.

124. "Report of the Committee on Birth Control," 1945, Mennonite Conference of Ontario Collection, Mennonite Archives of Ontario, Waterloo, Ontario.

125. Untitled typescript report, Evangelical Mennonite church of Blumenort, no date. In Mennonites in Canada files (1950-Birth Control), Mennonite Archives of Ontario.

126. Martens, *All in a Row*, 107.

127. Report on trial of Dorothea Palmer, in *Ottawa Journal*, 23 October 1936, p. 18.

128. Douglas Millar, "Mennonites in the Melting Pot" (unpublished research paper, n.d.), filed in Mennonites in Canada files, Mennonite Archives of Ontario, Waterloo, Ontario.

129. Wiebe, "Me Tarzan, Son of Menno," 18.

130. Royden Loewen, *Diaspora in the Countryside: Two Mennonite Communities and Mid-Twentieth-Century Rural Disjuncture* (Toronto: University of Toronto Press, 2006), 133, referring to Donald H. Parkerson and Jo Ann Parkerson, "'Fewer Children of Greater Spiritual Quality': Religion and the Decline of Fertility in Nineteenth-Century America," *Social Science History* 12 (1988): 49–70.

131. From *Migration North: Mennonites from Mexico*, film (Winnipeg: Mennonite Central Committee, 1995).

132. Karen Pauls, "Northfield Settlement, Nova Scotia: A New Direction for Immigrants from Belize," *Journal of Mennonite Studies* 22 (2004): 179.

133. Janet Mancini Billson, *Keepers of the Culture: The Power of Tradition in Women's Lives* (New York: Lexington Books, 1995), 224.

134. Konrad, *And in Their Silent Beauty Speak*, 279.

135. Sue Clemmer Steiner, "The Impact of Childbearing/Childlessness On Our Lives: Ten Stories," *MCC Committee Report on Women's Concerns Report* 55 (May–June 1984): 10.

136. *MCC Peace Section Task Force on Women in Church and Society*, 12 (December 1976): 4.

137. Martens, *In Her Own Voice*, 184.

138. Loewen, *From the Inside Out*, 246–47.

139. Koop and Dyck, "The Band Plays On," 80.

140. Klassen, "Practicing Conflict," 234.

141. Koop and Dyck, "The Band Plays On," 81.

142. Farah Morrow, "Lives Lived: Helen (Dueck) Enns," *Globe and Mail*, 1 February 2007, p. A16.

143. From Amy Epp, "The Unspoken Pain: How the Mennonite Community Deals with Rape" (unpublished paper, Mennonite Heritage Centre, 1993).

144. For a detailed discussion on this postwar migration, see my book *Women without Men*; also my article, "The 'Grab Bag' Mennonite Family in Post-War Canada," in *On the Case: Explorations in Social History*, ed. Franca Iacovetta and Wendy Mitchinson (Toronto: University of Toronto Press, 1998).

145. Both stories are from Epp, *Women without Men*, 145-6.

146. "Introduction," in *Households of Faith: Family, Gender, and Community in Canada, 1760–1969*, ed. Nancy Christie (Montreal & Kingston: McGill-Queen's University Press, 2002), 16.

147. Martens, *They Came From Wiesenfeld Ukraine to Canada*, 184.

148. Clayton F. Derstine, *The Home: From Four Angles* (Eureka, IL: The Author, 1919), 9.

149. Konrad, *And in Their Silent Beauty Speak*, 159.

150. Roth, *Willing Service*, 99.

151. Esther Patkau, *Canadian Women in Mission, 1895–1952–2002* (Canada: Canadian Women in Mission, 2002), 278.

152. By four women in British Columbia who wish to be known only as 'returned missionaries', "Four Experiences," *MCC Peace Section Task Force on Women in Church & Society*, 3 (March–April 1980): 5.

153. Beth E. Graybill, "'Finding My Place as a Lady Missionary': Mennonite Women Missionaries to Puerto Rico, 1945–1960," *Journal of Mennonite Studies* 17 (1999): 163.

154. Jennifer L. Baumbusch, "Unclaimed Treasures: Older Women's Reflections on Lifelong Singlehood," paper presented at the Canadian Historical Association annual meeting, Toronto, Ontario, 2002, p. 5.

155. Peter Ralph Friesen, "Esther Goossen: A Real Zest for Life," *Preservings* 14 (June 1999): 90.

156. Susan B. Peters to 'Helen,' 15 November 1946. Susan B. Peters Collection, Centre for Mennonite Brethren Studies, Winnipeg, Manitoba.

157. "Salome Bauman (1909-1986)," in *Women of Waterloo County*, ed. Ruth Russell (Kitchener-Waterloo, ON: Canadian Federation of University Women, 2000), 219. Adapted from Lorraine Roth's book *Willing Service*.

158. Cornelius (Chuck) Regehr, "Taking Counsel from Strength and Duty: Agatha Klassen," in Neufeldt, *Village of Unsettled Yearnings*, 292.

159. Koop and Dyck, "The Band Plays On," 128.

160. "Miss Gertrude Klassen: Private Social Worker," *Carillon News*, 18 March 1955.

161. Konrad, *And in Their Silent Beauty Speak*, 422.

162. Regehr, "Take Counsel from Strength and Duty: Agatha Klassen," 294.

163. *Diaries of our Pennsylvania German Ancestors, 1846–1925* (Kitchener, ON: Pennsylvania German Folklore Society of Ontario, 2002), 36; Konrad, *And in Their Silent Beauty Speak*, 159.

164. Linda Buhler, "Mennonite Burial Customs: Part Three," *Preservings* 10 (June 1997): 80.

165. Koop and Dyck, "The Band Plays On," 62.

166. "The Problems of the Single Girl," *The Canadian Mennonite* 5, 27 September and 4 October 1957, p.2.

167. John A. Harder, ed. and trans., *From Kleefeld with Love* (Kitchener, ON: Pandora Press, 2003), 74.

168. Gerry Epp, "Tribute to Margaret Epp," *Saskatchewan Mennonite Historian* 2, 1 (September 1997): 13.

169. Loewen, *From the Inside Out*, 313.

170. Katie Funk Wiebe, "Twenty-five Years Later," *Women's Concerns Report* 73 (July–August 1987): 9.

171. Barbara Murphy, *Why Women Bury Men: The Longevity Gap in Canada* (Winnipeg: J. Gordon Shillingford Publishing, 2002).

172. Loewen, "'The Children, the Cows, My Dear Man and My Sister'," 362–63.

173. Harvey Kroeker, "Aganetha Barkman Reimer," *Preservings* 6 (June 1995): 23.

174. Ernest P. Toews, "Elizabeth Reimer Toews, 1843–1918," *Preservings* 8 (June 1996): part 2, 14.

175. "New Centenarian Recalls Life under Cczar and Commissar," *Kitchener–Waterloo Record*, 23 November 1984, D3.

176. Elizabeth Wall Dyck, "'I Was Left Alone with My Little Children': Elizabeth Wall," in Neufeldt, *Village of Unsettled Yearnings*, 273.

177. *The Diaries of Susannah Cressman, 1911–1946*, selected and prepared by Anne Eby Millar, and edited and annotated by D. Douglas Millar (Kitchener, ON: N.p., 1997), 7.

178. Konrad, *And in Their Silent Beauty Speak*, 415–17.

179. Lorna Bergey, "Changes in Cultural Symbols for Ontario Mennonite Women of the Swiss Tradition during the 1950s and 60s: Stories We Need to Hear," *Mennogespräch* 8, 2 (September 1990): 1.

180. John Unrau, *The Balancing of the Clouds: Paintings of Mary Klassen* (Winnipeg: Windflower Communications, 1991), 46.

181. Harvey Kroeker, "Susanna Loewen Dueck Reimer (1852–1918)," *Preservings* 10 (June 1997): 54.

182. Neufeld, "Katherina Hiebert," 14.

183. Loewen, *From the Inside Out*, 309–10.

184. Born, *Maria's Century*, 117.

185. Loewen, *From the Inside Out*, 265.

186. For more detail on the problem of widows and remarriage amongst post-Second World War Mennonite refugees, see my book *Women without Men*, Chapter 6.

187. Katie Funk Wiebe, *Alone: A Search for Joy* (Hillsboro, KS, and Winnipeg: Kindred Press, 1987), 41.

188. Kauffman, "Mennonite: Family Life as Christian Community," 50.

189. George H. Epp, "'Widow' Epp," in Neufeldt, *Village of Unsettled Yearnings*, 230–36.

190. Anna (Pauls Thiessen) Paetkau, *Memories and Reflections of a Widow* (Winnipeg: J.M. Thiessen, 1991); and Katharina Ediger, *Under His Wings: Events in the Lives of Elder Alexander Ediger and his Family* (Kitchener, ON: The Author, 1994).

191. J.D. Graber and Leo Driedger, "Divorce and Remarriage," *Global Anabaptist Mennonite Encyclopedia Online*. 1989. Global Anabaptist Mennonite Encyclopedia Online. Accessed 5 March 2007. <http://www.gameo.org/encyclopedia/contents/d59me.html>.

192. For evidence of violence against women within Mennonite families, see for instance, Steven P. Martin, "The Presence of Violence in the Mennonite Church and Family Systems" (M.Th. thesis, Waterloo Lutheran Seminary, 1990); Isaac I. Block, *Assault on God's Image: Domestic Abuse* (Winnipeg: Windflower Communications, 1999). See also Mary Anne Hildebrand, "Domestic Violence: A Challenge to Mennonite Faith and Peace Theology," *The Conrad Grebel Review* 10, 1 (Winter 1992): 73–80.

193. Martin, "The Presence of Violence in the Mennonite Church and Family Systems," 23.

194. Block, *Assault on God's Image*, 80.

195. Carol Jean Penner, "Mennonite Silences and Feminist Voices: Peace Theology and Violence Against Women" (PhD thesis, Toronto School of Theology, 1999), 1.

196. B. Charles Hostetter, "The Husband's Part in Happy Home Building," *The Canadian Mennonite* 2 (27 August 1954): 6; and "The Wife's Part in Happy Home Building," *The Canadian Mennonite* 2 (3 September 1954): 6.

197. Derstine, *The Home*, 7.

198. Pauls, "Northfield Settlement, Nova Scotia," 178.

199. Ruth Derksen Siemens, "Quilt as Text and Text as Quilt: The Influence of Genre in the Mennonite Girls' Home of Vancouver (1930–1960)," *Journal of Mennonite Studies* 17 (1999): 118–29

200. Konrad, *And in Their Silent Beauty Speak*, 296.

201. Koop and Dyck, "The Band Plays On," 174.

202. Epp-Tiessen, "Gains and Losses," 152.

203. Harvey Kroeker, "A Notable Pioneer Woman: Elizabeth Dueck Kroeker (1879–1963)," *Preservings* 8 (June 1996): 55.

204. Martens, *In Her Own Voice*, 38.

205. Anna Bartsch, *The Hidden Hand in the Story of My Life*, (Nelson, BC: The Author, 1987), 194.

206. Jim and Helen Reusser, "Best Friends," *MCC Women's Concerns Report* 101 (March–April 1992): 10.

207. R. Marie Griffith, *God's Daughters: Evangelical Women and the Power of Submission* (Berkeley: University of California Press, 1997), 199.

208. Ibid.

209. Good Gingrich, "A Mother's Garden," 6.

210. Ibid.

211. "I Am," *MCC Women's Concerns Report* 74 (September–October 1987): 4.

212. Kerry L. Fast, "Religion, Pain, and the Body: Agency in the Life of an Old Colony Mennonite Woman," *Journal of Mennonite Studies* 22 (2004): 103–29.

CHAPTER 3

1. Roth, *Willing Service*, 28–30.

2. Agatha's story is told in Klassen, *Going by the Moon and the Stars*.

3. Information from Helen Loewen Warkentin Collection, Centre for Mennonite Brethren Studies, Winnipeg, Manitoba.

4. Elise Boulding, *The Underside of History: A View of Women Through Time* (Boulder, CO: Westview Press, 1976), 548.

5. Ursula King, "Religion and Gender: Embedded Patterns, Interwoven Frameworks," in *A Companion to Gender History*, ed. Meade and Wiesner-Hanks, 71.

6. Mary Lou Cummings, "Ordained into Ministry: Ann J. Allebach (1874–1918)," in *Full Circle: Stories of Mennonite Women*, ed. Mary Lou Cummings (Newton, KS: Faith and Life Press, 1978), 2–11.

7. Emma Richards was ordained as a Mennonite minister in 1973 in Illinois.

8. The emergence of the Salvation Army, with Catherine Booth as a key leader, is an example of this trend. Though there has been limited research on the influence of Protestant revivalism on Mennonite understandings of women's role,

there is piecemeal evidence that Ontario Swiss Mennonite women were attracted to the Mennonite Brethren in Christ, a group that split from the mainstream in mid-nineteenth century (becoming the Missionary Church in 1947) and that was characterized by a rejection of traditionalism and emphasis on inner spirituality.

9. "Mennonite Brethren General Conference Resolution, Sister's Participation," in *General Conference Yearbook* (1879), 4. Accessed April 12, 2006. <http://www.mbconf.ca/believe/wiml/resolutions.en.html>.

10. Wiebe, "Me Tarzan, Son of Menno," 17.

11. *Mennonite Confession of Faith: adopted by Mennonite General Conference, August 22, 1963* (Scottdale, PA: Herald Press, 1964).

12. David Ewert, "The Place of Women in the Church According to the New Testament," manuscript in Centre for Mennonite Brethren Studies, Winnipeg, Manitoba, 25-G-2. Published as "Women in the Church," *Mennonite Brethren Herald*, 25 February 1966, pp. 4–6.

13. Quoted in Patkau, *Canadian Women in Mission, 1895-1952-2002*, 152.

14. *MCC Women's Concerns Report* 108 (May-June 1993): 13.

15. Ardith Frey, "Call: A One-Time Event, or a Vocation?" *MCC Women's Concerns Report*, 175 (September-October 2004): 4.

16. *Jubilee Issue of the Waterloo-Kitchener United Mennonite Church, 1924–1974* (Waterloo, ON: The Church, 1974), 35.

17. For profiles of the first Mennonite minsters in Ontario, see Mary A. Schiedel, *Pioneers in Ministry: Women Pastors in Ontario Mennonite Churches, 1973–2003* (Kitchener, ON: Pandora Press, 2003).

18. Martha Smith Good, "A Wife and Husband Reflect on Ordination," *MCC Peace Section Task Force on Women in Church and Society* 43 (May–June 1982): 1.

19. Schiedel, *Pioneers in Ministry*, 35.

20. Martha Smith Good, "From Ministry to Pastor's Wife to Ministry: A Story of Change," *MCC Peace Section Task Force on Women in Church and Society* 38 (July–August 1981): 1.

21. Schiedel, *Pioneers in Ministry*, 29.

22. Pamela E. Klassen, "Speaking Out in God's Name: A Mennonite Woman Preaching," in *Undisciplined Women: Tradition and Culture in Canada*, ed. Pauline Greenhill and Diane Tye (Montreal and Kingston: McGill-Queen's University Press, 1997), 242–49.

23. Issue on "Women Pastors," *MCC Women's Concerns Report* 175 (September–October 2004), 15. Mennonite Brethren position is from a 1999 resolution.

24. Patkau, *Canadian Women in Mission*, 209.

25. Schiedel, *Pioneers in Ministry*, 35.

26. Koop and Dyck, "The Band Plays On," 242–49.

27. Klassen, "Speaking Out in God's Name," 244.
28. Ruth Unrau, "The Writer's Journal," in *Encircled: Stories of Mennonite Women*, ed. Ruth Unrau (Newton, KS: Faith and Life Press, 1986), 2.
29. Wilma L. Dyck, "The Minister's Wife," *The Mennonite* 72, (11 June 1957): 372.
30. Mrs. William Keeney, "The Minister's Wife—Her Spiritual Growth," *The Mennonite* 68 (17 February 1953): 101.
31. Mrs. Claude Boyer, "The Minister's Wife," *The Mennonite* 68 (23 June 1953): 390.
32. Koop and Dyck, "The Band Plays On," 226.
33. Roth, *Willing Service*, 61.
34. Shirley Martin, "Lizzy's Story," *Ontario Mennonite History* 11, 2 (September 1993): 11.
35. Reesor, *Check Rein*, 177.
36. Epp-Tiessen, *J.J. Thiessen*, 240.
37. Koop and Dyck, "The Band Plays On," 356.
38. Roth, *Willing Service*, 119.
39. Margaret Penner Toews, "Anna: The Bishop's Wife," *Preservings* 10 (June 1997): 23–25.
40. LaVerna Klippenstein, "The Diary of Tina Schulz," in *Mennonite Memories: Settling in Western Canada*, ed. Lawrence Klippenstein and Julius G. Toews (Winnipeg: Centennial Publications, 1977), 232.
41. Dennis, *Memories of Reesor*, 120.
42. Epp-Tiessen, *J.J. Thiessen*, 134.
43. Dyck, "The Minister's Wife," 372.
44. Anna Reimer Dyck, *Anna: From the Caucasus to Canada* (Hillsboro, KS: Mennonite Brethren Publishing House, 1979), 177.
45. Unrau, "The Writer's Journal," 4.
46. Dyck, "The Minister's Wife," 372.
47. Daisy Isaac Penner, "Margaret Loewen Isaac (1855–1930)," *Preservings* 12 (June 1998): 73.
48. Laureen Harder, *Their Richest Inheritance: A Celebration of The First Mennonite Church, Vineland, Ontario, 1801-2001* (Vineland, ON: The First Mennonite Church, 2001), 37.
49. Anna Ens, *In Search of Unity: Story of the Conference of Mennonites in Manitoba* (Winnipeg: CMBC Publications, 1996), 112–13.
50. Katherine Martens, *All in a Row: The Klassens of Homewood* (Winnipeg: Mennonite Literary Society, 1988), 35.
51. Ibid., 102.
52. Wiebe, "Me Tarzan, Son of Menno," 10.

53. Epp-Tiessen, *J.J. Thiessen*, 240.

54. Barbara Coffman, "Home Life: From John S. Coffman's Diaries," *The Christian Ministry* 2, 2 (April 1949): 77.

55. Veronica Barkowsky Thiessen, "History of the Yarrow United Mennonite Church," in *Village of Unsettled Yearnings. Yarrow, British Columbia: Mennonite Promise*, ed. Leonard Neufeldt (Victoria: TouchWood Editions, 2002), 47.

56. Marilyn Färdig Whiteley, *Canadian Methodist Women, 1766–1925: Marys, Marthas, Mothers in Israel* (Waterloo, ON: Wilfrid Laurier University Press, 2003), 119.

57. LaVerna Klippenstein, "The Changing Role of Women in the Church (1)," *Mennonite Reporter* 2, 7 (April 3, 1972): 5.

58. On the Mennonite deaconess movement in the United States, see, for instance, Rachel Waltner Goossen, "Piety and Professionalism: The Bethel Deaconesses of the Great Plains," *Mennonite Life* 49 (March 1994): 4–11.

59. Untitled document in Heinrich F. and Catherine Klassen Collection, Volume 1002, Centre for Mennonite Brethren Studies, Winnipeg, Manitoba.

60. Roth, *Willing Service*, 157–58.

61. Patkau, *Canadian Women in Mission*, 280.

62. Ens, *In Search of Unity*, 127.

63. "Testimony," Heinrich F. and Catherine Klassen Collection, Volume 1002, Centre for Mennonite Brethren Studies, Winnipeg, Manitoba.

64. Leonard Doell, *The Bergthaler Mennonite Church of Saskatchewan, 1892–1975* (Winnipeg: CMBC Publications, 1987), 74.

65. Frieda Esau Klippenstein, "Gender and Mennonites: A Response to Mennonites in Canada, 1939–1970: A People Transformed," *Journal of Mennonite Studies* 15 (1997): 144.

66. Loralyn Smith, "An Emerging Spirit" (research paper, University of Waterloo, 1992, Mennonite Archives of Ontario), 10.

67. Marlene O. Martens, ed., *Returning Thanks to God: Hoffnungsfelder Mennonite Churches 1928–2003* (Rabbit Lake, SK: Hoffnungsfelder Mennonite Churches, 2003), 57.

68. Koop and Dyck, "The Band Plays On," 128.

69. *50th Anniversary Highlights of the Vineland United Mennonite Church, 1936-1986: Reflect, Rejoice, Renew* (Vineland, ON: 50th Anniversary Committee, 1986), 88; *50th Anniversary of the Niagara United Mennonite Church, 1938–1988* (Niagara-on-the-Lake, ON: The Church, 1988), 35.

70. Esther Epp-Tiessen, *Altona: The Story of a Prairie Town* (Altona: D.W. Friesen & Sons, 1982), 339.

71. Susan Hiebert, "Missionsverein 1931–1981," in *Milestones and Memories: Bergthaler Mennonite Church of Morden, 1931–1981* (Morden, MB: Bergthaler Mennonite Church, 1981), 41.

72. Martens, *All in a Row*, 106.

73. Marie Funk, quoted in Ens, *In Search of Unity*, 126.

74. *The Canadian Mennonite*, 22 April 1969, 3.

75. Dennis Stoesz, *The Story of Home Street Mennonite Church, 1957–1982* (Winnipeg: The Church, 1985), 16.

76. Patkau, *Canadian Women in Mission*, 51.

77. Anne Harder, *The Vauxhall Mennonite Church* (Calgary: Mennonite Historical Society of Alberta, 2001), 9.

78. Unpublished notes for 40th anniversary of the church, 1988. In Mennonite Historical Society of Canada collection, Mennonite Archives of Ontario.

79. Gerald C. Ediger, *Crossing the Divide: Language Transition Among Canadian Mennonite Brethren, 1940–1970* (Winnipeg: Centre for Mennonite Brethren Studies, 2001), chapter 5.

80. N.N. Fransen, "Stimmberechtigung der Schwestern in unsern Gemeinden im Lichte der Bibel and unsere Praxis, gelesen in Winnipeg, 13 January 1959." Mennonite Archives of Ontario, Waterloo, Ontario.

81. "The Rosthern Mennonite Church—75 Years of Growth" (paper, Mennonite Heritage Centre, Winnipeg, n.d.).

82. Stoesz, *The Story of Home Street Mennonite Church*, 16.

83. Reference in Adolf Ens, *Becoming a National Church: A History of the Conference of Mennonites in Canada* (Winnipeg: CMU Press, 2004), 160.

84. Epp, *Women without Men*, 178–81.

85. Epp-Tiessen, *J.J. Thiessen*, 249.

86. Esther Patkau, *First Mennonite Church in Saskatoon, 1923–1982* (Saskatoon: The Church, 1982), 104–05. See also Epp-Tiessen, *J.J. Thiessen*, 248–50, for an account of this debate.

87. Epp-Tiessen, *J.J. Thiessen*, 249.

88. Patkau, *Canadian Women in Mission*, 152.

89. Peter D. Zacharias, *Footprints of a Pilgrim People: Story of the Blumenort Mennonite Church* (Gretna, MB: Blumenort Mennonite Church, 1985), 158–61.

90. Vernon Zehr and Leona Bender, *Cassel Mennonite Church, 1935–1985* (Tavistock, ON: The Church, 1985), 9.

91. Lillian Kennel, *History of the Wilmot Amish Mennonite Congregation: Steinmann and St. Agatha Mennonite Churches, 1824–1984* (Baden, ON: Steinmann Mennonite Church, 1984), 37.

92. Brent Bauman, *Forged Anew: A History of the Floradale Mennonite Church: Hembling–North Woolwich–Floradale, 1856–1996* (Floradale, ON: The Church, 1996), 74.

93. Frank Zacharias, "Reinland EMMC Historical Sketch," *EMMC Recorder* 25, 11 (December 1988): 5.

94. "Statement on Women Suffrage," *1978 EMC Yearbook* (Steinbach, MB: Evangelical Mennonite Conference, 1978), 14.

95. Neoma Jantz, "A New Position for Mennonite Brethren Women," *MCC Peace Section Task Force on Women in Church and Society*, 9 (October–December 1975): 2.

96. Katy Penner, *Diamonds in the Sand* (Winnipeg: Windflower Communications, 2001), 167.

97. Wiebe, "Me Tarzan, Son of Menno," 14.

98. Kerry Fast, "Struggling with Exclusion," *MCC Women's Concerns Report* 102 (May–June 1992): 13.

99. "General Conference Adopts Resolution on Women in the Church," *Ontario Mennonite Evangel* 15, 4 (April 1970): 6.

100. Ens, *In Search of Unity*, 238–39.

101. Koop and Dyck, "The Band Plays On," 81–82.

102. *Fiftieth Anniversary of the Niagara United Mennonite Church, 1938–1988*, 88–89.

103. Cornelius (Chuck) Regehr, "Take Counsel from Strength and Duty: Agatha Klassen," in Neufeldt, *Village of Unsettled Yearnings*, 295.

104. Unrau, "The Writer's Journal," 5.

105. Peter Penner, "The Foreign Missionary as Hero," in Neufeldt, *Village of Unsettled Yearnings*, 54–55.

106. Beth E. Graybill, "'Finding My Place as a Lady Missionary': Mennonite Women Missionaries in Puerto Rico, 1945–1960," *Journal of Mennonite Studies* 17 (1999): 155.

107. See obituary of Margarete (Siemens) Dueck in *Mennonite Brethren Herald*, 20 April 1990, 27.

108. Patkau, *Canadian Women in Mission*, 120.

109. Graybill, "'Finding My Place as a Lady Missionary'," 161.

110. Ibid., 152–73.

111. Roth, *Willing Service*, 92–93; and Lorraine Roth, "Margaret Elizabeth Brown Kanagy: An Exemplary Life of Christian Service," *Mennonite Historical Bulletin* 54, 3 (July 1993): 1–2.

112. Lorraine Roth, "Serving in the Mission Field," *MCC Women's Concerns Report*, 102 (May–June 1992): 6.

113. Patkau, *Canadian Women in Mission*, 32.

114. Peter Penner, *Russians, North Americans and Telugas: The Mennonite Brethren Mission in India 1885–1975* (Winnipeg, and Hillsboro, KS: Centre for Mennonite Brethren Studies, 1997), 162.

115. Katie Funk Wiebe, "Woman's Freedom—The Church's Necessity," *Direction* 1, 3 (July 1972). Accessed at <http://www.directionjournal.org>.

116. Katie Funk Wiebe, "Mennonite Brethren Women: Images and Realities of the Early Years," *Direction* 24, 2 (Fall 1995): 23–35. Accessed at <http://www.directionjournal.org>.*

117. "People," *Mennonite Reporter* 5 (15 September 1975): 11.

118. *Mennonite Brethren Church, Winkler, Manitoba: 1888–1963* (Winkler, MB: Mennonite Brethren Church, 1963), 37.

119. Gloria Neufeld Redekop, "The Understanding of Woman's Place among Mennonite Brethren in Canada: A Question of Biblical Interpretation," *The Conrad Grebel Review* 8, 3 (Fall 1990): 260–61.

120. "Mennonite Brethren General Conference Resolution Ordaining, Commissioning, and Licensing of Workers," *General Conference Yearbook* (1957): 106. Accessed at <http://www.mbconf.ca/believe/wiml/resolutions.en.html>.

121. Ewert, "The Place of Women in the Church."

122. See Ferne Burkhardt, "The Origins and Development of the Toronto Mennonite Mission: Women were key players, but won few medals" (manuscript, Mennonite Archives of Ontario, 1991).

123. Ibid., 24.

124. Alice Bachert's story is told in Roth, *Willing Service*, 73–77. See also Laureen Harder, *Risk and Endurance: A History of Stirling Avenue Mennonite Church* (Kitchener, ON: Stirling Avenue Mennonite Church, 2003), 91–93, 143–45.

125. By four women in British Columbia who wish to be known only as 'returned missionaries', "Four Experiences," *MCC Peace Section Task Force on Women in Church & Society*, 3 (March–April 1980): 4–5.

126. Roth, *Willing Service*, 84.

127. Penner, *Russians, North Americans and Telugas*, 130.

128. J.P. Kliewer to Sisters 'Wall and Warkentin,' 29 July 1957. Helen Loewen Warkentin collection, Centre for Mennonite Brethren Studies, Winnipeg, Manitoba.

129. Helen L. Warkentin, to "Dear Tien, Sarah and the others of the Home family," 14 August 1957, and to "Dear Tien," 22 September 1957, and "Dear Tien," 27 October 1957. Helen Loewen Warkentin collection, Centre for Mennonite Brethren Studies, Winnipeg, Manitoba.

130. A.E. Janzen to Miss Mary C. Wall and Sister Helen Warkentin, 27 December 1957. Helen Loewen Warkentin collection, Centre for Mennonite Brethren Studies, Winnipeg, Manitoba.

131. A.E. Janzen to "Dear Sister Warkentin," 21 January 1958. Helen Loewen Warkentin collection, Centre for Mennonite Brethren Studies, Winnipeg, Manitoba.

132. Roth, *Willing Service*, 106–07. See also Ferne Burkhardt, *A Mighty Flood: The House of Friendship Story* (Kitchener, ON: House of Friendship, 1989).

133. "Women in Church Vocations," *Mennonite Encyclopedia*, vol. 4 (Scottdale, PA: Mennonite Publishing House, 1959), 972.

134. "Women in Church Vocations Handbook," Women in Church Vocations Collection, XXII F 4, Volume 810, Mennonite Heritage Centre, Winnipeg, Manitoba.

135. Elaine Sommers Rich, "Woman's Place in the World," a speech given at a General Conference Girls' Vocational Conference, Wichita, Kansas, 23 April 1955. Women in Church Vocations Collection, XXII F 4, Volume 810, Mennonite Heritage Centre, Winnipeg, Manitoba.

136. Gloria Neufeld Redekop, *The Work of Their Hands: Mennonite Women's Societies in Canada* (Waterloo, ON: Wilfrid Laurier University Press, 1996).

137. Report of Maria Vogt Derksen in *Fifty Years Ebenezer Verein, 1936–1986* (Steinbach, MB: Ebenezer Verein, 1987), 14.

138. Elsie Neufeld, "Unity in Women's Work," *The Canadian Mennonite* (16 May 1958): 4.

139. Ibid.

140. Redekop, *The Work of Their Hands*, 113.

141. *South Western Ontario Women in Mission, 1925–1987* (Leamington, ON: South Western Ontario Women in Mission, 1987), 74.

142. Thiessen, "History of the Yarrow United Mennonite Church," in Neufeldt, *Village of Unsettled Yearnings*, 46.

143. Patkau, *Canadian Women in Mission*, 9–10.

144. See the article on Mary Ann Cressman, founder and leader of the Mennonite women's organization in Ontario, in *Women of Waterloo County*, ed. Ruth Russell (Kitchener-Waterloo, ON: Canadian Federation of University Women, 2000), 59–63. Also Roth, *Willing Service*, for stories of many of the earlier leaders of Ontario Mennonite women's organizations.

145. "Introduction," in *Women and Twentieth-Century Protestantism*, ed. Margaret Lamberts Bendroth and Virginia Lieson Brereton (Urbana and Chicago: University of Illinois Press, 2002), xiv. The takeover of the Mennonite Women's Missionary Society is discussed in Sharon Klingelsmith, "Women in the Mennonite Church, 1880–1920," *Mennonite Quarterly Review* 54, 31 (July 1980): 163–207.

146. *History of Alberta Mennonite Women in Mission, 1947–1977* (Coaldale, AB: Women in Mission, 1978), 85.

147. Katie Hooge, *The History of the Canadian Women in Mission, 1952-1977* (Winnipeg: Women in Mission, 1977), 7.

148. Lorna L. Bergey, "Changes in Cultural Symbols for Ontario Mennonite Women of the Swiss Tradition during the 1950s & 60s: Stories We Need to Hear," *Mennogespräch* 8, 2 (September 1990): 2.

149. Patkau, *Canadian Women in Mission*, 20.

150. *Fifty Years Ebenezer Verein*, 15.

151. *South Western Ontario Women in Mission*, 41.

152. Susan Hiebert, "Missionsverein 1931–1981," in *Milestones and Memories: Bergthaler Mennonite Church of Morden, 1931–1981* (Morden, MB: Bergthaler Mennonite Church, 1981), 41.

153. *History of Alberta Mennonite Women in Mission*, 109; *South Western Ontario Women in Mission*, 39.

154. Roth, *Willing Service*, 40–41.

155. Mrs. Milton Fast, "Sewing Circle Report for the 1965 Annual Conf.," *1965 Yearbook of the Evangelical Mennonite Conference*, 15–16.

156. Katie Funk Wiebe, "Rempel, Redekop and Reflections About Women's Organizations Among the Brethren," in *Bridging Troubled Waters: The Mennonite Brethren at Mid-Twentieth Century*, ed. Paul Toews (Winnipeg: Kindred Press, 1995), 177.

157. *Fifty Years Ebenezer Verein*, 13.

158. Harder, *The Vauxhall Mennonite Church*, 7.

159. Quoted in Neufeld Redekop, *The Work of Their Hands*, 47.

160. *Fifty Years Ebenezer Verein*, 15.

161. Quoted in Neufeld Redekop, *The Work of Their Hands*, 43.

162. Neufeld, "Unity in Women's Work."

163. *Fifty Years Ebenezer Verein*, 14.

164. Roth, *Willing Service*, 36.

165. *MCC Women's Activities Letter* 50 (February 1948).

166. Harder, *Risk and Endurance*, 63–64.

167. Neufeld Redekop, *The Work of Their Hands*, 51.

168. Gladys V. Goering, *Women in Search of Mission: A History of the General Conference Mennonite Women's Organization* (Newton, KS: Faith and Life Press, 1980).

169. Dorothy M. Swartzentruber, "Ontario Auxiliary Review Forty Year's Women's Work," *The Canadian Mennonite*, 5 (31 May 1957): 3.

170. "Dorcas Mission Circle Serves in Many Ways," *The Canadian Mennonite*, 7 (3 January 1958): 7.

171. Fast, "Sewing Circle Report for the 1965 Annual Conf.," 15–16.

172. Lucille Marr, "'The Time for the Distaff and Spindle': The Ontario Mennonite Women's Sewing Circles and the Mennonite Central Committee," *Journal of Mennonite Studies* 17 (1999): 130.

173. Patkau, *Canadian Women in Mission*, 10.

174. *Saskatchewan Women in Mission* (Regina: Saskatchewan Women in Mission, 1977), 14.

175. *Fifty Years Ebenezer Verein*, 12.

176. Harder, *Risk and Endurance*, 63.

177. Ens, *In Search of Unity*, 91.

178. Patkau, *Canadian Women in Mission*, 50.

179. Klippenstein, "Gender and Mennonites," 146.

180. Epp-Tiessen, *J.J. Thiessen*, 185.

181. *Fifty Years Ebenezer Verein*, 15.

182. Koop and Dyck, "The Band Plays On," 81.

183. Katie Funk Wiebe, "The Place of Women in the Work of the Church," *The Canadian Mennonite* 11 (1 March 1963): 5.

184. Klassen, *Going by the Moon and the Stars*, 58.

185. *History of Alberta Mennonite Women in Mission*, 9.

186. Marr, "'The Time for the Distaff and Spindle'," 130–51.

187. Ibid., 141.

188. Bergey, "Changes in Cultural Symbols for Ontario Mennonite Women." See also Marr, "'The Time for the Distaff and Spindle'" for a detailed account of the Cutting Room's history.

189. Menno Wiebe, "Women's Conference More than Peripheral," *Mennonite Reporter* 2, (24 July 1972): 4.

190. *South Western Ontario Women in Mission*, 16.

191. Ibid., 22.

192. Patkau, *Canadian Women in Mission*, 22-3.

193. Burkhardt, "The Origins and Development of the Toronto Mennonite Mission," 22.

194. Letters in Matheson Island Nursing Station collection, Volume 964, XXIII-F, Box 1, Mennonite Heritage Centre, Winnipeg, Manitoba.

195. See for instance Report #18, "Focus on the Auxiliary Syndrome," in *MCC Peace Section Task Force on Women in Church and Society* (February 1978).

196. Lydia Klassen, Introductory statement to President's Meeting of Mennonite Brethren women's societies, 14 November 1970. In Heinrich F. and Catherine Klassen Collection, Volume 1002, Centre for Mennonite Brethren Studies, Winnipeg, Manitoba.

197. *South Western Ontario Women in Mission*, 26.

198. Neufeld Redekop, *The Work of Their Hands*, 103.

199. Anne Bargen, "Sewing Circles Are Not Gossip Centres," *The Canadian Mennonite* 5 (1 March 1957): 4.

200. Ens, *In Search of Unity*, 224.

201. For a detailed analysis of the transition in naming women's organizations, see Neufeld Redekop, *The Work of Their Hands*, especially chapter 6.

202. *Menno Place: Encompassed by Compassion: Mennonite Benevolent Society Fiftieth Anniversary, 1953–2003* (Abbotsford, BC: Mennonite Benevolent Society, 2003), 24.

203. "Men, Women and Decision-making in Mennonite Central Committee," *MCC Task Force on Women in Church and Society* 3 (December 1973): 4.

204. "General Conference Structure Study," *MCC Peace Section Task Force on Women in Church and Society* 3 (December 1973): 5.

205. "Women in Mennonite Church Structures," *MCC Peace Section Task Force on Women in Church and Society* 5 (April 1974): 6. Ten years later there had been a shift. While in 1975, zero women were in top level administrative positions at Mennonite Central Committee (MCC) Canada compared to six men, ten years later that ratio was 1:15. In a report on a statistical survey gathered by the MCC women's concerns office, it was observed that MCC Canada lagged behind MCC US. Of three large North American church organizations surveyed in 1985, the General Conference (GC) Mennonite Church showed the greatest gender parity in representation on its main boards (overall rate of 40 percent), with MCC (18 percent) and the Mennonite Church (30 percent) lagging behind. However, the Canadian GC body—Conference of Mennonites in Canada—lagged behind other GC boards in including women. See statistics in special issue of *Women's Concerns Report*, "Women and Decision-Making in Mennonite Institutions" 63 (Sept.–Oct. 1985).

206. Koop and Dyck, "The Band Plays On," 126.

207. Mary Enns, *Selma Redekopp: An Unusual Woman* (Winnipeg: Estate of Henry W. Redekopp, 1990), 62.

208. Ibid., 61.

209. Ibid., 75.

210. Ibid., 83.

211. Helena Penner Hiebert, "Granny's Stories," quoted in Esther Epp-Tiessen, "Gains and Losses: The Experience of Mennonite Women Immigrants of Late Nineteenth Century," *Journal of Mennonite Studies* 18 (2000): 153.

212. *History of the Whitewater Mennonite Church, 1927–1987* (Boissevain, MB: Whitewater Mennonite Church, 1987), 86.

213. Klassen, *Going by the Moon and the Stars*. See also Sydney Stahl Weinberg, *The World of Our Mothers: The Lives of Jewish Immigrant Women* (Chapel Hill: University of North Carolina Press, 1988), 19; and Marlene Epp, "'My Mom Was a Preacher': Female Religion in the Soviet Era," *Sophia* 5, 1 (Winter 1995): 14–15.

214. Justina D. Neufeld, *A Family Torn Apart* (Kitchener, ON: Pandora Press, 2003), 59.

215. Katie Friesen, *Into the Unknown* (Steinbach, MB: The Author, 1986), 27.

216. For more detail, see my book *Women without Men*, especially Chapter 7.

217. From a personal interview with Gloria Gonzalez (a pseudonym), Kitchener, Ontario, October 2000. See my article, "Pioneers, Refugees, Exiles, and Transnationals: Gendering Diaspora in an Ethno-Religious Context," *Journal of the Canadian Historical Association* 12 (2001): 137–53.

218. Daphne N. Winland, "Christianity and Community: Conversion and Adaptation among Hmong Refugee Women," *Canadian Journal of Sociology* 19, 1 (1994): 21–45.

219. Daphne Abergel, "Women and Religion: 'Mennonite Hmong'," *Refuge: Canada's Periodical on Refugees* 6, 3 (February 1987): 9.

220. Plett, *Johann Plett*, p. 522.

221. Martens, *All in a Row*, 8.

222. Ibid., 37.

223. Royden Loewen, *Blumenort: A Mennonite Community in Transition, 1874–1982* (Steinbach, MB: Blumenort Mennonite Historical Society, 1983), 179.

224. Wiebe, *The Storekeeper's Daughter*, 84.

225. Reesor, *Check Rein*, 188.

226. Hilda J. Born, *Maria's Century: A Family Saga* (Abbotsford, BC: The Author, 1997), 69–70.

227. Nancy-Lou Gellermann Patterson, *Swiss–German and Dutch–German Mennonite Traditional Art in the Waterloo Region, Ontario* (Ottawa: National Museum of Canada, 1979), 144.

228. Elizabeth and Irwin Steckly, *Joseph Reschly and Anna Schweitzer Family History and Genealogy*, 2nd edition (Stratford, ON: The Authors, 2003), 281.

229. Donald Martin, *Old Order Mennonites of Ontario: Gelassenheit, Discipleship, Brotherhood* (Kitchener, ON: Pandora Press, 2003), 161.

230. Winland, "Christianity and Community," 22.

CHAPTER 4

1. Malinda Bricker to John S. Coffman, 1 March 1895. John S. Coffman Collection, Archives of the Mennonite Church, Goshen, Indiana.

2. Helen Erb Burkholder's story is from a personal interview with the author. See Marlene Epp, "Alternative Service and Alternative Gender Roles: Conscientious Objectors in B.C. During World War II," *BC Studies* 105–106 (Spring/Summer 1995): 139–58.

3. Peter and Elfrieda Dyck, *Up from the Rubble: The Epic Rescue of Thousands of War-Ravaged Mennonite Refugees* (Scottdale, PA: Herald Press, 1991).

4. Wiebe, "Me Tarzan, Son of Menno," 16.

5. Joanne Hess Siegrist, *Mennonite Women of Lancaster Pennsylvania: A Story in Photographs from 1855–1935* (Intercourse, PA: Good Books, 1996), 14.

6. Margaret C. Reynolds, "River Brethren Breadmaking Ritual," in *Strangers at Home: Amish and Mennonite Women in History*, ed. Kimberly D. Schmidt, et al. (Baltimore: The Johns Hopkins University Press, 2002), 93.

7.   R. Marie Griffith, *God's Daughters: Evangelical Women and the Power of Submission* (Berkeley: University of California Press, 1997), 162.

8.   Henry Klippenstein, *Thicker than Water: The Uncensored, Unabridged and Completely Unbiased Account of the Life and Times of the Dietrich Klippenstein Family* (North Vancouver: Loon Books, 2004), 62.

9.   Leonard N. Neufeldt, ed., *Before We Were the Land's: Yarrow, British Columbia: Mennonite Promise* (Victoria: TouchWood Editions, 2002), 34.

10.   Pamela Klassen, "Women's Sexuality and the Messages of Dress," *MCC Women's Concerns Report* 107 (March–April 1993): 4.

11.   Pamela Klassen, "What's Bre(a)d in the Bone: The Bodily Heritage of Mennonite Women," *Mennonite Quarterly Review* 68, 2 (April 1994): 237.

12.   Siegrist, *Mennonite Women of Lancaster Pennsylvania*, 8.

13.   Some of the literature on this topic includes: Ruth Barnes and Joanne B. Eicher, eds., *Dress and Gender: Making and Meahing in Cultural Contexts* (New York: St. Martin's Press, 1992); Linda B. Arthur, ed., *Religion, Dress and the Body* (Oxford, UK: Berg, 1999).

14.   Linda B. Arthur, "Introduction: Dress and the Social Control of the Body," and Beth Graybill and Linda B. Arthur, "The Social Control of Women's Bodies in Two Mennonite Communities," in *Religion, Dress and the Body*, ed. Arthur, 1–7, 9–29.

15.   For a discussion of the dress issue in Ontario, see Marlene Epp, "Carrying the Banner of Nonconformity: Ontario Mennonite Women and the Dress Question," *The Conrad Grebel Review* 8, 3 (Fall 1990): 237–57.

16.   Beth E. Graybill, "'To Remind Us of Who We Are': Multiple Meanings of Conservative Women's Dress," in Schmidt, *Strangers at Home*, 61.

17.   Mary Hunsberger Schiedel, *A Journey of Faith: The History of Shantz Mennonite Church, 1840–2000* (Baden, ON: Shantz Mennonite Church, 2000), 38.

18.   Margaret L. Bendroth, "Fundamentalism and Femininity: The Reorientation of Women's Role in the 1920s," *Evangelical Studies Bulletin* 5 (March 1988): 1–4.

19.   Letha Dawson Scanzoni and Susan Setta, "Women in Evangelical, Holiness, and Pentecostal Traditions," in *Women and Religion in America, Vol. 3: 1900–1968*, ed. Rosemary Radford Ruether and Rosemary Skinner Keller (San Francisco: Harper and Row, 1986), 233.

20.   See Epp, "Carrying the Banner of Nonconformity," 242.

21.   Graybill, "'To Remind Us of Who We Are'," 64–65.

22.   Harold S. Bender, "An Exegesis of I Cor. 11:1–16" (paper, 1922), 19. Mennonite Historical Library, Goshen, Indiana.

23.   Ezra Stauffer, "The Christian Woman's Spiritual Service," *The Christian Ministry* 2 (January 1949): 33–35.

24. Oscar Burkholder, "The Devotional Covering," *Gospel Herald* 23 (17 April 1930): 67–68; "As it was in the days of Sodom, Attention women!" *Christian Review* 2 (October 1928): 14.

25. Esther F. Rupel, "The Dress of the Brethren (and Church of the Brethren)," *Brethren Life and Thought* 31 (Summer 1986): 140.

26. T.D. Regehr, *Faith, Life and Witness in the Northwest, 1903-2003: Centennial History of the Northwest Mennonite Conference* (Kitchener, ON: Pandora Press, 2003), 107.

27. E. Reginald Good, *Frontier Community to Urban Congregation: First Mennonite Church, Kitchener: 1813–1988* (Kitchener, ON: First Mennonite Church, 1988), 109.

28. Burkholder, "As it was in the days of Sodom," 14.

29. More detailed discussions of this church split can be found in Good, *Frontier Community to Urban Congregation*; Epp, "Carrying the Banner of Nonconformity"; and Laureen Harder, *Risk and Endurance: A History of Stirling Avenue Mennonite Church* (Kitchener, ON: Stirling Avenue Mennonite Church, 2003).

30. Harder, *Risk and Endurance*, 46–47.

31. Ibid., 42.

32. *The Diaries of Susannah Cressman, 1911-1946*, selected and prepared by Anne Eby Millar, and edited and annotated by D. Douglas Millar (Kitchener, ON: N.p., 1997).

33. Ibid., 51, 61.

34. Harder, *Risk and Endurance*, 69-70.

35. Epp, "Carrying the Banner of Nonconformity," 247.

36. Ibid., 247.

37. Lorraine Roth, "Serving in the Mission Field," *MCC Women's Concerns Report* 102 (May–June 1992): 5.

38. Isaac R. Horst and Sam Steiner, "Conservative Mennonite Church of Ontario," *Global Anabaptist Mennonite Encyclopedia Online*. 2001. Accessed 8 June 2007: <http://www.gameo.org/encyclopedia/contents/c6674me.html>.

39. Oscar Burkholder, "The Ministry and Christian Living," *The Sword and Trumpet* 13 (August 1945): 421.

40. Loralyn Smith, "An Emerging Spirit" (research paper, 1992, Mennonite Archives of Ontario), 8.

41. L.N. Snyder, Interview 7095, Fairview Mennonite Home Oral History Project, Mennonite Archives of Ontario, Waterloo, Ontario.

42. Reesor, *Check Rein*, 184.

43. Fred Habermehl, *Twigs, Branches & Roots: Waterloo County Habermehl Family* (Niagara Falls, ON: Paul Heron Publishing Ltd., 1997).

44. Lorraine Roth, *Willing Service: Stories of Ontario Mennonite Women* (Waterloo, ON: Mennonite Historical Society of Ontario, 1992), 56.

45. See Kimberly D. Schmidt, "Schism: Where Women's Outside Work and Insider Dress Collided," in Schmidt, *Strangers at Home*, 208–33.

46. Interview, Lorraine Roth, 14 March 1990.

47. Harder, *Risk and Endurance*, 56-7.

48. Epp, "Carrying the Banner of Nonconformity," 254. Story is of Elizabeth Jutzi Nafziger, told in Roth, *Willing Service*, 121–22.

49. Janet Martin, "Distinctive Dress and the Newcomer," *MCC Women's Concerns Report* 107 (March–April 1993): 6.

50. Roth, *Willing Service*, 199–200.

51. See Laureen Harder, *Their Richest Inheritance: A Celebration of The First Mennonite Church Vineland, Ontario, 1801–2001* (Vineland, ON: The First Mennonite Church, 2001), 37.

52. Roth, *Willing Service*, 36.

53. Harder, *Risk and Endurance*, 29.

54. Mary Martin, "Women and Dress," *Women's Concerns Report* 107 (March–April 1993): 1.

55. Anne Friesen, "A Treasure Chest—'for when they shall ask,'" *Saskatchewan Mennonite Historian* 4, 2 (September 1999): 19.

56. The groups were the Saskatchewan Bergthaler, Manitoba Chortitzer, and Sommerfelder. Leonard Doell, *The Bergthaler Mennonite Church of Saskatchewan, 1892–1975* (Winnipeg: CMBC Publications, 1987), 71.

57. Marlene O. Martens, ed. *Returning Thanks to God: Hoffnungsfelder Mennonite Churches, 1928–2003* (Rabbit Lake, SK: Hoffnungsfelder Mennonite Churches, 2003), 56.

58. Patkau, *Canadian Women in Mission*, 133.

59. Konrad, *And in Their Silent Beauty Speak*, 46–47.

60. Gudrun L. (Wohlgemut) Mathies, "Refugee Pilgrimage: A Story of God's Care. Lina (Heinrich) Wohlgemut: From Poland to Canada," *Ontario Mennonite History* 13, 1 (March 1995): 13.

61. Janet Mancini Billson, *Keepers of the Culture: The Power of Tradition in Women's Lives* (New York: Lexington Books, 1995), 208.

62. John R. Rice, *Bobbed Hair, Bossy Wives, and Women Preachers* (Wheaton: Sword of the Lord, 1941).

63. Alison Prentice, et al., *Canadian Women: A History* (Toronto: Harcourt Brace Jovanovich, 1988), 252.

64. "Statement on Faith and Practice," Mennonite Conference of Ontario records, II-2.1.1.3, Mennonite Archives of Ontario, Waterloo, Ontario.

65. Loewen, *Blumenort: A Mennonite Community in Transition, 1874–1982*, 583. Other dangers included worldly magazines, radio, television, hockey games, 4–H clubs, picnics, wiener roasts, inter-school sports, dating, summer vacations, late-night Christmas carolling, finger rings, musical instruments, and wedding dresses.

66. Koop and Dyck, "The Band Plays On," 336.

67. Katie Friesen, *Into the Unknown* (Steinbach, MB: The Author, 1986), 115.

68. Dennis Stoesz, *The Story of Home Street Mennonite Church, 1957–1982* (Winnipeg: Home Street Mennonite Church, 1985), 36.

69. Harvey Neufeldt, "M Hank," in Neufeldt, ed., *Village of Unsettled Yearnings*, 302.

70. Linda Buhler, "Agnes Toews Kornelsen, Hairdresser," *Preservings* 5 (January 1995): 12.

71. Martens, *All in a Row*, 130.

72. Ibid., 129.

73. Koop and Dyck, "The Band Plays On," 116.

74. Martens, *All in a Row*, 129.

75. Hilda J. Born, *Maria's Century: A Family Saga* (Abbotsford, BC: The Author, 1997), 76.

76. Martens, *All in a Row*, 130.

77. Chornoboy, *Faspa*, 18–19.

78. Konrad, *And in Their Silent Beauty Speak*, 265.

79. Koop and Dyck, "The Band Plays On," 230.

80. Magdalene Redekop, "Through the Mennonite Looking Glass," in *Why I Am a Mennonite: Essays on Mennonite Identity*, ed. Harry Loewen (Kitchener, ON: Herald Press, 1988), 229.

81. Martens, *All in a Row*, 128–29.

82. Ibid., 130–31.

83. Harry Loewen, "From Russia to Canada: My Mother Was Betrayed by the Church," *Mennonite Reporter* 20 (1 October 1990): 9.

84. Harvey Neufeldt, "Creating the Brotherhood: Status and Control in the Yarrow Mennonite Community, 1928–1960," in *Canadian Papers in Rural History*, vol. 9, ed. Donald H. Akenson (Gananoque, ON: Langdale Press, 1994), 225–26.

85. Klassen, "Women's Sexuality and the Messages of Dress," 4.

86. Koop and Dyck, "The Band Plays On," 231.

87. Martens, *All in a Row*, 31.

88. *Chilliwack Progress*, 27 May 1942, p. 8. In Mennonites in Canada files, 1940-Yarrow, Mennonite Archives of Ontario, Waterloo, Ontario.

89. Esther Epp-Tiessen, *J.J. Thiessen*, 229.

90. Katie Funk Wiebe, "Images and Realities of the Early Years," *Mennonite Life* 36, 3 (September 1981): 27.

91. M.J. Heisey, *Peace and Persistence: Tracing the Brethren in Christ Peace Witness Through Three Generations* (Kent, OH: Kent State University Press, 2003), 19.

92. Redekop, "Through the Mennonite Looking Glass," 239.

93. Rachel Waltner Goossen, *Women Against the Good War: Conscientious Objection and Gender on the American Home Front, 1941–1947* (Chapel Hill, NC: University of North Carolina Press, 1997), 93.

94. Heisey, *Peace and Persistence*, 136.

95. For a summary of the Canadian Alternative Service program in World War II, see Regehr, *Mennonites in Canada*, chapter 2.

96. Roth, *Willing Service*, 168.

97. Plett, *Johann Plett*, 197.

98. Patkau, *Canadian Women in Mission,*102.

99. Koop and Dyck, "The Band Plays On," 60.

100. Marjorie Kaethler and Susan D. Shantz, *Quilts of Waterloo County: A Sampling* (Waterloo, ON: The Authors, 1990), 29.

101. Edna Ramseyer, "Will Ye Heed the Call?" *Missionary News and Notes* (November 1943): 1. In Marlene Epp, "Nonconformity and Nonresistance: What Did It Mean to Mennonite Women?" in *Changing Roles of Women within the Christian Church in Canada*, ed. Elizabeth Gillan Muir and Marilyn Färdig Whiteley (Toronto: University of Toronto Press, 1995), 68.

102. H.R. Baerg to David J. Braun, 10 May 1973. Miscellaneous Conscientious Objector material, Volume 1159, Mennonite Heritage Centre, Winnipeg, Manitoba.

103. "Horne Lake 'High' Spots," *The Beacon* 2, 2 (February 1943): 12. Quoted in Epp, "Alternative Service and Alternative Gender Roles," 146.

104. Epp, "Alternative Service and Alternative Gender Roles," 149.

105. C.F. Derstine, "Canadian Conscientious Objectors in Camp," *Gospel Herald* 34 (13 August 1942): 426–27.

106. Questionnaire re: CO Service from Ben and Martha Rempel, Miscellaneous Conscientious Objector material, Volume 1159, Mennonite Heritage Centre, Winnipeg, Manitoba.

107. The stories of Helen Erb Burkholder and Clara Lebold Roth are based on interviews with the author. See Epp, "Alternative Service and Alternative Gender Roles."

108. Interview with Annie Martin by the author. See also Lorraine Roth, "Conscientious Objection: The Experiences of Some Canadian Mennonite Women During World War II," *Mennonite Quarterly Review* 66, 4 (October 1992): 544.

109. From an interview by Lorraine Roth; see Epp, "Alternative Service and Alternative Gender Roles," 154.

110. Prentice, *Canadian Women*, 311. For a detailed study of Canadian women's workforce and military participation in World War II, see Ruth Roach Pierson, *'They're Still Women After All': The Second World War and Canadian Womanhood* (Toronto: McClelland and Stewart, 1986).

111. Harder, *Risk and Endurance*, 101.

112. Koop and Dyck, "The Band Plays On," 335.

113. "Girls Man the Farm Front," *Star Weekly*, 14 August 1943.

114. "Who's Who," *The Beacon* 2, 5 (May 1943): 15.

115. Harder, *Risk and Endurance*, 103.

116. Koop and Dyck, "The Band Plays On," 9.

117. Ibid., 84.

118. *Church and Mission News* 9, 1 (January 1944): 3.

119. Jake Unrau, with Johann D. Funk, *Living in the Way: The Pilgrimage of Jake & Trudie Unrau* (Winnipeg: CMBC Publications, 1996), 21.

120. K.S. Toews, "German English Academy, Rosthern, Saskatchewan," *The Mennonite* 59 (22 August 1944): 4.

121. Kelly G.I. Harms, *Grace Upon Grace: A History of the Mennonite Home of Rosthern* (Rosthern, SK: Mennonite Nursing Homes, 1994), 71.

122. Nicholas N. Driedger, *The Leamington United Mennonite Church: Establishment and Development, 1925–72* (Altona, MB: D.W. Friesen, 1973), 94.

123. Esther Epp-Tiessen, *Altona: The Story of a Prairie Town* (Altona, MB: D.W. Friesen, 1982), 196.

124. Loewen, *Blumenort*, 615.

125. Royden Loewen, "Rurality, Ethnicity, and Gender Patterns of Cultural Continuity during the 'Great Disjuncture' in the R.M. of Hanover, 1945–1961," *Journal of the Canadian Historical Association* 4 (1993): 161–82.

126. Neufeldt, *Before We Were the Land's*, 37.

127. Roth, "Conscientious Objection," 540.

128. Loewen, ed., *From the Inside Out*, 257.

129. *The Diaries of Susannah Cressman*, 77.

130. Correspondence between Mary Faust and N.N. Driedger, reproduced in *Mennonite Peace Perspectives from Essex and Kent*, ed. Victor D. Kliewer (Leamington, ON: The Essex–Kent Mennonite Historical Association, 2001), 48–52.

131. Harder, *Risk and Endurance*, 104.

132. Epp-Tiessen, *J.J. Thiessen*, 154–55.

133. *The Diaries of Susannah Cressman*, 69.

134. John B. Toews, *With Courage to Spare* (Hillsboro, KS: General Conference of Mennonite Brethren Churches, 1978), 79.

135. Clara Snider to Workers of the Nonresistant Relief Organization, 16 December 1942. John Coffman letters, Mennonite Archives of Ontario, Waterloo, Ontario.

136. *Missionary News and Notes*, April 1941, 61.

137. Arlene Sitler, "A Challenge to Mennonite Women," *Women's Activities Letter* 18 (February 1946): 1–3.

138. See unpublished manuscript on the letters of Alice Snyder to her mother, by M. Lucille Marr. Used with permission.

139. Linda Huebert Hecht, "Legacy of Service: Dorothy M. Swartzentruber Sauder's Career in Church Work at Home and Abroad," *Ontario Mennonite History* 19, 2 (November 2001): 9–15.

140. Siemens, "Quilt as Text and Text as Quilt," 126–27.

141. A recent detailed and long-range study by James Urry challenges the notion of Mennonites as non-political; see *Mennonites, Politics, and Peoplehood: Europe, Russia, Canada, 1525–1980* (Winnipeg: University of Manitoba Press, 2006).

142. "Excerpts from Diaries of Barbara (Bowman) Shuh," in *Diaries of our Pennsylvania German Ancestors, 1846–1925*, Volume 15 of *Canadian-German Folklore* (Kitchener, ON: The Pennsylvania German Folklore Society of Ontario, 2002), 59.

143. Koop and Dyck, "The Band Plays On, 60.

144. *The Diaries of Susannah Cressman*, 180.

145. Ibid., 43.

146. Alfred J. Kitchen, Social Worker, to Mr. C.W. Lundy, Director of Welfare, Victoria, B.C., 5 November 1945. Saskatchewan Archives Board, photocopy in Mennonites in Canada files, Mennonite Archives of Ontario Waterloo, Ontario.

147. Martens, *All in a Row*, 89.

148. Ibid.

149. "Family Allowance Study Committee," *Calendar of Appointments of the Mennonite Conference of Ontario* (1945–46): 41.

150. Roth, *Willing Service*, 51.

151. Irene Friesen Petkau, and Peter A. Petkau, *Blumenfeld: Where Land and People Meet* (Winkler, MB: Blumenfeld Historical Committee, 1981), 177.

152. Harder, *Risk and Endurance*, 64.

153. Roth, *Willing Service*, 170.

154. Epp-Tiessen, *Altona*, 181–83.

155. "Women's Coop Guild," FSMC, Box 3896, file 2, Mennonite Heritage Centre, Winnipeg, Manitoba.

156. *The Diaries of Susannah Cressman*, 11.

157. Ibid., 97.

158. Ibid., 36.

159. Ibid., 60.

160. Ibid., 184.

161. Ibid., 201.

162. Koop and Dyck, "The Band Plays On," 47.

163. Ibid., 189.

164. Loewen, *Blumenort*, 615.

165. Wiebe, *Alone: A Search for Joy* (Hillsboro, KS, and Winnipeg: Kindred Press, 1987), 26.

166. "The Lives of Mennonite Women," Prairie Public Television, <http://www.prairiepublic.org>. Accessed on May 11, 2006.

167. Reesor, *Check Rein*, 152.

CHAPTER 5

1. E. Reginald Good, *Anna's Art: The Fraktur Art of Anna Weber, a Waterloo County Mennonite Artist, 1814–1888* (Kitchener, ON: Pochauna Publications, 1976).

2. Ibid., 17.

3. Abe Dueck, "Esther (Hiebert) Horch: A Gifted and Generous Woman," *Profiles of Mennonite Faith, Mennonite Brethren Historical Commission*. Accessed June 12, 2006. <http://www.mbhistory.org/profiles/horch.en.html>.

4. Wiebe, "Me Tarzan, Son of Menno," 11. Prips (a coffee-like beverage made of roasted grain) and Schinkefleisch (fried ham) are two typical Russian Mennonite foods.

5. Martens, *All in a Row*, 146–47.

6. Hasia R. Diner, and Beryl Lieff Benderly, *Her Works Praise Her: A History of Jewish Women in America from Colonial Times to the Present* (New York: Basic Books, 2002).

7. Joanne Hess Siegrist, *Mennonite Women of Lancaster Pennsylvania: A Story in Photographs from 1855–1935* (Intercourse, PA: Good Books, 1996), 7.

8. Magdalene Redekop, "Through the Mennonite Looking Glass," in *Why I Am a Mennonite*, ed. Loewen, 240, 242. Borscht is a cabbage and vegetable soup, and varenike are dumplings like perogies, both foods with Ukrainian origins.

9. Di Brandt, *Questions I asked my mother* (Winnipeg: Turnstone Press, 1987), 8.

10. Eleanor Martens, "The Artist as Homemaker: A Portrait," *Sophia* 3, 1 (Winter 1993): 13.

11. Shirley Martin, "Lizzy's Story," *Ontario Mennonite History* 11, 2 (September 1993): 11.

12. Henry Wiebe, ed., *Memories of Our Parents* (Kitchener, ON: Evenstone Press, 1992), 200.

13. Martens, "The Artist as Homemaker," 13.

14. Linda Buhler, "Sarah Sawatzky Funk: Matriarch of Kronsgart'," *Preservings* 10 (June 1997): 42.

15. Nancy-Lou Gellermann Patterson, *Swiss-German and Dutch-German Mennonite Traditional Art in the Waterloo Region, Ontario* (Ottawa: National Museums of Canada, 1979), 42–43.

16. Marjorie Hildebrand, ed., *Reflections of a Prairie Community: A Collection of Stories and Memories of Burwalde S.D. #529* (Winkler, MB: Friends of the Former Burwalde School District #529, 2004), 82.

17. Reesor, *Check Rein*, 281.

18. Patterson, *Swiss-German and Dutch-German Mennonite Traditional Art*, 44.

19. Konrad, *And in Their Silent Beauty Speak*, 242.

20. Nancy-Lou Patterson, *The Language of Paradise: Folk Art from Mennonite and other Anabaptist Communities of Ontario* (London, ON: London Regional Art Gallery, 1985), 18.

21. Ibid., 31.

22. Marjorie Kaethler, and Susan D. Shantz, *Quilts of Waterloo County: A Sampling* (Waterloo, ON: The Authors, 1990), 8.

23. Ibid.,11.

24. Ibid., 22.

25. William F. Forbes, et al., *Present Faces of Waterloo Past* (Waterloo, ON: Gerontology Program of University of Waterloo, 1988), 6.

26. Susan H. Clark, "Quilting in Waterloo County," in *Women of Waterloo County*, ed. Ruth Russell (Kitchener-Waterloo: Canadian Federation of University Women, 2000), 101.

27. Louise Stoltzfus, *Amish Women: Life and Stories* (Intercourse, PA: Good Books, 1994), 12.

28. Siemens, "Quilt as Text and Text as Quilt," 118–29.

29. Dennis, *Memories of Reesor: The Mennonite Settlement in Northern Ontario, 1925-1948*, 111.

30. Kaethler and Shantz, *Quilts of Waterloo County*, 35.

31. Dennis, *Memories of Reesor*, 87.

32. Roth, *Willing Service*, 146.

33. Susan M. Burke, "Perpetuation and Adaptation: The Germanic Textiles of Waterloo County 1800–1900," in *From Pennsylvania to Waterloo: Pennsylvania-German Folk Culture in Transition*, ed. Susan M. Burke and Matthew H. Hill (Kitchener, ON: Joseph Schneider Haus, 1991), 79–80.

34. Roth, *Willing Service*, 118.

35. Patterson, *Swiss-German and Dutch-German Mennonite Traditional Art*, 129.

36. John Unrau, *The Balancing of the Clouds: Paintings of Mary Klassen* (Winnipeg: Windflower Communications, 1991), 12. See also Lori Matties, "Pioneer Painter: The Watercolours of Mary Klassen," *Sophia* 4, 3 (Fall 1994): 18–19.

37. Unrau, *The Balancing of the Clouds*, 33.

38. Carol Dyck, "A Golden Braid," *MCC Women's Concerns Report* 75 (November–December 1987): 5.

39. Debra Fieguth, "A House Overflowing: Portrait of a Family of Artists," *Sophia* 4, 3 (Fall 1994): 6–7.

40. *Gnadenthal, 1880–1980* (Winkler, MB: Gnadenthal History Book Committee, 1982), 91.

41. Clayton F. Derstine, *Manual of Sex Education* (Kitchener, ON: The Author, 1942), 65.

42. "Reminiscences of Grandmother Snider," *Waterloo Historical Society* 66 (1978): 12.

43. Hildebrand, *Reflections of a Prairie Community*, 75.

44. Martens, *All in a Row*, 93.

45. Chornoboy, *Faspa*, 132–35.

46. Sara Brooks Sundberg, "A Female Frontier: Manitoba Farm Women in 1922," *Prairie Forum* 15–16 (1990–1991): 193.

47. Martens, *All in a Row*, 93.

48. Janet Mancini Billson, *Keepers of the Culture: The Power of Tradition in Women's Lives* (New York: Lexington Books, 1995), 206.

49. Ibid., 206.

50. Loewen, ed., *From the Inside Out*, 294–307.

51. Hilda J. Born, *Maria's Century: A Family Saga* (Abbotsford, BC: The Author, 1997), 123.

52. Micaela di Leonardo, "The Female World of Cards and Holidays: Women, Families, and the Work of Kinship," *Signs* 12, 3 (1987): 440–53.

53. L. Marie Enns, *Preacher's Kids on the Homestead* (Belleville, ON: Guardian Books, 2005), 115.

54. Hildebrand, *Reflections of a Prairie Community*, 11.

55. Chornoboy, *Faspa*, 36–37.

56. Wiebe, *The Storekeeper's Daughter*, 163.

57. Klassen, "What's Bre(a)d in the Bone," 241.

58. Hostetler, *Mennonite Life*, 15–16.

59. Such depictions have been popularized especially by renowned journalist and cookbook writer Edna Staebler (d. 2006), who spent substantial amount of time exploring the foodways of Old Order Mennonites of Pennsylvania German culture. See

for instance one of her best-known cookbooks, *Food That Really Schmecks* (Toronto: McGraw-Hill Ryerson, 1968).

60. Wiebe, *Memories of Our Parents*, 204, 209.

61. Enns, *Preacher's Kids on the Homestead*, 69.

62. Edward R. Giesbrecht, "The Everydayness of a Dairy Farm," in *Village of Unsettled Yearnings. Yarrow, British Columbia: Mennonite Promise*, ed. Leonard Neufeldt (Victoria: TouchWood Editions, 2002), 187.

63. Konrad, *And in Their Silent Beauty Speak*, 241.

64. Groening, "Grandmother Remembers."

65. Doris Penner, "Memories of *Schaaldouak* Make Nostalgic Afternoon," *The Carillon*, 15 May 2000.

66. Carol Counihan and Penny van Esterik, "Introduction," in *Food and Culture: A Reader* (New York: Routledge, 1997), 3.

67. Anne Harder, *The Vauxhall Mennonite Church* (Calgary: Mennonite Historical Society of Alberta, 2001), 13.

68. Roth, *Willing Service*, 128.

69. Herman A. Neufeld, *Mary Neufeld and the Repphun Story, from The Molotschna to Manitoba* (North Hollywood: The Carole Joyce Gallery, 1987), 200.

70. Anne Bower, "Bound Together: Recipes, Lives, Stories, and Readings," in *Recipes for Reading: Community Cookbooks, Stories, Histories*, ed. Anne L. Bower (Amherst, MA: University of Massachusetts Press, 1997), 2.

71. Matthew Bailey-Dick, "The Kitchenhood of all Believers: A Journey into the Discourse of Mennonite Cookbooks," *Mennonite Quarterly Review* 79, 2 (April 2005): 155.

72. Lydia Penner, "*The Mennonite Treasury of Recipes*, a Canadian Bestseller," in *Fifty Years Ebenezer Verein, 1936–1986* (Steinbach, MB: Ebenezer Verein, 1987), 53–54.

73. Pat Gerber Pauls, *Canadian Mennonite Cookbook* (Altona: Friesen Stationers, 1978), iii.

74. Bailey-Dick, "Kitchenhood of all Believers," 153–63. Doris Janzen Longacre's cookbook, *More-with-Less Cookbook: suggestions by Mennonites on how to eat better and consume less of the world's limited food resources* (Scottdale, PA: Herald Press, 1976), introduced the world to 'eating simply,' now has its own Internet home page, and was celebrated in a twenty-fifth anniversary edition in 2000.

75. Perhaps the best example of this is the two-volume *Mennonite Foods and Folkways from South Russia*, by Norma Jost Voth (Intercourse, PA: Good Books, 1990).

76. In urban areas with population 1000 to 5000, these numbers jumped to 94.1 percent, 81.6 percent, 34 percent, 56.3 percent, and 66.5 percent, respectively. Prentice, et al., *Canadian Women: A History*, 245.

77. Loewen, *Blumenort*, 615.

78. Anna Reimer Dyck, *Anna: From the Caucasus to Canada* (Hillsboro, KS: Mennonite Brethren Publishing House, 1979), 178.

79. Born, *Maria's Century*, 84.

80. Hildebrand, *Reflections of a Prairie Community*, 35.

81. Yvonne Mathews-Klein, "How They Saw Us: Images of Women in National Film Board Films of the 1940s and 1950s," *Atlantis* 4, 2 (Spring 1979): 26.

82. LaVerna Klippenstein, "The Changing Role of Women in the Home (2)," *Mennonite Reporter* 2, (17 April 1972): 5.

83. Personal conversation with Amsey and Salome Martin, Yatton, Ontario, 2004.

84. Koop and Dyck, "The Band Plays On," 128.

85. Reesor, *Check Rein*, 284.

86. Hildebrand, *Reflections of a Prairie Community*, 79.

87. Roth, *Willing Service*, 28. See also "Excerpts from Diaries of Barbara (Bowman) Shuh," in *Diaries of our Pennsylvania German Ancestors, 1846–1925*, Volume 15 of *Canadian–German Folklore* (Kitchener, ON: The Pennsylvania German Folklore Society of Ontario, 2002), 45–70.

88. Shirley B. Bergen, "Life of Mrs. Dr. Thiessen (nee Catherine Bornn)—1842–1915," paper in Katherina Thiessen Collection, Volume 5028, Mennonite Heritage Centre, Winnipeg, Manitoba.

89. *Lowe Farm: 75th Anniversary, 1899–1974* (Lowe Farm, MB: N.p., 1974), 48.

90. Koop and Dyck, "The Band Plays On," 225.

91. Forbes, *Present Faces of Waterloo Past*, 24.

92. C. Alfred Friesen, *History of the Mennonite Settlement at Niagara-on-the-Lake, 1934–1984: Memoirs of the Virgil-Niagara Mennonites* (Virgil, ON: Virgil-Niagara Mennonite Jubilee Committee, 1985), 127.

93. Alfred J. Kitchen, Social Worker, to Mr. C.W. Lundy, Director of Welfare, Victoria, B.C., 5 November 1945. Saskatchewan Archives Board, photocopy in Mennonites in Canada files, Mennonite Archives of Ontario.

94. Neufeldt, *Before We Were the Land's*, 163–64.

95. Kimberly D. Schmidt, "'Sacred Farming' or 'Working Out': The Negotiated Lives of Conservative Mennonite Farm Women," *Frontiers: A Journal of Women's Studies* 22, 1 (2001): 79–102.

96. Martens, ed. and trans., *They Came From Wiesenfeld Ukraine to Canada*, 67.

97. Mary Regehr, "Motherhood: Changing and Growing," *MCC Committee on Women's Concerns Report* 62 (July–August 1985): 8.

98. Katherine Friesen, "Domestic Work in the Depression Era," *MCC Women's Concerns Report* 79 (July–August 1988): 4.

99. Forbes, *Present Faces of Waterloo Past*, 22.

100. Roth, *Willing Service*, 146.

101. Lorna Bergey, "Changes in Cultural Symbols for Ontario Mennonite Women of the Swiss Tradition during the 1950s and 1960s: Stories We Need To Hear," *Mennogespräch* 8, 2 (September 1990): 9.

102. Winland, "Christianity and Community," 21–45.

103. Frieda Esau Klippenstein, "Scattered but Not Lost: Mennonite Domestic Servants in Winnipeg, 1920s–50s," in *Telling Tales*, ed. Cavanaugh and Warne; and Siemens, "Quilt as Text and Text as Quilt," 118–29.

104. Friesen, *Memoirs of the Virgil-Niagara Mennonites*, 108.

105. Loewen, *Blumenort*, 583.

106. Harder, *Their Richest Inheritance*, 33.

107. Wilma Toews, "Homemaking—A Challenging Vocation," *Mennonite Life* 11, 4 (October 1956): 191.

108. *History of the Whitewater Mennonite Church: Boissevain, Manitoba, 1927–1987* (Boissevain, MB: The Church, 1987), 86.

109. "Women's Broadcast Heard over CFAM," *Canadian Mennonite* 5 (4 October 1957): 9.

110. *MCC Peace Section Task Force on Women in Church and Society* (October-December 1975): 8.

111. Anne Bargen, "Conversation with Mothers: Too Gifted to Become a Mere Housewife?" *The Canadian Mennonite* 4 (7 September 1956): 2.

112. Anne Bargen, "Conversation with Mothers: A Man Can Build a House, But it Takes a Woman to Make a Home," *The Canadian Mennonite* 5 (1 February 1957): 4.

113. Saundra Plett, "Attitudes Toward Women as Reflected in Mennonite Brethren Periodicals," *Direction* 9, 1 (January 1980). Accessed at <www.directionjournal.org>.

114. Toews, "Homemaking—A Challenging Vocation," 163.

115. Mary Lou Driedger, "A Career of the Heart: Aunt Olly Penner Earned a Lasting Place in Many Youthful Lives," *Mennonite Mirror* 18 (May–June 1989): 4–5.

116. Hubert R. Pellman, *Mennonite Broadcasts: The First 25 Years* (Harrisonburg, VA: Mennonite Broadcasts, 1979), 11. Also Ruth Brunk Stoltzfus, *A Way Was Opened: A Memoir* (Scottdale, PA: Herald Press, 2003).

117. Prentice, et al., *Canadian Women: A History*, 311.

118. Quoted in Patkau, *Canadian Women in Mission*, 336.

119. Alice B. Hershberger, "Women's Work," *Christian Living* 8 (March 1961): 39.

120. Anna L. Schroeder, "A Woman's Place," *Christian Living* 13 (September 1966): 40.

121. Interview with Dr. Iva Taves by the author, Kitchener, Ontario, 1989.

122. "The Lives of Mennonite Women," Prairie Public Television, <http://www.prairiepublic.org>. Accessed May 11, 2006.

123. "Church Service for Women," *Gospel Herald* 52 (27 January 1959): 75.

124. Oscar Burkholder, "Why Christian Married Women Work," *The Canadian Mennonite* 3 (21 January 1955): 7.

125. Reesor, *Check Rein*, 354.

126. Neufeld, *Mary Neufeld and the Repphun Story*, 217.

127. Konrad, *And in Their Silent Beauty Speak*, 296.

128. Hedy Durksen, "Where Do We Stand?" *The Canadian Mennonite* 10 (30 March 1962): 8.

129. Agnes Eby, "Working Mother: Service on the Home Front," *MCC Peace Section Task Force on Women in Church and Society* 21 (August–September 1978): 2–3.

130. Born, *Maria's Century*, 88.

131. The Concordia Hospital in Winnipeg, established by Mennonites as a maternity home in 1928, had a training program for practical nurses in the 1960s. See Abe J. Dueck, *Concordia Hospital, 1928–1978* (Winnipeg: Christian Press, 1978), 24.

132. Nettie Neufeld, "Aganetha 'Agnes' Fast," *Preservings* 10 (June 1997): 38–40.

133. Marjorie Wiebe Hildebrandt, "Agatha Wiebe (1887–1979) Registered Nurse," *Preservings* 14 (1999): 80.

134. Konrad, *And in Their Silent Beauty Speak*, 282.

135. Hilda Lohrenz Bergen, *Immigrants' Daughter* (Edmonton: The Author, 1997), 55.

136. "Editorial," *The Christian Nurse* 3 (April 1947): 2.

137. Minutes, Meeting of Mennonite Nurses Association of Ontario, 20 May 1946, Mennonite Conference of Ontario Collection, Mennonite Nurses Association, II-5-9, Mennonite Archives of Ontario, Waterloo, Ontario.

138. D. Plett, "First Woman Teacher Maria Friesen Redenzel 1844–1925," *Preservings* 8 (June 1996): 9.

139. Elfrieda Neufeld, "Anna Vogt: Kindergarten Pioneer," *Preservings* 8 (June 1996): 26–27.

140. Susan Shantz, "Profile: Nellie Kinsie," *The Marketplace* 11, 3 (June 1981): 1, 4–5.

141. John Dyck, "Helena Penner Hiebert (1874–1970): True Pioneer," *Preservings* 10 (June 1997): 7–10.

142. On the establishment of Mennonite high schools and colleges during the 1940s, see Regehr, *Mennonites in Canada*, ch. 11.

143. "Association Decides to Admit Women Students," *The Canadian Mennonite* 4 (30 November 1956): 11.

144. Born, *Maria's Century*, 74.

145. Hedy Durksen, "The Ladies' Class," *The Canadian Mennonite* 9 (23 June 1961): 7.

146. Konrad, *And in Their Silent Beauty Speak*, 212–13.

147. Koop and Dyck, "The Band Plays On," 114.

148. Friesen, "Domestic Work in the Depression Era," 5.

149. Gordon and Erma (Martin) Bauman, *Memories of Our Lives* (Tavistock, ON: The Authors, 2001), 22.

150. Konrad, *And in Their Silent Beauty Speak*, 225.

151. Linda Matties, "The Mary-Martha Complex in the Post-Modern Church," *MCC Women's Concerns Report* 102 (May–June 1992): 10.

152. Anna Ens, "Conference of Mennonites Bible Schools in Manitoba," *Mennonite Historian* 28, 1 (March 2002): 1, 4–5.

153. Agatha E. Klassen, ed., *Yarrow: A Portrait in Mosaic*, rev. ed. (Yarrow, BC: The Author, 1976), 89.

154. Roth, *Willing Service*, 127.

155. Wiebe, "Me Tarzan, Son of Menno," 11–12.

156. Abe Dueck, "A Tribute to Esther Horch, 1909–1994," *Mennonite Historian* 20, 1 (March 1994): 7.

157. Loewen, *From the Inside Out*, 5.

158. Plett, *Johann Plett*, 697.

159. Julie C. Chychota, "Mary Eidse Friesen (1923–1996)," in *The Small Details of Life: 20 Diaries by Women in Canada, 1830–1996*, ed. Kathryn Carter (Toronto: University of Toronto Press, 2002), 445–53.

160. Loewen, *From the Inside Out*, 312.

161. Martens and Harms, eds., *In Her Own Voice*, 108.

162. Roth, *Willing Service*, 165.

163. Barbara Sherk, quoted in Carol Penner, "Let Me Introduce You to Barbara Sherk ...," *Ontario Mennonite History* 11, 2 (September 1993): 13.

164. Ibid., 12–14.

165. Patterson, *Swiss-German and Dutch-German Mennonite Traditional Art*, 89.

166. Roth, *Willing Service*, 129.

167. Koop and Dyck, "The Band Plays On," 237.

168. Anita Epp, "Books of Mennonite Author Reach 40,000 Circulation in '56," *The Canadian Mennonite* 5 (31 May 1957): 1.

169. Katie Funk Wiebe, "A Tale of Seduction," in *Why I am a Mennonite: Essays on Mennonite Identity*, ed. Loewen, 329.

170. Katie Funk Wiebe, *MCC Peace Section Task Force on Women in Church & Society Report* 37 (May–June 1981): 4.

171. Ibid., 5.

172. Al Reimer, "Where Was/Is the Woman's Voice? The Re-Membering of the Mennonite Woman," *Mennonite Life* 47, 1 (March 1992): 20–25.

173. "AMUS Report Urges Better Reading," *The Canadian Mennonite* 2 (5 November 1954): 3.

174. Koop and Dyck, "The Band Plays On," 58.

175. Ibid., 252.

176. Eileen Klassen Hamm, "Readers' Groups," *MCC Women's Concerns Report* 131 (March-April 1997): 6.

CONCLUSION

1. Lois Barrett Janzen, "Women, the Ministry, and Mennonites," *The Mennonite* 87 (18 January 1972): 38.

2. For background, see Winland, "Revisiting a Case Study of Hmong Refugees and Ontario Mennonites," 169–76.

3. "An Interview with Heidi Quiring, Miss Canada, 1979," *Forum* 13 (October 1979): 2–5.

4. Mary Regehr Dueck, "The Role of Women (3): Young Maidens Dare Not Prophesy," *Mennonite Reporter* 3 (2 April 1973): 7.

5. Katherine Wiens, "Reader Response," *MCC Task Force on Women in Church and Society* 3 (December 1973): 7.

6. Margaret Loewen Reimer, "Canadian Conference Divided Over Teenage Election," *MCC Peace Section Task Force on Women in Church and Society* 9 (October–December 1975): 2.

7. Quoted in Patkau, *Canadian Women in Mission*, 170.

8. Claire Ewert, "Liberating People Is the Issue," *Mennonite Reporter* 5 (18 August 1975): 8.

9. Lois Gunden Clemens, *Woman Liberated* (Scottale, PA: Herald Press, 1971); Marabel Morgan, *The Total Woman* (Old Tappan, NJ: Fleming H. Revell, 1973).

10. Marian Claassen Franz, "Easy to Love the Enemy," *The Mennonite* 85 (30 June 1970): 451.

11. Esther Jantzen, "Women—The Revolution Brewing Now"; and Norman J. Schmidt, "Responses to the Women's Revolution," *The Mennonite* 85 (30 June 1970): 448, 550.

12. Ruth Ann Soden, "Traditions Yielding as More Women Vote at Mennonite Meet," *Kitchener–Waterloo Record*, 18 August 1971, p. 57.

13. Herta Funk, "Equal Opportunity to Serve," *The Mennonite* 90 (4 February 1975): 68.

14. "Ten-Year Celebration of the Committee on Women's Concerns," *MCC Committee on Women's Concerns Report* 50 (July–August 1983).

15. Linda Gehman Peachey, "Vision for the Future in MCC U.S," *MCC Women's Concerns Report* (November–December 2004). <http://www.mcc.org/womensconcerns/articles/2004/december.html>. Accessed January 26, 2006. For reflections on the history of Mennonite Central Committee's work on women's concerns (though

mainly in the US), and on the *Report*, see the articles in "Gifts of the Red Tent: Women Creating," thematic issue of *The Conrad Grebel Review* 23, 1 (Winter 2005).

16. Janet Mancini Billson, *Keepers of the Culture: The Power of Tradition in Women's Lives* (New York: Lexington Books, 1995).

BIBLIOGRAPHY

PUBLISHED SOURCES:

Abergel, Daphne. "Women and Religion: 'Mennonite Hmong.'" *Refuge: Canada's Periodical on Refugees* 6, 3 (February 1987): 9.

"AMUS Report Urges Better Reading." *The Canadian Mennonite* 2 (5 November 1954): 3.

"An Interview with Heidi Quiring, Miss Canada, 1979." *Forum* 13 (October 1979): 2–5.

"A People Apart." *The Record* (October 27–28, 2000).

Armstrong, John A. "Mobilized and Proletarian Diasporas." *American Political Science Review* 70 (June 1976): 393–408.

Arthur, Linda B., ed. *Religion, Dress and the Body*. Oxford, UK: Berg, 1999.

_____. "Introduction: Dress and the Social Control of the Body." In *Religion, Dress and the Body*, edited by Linda B. Arthur, 1–7. Oxford, UK: Berg, 1999.

"Association Decides to Admit Women Students." *The Canadian Mennonite* 4 (30 November 1956): 11.

Bailey-Dick, Matthew. "The Kitchenhood of all Believers: A Journey into the Discourse of Mennonite Cookbooks." *Mennonite Quarterly Review* 79, 2 (April 2005): 153–63.

Bargen, Anne. "Conversation with Mothers: Too Gifted to Become a Mere Housewife?" *The Canadian Mennonite* 4 (7 September 1956): 2.

_____. "Conversation with Mothers: A Man Can Build a House, But it Takes a Woman to Make a Home." *The Canadian Mennonite* 5 (1 February 1957): 4.

_____. "Sewing Circles Are Not Gossip Centres." *The Canadian Mennonite* 5 (1 March 1957): 4.

Barkman, Cathy. "Anna Toews (1868–1933): Midwife." *Preservings* 10 (June 1997): 50–53.

Barnes, Ruth, and Joanne B. Eicher, eds. *Dress and Gender: Making and Meaning in Cultural Contexts*. New York: St. Martin's Press, 1992.

Barrington, Eleanor. *Midwifery is Catching*. Toronto, ON: NC Press Ltd., 1985.

Bartsch, Anna. *The Hidden Hand in the Story of My Life*. Nelson, BC: The Author, 1987.

Bauman, Brent. *Forged Anew: A History of the Floradale Mennonite Church: Hembling–North Woolwich–Floradale, 1856–1996*. Floradale, ON: The Church, 1996.

Bendroth, Margaret L. "Fundamentalism and Femininity: The Reorientation of Women's Role in the 1920s." *Evangelical Studies Bulletin* 5 (March 1988): 1–4.

_____. *Fundamentalism and Gender, 1875 to the Present*. New Haven, CT: Yale University Press, 1993.

_____, and Virginia Lieson Brereton, eds. *Women and Twentieth-Century Protestantism*. Urbana and Chicago, IL: University of Illinois Press, 2002.

Benoit, Cecila, and Dena Carroll. "Canadian Midwifery: Blending Traditional and Modern Practices." In *On All Frontiers: Four Centuries of Canadian Nursing*, edited by Christina Bates, Dianne Dodd, and Nicole Rousseau, 27–41. Ottawa, ON: University of Ottawa Press, 2005.

Bergen, Hilda Lohrenz. *Immigrants' Daughter*. Edmonton, AB: The Author, 1997.

Bergen, Karen. "Maria Dueck Ginter (1909–1990): Chiropractor." *Preservings* 14 (June 1999): 85–87.

Bergen, Shirley. "Dr. Katherina Born Thiessen: A Woman Who Made a Difference." *Mennonite Historian* 23, 3 (September 1997): 8.

Bergey, Lorna L. "Changes in Cultural Symbols for Ontario Mennonite Women of the Swiss Tradition during the 1950s and 1960s: Stories We Need to Hear." *Mennogespräch* 8, 2 (September 1990): 9–12.

Bernier, Jacques. *Disease, Medicine and Society in Canada: A Historical Overview*. Ottawa, ON: Canadian Historical Association, 2003.

Biggs, C. Lesley. "The Case of the Missing Midwives: A History of Midwifery in Ontario from 1795–1900." *Ontario History* 75, 1 (March 1983): 21–36.

_____. "Rethinking the History of Midwifery in Canada." In *Reconceiving Midwifery*, edited by Ivy Lynn Bourgeault, et al., 17–45. Montreal, PQ, and Kingston, ON: McGill-Queen's University Press, 2004.

Billson, Janet Mancini. *Keepers of the Culture: The Power of Tradition in Women's Lives*. New York: Lexington Books, 1995.

Block, Isaac I. *Assault on God's Image: Domestic Abuse*. Winnipeg, MB: Windflower Communications, 1991.

Bloomfield, Elizabeth. *Waterloo Township through Two Centuries*. Waterloo, ON: Waterloo Historical Society, 1995.

Born, Hilda J. *Maria's Century: A Family Saga*. Abbotsford, BC: The Author, 1997.

Borst, Charlotte G. *Catching Babies: The Professionalization of Childbirth, 1870–1920*. Cambridge, MA: Harvard University Press, 1995.

Boyer, Mrs. Claude. "The Minister's Wife." *The Mennonite* 68 (23 June 1953): 390–91.

Boulding, Elise. *The Underside of History: A View of Women through Time*. Boulder, CO: Westview Press, 1976.

Bower, Anne. "Bound Together: Recipes, Lives, Stories, and Readings." In *Recipes for Reading: Community Cookbooks, Stories, Histories*, edited by Anne L. Bower, 1–14. Amherst, MA: University of Massachusetts Press, 1997.

Boyd, Stephen B. "Theological Roots of Gender Reconciliation in 16th Century Anabaptism: A Prolegomenon." *Journal of Mennonite Studies* 17 (1999): 34–52.

Brouwer, Ruth Compton. *New Women for God: Canadian Presbyterian Women and Indian Missions, 1876–1914*. Toronto, ON: University of Toronto Press, 1990.

———. "Transcending the 'Unacknowledged Quarantine': Putting Religion into English-Canadian Women's History." *Journal of Canadian Studies* 27 (Autumn 1992): 47–61.

Buckley, Suzanne. "Ladies or Midwives? Efforts to Reduce Infant and Maternal Mortality." In *A Not Unreasonable Claim: Women and Reform in Canada, 1880s–1920s*, edited by Linda Kealey, 131–49. Toronto, ON: The Women's Press, 1979.

Buhler, Linda. "Agnes Toews Kornelsen, Hairdresser." *Preservings* 5 (January 1995): 12.

———. "The Apple Tree." *Preservings* 6 (June 1995): 27.

———. "Mennonite Burial Customs: Part Three." *Preservings* 10 (June 1997): 78–80.

———. "Sarah Sawatzky Funk: Matriarch of Kronsgart." *Preservings* 10 (June 1997): 40–42.

Buhler, Sara. "'I chose some cups and saucers': Gender, Tradition, and Subversive Elements in my Grandmother's Life Stories." *Ethnologies* 21, 1 (1999): 47–63.

Brandt, Di. *Questions I asked my mother*. Winnipeg, MB: Turnstone Press, 1987.

Burke, Susan M. "Perpetuation and Adaptation: The Germanic Textiles of Waterloo County 1800-1900." In *From Pennsylvania to Waterloo: Pennsylvania–German Folk Culture in Transition*, edited by Susan M. Burke and Matthew H. Hill, 79–95. Kitchener, ON: Joseph Schneider Haus, 1991.

———, and Matthew H. Hill, eds. *From Pennsylvania to Waterloo: Pennsylvania–German Folk Culture in Transition*. Kitchener, ON: Joseph Schneider Haus, 1991.

Burkhardt, Ferne. *A Mighty Flood: The House of Friendship Story*. Kitchener, ON: House of Friendship, 1989.

Burkholder, Oscar. "As it was in the days of Sodom, Attention women!" *Christian Review* 2 (October 1928): 14.

_____. "The Devotional Covering." *Gospel Herald* 23 (17 April 1930): 67–68.

_____. "The Ministry and Christian Living." *The Sword and Trumpet* 13 (August 1945): 417–23.

_____. "Why Christian Married Women Work." *The Canadian Mennonite* 3 (21 January 1955): 7.

Canada. Dominion Bureau of Statistics. *Eighth census of Canada, 1941. Vol. 3. Ages of the population classified by sex, conjugal condition, racial origin, religious denomination, birthplace*. Ottawa, ON: Edmond Cloutier, Printer to the King's Most Excellent Majesty, 1946.

Cannon, Steve. "When Dreams Die: Drayton Farm Tragedy Compels Family to Rejoin Mexican Mennonite Colony." *The Record* (27 October 2000): A1, A9.

_____. "The Long Road Home: Back in Mexico, a Mennonite Widow Faces an Uncertain Future." *The Record* (28 October 2000): H1–2.

Cavanaugh, Catherine A., and Randi Warne, eds. *Telling Tales: Essays in Western Women's History*. Vancouver, BC: University of British Columbia Press, 2000.

Chornoby, Eleanor Hildebrand. *Faspa: A Snack of Mennonite Stories*. Winnipeg, MB: The Author, 2003.

Christie, Nancy, ed. *Households of Faith: Family, Gender, and Community in Canada, 1760–1969*. Montreal, PQ, and Kingston, ON: McGill-Queen's University Press, 2002.

Church and Mission News 9, 1 (January 1944).

"Church Service for Women." *Gospel Herald* 52 (27 January 1959): 75.

Chychota, Julie C. "Mary Eidse Friesen (1923–1996)." In *The Small Details of Life: 20 Diaries by Women in Canada, 1830–1996*, edited by Kathryn Carter, 445–53. Toronto, ON: University of Toronto Press, 2002.

Clark, Susan H. "Quilting in Waterloo County." In *Women of Waterloo County*, edited by Ruth Russell, 99–103. Kitchener–Waterloo, ON: Canadian Federation of University Women, 2000.

Clemens, Lois Gunden. *Woman Liberated*. Scottdale, PA: Herald Press, 1971.

Clifford, James. "Diasporas." *Cultural Anthropology* 9, 3 (August 1994): 302–38.

Cockburn, Cynthia. *The Space Between Us: Negotiating Gender and National Identities in Conflict*. London, UK: Zed Books, 1998.

Coffman, Barbara. "Home Life: From John S. Coffman's Diaries." *The Christian Ministry* 2, 2 (April 1949): 77–84.

"Congolese Mennonite Brethren Conference Ordains Women Pastors." *MCC Women's Concerns Report* 175 (September–October 2004): 15.

Connor, J.T.H. "'Larger Fish to Catch Here than Midwives': Midwifery and the Medical Profession in Nineteenth-Century Ontario." In *Caring and Curing: Historical Perspectives on Women and Healing in Canada,* edited by Dianne Dodd and Deborah Gorham, 103–34. Ottawa, ON: University of Ottawa Press, 1994.

Counihan, Carol, and Penny van Esterik, eds. *Food and Culture: A Reader.* New York: Routledge, 1997.

Cummings, Mary Lou, ed. *Full Circle: Stories of Mennonite Women.* Newton, KS: Faith and Life Press, 1978.

_____. "Ordained into Ministry: Ann J. Allebach (1874–1918)." In *Full Circle: Stories of Mennonite Women,* edited by Mary Lou Cummings, 2-11. Newton, KS: Faith and Life Press, 1978.

Danylewycz, Marta. *Taking the Veil: An Alternative to Marriage, Motherhood, and Spinsterhood in Quebec, 1840–1902.* Toronto, ON: McClelland and Stewart, 1987.

Dennis, Hedy Lepp. *Memories of Reesor: The Mennonite Settlement in Northern Ontario, 1925–1948.* Leamington, ON: Essex-Kent Mennonite Historical Association, 2001.

Derstine, Clayton F. "Canadian Conscientious Objectors in Camp." *Gospel Herald* 34 (13 August 1942): 426–27.

_____. *The Home: From Four Angles.* Eureka, IL: The Author, 1919.

_____. *Manual of Sex Education for Parents, Teachers and Students.* Kitchener, ON: The Author, 1942.

di Leonardo, Micaela. "The Female World of Cards and Holidays: Women, Families, and the Work of Kinship." *Signs* 12, 3 (1987): 440–53.

Diner, Hasia R. "Insights and Blind Spots: Writing History from Inside and Outside." In *Strangers at Home: Amish and Mennonite Women in History,* edited by Kimberly D. Schmidt, et al., 21–38. Baltimore, MD: The Johns Hopkins University Press, 2002.

_____., and Beryl Lieff Benderly. *Her Works Praise Her: A History of Jewish Women in America from Colonial Times to the Present.* New York: Basic Books, 2002.

Dodd, Dianne. "Helen MacMurchy, Popular Midwifery and Maternity Services for Canadian Pioneer Women." In *Caring and Curing: Historical Perspectives on Women and Healing in Canada,* edited by Dianne Dodd and Deborah Gorham, 135–62. Ottawa, ON: University of Ottawa Press, 1994.

Doell, Leonard. *The Bergthaler Mennonite Church of Saskatchewan, 1892–1975.* Winnipeg, MB: CMBC Publications, 1987.

"Dorcas Mission Circle Serves in Many Ways." *The Canadian Mennonite* 7 (3 January 1958): 7.

Driedger, Mary Lou. "A Career of the Heart: Aunt Olly Penner Earned a Lasting Place in Many Youthful Lives." *Mennonite Mirror* 18 (May–June 1989): 4–5.

Driedger, Michael D. *Obedient Heretics: Mennonite Identities in Lutheran Hamburg and Altona During the Confessional Age.* Aldershot, UK: Ashgate, 2002.

Driedger, Nicholas N. *The Leamington United Mennonite Church: Establishment and Development, 1925–1972.* Altona, MB: D.W. Friesen, 1973.

Dueck, Abe J. *Concordia Hospital, 1928–1978* .Winnipeg, MB: Christian Press, 1978.

_____. "A Tribute to Esther Horch, 1909–1994." *Mennonite Historian* 20, 1 (March 1994): 7.

Dueck, Abe. "Esther (Hiebert) Horch: A Gifted and Generous Woman." *Profiles of Mennonite Faith, Mennonite Brethren Historical Commission.* Accessed 12 June 2006. <http://www.mbhistory.org/profiles/horch.en.html>.

Dueck, Mary Regehr. "The Role of Women (3): Young Maidens Dare Not Prophesy." *Mennonite Reporter* 3 (2 April 1973): 7.

Durksen, Hedy. "The Ladies' Class." *The Canadian Mennonite* 9 (23 June 1961): 7.

_____. "Where Do We Stand?" *The Canadian Mennonite* 10 (30 March 1962): 8.

Dyck, Anna Reimer. *Anna: From the Caucasus to Canada.* Hillsboro, KS: Mennonite Brethren Publishing House, 1979.

Dyck, Anne W. Untitled. *MCC Peace Section Task Force on Women in Church and Society* 12 (December 1976): 4.

Dyck, Carol. "A Golden Braid." *MCC Women's Concerns Report* 75 (November–December 1987): 5–6.

Dyck, Cornelius J., and Wilma L. Dyck, eds. *A Pilgrim People.* Saskatoon, SK: Renata and Allan Klassen, 1987.

Dyck, Elizabeth Wall. "'I Was Left Alone with My Little Children': Elizabeth Wall." In *Village of Unsettled Yearnings. Yarrow, British Columbia: Mennonite Promise*, edited by Leonard Neufeldt, 270–75. Victoria, BC: TouchWood Editions, 2002.

Dyck, John. "Helena Penner Hiebert (1874–1970): True Pioneer." *Preservings* 10 (June 1997): 7–10.

Dyck, Peter, and Elfrieda Dyck. *Up From the Rubble: The Epic Rescue of Thousands of War-Ravaged Mennonite Refugees.* Scottdale, PA: Herald Press, 1991.

Dyck, Wilma L. "The Minister's Wife." *The Mennonite* 72 (11 June 1957): 372–73.

Eby, Agnes. "Working Mother: Service on the Home Front." *MCC Peace Section Task Force on Women in Church and Society* 21 (August–September 1978): 2–3.

Ediger, Gerald C. *Crossing the Divide: Language Transition Among Canadian Mennonite Brethren, 1940–1970.* Winnipeg, MB: Centre for Mennonite Brethren Studies, 2001.

Ediger, Katharina. *Under his Wings: Events in the Lives of Elder Alexander Ediger and his Family.* Kitchener, ON: The Author, 1994.

"Editorial." *The Christian Nurse* 3 (April 1947): 2.

"EnGendering the Past: Women and Men in Mennonite History." Thematic issue of *Journal of Mennonite Studies* 17 (1999).

Enloe, Cynthia. *The Curious Feminist: Searching for Women in a New Age of Empire.* Berkeley, CA: University of California Press, 2004.

Enns, L. Marie. *Preacher's Kids on the Homestead.* Belleville, ON: Guardian Books, 2005.

Enns, Mary. *Selma Redekopp: An Unusual Woman.* Winnipeg, MB: The Estate of Henry R. Redekopp, 1990.

Ens, Adolf. *Becoming a National Church: A History of the Conference of Mennonites in Canada.* Winnipeg, MB: CMU Publications, 2004.

Ens, Anna. *In Search of Unity: Story of the Conference of Mennonites in Manitoba.* Winnipeg, MB: CMBC Publications, 1996.

_____ "Conference of Mennonites Bible Schools in Manitoba." *Mennonite Historian* 28, 1 (March 2002): 1, 4–5.

Ens, Anna Epp, ed. *The House of Heinrich: The Story of Heinrich Epp (1811–1863) of Rosenort, Molotschna and His Descendants.* Winnipeg, MB: Epp Book Committee, 1980.

Epp, Anita. "Books of Mennonite Author Reach 40,000 Circulation in '56." *The Canadian Mennonite* 5 (31 May 1957): 1, 4.

Epp, Dick H. *From Between the Tracks: 1927–1952.* Saskatoon, SK: Eppisode Publications, 2004.

Epp, Frank H. *Mennonites in Canada, 1786–1920: The History of a Separate People.* Toronto, ON: Macmillan of Canada, 1974.

_____. *Mennonites in Canada, 1920–1940: A People's Struggle for Survival.* Toronto, ON: Macmillan of Canada, 1982.

Epp, Frank H., and Marlene G. Epp. "The Diverse Roles of Ontario Mennonite Women." In *Looking into My Sister's Eyes: An Exploration in Women's History*, edited by Jean Burnet, 223–42. Toronto, ON: Multicultural History Society of Ontario, 1986.

Epp, George H. "'Widow' Epp." In *Village of Unsettled Yearnings. Yarrow, British Columbia: Mennonite Promise*, edited by Leonard Neufeldt, 230–36. Victoria, BC: TouchWood Editions, 2002.

Epp, Gerry. "Tribute to Margaret Epp." *Saskatchewan Mennonite Historian* 2, 1 (September 1997): 13–14.

Epp, Irma, Lillian Harms, and Lora Sawatsky. "Midwifery: A Ministry." In *Village of Unsettled Yearnings. Yarrow, British Columbia: Mennonite Promise*, edited by Leonard Neufeldt, 17–22. Victoria, BC: TouchWood Editions, 2002.

Epp, Marlene. "Women in Canadian Mennonite History: Uncovering the 'Underside'." *Journal of Mennonite Studies* 5 (1987): 90–107.

_____. "The Mennonite Girls' Homes of Winnipeg: A Home Away from Home." *Journal of Mennonite Studies* 6 (1988):100–14.

_____. "Carrying the Banner of Nonconformity: Ontario Mennonite Women and the Dress Question." *The Conrad Grebel Review* 8, 3 (Fall 1990): 237–57.

_____. "Nonconformity and Nonresistance: What Did It Mean to Mennonite Women?" In *Changing Roles of Women within the Christian Church in Canada*, edited by Elizabeth Gillan Muir and Marilyn Färdig Whiteley, 55–74. Toronto, ON: University of Toronto Press, 1995.

_____. "'My Mom Was a Preacher': Female Religion in the Soviet Era." *Sophia* 5 (Winter 1995): 14–15.

_____. "Alternative Service and Alternative Gender Roles: Conscientious Objectors in B.C. During World War II." *BC Studies* 105–106 (Spring–Summer 1995): 139–58.

_____. "The 'Grab Bag' Mennonite Family in Post-War Canada." In *On the Case: Explorations in Social History*, edited by Franca Iacovetta and Wendy Mitchinson, 338–57. Toronto, ON: University of Toronto Press, 1998.

_____. *Women without Men: Mennonite Refugees of the Second World War.* Toronto, ON: University of Toronto Press, 2000.

_____. "Pioneers, Refugees, Exiles, and Transnationals: Gendering Diaspora in an Ethno-Religious Context." *Journal of the Canadian Historical Association* 12 (2001): 137–53.

_____, Franca Iacovetta, and Frances Swyripa, eds. *Sisters or Strangers? Immigrant, Ethnic, and Racialized Women in Canadian History.* Toronto, ON: University of Toronto Press, 2004.

Epp-Tiessen, Esther. *Altona: The Story of a Prairie Town.* Altona, MB: D.W. Friesen and Sons, 1982.

_____. "Gains and Losses: The Experience of Mennonite Women Immigrants of Late Nineteenth Century." *Journal of Mennonite Studies* 18 (2000): 146–56.

_____. *J.J. Thiessen: A Leader for His Time.* Winnipeg, MB: CMBC Publications, 2001.

Ewert, Claire. "Liberating people Is the Issue." *Mennonite Reporter* 5 (18 August 1975): 8.

Ewert, David. "Women in the Church." *Mennonite Brethren Herald* 5 (25 February 1966): 4–6.

"Excerpts from Diaries of Barbara (Bowman) Shuh." In *Diaries of our Pennsylvania German Ancestors, 1846–1925*, Volume 15 of *Canadian-German Folklore*, 45–70. Kitchener, ON: The Pennsylvania German Folklore Society of Ontario, 2002.

"Family Allowance Study Committee." *Calendar of Appointments of the Mennonite Conference of Ontario* (1945–46): 41.

Fast, Henry. *Gruenfeld (now Kleefeld): First Mennonite Village in Western Canada, 1874–1910.* Kleefeld, MB: The Author, 2006.

Fast, Kerry. "Struggling with Exclusion." *MCC Women's Concerns Report* 102 (May–June 1992): 12–15.

———. "Religion, Pain, and the Body: Agency in the Life of an Old Colony Mennonite Woman." *Journal of Mennonite Studies* 22 (2004): 103–29.

Fast, Mrs. Milton. "Sewing Circle Report for the 1965 Annual Conf." *1965 Yearbook of the Evangelical Mennonite Conference*, 15–16.

Fieguth, Debra. "A House Overflowing: Portrait of a Family of Artists." *Sophia* 4, 3 (Fall 1994): 6–7.

Fiftieth Anniversary of the Mennonite Settlement in North Kildonan, 1928–1978. Winnipeg, MB: Anniversary Committee, 1978.

Fiftieth Anniversary Highlights of the Vineland United Mennonite Church, 1936–1986: Reflect, Rejoice, Renew. Vineland, ON: 50th Anniversary Committee, 1986.

Fiftieth Anniversary of the Niagara United Mennonite Church, 1938–1988. Niagara-on-the-Lake, ON: The Church, 1988.

Fifty Years Ebenezer Verein, 1936–1986. Steinbach, MB: Ebenezer Verein, 1987.

"Focus on the Auxiliary Syndrome." *MCC Peace Section Task Force on Women in Church and Society* 18 (February 1978).

Forbes, William F., et al. *Present Faces of Waterloo Past.* Waterloo, ON: Gerontology Program of University of Waterloo, 1988.

"Four Experiences." *MCC Peace Section Task Force on Women in Church & Society* 3 (March–April 1980): 4–5.

Franz, Marian Claassen. "Easy to Love the Enemy." *The Mennonite* 85 (30 June 1970): 451.

Freeman, Leonard. *Up Amos Avenue: From a Path in the Woods to a Street in the City.* Waterloo, ON: The Author, 1997.

Frey, Ardith. "Call: A One-Time Event, or a Vocation?" *MCC Women's Concerns Report* 175 (September–October 2004): 4–5.

Friedmann, Robert. "Gelassenheit." *Global Anabaptist Mennonite Encyclopedia Online.* 1955. Accessed 20 Jan 2006. <http://www.gameo.org/encyclopedia/contents/g448.html>.

Friesen, Anne. "A Treasure Chest—'for when they shall ask'." *Saskatchewan Mennonite Historian* 4, 2 (September 1999): 19–20.

Friesen, Bert. *Where We Stand: An Index of Peace and Social Concerns Statements by Mennonites and Brethren in Christ in Canada, 1787–1982.* Winnipeg, MB: Mennonite Central Committee Canada, 1986.

Friesen, C. Alfred. *History of the Mennonite Settlement at Niagara-on-the-Lake, 1934–1984: Memoirs of the Virgil-Niagara Mennonites.* Virgil, ON: Virgil-Niagara Mennonite Jubilee Committee, 1985.

Friesen, John, ed. *Mennonites in Russia, 1788–1988.* Winnipeg, MB: CMBC Publications, 1989.

Friesen, Katherine. "Domestic work in the Depression Era." *MCC Women's Concerns Report* 79 (July–August 1988): 4–5.

Friesen, Katie. *Into the Unknown*. Steinbach, MB: The Author, 1986.

Friesen, Les. *Menno Place: Encompassed by Compassion: Mennonite Benevolent Society Fiftieth Anniversary, 1953–2003*. Abbotsford, BC: Mennonite Benevolent Society, 2003.

Friesen, Peter Ralph. "Esther Goossen: A Real Zest for Life." *Preservings* 14 (June 1999): 89–90.

Froese, Hilda. "The Ministry of Women in the Christian Church." *Mennonite Brethren Herald* 3 (22 May 1964): 13.

Funk, Herta. "Equal Opportunity to Serve." *The Mennonite* 90 (4 February 1975): 68–69.

_____, ed. *Study Guide: Women in the Bible and Early Anabaptism*. Newton, KS: Faith and Life Press, 1975.

Gagan, Rosemary R. *A Sensitive Independence: Canadian Methodist Missionaries in Canada and the Orient, 1881–1925*. Kingston, ON, and Montreal, PQ: McGill-Queen's University Press, 1992.

"Garments for Relief." *Women's Activities Letter* 50 (February 1948): 4–5.

"General Conference Adopts Resolution on Women in the Church." *Ontario Mennonite Evangel* 15, 4 (April 1970): 6.

"General Conference Structure Study." *MCC Task Force on Women in Church and Society* 3 (December 1973): 5.

Giesbrecht, Edward R. "The Everydayness of a Dairy Farm." In *Village of Unsettled Yearnings. Yarrow, British Columbia: Mennonite Promise*, edited by Leonard Neufeldt, 184–91. Victoria, BC: TouchWood Editions, 2002.

"Gifts of the Red Tent: Women Creating." Thematic issue of *The Conrad Grebel Review* 23, 1 (Winter 2005).

Gingerich, Orland. *The Amish of Canada*. Waterloo, ON: Conrad Press, 1972.

"Girls Man the Farm Front." *Star Weekly*, 14 August 1943.

Gnadenthal, 1880–1980. Winkler, MB: Gnadenthal History Book Committee, 1982.

Goering, Gladys V. *Women in Search of Mission: A History of the General Conference Mennonite Women's Organization*. Newton, KS: Faith and Life Press, 1980.

Good, E. Reginald. *Anna's Art: The Fraktur Art of Anna Weber, a Waterloo County Mennonite Artist, 1814–1888*. Kitchener, ON: Pochauna Publications, 1976.

_____. *Frontier Community to Urban Congregation: First Mennonite Church, Kitchener, 1813–1988*. Kitchener, ON: First Mennonite Church, 1988.

Good, Martha Smith. "From Ministry to Pastor's Wife to Ministry: A Story of Change." *MCC Peace Section Task Force on Women in Church and Society* 38 (July–August 1981): 1.

_____. "A Wife and Husband Reflect on Ordination." *MCC Peace Section Task Force on Women in Church and Society* 43 (May–June 1982): 1–3.

Goossen, Rachel Waltner. "Piety and Professionalism: The Bethel Deaconesses of the Great Plains." *Mennonite Life* 49 (March 1994): 4–11.

_____. *Women Against the Good War: Conscientious Objection and Gender on the American Home Front, 1941–1947.* Chapel Hill, NC: The University of North Carolina Press, 1997.

_____. "A Gender Gap Among Mennonite Peacemakers?" *Mennonite Quarterly Review* 73, 3 (July 1999): 539–45.

Graber, J.D., and Leo Driedger. "Divorce and Remarriage." *Global Anabaptist Mennonite Encyclopedia Online.* 1989. Accessed 5 March 2007. <http://www.gameo.org/encyclopedia/contents/d59me.html>.

Graybill, Beth E. "'Finding My Place as a Lady Missionary': Mennonite Women Missionaries to Puerto Rico, 1945–1960." *Journal of Mennonite Studies* 17 (1999): 152–73.

_____. "'To Remind Us of Who We Are': Multiple Meanings of Conservative Women's Dress." In *Strangers at Home: Amish and Mennonite Women in History*, edited by Kimberly D. Schmidt, et al., 53–77. Baltimore, MD: The Johns Hopkins University Press, 2002.

_____, and Linda B. Arthur. "The Social Control of Women's Bodies in Two Mennonite Communities." In *Religion, Dress and the Body*, edited by Linda B. Arthur, 9–29. Oxford, UK: Berg, 1999.

Griffith, R. Marie. *God's Daughters: Evangelical Women and the Power of Submission.* Berkeley, CA: University of California Press, 1997.

Guenter, Jacob G., ed. *Osler—The Early Years and the One Room School #1238 (1905–1947).* Osler, SK: Osler Historical Museum, 1999.

Habermehl, Fred. *Twigs, Branches & Roots: Waterloo County Habermehl Family.* Niagara Falls, ON: Paul Heron Publishing, 1997.

Hamm, Eileen Klassen. "Readers' Groups." *MCC Women's Concerns Report* 131 (March–April 1997): 6.

Harder, Anne. *The Vauxhall Mennonite Church.* Calgary, AB: Mennonite Historical Society of Alberta, 2001.

Harder, John A., ed. and trans. *From Kleefeld with Love.* Kitchener, ON: Pandora Press, 2003.

Harder, Laureen. *Their Richest Inheritance: A Celebration of The First Mennonite Church, Vineland, Ontario, 1801–2001.* Vineland, ON: The First Mennonite Church, 2001.

_____. *Risk and Endurance: A History of Stirling Avenue Mennonite Church.* Kitchener, ON: Stirling Avenue Mennonite Church, 2003.

Harder, Lydia. "Discipleship Reexamined: Women in the Hermeneutical Community." In *The Church as Theological Community: Essays in Honour of David Schroeder*, edited by Harry Huebner, 199–220. Winnipeg, MB: CMBC Publications, 1990.

Harms, Kelly G.I. *Grace Upon Grace: A History of the Mennonite Home of Rosthern.* Rosthern, SK: Mennonite Nursing Homes Inc., 1994.

Harms, Patricia. "'Gott es hiea uck': Gender and Identity in an Immigrant Family from Paraguay." *Journal of Mennonite Studies* 22 (2004): 39–57.

Hecht, Linda A. Huebert. "An Extraordinary Lay Leader: The Life and Work of Helene of Freyberg, Sixteenth-Century Noblewoman and Anabaptist from the Tirol." *Mennonite Quarterly Review* 66, 3 (July 1992): 312–41.

_____. "A Brief Moment in Time: Informal Leadership and Shared Authority Among Sixteenth Century Anabaptist Women." *Journal of Mennonite Studies* 17 (1999): 52–74.

_____. "Legacy of Service: Dorothy M. Swartzentruber Sauder's Career in Church Work at Home and Abroad." *Ontario Mennonite History* 19, 2 (November 2001): 9–15.

_____, and C. Arnold Snyder, eds. *Profiles of Anabaptist Women: Sixteenth Century Reforming Pioneers.* Waterloo, ON: Wilfrid Laurier University Press, 1996.

Heisey, M.J. *Peace and Persistence: Tracing the Brethren in Christ Peace Witness Through Three Generations.* Kent, OH: Kent State University Press, 2003.

"Helena Jansen (1822–1897)." *Preservings* 10 (June 1997): 20.

Hershberger, Alice B. "Women's Work." *Christian Living* 8 (March 1961): 8–10, 39.

Hildebrand, Marjorie, ed. *Reflections of a Prairie Community: A Collection of Stories and Memories of Burwalde S.D. #529.* Winkler, MB: Friends of the Former Burwalde School District #529, 2004.

Hildebrandt, Marjorie Wiebe. "Agatha Wiebe (1887-1979) Registered Nurse." *Preservings* 14 (June 1999): 80–81.

Hildebrand, Mary Anne. "Domestic Violence: A Challenge to Mennonite Faith and Peace Theology." *The Conrad Grebel Review* 10, 1 (Winter 1992): 73–80.

History of Alberta Mennonite Women in Mission, 1947–1977. Coaldale, AB: Women in Mission, 1978.

History of the Whitewater Mennonite Church: Boissevain, Manitoba, 1927–1987. Boissevain, MB: The Church, 1987.

Hooge, Katie. *The History of the Canadian Women in Mission, 1952–1977.* Winnipeg, MB: Women in Mission, 1977.

"Horne Lake 'High' Spots." *The Beacon* 2, 2 (February 1943): 12.

Horst, Isaac R., and Sam Steiner. "Conservative Mennonite Church of Ontario." *Global Anabaptist Mennonite Encyclopedia Online.* 2001. Accessed 8 June 2007. <http://www.gameo.org/encyclopedia/contents/c6674me.html>.

Hostetler, John A. *Mennonite Life.* Scottdale, PA: Herald Press, 1954.

Hostetter, B. Charles. "The Husband's Part in Happy Home Building." *The Canadian Mennonite* 2 (27 August 1954): 6.

———. "The Wife's Part in Happy Home Building." *The Canadian Mennonite* 2 (3 September 1954): 6.

Huang, Shirlena, Peggy Teo, and Brenda S.A. Yeoh. "Diasporic Subjects and Identity Negotiation: Women in and from Asia." *Women's Studies International Forum* 23, 4 (2000): 391–98.

"I Am." *MCC Women's Concerns Report* 74 (September–October 1987): 3–5.

Iacovetta, Franca. "Manly Militants, Cohesive Communities, and Defiant Domestics: Writing about Immigrants in Canadian Historical Scholarship." *Labour/Le Travail* 36 (Fall 1995): 217–52.

———. "Post-Modern Ethnography, Historical Materialism, and Decentring the (Male) Authorial Voice: A Feminist Conversation." *Histoire sociale/Social History* 32, 64 (November 1999): 275–93.

Irwin, Joyce L. *Womanhood in Radical Protestantism, 1525–1675.* New York: E. Mellen Press, 1979.

Jantz, Neoma. "A New Position for Mennonite Brethren Women." *MCC Peace Section Task Force on Women in Church and Society* 9 (October–December 1975): 2.

Jantzen, Esther. "Women—The Revolution Brewing Now." *The Mennonite* 85 (30 June 1970): 448–49.

Janzen, Lois Barrett. "Women, the Ministry, and Mennonites." *The Mennonite* 87 (18 January 1972): 37–39.

Jubilee Issue of the Waterloo–Kitchener United Mennonite Church, 1924–1974. Waterloo, ON: The Church, 1974.

Kaethler, Marjorie, and Susan D. Shantz. *Quilts of Waterloo County: A Sampling.* Waterloo, ON: The Author, 1990.

Kauffman, J. Howard. "Mennonite: Family Life as Christian Community." In *Faith Traditions and the Family*, edited by Phyllis D. Airhart and Margaret Lamberts Bendroth, 38–52. Louisville, KY: Westminster John Knox Press, 1996.

Kauffman, J. Howard. "Intermarriage." *Global Anabaptist Mennonite Encyclopedia Online.* 1989. Accessed 1 Feb 2006. <http://www.gameo.org/encyclopedia/contents/i587me.html>.

Kauffman, Thelma Reimer. "Hop Season." In *Village of Unsettled Yearnings. Yarrow, British Columbia: Mennonite Promise*, edited by Leonard Neufeldt, 175–83. Victoria, BC: TouchWood Editions, 2002.

Keeney, Mrs. William. "The Minister's Wife—Her Spiritual Growth." *The Mennonite* 68 (17 February 1953): 101.

Kennel, Lillian. *History of the Wilmot Amish Mennonite Congregation: Steinmann and St. Agatha Mennonite Churches, 1824–1984.* Baden, ON: Steinmann Mennonite Church, 1984.

Kerber, Linda, et al. "Beyond Roles, Beyond Spheres: Thinking about Gender in the Early Republic." *William and Mary Quarterly* 46 (July 1989): 565–85.

King, Ursula. "Religion and Gender: Embedded Patterns, Interwoven Frameworks." In *A Companion to Gender History*, edited by Teresa A. Meade and Merry E. Wiesner-Hanks, 70–85. Malden, MA: Blackwell Publishing, 2004.

Klassen, Agatha E., ed. *Yarrow: A Portrait in Mosaic*, rev. ed. Yarrow, BC: The Author, 1976.

Klassen, Irene. *Pieces and Patches of my Crazy Quilt*. Belleville, ON: Guardian Books, 2000.

Klassen, Pamela E. "Women's Sexuality and the Messages of Dress." *MCC Women's Concerns Report* 107 (March–April 1993): 4–5.

_____. *Going by the Moon and the Stars: Stories of Two Russian Mennonite Women*. Waterloo, ON: Wilfrid Laurier University Press, 1994.

_____. "Submerged in Love: An Interpretation of the Diary of Lydia Reimer, 1922–24." *Studies in Religion/Sciences Religieuses* 23, 4 (1994): 429–39.

_____. "What's Bre(a)d in the Bone: The Bodily Heritage of Mennonite Women." *Mennonite Quarterly Review* 68, 2 (April 1994): 229–47.

_____. "Speaking Out in God's Name: A Mennonite Woman Preaching." In *Undisciplined Women: Tradition and Culture in Canada*, edited by Pauline Greenhill and Diane Tye, 242–49. Montreal, PQ, and Kingston, ON: McGill-Queen's University Press, 1997.

_____. "Practicing Conflict: Weddings as Sites of Contest and Compromise." *Mennonite Quarterly Review* 72, 2 (April 1998): 225–41.

Klassen, Paul. *From the Steppes to the Prairies: A History of the Agneta and David Klassen Family in Russia and Canada*. Winnipeg, MB: City Press, 1998.

Kliewer, Victor D., ed. *Mennonite Peace Perspectives from Essex and Kent*. Leamington, ON: The Essex-Kent Mennonite Historical Association, 2001.

Klingelsmith, Sharon. "Women in the Mennonite Church, 1880–1920." *Mennonite Quarterly Review* 54, 3 (July 1980): 163–207.

Klippenstein, Frieda Esau. "'Doing What We Could': Mennonite Domestic Servants in Winnipeg, 1920s to 1950s." *Journal of Mennonite Studies* 7 (1989): 145–66.

_____. "Gender and Mennonites: A Response to Mennonites in Canada, 1939–1970: A People Transformed." *Journal of Mennonite Studies* 15 (1997): 142–49.

_____. "Scattered but Not Lost: Mennonite Domestic Servants in Winnipeg, 1920s–50s." In *Telling Tales: Essays in Western Women's History*, edited by Catherine A. Cavanaugh and Randi R. Warne, 200–31. Vancouver, BC: University of British Columbia Press, 2000.

Klippenstein, Henry. *Thicker than Water: The Uncensored, Unabridged and Completely Unbiased Account of the Life and Times of the Dietrich Klippenstein Family*. North Vancouver, BC: Loon Books, 2004.

Klippenstein, LaVerna. "The Diary of Tina Schulz." In *Mennonite Memories: Settling in Western Canada*, edited by Lawrence Klippenstein and Julius G. Toews, 219–32. Winnipeg, MB: Centennial Publications, 1977.

_____. "The Changing Role of Women in the Church (1)." *Mennonite Reporter* 2 (3 April 1972): 5.

_____. "The Changing Role of Women in the Home (2)." *Mennonite Reporter* 2 (17 April 1972): 5.

Klippenstein, Lawrence, and Julius G. Toews, eds. *Mennonite Memories: Settling in Western Canada*. Winnipeg, MB: Centennial Publications, 1977.

Kobelt-Groch, Marion. "'Hear My Son the Instructions of Your Mother': Children and Anabaptism." *Journal of Mennonite Studies* 17 (1999): 22–33.

Kolmerton, Carol A. *Women in Utopia: The Ideology of Gender in the American Owenite Communities*. Bloomington, IN: Indiana University Press, 1990.

Konrad, Anne. *And in Their Silent Beauty Speak: A Mennonite Family in Russia and Canada, 1790–1990*. Toronto, ON: The Author, 2004.

Kroeker, Harvey. "Aganetha Barkman Reimer." *Preservings* 6 (June 1995): 23–24.

Kroeker, Harvey. "A Notable Pioneer Woman: Elizabeth Dueck Kroeker (1879–1963)." *Preservings* 8 (June 1996): 55–57, 60.

Kroeker, Harvey. "Susanna Loewen Dueck Reimer (1852–1918)." *Preservings* 10 (June 1997): 54.

Langford, Nanci. "Childbirth on the Canadian Prairies, 1880–1930." In *Telling Tales: Essays in Western Women's History*, edited by Catherine A. Cavanaugh and Randi R. Warne, 147–73. Vancouver, BC: University of British Columbia Press, 2000.

Lerner, Gerda. *The Majority Finds its Past: Placing Women in History*. New York: Oxford University Press, 1979.

_____. *Women and History*. New York: Oxford University Press, 1986.

Light, Beth, and Pierson, Ruth Roach, eds. *No Easy Road: Women in Canada 1920s to 1960s*. Toronto, ON: New Hogtown Press, 1990.

Lindström, Varpu. *Defiant Sisters: A Social History of Finnish Immigrant Women in Canada*. Toronto, ON: Multicultural History Society of Ontario, 1988.

"The Lives of Mennonite Women." Prairie Public Television. Accessed 11 May 2006. <http://www.prairiepublic.org>.

Loewen, Harry. "From Russia to Canada: My Mother Was Betrayed by the Church." *Mennonite Reporter* 20 (1 October 1990): 9.

Loewen, Royden. *Blumenort: A Mennonite Community in Transition, 1874–1982*. Steinbach, MB: Blumenort Mennonite Historical Society, 1983.

_____. "'The Children, the Cows, My Dear Man and My Sister': The Transplanted Lives of Mennonite Farm Women, 1874–1900." *Canadian Historical Review* 73, 3 (1992): 344–73.

_____. *Family, Church and Market: A Mennonite Community in the Old and the New Worlds, 1850–1930*. Toronto, ON: University of Toronto Press, 1993.

Loewen, Royden. "Rurality, Ethnicity, and Gender Patterns of Cultural Continuity during the 'Great Disjuncture' in the R.M. of Hanover, 1945–1961." *Journal of the Canadian Historical Association* 4 (1993): 161–82.

_____. *From the Inside Out: The Rural Worlds of Mennonite Diarists, 1863–1929*. Winnipeg, MB: University of Manitoba Press, 1999.

_____. *Hidden Worlds: Revisiting the Mennonite Migrants of the 1870s*. Winnipeg, MB: University of Manitoba Press, 2001.

_____. *Diaspora in the Countryside: Two Mennonite Communities and Mid-Twentieth-Century Rural Disjuncture*. Toronto, ON: University of Toronto Press, 2006.

Longacre, Doris Janzen. *More-with-Less Cookbook: Suggestions by Mennonites on How to Eat Better and Consume Less of the World's Limited Food Resources*. Scottdale, PA: Herald Press, 1976.

Lowe Farm: 75ᵗʰ Anniversary, 1899–1974. Lowe Farm, MB: N.p., 1974.

"Margarete Dueck." *Mennonite Brethren Herald* 29 (20 April 1990): 27.

Marks, Lynne. *Revivals and Roller Rinks: Religion, Leisure, and Identity in Late-Nineteenth-Century Small-Town Ontario*. Toronto, ON: University of Toronto Press, 1996.

Marr, M. Lucille. "Anabaptist Women of the North: Peers in the Faith, Subordinates in Marriage." *Mennonite Quarterly Review* 61, 4 (October 1987): 347–62.

_____. "'The Time for the Distaff and Spindle': The Ontario Mennonite Women's Sewing Circles and the Mennonite Central Committee." *Journal of Mennonite Studies* 17 (1999): 130–51.

_____. *The Transforming Power of a Century : Mennonite Central Committee and its Evolution in Ontario* .Kitchener, ON: Pandora Press, 2003.

Martens, Eleanor. "The Artist as Homemaker: A Portrait." *Sophia* 3, 1 (Winter 1993): 13.

Martens, Katherine. *All in a Row: The Klassens of Homewood*. Winnipeg, MB: Mennonite Literary Society, 1988.

_____, and Heidi Harms, eds. *In Her Own Voice: Childbirth Stories from Mennonite Women*. Winnipeg, MB: University of Manitoba Press, 1997.

_____, ed. and trans. *They Came from Wiesenfeld Ukraine to Canada: Family Stories*. Winnipeg, MB: The Author, 2005.

Martens, Marlene O., ed. *Returning Thanks to God: Hoffnungsfelder Mennonite Churches, 1928–2003*. Rabbit Lake, SK: Hoffnungsfelder Mennonite Churches, 2003.

Martin, Donald. *Old Order Mennonites of Ontario: Gelassenheit, Discipleship, Brotherhood*. Kitchener, ON: Pandora Press, 2003.

Martin, Janet. "Distinctive Dress and the Newcomer." *MCC Women's Concerns Report* 107 (March–April 1993): 5–6.

Martin, Mary. "Women and Dress." *Women's Concerns Report* 107 (March–April 1993): 1.

Martin, Shirley. "Lizzy's Story." *Ontario Mennonite History* 11, 2 (September 1993): 11.

Martin, Terry R. "The Russian Mennonite Encounter with the Soviet State, 1917–1955." *The Conrad Grebel Review* 20, 1 (2002): 5–59.

Mathews-Klein, Yvonne. "How They Saw Us: Images of Women in National Film Board Films of the 1940s and 1950s." *Atlantis* 4, 2 (Spring 1979): 20–33.

Mathies, Gudrun L. (Wohlgemut). "Refugee Pilgrimage: A Story of God's Care. Lina (Heinrich) Wohlgemut: From Poland to Canada." *Ontario Mennonite History* 13, 1 (March 1995): 8–14.

Matties, Linda. "The Mary-Martha Complex in the Post-Modern Church." *MCC Women's Concerns Report* 102 (May–June 1992): 9–12.

Matties, Lori. "Pioneer Painter: The Watercolours of Mary Klassen." *Sophia* 4, 3 (Fall 1994): 18–19.

MCC Peace Section Task Force on Women in Church and Society, 9 (October–December 1975).

_____, 12 (December 1976).

MCC Women's Concerns Report 108 (May–June 1993).

_____, 175 (September–October, 2004).

McLaren, Angus. *A History of Contraception: From Antiquity to the Present Day*. Oxford: Basil Blackwell, 1990.

McManus, Sheila. "Gender(ed) Tensions in the Work and Politics of Alberta Farm Women, 1905–29." In *Telling Tales: Essays in Western Women's History*, edited by Catherine A. Cavanaugh and Randi R. Warne, 123–46. Vancouver, BC: University of British Columbia Press, 2000.

McPherson, Kathryn. "Was the 'Frontier' Good for Women?: Historical Approaches to Women and Agricultural Settlement in the Prairie West, 1870–1925." *Atlantis* 25, 1 (Fall/Winter 2000): 75–86.

Meade, Teresa A., and Merry E. Wiesner-Hanks, eds. *A Companion to Gender History*. Malden, MA: Blackwell Publishing, 2004.

"Men, Women and Decision-making in Mennonite Central Committee." *MCC Task Force on Women in Church and Society* 3 (December 1973): 4.

Menno Place: Encompassed by Compassion: Mennonite Benevolent Society Fiftieth Anniversary, 1953–2003. Abbotsford, BC: Mennonite Benevolent Society, 2003.

Mennonite Brethren Church, Winkler, Manitoba, 1888–1963. Winkler, MB: Mennonite Brethren Church, 1963.

"Mennonite Brethren General Conference Resolution Ordaining, Commissioning, and Licensing of Workers>" *General Conference Yearbook* (1957): 106. Accessed 12 April 2006. <http://www.mbconf.ca/believe/wiml/resolutions.en.html>.

"Mennonite Brethren General Conference Resolution, Sister's Participation." In *General Conference Yearbook* (1879): 4. Accessed 12 April 2006. <http://www.mbconf.ca/believe/wiml/resolutions.en.html>.

"Mennonite Central Committee Relief Notes." *Missionary News and Notes* 15 (April 1941): 61.

Mennonite Confession of Faith: Adopted by Mennonite General Conference, August 22, 1963. Scottdale, PA: Herald Press, 1964.

The Mennonite Treasury of Recipes. Steinbach, MB: Derksen Printers, 1961.

Milestones and Memories: Bergthaler Mennonite Church of Morden, 1931–1981. Morden, MB: Bergthaler Mennonite Church, 1981.

Millar, Anne Eby, and D. Douglas Millar. *The Diaries of Susannah Cressman, 1911–1946.* Kitchener, ON: N.p., 1997.

"Miss Gertrude Klassen: Private Social Worker." *Carillon News*, 18 March 1955.

Missionary News and Notes (April 1941).

Mitchinson, Wendy. *Giving Birth in Canada, 1900–1950.* Toronto, ON: University of Toronto Press, 2002.

Morgan, Marabel. *The Total Woman.* Old Tappan, NJ: Fleming H. Revell, 1973.

Morrow, Farah. "Lives Lived: Helen (Dueck) Enns." *Globe and Mail*, 1 February 2007, p. A16.

Muir, Elizabeth Gillan and Whiteley, Marilyn Färdig, eds., *Changing Roles of Women within the Christian Church in Canada.* Toronto, ON: University of Toronto Press, 1995.

Murphy, Barbara. *Why Women Bury Men: The Longevity Gap in Canada.* Winnipeg, MB: J. Gordon Shillingford Publishing, 2002.

Neufeld, Elfrieda. "Anna Vogt: Kindergarten Pioneer." *Preservings* 8 (June 1996): 26–27.

Neufeld, Elsie. "Unity in Women's Work." *The Canadian Mennonite* 6 (16 May 1958): 4.

Neufeld, Herman A. *Mary Neufeld and the Repphun Story, from the Molotschna to Manitoba.* North Hollywood, CA: The Carole Joyce Gallery, 1987.

Neufeld, Justina D. *A Family Torn Apart.* Kitchener, ON: Pandora Press, 2003.

Neufeld, Margaret Klassen. "My Grandmother Was an Undertaker: A Tribute to Anganetha Dyck Bergen Baerg (1859–1942)." *Mennonite Historian* 24, 1 (March 1998): 2, 9.

Neufeld, Nettie. "Aganetha 'Agnes' Fast." *Preservings* 10 (June 1997): 38–40.

Neufeld, Regina Doerksen. "Katherina Hiebert (1855–1910): Midwife." *Preservings* 10 (June 1997): 14–16.

_____. "Katharina Hiebert: Manitoban Pioneer Midwife." *Mennonite Historical Bulletin* 61 (July 2000): 4.

Neufeldt, Harvey. "Creating the Brotherhood: Status and Control in the Yarrow Mennonite Community, 1928–1960." In *Canadian Papers in Rural History Vol. 9*, edited by Donald H. Akenson, 211–38. Gananoque, ON: Langdale Press, 1994.

Neufeldt, Harvey. "M. Hank." In *Village of Unsettled Yearnings. Yarrow, British Columbia: Mennonite Promise*, edited by Leonard Neufeldt, 298–304. Victoria, BC: Touch-Wood Editions, 2002.

_____, et al., eds. *First Nations and First Settlers in the Fraser Valley (1890–1960)*. Kitchener, ON: Pandora Press, 2004.

Neufeldt, Leonard N., ed. *Before We Were the Land's: Yarrow, British Columbia: Mennonite Promise*. Victoria, BC: TouchWood Editions, 2002.

_____, ed. *Village of Unsettled Yearnings. Yarrow, British Columbia: Mennonite Promise*. Victoria, BC: TouchWood Editions, 2002.

"New Centenarian Recalls Life under Czar and Commissar." *Kitchener–Waterloo Record*, 23 November 1984, p. D3.

Nickel, Janis E. "In the Name of Harmony Voices Are Lost." *MCC Women's Concerns Report* 121 (July–August 1995): 5–6.

"The Ontario Mennonite Bible School." *Church and Mission News* 9, 1 (January 1944): 3.

Oppenheimer, Jo. "Childbirth in Ontario: The Transition from Home to Hospital in the Early Twentieth Century." In *Delivering Motherhood: Maternal Ideologies and Practices in the 19th and 20th Centuries*, edited by Katherine Arnup, et al. London & New York: Routledge, 1990.

Paetkau, Anna (Pauls Thiessen). *Memories and Reflections of a Widow*. Winnipeg, MB: J.M. Thiessen, 1991.

Parkerson, Donald H., and Jo Ann Parkerson. "'Fewer Children of Greater Spiritual Quality': Religion and the Decline of Fertility in Nineteenth-Century America." *Social Science History* 12 (1988): 49–70.

Parr, Joy. "Gender History and Historical Practice." *Canadian Historical Review* 76, 3 (September 1995): 354–76.

Patkau, Esther. *First Mennonite Church in Saskatoon, 1923–1982*. Saskatoon, SK: The Church, 1982.

_____. *Canadian Women in Mission, 1895–1952–2002*. Canada: Canadian Women in Mission, 2002.

Patterson, Nancy-Lou. *The Language of Paradise: Folk Art from Mennonite and Other Anabaptist Communities of Ontario*. London, ON: London Regional Art Gallery, 1985.

Patterson, Nancy-Lou Gellermann. *Swiss-German and Dutch-German Mennonite Traditional Art in the Waterloo Region, Ontario*. Ottawa, ON: National Museums of Canada, 1979.

Pauls, Karen. "Northfield Settlement, Nova Scotia: A New Direction for Immigrants from Belize." *Journal of Mennonite Studies* 22 (2004): 167–84.

Pauls, Pat Gerber. *Canadian Mennonite Cookbook*. Altona, MB: Friesen Stationers, 1978.

Peachey, Linda Gehman. "Vision for the Future in MCC U.S." *MCC Women's Concerns Report* (November–December 2004). Retrieved 26 January 2006. <http://www. mcc.org/womensconcerns/articles/2004/december.html>.

Pellman, Hubert R. *Mennonite Broadcasts: The First 25 Years*. Harrisonburg, VA: Mennonite Broadcasts, 1979.

Penner, Carol. "Mennonite Women's History: A Survey." *Journal of Mennonite Studies* 9 (1991): 122–35.

Penner, Carol. "Let Me Introduce You to Barbara Sherk...." *Ontario Mennonite History* 11, 2 (September 1993): 12–14.

_____. Review of *She Has Done a Good Thing: Mennonite Women Leaders Tell Their Stories*. Scottdale, PA: Herald Press, 1999. *The Conrad Grebel Review* 19, 3 (Fall 2001):103–04.

Penner, Daisy Isaac. "Margaret Loewen Isaac (1855–1930)." *Preservings* 12 (June 1998): 73.

Penner, Doris. "Memories of *Schaaldouak* Make Nostalgic Afternoon." *The Carillon*, 15 May 2000.

Penner, Katy. *Diamonds in the Sand*. Winnipeg, MB: Windflower Communications, 2001.

Penner, Lydia. "The Mennonite Treasury of Recipes, a Canadian Bestseller." In *Fifty Years Ebenezer Verein, 1936–1986*, 53–54. Steinbach, MB: Ebenezer Verein, 1987.

Penner, Peter. *Russians, North Americans and Telugas: The Mennonite Brethren Mission in India 1885–1975*. Winnipeg, MB, and Hillsboro, KS: Centre for Mennonite Brethren Studies, 1997.

_____. "The Foreign Missionary as Hero." In *Village of Unsettled Yearnings. Yarrow, British Columbia: Mennonite Promise*, edited by Leonard Neufeldt, 50–61. Victoria, BC: TouchWood Editions, 2002.

"People," *Mennonite Reporter* 5 (15 September 1975): 11.

Peters, Alan. "The Impact of the Family in Mennonite History: Some Preliminary Observations." *Direction* 1, 3 (July 1972): 74–81.

Peters, Elizabeth, ed. *Gnadenthal, 1880-1980*. Winkler, MB: Gnadenthal History Book Committee, 1982.

Peters, John F. "Traditional Customs of Remarriage among Some Canadian Mennonite Widow(er)s." *Journal of Mennonite Studies* 10 (1992): 118–29.

Petkau, Irene Friesen, and Peter A. Petkau. *Blumenfeld: Where Land and People Meet*. Winkler, MB: Blumenfeld Historical Committee, 1981.

Piecework: A Women's Peace Theology. Winnipeg, MB: Mennonite Central Committee Canada, 1997.

Pierson, Ruth Roach. *'They're Still Women After All': The Second World War and Canadian Womanhood.* Toronto, ON: McClelland and Stewart, 1986.

Plett, D. "First Woman Teacher Maria Friesen Redenzel 1844–1925." *Preservings* 8 (June 1996): 9.

Plett, Delbert F. "Maria Koop Plett 1868-1918 Journal." *Preservings* 10 (June 1997): 33–35.

_____. "Letters: Anna Klassen Goossen, 1839–1927." *Preservings* 10 (June 1997): 16–17.

_____. "Klaas Reimer's Kjist?" *Preservings* 12 (June 1998): 92–94.

_____, ed. *Old Colony Mennonites in Canada, 1875–2000.* Steinbach, MB: Crossway Publications, 2000.

_____. *Johann Plett: A Mennonite Family Saga.* Steinbach, MB: Crossway Publications, 2003.

Plett, Saundra. "Attitudes Toward Women as Reflected in Mennonite Brethren Periodicals." *Direction* 9, 1 (January 1980): 13–24. Accessed 11 April 2006. <http://www.directionjournal.org>.

Prentice, Alison, et al. *Canadian Women: A History.* Toronto, ON: Harcourt Brace Jovanovich, 1988.

Ramseyer, Edna. "Will Ye Heed the Call?" *Missionary News and Notes* (November 1943): 1.

Rayaprol, Aparna. *Negotiating Identities: Women in the Indian Diaspora.* New York: Oxford University Press, 1997.

Redekop, Gloria Neufeld. "The Understanding of Woman's Place among Mennonite Brethren in Canada: A Question of Biblical Interpretation." *The Conrad Grebel Review* 8, 3 (Fall 1990): 259–74.

_____. *The Work of Their Hands: Mennonite Women's Societies in Canada.* Waterloo, ON: Wilfrid Laurier University Press, 1996.

Redekop, Magdalene. "Through the Mennonite Looking Glass." In *Why I Am a Mennonite: Essays on Mennonite Identity*, edited by Harry Loewen, 226–53. Kitchener, ON: Herald Press, 1988.

Redekop, Paul. "The Mennonite Family in Tradition and Transition." *Journal of Mennonite Studies* 4 (1986): 77–93.

Reesor, Ruth. *Check Rein: A Journey of Remembrance.* Ontario: Pennsylvania German Folklore Society of Ontario, 2003.

Regehr, Cornelius (Chuck). "Taking Counsel from Strength and Duty: Agatha Klassen." In *Village of Unsettled Yearnings. Yarrow, British Columbia: Mennonite Promise*, edited by Leonard Neufeldt, 290–97. Victoria, BC: TouchWood Editions, 2002.

Regehr, Mary. "Motherhood: Changing and Growing." *MCC Committee on Women's Concerns Report* 62 (July–August 1985): 8–9.

Regehr, T.D. *Mennonites in Canada, 1939–1970: A People Transformed*. Toronto, ON: University of Toronto Press, 1996.

———. *Faith, Life and Witness in the Northwest, 1903–2003: Centennial History of the Northwest Mennonite Conference*. Kitchener, ON: Pandora Press, 2003.

Regier, Katharina Wiens Bahmann Dyck. *Our Heritage. Remembrances of My Life in Russia 1866–1895*. Fort Worth, TX: Marvin W. Bahnman, 1997.

"Regier Receives 'Emeritus Stole' for 40 Years in Ministry." *Canadian Mennonite*, 8, 15 (2 August 2004): 5.

Reimer, Al. "Where Was/Is the Woman's Voice? The Re-Membering of the Mennonite Woman." *Mennonite Life* 41,1 (March 1992): 20–05.

Reimer, Margaret Loewen. "Canadian Conference Divided Over Teenage Election." *MCC Peace Section Task Force on Women in Church and Society* 9 (October–December 1975): 1–2.

———. *One Quilt Many Pieces: A Guide to Mennonite Groups in Canada*. Waterloo, Scottdale: Herald Press, 2008.

"Reminiscences of Grandmother Snider." *Waterloo Historical Society* 66 (1978): 5–17.

Rempel, Margaret Thiessen. "Margaretha Frantz Enns (1892–1959)." *Preservings* 10 (June 1997): Part 2, 56–60.

"Resolutions Committee Report." *Calendar of Appointments, Mennonite Conference of Ontario* (1944–1945), 44–45.

Reusser, Jim, and Helen Reusser. "Best Friends." *MCC Women's Concerns Report* 101 (March–April 1992): 9–12.

Reynolds, Margaret C. *Plain Women: Gender and Ritual in the Old Order River Brethren*. University Park, PA: Pennsylvania State University Press, 2001.

———. "River Brethren Breadmaking Ritual." In *Strangers at Home: Amish and Mennonite Women in History*, edited by Kimberly D. Schmidt, et al., 78–101. Baltimore, MD: The Johns Hopkins University Press, 2002.

Rice, John R. *Bobbed Hair, Bossy Wives, and Women Preachers*. Wheaton: Sword of the Lord, 1941.

Rich, Elaine Sommers. *Mennonite Women: A Story of God's Faithfulness, 1683–1983*. Scottdale, PA: Herald Press 1983.

Roth, Lorraine. "Use of Maiden Names—Women's Liberation in the Nineteenth Century?" *Mennonite Family History* 8, 4 (October 1989): 147.

———. "Conscientious Objection: The Experiences of Some Canadian Mennonite Women During World War II." *Mennonite Quarterly Review* 66, 4 (October 1992): 539–45.

———. *Willing Service: Stories of Ontario Mennonite Women*. Waterloo, ON: Mennonite Historical Society of Ontario, 1992.

———. "Serving in the Mission Field." *MCC Women's Concerns Report* 102 (May–June 1992): 4–6.

_____. "Margaret Elizabeth Brown Kanagy: An Exemplary Life of Christian Service." *Mennonite Historical Bulletin* 54, 3 (July 1993): 1–2.

_____. *The Amish and Their Neighbours: The German Block, Wilmot Township 1822–1860.* Waterloo, ON: Mennonite Historical Society of Ontario, 1998.

Ruiz, Miriam. "A New Breed of Mennonite Women." *MCC Women's Concerns Report* 119 (March–April 1995): 7–9.

Rupel, Esther F. "The Dress of the Brethren (and Church of the Brethren)." *Brethren Life and Thought* 31 (Summer 1986): 135–50.

Russell, Ruth, ed. *Women of Waterloo County.* Kitchener–Waterloo, ON: Canadian Federation of University Women, 2000.

Saskatchewan Women in Mission. SK: Saskatchewan Women in Mission, 1977.

Scanzoni, Letha Dawson, and Susan Setta. "Women in Evangelical, Holiness, and Pentecostal Traditions." In *Women and Religion in America, Vol 3: 1900–1968,* edited by Rosemary Radforth Ruether and Rosemary Skinner Keller. San Francisco, CA: Harper and Row, 1986.

Scharfenberg, Lorilee G. "Helena (Klassen) Eidse (1861–1938)." *Preservings* 8 (June 1996): 51–54.

Scharfenberg, Lori. "Helena Eidses' Medical Bag." *Preservings* 9 (December 1996): Part 2, 53.

Scharfenberg, Lori Loewen. "Anna Bartel Eidse, 1889–1954." *Preservings* 9 (December 1996), Part 1, 30–31.

Scharfenberg, Lorilee. "Helena Brandt Klassen." *Rootsweb.* 2002. Accessed 19 September 2005. <http://freepages.genealogy.rootsweb.com/~eidse/midwife.html>.

Schiedel, Mary Hunsberger. *A Journey of Faith: The History of Shantz Mennonite Church, 1840–2000.* Baden, ON: Shantz Mennonite Church, 2000.

Schiedel, Mary A. *Pioneers in Ministry: Women Pastors in Ontario Mennonite Churches, 1973–2003.* Kitchener, ON: Pandora Press, 2003.

Schmidt, Kimberly D. "'Sacred Farming' or 'Working Out': The Negotiated Lives of Conservative Mennonite Farm Women." *Frontiers: A Journal of Women's Studies* 22, 1 (2001): 79–102.

_____. "Schism: Where Women's Outside Work and Insider Dress Collided." In *Strangers at Home: Amish and Mennonite Women in History,* edited by Kimberly D. Schmidt, et al., 208–33. Baltimore, MD: The Johns Hopkins University Press, 2002.

_____, and Steven D. Reschly. "A Women's History for Anabaptist Traditions: A Framework of Possibilities, Possibly Changing the Framework." *Journal of Mennonite Studies* 18 (2000): 29–46.

_____, et al., eds. *Strangers at Home: Amish and Mennonite Women in History.* Baltimore, MD: The Johns Hopkins University Press, 2002.

Schmidt, Norman J. "Responses to the Women's Revolution." *The Mennonite* 85 (30 June 1970): 450–51.

Schroeder, Anna L. "A Woman's Place." *Christian Living* 13 (September 1966): 40.

Schwartz, Linda. "Self-Perception among Mennonite Brethren Women Students on Women in Ministry." *MCC Women's Concerns Report* 108 (May–June 1993): 13–14.

Shantz, Lester B. *A Shantz Family in Canada, 1800–2000: Ancestors and Descendants of Samuel Y. Shantz.* Hamilton, ON: The Author, 1997.

Shantz, Susan. "Profile: Nellie Kinsie." *The Marketplace* 11, 3 (June 1981): 1, 4–5.

Siegrist, Joanne Hess. *Mennonite Women of Lancaster Pennsylvania: A Sstory in Photographs from 1855–1935.* Intercourse, PA: Good Books, 1996.

Siemens, Ruth Derksen. "Quilt as Text and Text as Quilt: The Influence of Genre in the Mennonite Girls' Home of Vancouver (1930–1960)." *Journal of Mennonite Studies* 17 (1999): 118–29.

Singer, Lisa. "'God Could Not be Everywhere—So He Made Mothers': The Unrecognized Contributions of Early Jewish Women Pioneers, 1880–1920." In *A Sharing of Diversities: Proceedings of the Jewish Mennonite Ukrainian Conference 'Building Bridges,'* edited by Fred Stambrook and Bert Friesen, 101–12. Regina, SK: Canadian Plains Research Center, 1999.

Sitler, Arlene. "A Challenge to Mennonite Women." *Women's Activities Letter* 18 (February 1946): 1–3.

Soden, Ruth Ann. "Traditions Yielding as More Women Vote at Mennonite Meet." *Kitchener–Waterloo Record,* 18 August 1971, p. 57.

South Western Ontario Women in Mission, 1925–1987. Leamington, ON: South Western Ontario Women in Mission, 1987.

Sprunger, Keith. "God's Powerful Army of the Weak: Anabaptist Women of the Radical Reformation" In *Triumph Over Silence: Women in Protestant History,* edited by Richard L. Greaves, 45–74. Westport, CT: Greenwood Press, 1985.

Staebler, Edna. *Food That Really Schmecks.* Toronto, ON: McGraw-Hill Ryerson, 1968.

"Statement on Women Suffrage." *1978 EMC Yearbook.* Steinbach, MB: Evangelical Mennonite Conference, 1978.

Stauffer, Ezra. "The Christian Woman's Spiritual Service." *The Christian Ministry* 2 (January 1949): 33–35.

Stauffer, Joseph S. "The Family Book." *Waterloo Historical Society* 55 (1967): 16–17.

Steckley, Elizabeth, and Irwin Steckley. *Joseph Reschly and Anna Schweitzer Family History and Genealogy.* Second edition. Stratford, ON: The Authors, 2003.

Steiner, Sue Clemmer. "The Impact of Childbearing/Childlessness On Our Lives: Ten Stories." *MCC Committee Report on Women's Concerns Report* 55 (May–June 1984): 10.

Steinman, Carol M. *Refined by Fire: The Story of Hagey/Preston Mennonite Church, 1800–2000.* Kitchener, ON: Pandora Press, 2000.

Stoesz, Dennis. *The Story of Home Street Mennonite Church, 1957–1982.* Winnipeg, MB: The Church, 1985.

Stoltzfus, Louise. *Amish Women: Lives and Stories.* Intercourse, PA: Good Books, 1994.

———. *Quiet Shouts: Stories of Lancaster Mennonite Women Leaders.* Scottdale, PA: Herald Press, 1999.

Stoltzfus, Ruth Brunk. *A Way Was Opened: A Memoir.* Scottdale, PA: Herald Press, 2003.

Strachan, Glenda. "Present at the Birth: Midwives, 'Handywomen' and Neighbours in Rural New South Wales, 1850–1900." *Labour History* 81 (2001): 13–28.

Strong-Boag, Veronica. "Pulling in Double Harness or Hauling a Double Load: Women, Work and Feminism on the Canadian Prairie." *Journal of Canadian Studies* 21, 3 (Fall 1986): 32–52.

Sundberg, Sara Brooks. "A Female Frontier: Manitoba Farm Women in 1922." *Prairie Forum* 15–16 (1990–1991): 185–204.

Swartley, Mary, and Rhoda Keener, eds. *She Has Done a Good Thing: Mennonite Women Leaders Tell Their Stories.* Scottdale, PA: Herald Press, 1999.

Swartzentruber, Dorothy M. "Ontario Auxiliary Review Forty Year's Women's Work." *The Canadian Mennonite* 5 (31 May 1957): 3–4.

Swyripa, Frances. *Wedded to the Cause: Ukrainian–Canadian Women and Ethnic Identity, 1881–1981.* Toronto, ON: University of Toronto Press, 1992.

"Ten-Year Celebration of the Committee on Women's Concerns." *MCC Committee on Women's Concerns Report* 50 (July–August 1983).

"The Problems of the Single Girl." *The Canadian Mennonite* 5 (27 September and 4 October 1957): 2.

Thiessen, Veronica Barkowsky. "History of the Yarrow United Mennonite Church." In *Village of Unsettled Yearnings. Yarrow, British Columbia: Mennonite Promise*, edited by Leonard Neufeldt, 44–49. Victoria, BC: TouchWood Editions, 2002.

Toews, Ernest P. "Elizabeth Reimer Toews, 1843–1918." *Preservings* 8 (June 1996): Part 2, 12–14.

Toews, John B. *With Courage to Spare.* Hillsboro, KS: General Conference of Mennonite Brethren Churches, 1978.

Toews, K.S. "German English Academy, Rosthern, Saskatchewan." *The Mennonite* 59 (22 August 1944): 4.

Toews, Margaret Penner. "Anna: The Bishop's Wife." *Preservings* 10 (June 1997): 23–25.

Toews, Wilma. "Homemaking—A Challenging Vocation." *Mennonite Life* 11, 4 (October 1956): 163–64, 191.

Towell, Larry. *The Mennonites.* London: Phaidon, 2000.

Umble, Jenifer Hiett. "Women and Choice: An Examination of the *Martyrs Mirror*." *Mennonite Quarterly Review* 64, 2 (April 1990): 135–45.

Unrau, Jake, with Johann D. Funk. *Living in the Way: The Pilgrimage of Jake & Trudie Unrau*. Winnipeg, MB: CMBC Publications, 1996.

Unrau, John. *The Balancings of the Clouds: Paintings of Mary Klassen*. Winnipeg, MB: Windflower Communications, 1991.

Unrau, Ruth. "Singing the Lord's Song in Foreign Lands: Anna Enns Epp, 1902–1958." In *Encircled: Stories of Mennonite Women*, edited by Ruth Unrau, 285–97. Newton, KS: Faith and Life Press, 1986.

_____. "The Writer's Journal." In *Encircled: Stories of Mennonite Women*, edited by Ruth Unrau, 1–7. Newton, KS: Faith and Life Press, 1986.

_____, ed. *Encircled: Stories of Mennonite Women*. Newton, KS: Faith and Life Press, 1986.

Urry, James. *Mennonites, Politics, and Peoplehood: Europe, Russia, Canada, 1525–1980*. Winnipeg, MB: University of Manitoba Press, 2006.

van Braght, Thielman J. *The Bloody Theater or Martyrs Mirror of the Defenseless Christians*. Scottdale: Herald Press, 1968 8th edition. First published in 1660.

Vertovec, Steven, and Robin Cohen, eds. *Migration, Diasporas and Transnationalism*. Cheltenham, UK: Edward Elgar Publishing Ltd., 1999.

Visweswaran, Kamala. *Fictions of Feminist Ethnography*. Minneapolis, MN: University of Minnesota Press, 1994.

Voth, Norma Jost. *Mennonite Foods and Folkways from South Russia*. Intercourse, PA: Good Books, 1990.

Warne, Randi R. *Literature as Pulpit: The Christian Social Activism of Nellie L. McClung*. Waterloo, ON: Wilfrid Laurier University Press, 1987.

Weinberg, Sydney Stahl. *The World of Our Mothers: The Lives of Jewish Immigrant Women*. Chapel Hill, NC: University of North Carolina Press, 1988.

Whiteley, Marilyn Färdig. *Canadian Methodist Women, 1766–1925: Marys, Marthas, Mothers in Israel*. Waterloo, ON: Wilfrid Laurier University Press, 2005.

"Who's Who." *The Beacon* 2, 5 (May 1943): 15.

Wiebe, Henry, ed. *Memories of Our Parents*. Kitchener, ON: Evenstone Press, 1992.

Wiebe, Katie Funk. "The Place of Women in the Work of the Church." *The Canadian Mennonite* 11 (1 March 1963): 5.

_____. "Woman's Freedom—The Church's Necessity." *Direction* 1, 3 (July 1972): 82–84.

_____. Quote. *MCC Peace Section Task Force on Women in Church & Society* 37 (May–June 1981): 4.

_____. "Mennonite Brethren Women: Images and Realities of the Early Years." *Mennonite Life* 36, 3 (September 1981): 22–28.

_____. *Alone: A Search for Joy.* Hillsboro, KS, and Winnipeg, MB: Kindred Press, 1987.

_____. "Twenty-five Years Later." *Women's Concerns Report* 73 (July–August 1987): 8–9.

_____. "A Tale of Seduction." In *Why I Am a Mennonite: Essays on Mennonite Identity,* edited by Harry Loewen, 324–36. Kitchener, ON, and Scottdale, PA: Herald Press, 1988.

_____. "Rempel, Redekop and Reflections About Women's Organizations Among the Brethren." In *Bridging Troubled Waters: The Mennonite Brethren at Mid-Twentieth Century,* edited by Paul Toews, 175–82. Winnipeg, MB: Kindred Press, 1995.

_____. "Mennonite Brethren Women: Images and Realities of the Early Years." *Direction* 24, 2 (Fall 1995): 23–35.

_____. *The Storekeeper's Daughter: A Memoir.* Scottdale, PA: Herald Press, 1997.

_____. "Me Tarzan, Son of Menno—You Jane, Mennonite Mama." *Journal of Mennonite Studies* 17 (1999): 9–21.

_____, ed. *Women Among the Brethren: Stories of 15 Mennonite Brethren and Krimmer Mennonite Brethren Women.* Hillsboro, KS: General Conference of Mennonite Brethren Churches, 1979.

Wiebe, Menno. "Women's Conference More than Peripheral." *Mennonite Reporter* 2 (24 July 1972): 4.

Wiens, Katherine. "Reader Response." *MCC Task Force on Women in Church and Society* 3 (December 1973): 7.

Winland, Daphne N. "Christianity and Community: Conversion and Adaptation among Hmong Refugee Women." *Canadian Journal of Sociology* 19, 1 (1994): 21–45.

_____. "Revisiting a Case Study of Hmong Refugees and Ontario Mennonites." *Journal of Mennonite Studies* 24 (2006): 169–76.

"Women and Decision-Making in Mennonite Institutions." *MCC Women's Concerns Report* 63 (September–October 1985).

"Women at World Conference." *Missionary Sewing Circle Monthly* 25 (September 1952): 8.

"Women in Church Vocations." *Mennonite Encyclopedia,* vol. 4. Scottdale, PA: Mennonite Publishing House, 1959, 972.

"Women in Mennonite Church Structures." *MCC Task Force on Women in Church and Society* 5 (April 1974): 6.

"Women's Broadcast Heard over CFAM." *The Canadian Mennonite* 5 (4 October 1957): 9.

"Women Still in the Cold." *The Canadian Mennonite* 17 (22 April 1969): 3.

Yoder, Anne. "The Diaries of North American Mennonite Women, 1850–1950." *Mennonite Historical Bulletin* 54, 1 (January 1993): 5–9.

Zacharias, Frank. "Reinland EMMC Historical Sketch." *EMMC Recorder* 25, 11 (December 1988): 4–5.

Zacharias, Peter D. *Footprints of a Pilgrim People: Story of the Blumenort Mennonite Church*. Gretna, MB: Blumenort Mennonite Church, 1985.

Zehr, Vernon, and Leona Bender. *Cassel Mennonite Church, 1935–1985*. Tavistock, ON: The Church, 1985.

UNPUBLISHED SOURCES:

Bauman, Gordon, and Erma (Martin). *Memories of Our Lives*. Manuscript, 2001, Mennonite Archives of Ontario, Waterloo, Ontario.

Baumbusch, Jennifer L. "Unclaimed Treasures: Older Women's Reflections on Life-long Singlehood." Paper presented at the Canadian Historical Association annual meeting, Toronto, Ontario, 2002.

Bender, Harold S. "An Exegesis of I Cor. 11:1-16." Paper, 1922, Mennonite Historical Library, Goshen, Indiana.

Bergen, Shirley B. "Life of Mrs. Dr. Thiessen (nee Catherine Bornn)—1842–1915." Paper, n.d. Katherina Thiessen Collection, Volume 5028, Mennonite Heritage Centre, Winnipeg, Manitoba.

Burkhardt, Ferne. "The Origins and Development of the Toronto Mennonite Mission: Women Were Key Players, but Won Few Medals." Manuscript, 1991, Mennonite Archives of Ontario, Waterloo, Ontario.

Epp, Amy. "The Unspoken Pain: How the Mennonite Community Deals with Rape." Research paper, 1993, Mennonite Heritage Centre, Winnipeg, Manitoba.

Gingrich, Luann Good. "A Mother's Garden: Planting Seeds of Hope." Manuscript, 1997. In author's possession.

Groening, Margaret Heinrichs. "Grandmother Remembers," "Jugendvereins of the 1930–1965 [sic]," and "Reminiscences." Manuscripts, no date. Used with permission from Roger Groening.

Klassen, Pamela. "'Queen for the Day': Mennonites, Weddings, Women, and Dress." Paper, Drew University, 1993.

Koop, Heidi, comp., and Helga Dyck, ed. "The Band Plays On: Mennonite Pioneers of North Kildonan Reflect." Manuscript, 1998, Mennonite Heritage Centre, Winnipeg, Manitoba.

Marks, Lynne. "Challenging Binaries: Working-Class Women and Lived Religion in North America." Notes from paper presented at "Labouring Feminism and Feminist Working Class History in North America and Beyond," Munk Centre for International Studies, University of Toronto, Fall 2005.

Marr, M. Lucille. Book manuscript on the letters of Alice Snyder to her mother. Used with permission.

Martin, Steven P. "The Presence of Violence in the Mennonite Church and Family Systems." MTh thesis, Waterloo Lutheran Seminary, 1990.

Millar, Douglas. "Mennonites in the Melting Pot." Research paper, no date, Mennonites in Canada files, Mennonite Archives of Ontario, Waterloo, Ontario.

Penner, Carol. "Mennonite Silences and Feminist Voices: Peace Theology and Violence Against Women." PhD thesis, Toronto School of Theology, 1999.

Regehr, Olga Dyck. "From Refugee to Suburbanite: The Survival and Acculturation of North Kildonan Mennonite Immigrant Women, 1927–1947." MA thesis, University of Winnipeg, 2006.

"The Rosthern Mennonite Church—75 Years of Growth." Paper, no date, Mennonite Heritage Centre, Winnipeg, Manitoba.

Roth, Lorraine. Manuscript on Barbara Schultz Oesch. No date. Used with permission.

Smith, Loralyn. "An Emerging Spirit." Research paper, 1992, Mennonite Archives of Ontario, Waterloo, Ontario.

Steinmann, Roselynn. "The Marriage and Childbirth Experiences of Mennonite Women within the Context of the Amish Community." Research paper, 1992, Mennonite Heritage Centre, Winnipeg, Manitoba.

Werner, Hans, and Jenifer Waito. "'One of our own': Ethnicity Politics and the Medicalization of Childbirth in Manitoba." Paper, 2007. Used with permission.

OTHER MEDIA:

Global Anabaptist Mennonite Encyclopedia Online (GAMEO). <www.gameo.org>.

Migration North: Mennonites from Mexico, video. Winnipeg: Mennonite Central Committee, 1995.

INTERVIEWS:

Amsey and Salome Martin, conversation with author, Yatton, Ontario, 2004.

Gloria Gonzalez (pseudonym), interview with author, Kitchener, Ontario, October 2000.

Iva Taves, interview with author, Kitchener, Ontario, 1989.

Lorraine Roth, interview with author, Waterloo, Ontario, 14 March 1990.

L.N. Snyder, interview 7095, Fairview Mennonite Home Oral History Project, Mennonite Archives of Ontario, Waterloo, Ontario.

ARCHIVAL DOCUMENTS:

A. E. Janzen to Miss Mary C. Wall and Sister Helen Warkentin, 27 December 1957. Helen Loewen Warkentin collection, Centre for Mennonite Brethren Studies, Winnipeg, Manitoba.

A.E. Janzen to "Dear Sister Warkentin," 21 January 1958. Helen Loewen Warkentin collection, Centre for Mennonite Brethren Studies, Winnipeg, Manitoba.

Alfred J. Kitchen, Social Worker, to Mr. C.W. Lundy, Director of Welfare, Victoria, B.C., 5 November 1945. Saskatchewan Archives Board, photocopy in Mennonites in Canada files, Mennonite Archives of Ontario.

Chilliwack Progress, 27 May 1942, 8. In Mennonites in Canada files, 1940-Yarrow, Mennonite Archives of Ontario, Waterloo, Ontario.

Clara Snider to Workers of the Nonresistant Relief Organization, 16 December 1942. John Coffman letters, Mennonite Archives of Ontario, Waterloo, Ontario.

Fransen, N.N. "Stimmberechtigung der schwestern in unsern gemeinden im lichte der bibel and unsere praxis, gelesen in Winnipeg, 13 January 1959." In Mennonite Archives of Ontario, Waterloo, Ontario.

H.R. Baerg to David J. Braun, 10 May 1973. Miscellaneous Conscientious Objector material, Volume 1159, Mennonite Heritage Centre, Winnipeg, Manitoba.

Heinrich F. and Catherine Klassen Collection, Volume 1002, Centre for Mennonite Brethren Studies, Winnipeg, Manitoba.

Helen Loewen Warkentin Collection, Centre for Mennonite Brethren Studies, Winnipeg, Manitoba.

Helen L. Warkentin, to "Dear Tien, Sarah and the others of the Home family," 14 August 1957, and to "Dear Tien," 22 September 1957, and "Dear Tien," 27 October 1957. Helen Loewen Warkentin collection, Centre for Mennonite Brethren Studies, Winnipeg, Manitoba.

J.P. Kliewer to Sisters 'Wall and Warkentin', 29 July 1957. Helen Loewen Warkentin collection, Centre for Mennonite Brethren Studies, Winnipeg, Manitoba.

Klassen, Lydia. "Introductory statement to President's Meeting of Mennonite Brethren women's societies." 14 November 1970. Heinrich F. and Catherine Klassen Collection, Volume 1002, Centre for Mennonite Brethren Studies, Winnipeg, Manitoba.

Letters in Matheson Island Nursing Station collection, Volume 964, XXIII-F, Box 1, Mennonite Heritage Centre, Winnipeg, Manitoba.

Malinda Bricker to John S. Coffman, 1 March 1895. John S. Coffman Collection, Archives of the Mennonite Church, Goshen, Indiana.

Minutes, Meeting of Mennonite Nurses Association of Ontario, 20 May 1946. Mennonite Conference of Ontario Collection, Mennonite Nurses Association, II-5-9, Mennonite Archives of Ontario, Waterloo, Ontario.

Questionnaire re: CO Service from Ben and Martha Rempel, Miscellaneous Conscientious Objector material, Volume 1159, Mennonite Heritage Centre, Winnipeg, Manitoba.

"Report of the Committee on Birth Control," 1945, Mennonite Conference of Ontario Collection, Mennonite Archives of Ontario, Waterloo, Ontario.

Report on trial of Dorothea Palmer, in *Ottawa Journal*, 23 October, 1936, p. 18. In Dorothea Palmer Collection, Doris Lewis Rare Book Room, University of Waterloo.

Rich, Elaine Sommers. "Woman's Place in the World." Women in Church Vocations Collection, XXII F 4, Volume 810, Mennonite Heritage Centre, Winnipeg, Manitoba .

"Statement on Faith and Practice," Mennonite Conference of Ontario records, II-2.1.1.3, Mennonite Archives of Ontario, Waterloo, Ontario.

Susan B. Peter to 'Helen', 15 November 1946. Susan B. Peters Collection, Centre for Mennonite Brethren Studies, Winnipeg, Manitoba.

"Testimony." Heinrich F. and Catherine Klassen Collection, Volume 1002, Centre for Mennonite Brethren Studies, Winnipeg, Manitoba.

Unpublished notes for 40th anniversary of Crystal City Mennonite Church, 1988. In Mennonite Historical Society of Canada collection. Mennonite Archives of Ontario, Waterloo, Ontario.

Untitled typescript report, Evangelical Mennonite Church of Blumenort, no date. In Mennonites in Canada files (1950-Birth Control), Mennonite Archives of Ontario, Waterloo, Ontario.

"Women in Church Vocations Handbook." Women in Church Vocations Collection, XXII F 4, Volume 810, Mennonite Heritage Centre, Winnipeg, Manitoba.

"Women's Coop Guild," FSMC, Box 3896, file 2, Mennonite Heritage Centre, Winnipeg, Manitoba.

INDEX